Framing the global economic downturn

Crisis rhetoric and the politics of recessions

Framing the global economic downturn

Crisis rhetoric and the politics of recessions

Edited by Paul 't Hart and Karen Tindall

ANU
THE AUSTRALIAN NATIONAL UNIVERSITY

E PRESS

ANU
E PRESS

the Australia and New Zealand
School of Government

Published by ANU E Press
The Australian National University
Canberra ACT 0200, Australia
Email: anuepress@anu.edu.au
This title is also available online at: http://epress.anu.edu.au/global_economy_citation.
html

National Library of Australia
Cataloguing-in-Publication entry

Title:	Framing the global economic downturn : crisis rhetoric and the politics of recessions / editor, Paul 't Hart, Karen Tindall.
ISBN:	9781921666049 (pbk.) 9781921666056 (pdf)
Series:	Australia New Zealand School of Government monograph
Subjects:	Financial crises.
	Globalization--Economic aspects.
	Bankruptcy--International cooperation.
	Crisis management--Political aspects.
	Political leadership.
	Decision-making in public administration.
Other Authors/Contributors:	
	Hart, Paul 't
	Tindall, Karen.
Dewey Number:	352.3

Cover design by John Butcher
Cover images sourced from AAP

Funding for this monograph series has been provided by the Australia and New
Zealand School of Government Research Program.

John Wanna, *Series Editor*

Professor John Wanna is the Sir John Bunting Chair of Public Administration at the Research School of Social Sciences at The Australian National University and is the director of research for the Australian and New Zealand School of Government (ANZSOG). He is also a joint appointment with the Department of Politics and Public Policy at Griffith University and a principal researcher with two research centres: the Governance and Public Policy Research Centre and the nationally-funded Key Centre in Ethics, Law, Justice and Governance at Griffith University.

Table of Contents

Part V. Comparisons and reflections

The contributors

Editors

Paul 't Hart is Professor of Political Science at The Australian National University, Professor of Public Administration at Utrecht University, the Netherlands, and adjunct professor at the Australia New Zealand School of Government.

Karen Tindall is completing a PhD on government responses to large-scale consular emergencies at the Research School of Social Sciences, The Australian National University.

Case study authors (Parts II–IV)

Isaac Ijjo Donato, Anastasia Glushko, Justin Pritchard, Adam Masters, Natalie Windle, Tully Fletcher, Michael Jones and *Faith Benjaathonsirikul* study political science (Hons) at The Australian National University.

Matthew Laing is completing a PhD in political science at the Research School of Social Sciences, The Australian National University.

Theme chapter authors (Part V)

Arjen Boin is an associate professor at the Public Administration Institute, Louisiana State University.

Brendan McCaffrie is completing a PhD in political science in the College of Arts and Social Science, The Australian National University.

Allan McConnell is a professor in the Department of Politics, Strathclyde University, Glasgow.

Bengt Sundelius is Professor of Government at Uppsala University and at the Swedish National Defence College.

Part I. Setting the stage

1. From 'market correction' to 'global catastrophe': framing the economic downturn

Paul 't Hart and Karen Tindall

1. Economic rhetoric in times of turbulence

The global downturn that followed the collapse of major US financial institutions is no doubt the most significant economic crisis of our times. Its effects on corporate and governmental balance sheets have been devastating. It destroyed the employment and compromised the wellbeing of tens of millions of people. At the time of writing, it continues to pose major challenges to public policymakers and economic actors around the world.

Although it had been bubbling away for more than a year in the form of a US-based 'credit crunch', the crisis deepened and widened to a truly global and whole-of-economy phenomenon during a number of critical months in 2008. This volume studies how public policymakers in a range of polities responded to the cascading problems in financial institutions and their growing impact on the 'real' economy. In particular, our focus is on how these public leaders described and explained the downturn to the public and sought to persuade it of the courses of action they proposed to tackle the crisis.

Ours is, therefore, a study of crisis rhetoric, embedded in a broader perspective of the challenges of leadership and governance in times of crisis. When nagging problems such as financial-sector instability escalate, policymakers face the challenge of switching from 'business as usual' into 'crisis management' mode. Doing so entails much more than turning to emergency plans and invoking emergency powers. The very act of perceiving a certain set of events as a 'crisis' and publicly labelling it as such involves numerous judgment calls. When are economic conditions considered to be so bad one can start using the otherwise dreaded 'r', 'c', or 'd' words (recession, crisis, depression) to describe them? What does using those words do in terms of public perceptions and emotions? How does one use the language of crisis without sounding defeatist or opportunistic? How does one persuade audiences not just that a crisis is occurring, but that it has done so for particular reasons and should be met with particular responses?

These are questions in which issues of fact, speculation, values and interests are intimately intertwined. Policymakers will grapple with these problems in their own minds, particularly when situations are fast moving, uncertain, ambiguous or when different bodies of evidence and advice seem to pull them in different directions. At the same time, however, policymakers can seldom afford to wait until they really know what's going on before communicating about it publicly. In the case of economic turbulence, for example, markets, media and mass audiences will be talking about the issues constantly, and if the voices of key leaders are absent from those debates, governments will be on the back foot and will in effect lose credibility.

Risk and crisis communication is a tricky business in any sector—witness the recent dilemmas regarding the global 'swine flu' outbreak: how should one respond to and talk to the public about a virus with ominous potential but whose current manifestations are quite mild? Such communication is especially tricky in the world of finance and economics. If, as is often observed, economics is essentially about psychology, then the ill-considered use of terms such as crisis, recession or depression by authority figures can generate self-fulfilling prophecies. That is a scary thought in an age when truly massive capital flows can be redirected across the world in a matter of seconds. If, however, key economic or political elites maintain an upbeat, business-as-usual facade when public sentiment is already heading south, they might look out of touch, inept or impotent—which will create a backlash in markets in a different way. Talking up the economy makes sense for public leaders only when there is at least some basis in fact and when the intended audience has not already made up its mind in the other direction. Timing and the tone of conveying both good and bad news about the economy in an overall climate of uncertainty and anxiety are, therefore, crucial.

2. A leadership perspective on economic crisis management

This volume analyses the economic rhetoric of key government figures during the escalation of the US and later global financial crisis in 2008–09. Its chief analytical tools come not from economics but from crisis research—an interdisciplinary body of work dealing with how individuals, groups, organisations and societies prepare for and respond to unpleasant, unscheduled and uncertain events. In particular, we draw on insights about the recurrent challenges and patterns of public leadership in times of crisis. Since our main objects of interest are public office-holders, we focus on how crises can affect their political capital and policy commitments. We focus on these leaders in turn and examine how they try to shape debates about crises to achieve their political and policy aims.

There is wide agreement in the literature that crises can be said to occur when the problems confronting a society are widely perceived as threatening and urgent, yet also involve high levels of uncertainty (Boin et al. 2005). First, there must be a feeling that core values or the vital systems of a community are under *threat*. Think of widely shared values such as safety and security, welfare, health, integrity and fairness, becoming shaky or even meaningless as a result of (looming) violence, destruction, damage or other forms of adversity. This explains why the prospect of war or natural disasters (floods, earthquakes, hurricanes, heat waves) usually evokes a deep sense of crisis. The threat of death, damage, destruction or bodily mutilation violates deeply embedded societal values of safety and security.

Physical damage is, of course, only one type of threat that can trigger a crisis. As the global financial crisis amply demonstrates, if the key institutions on which an economic system relies are threatened, then a sociopolitical crisis can follow, particularly if the job security of citizens is threatened. The size of the threat, however, cannot be derived by counting the numbers of bodies, jobs or dollars affected. Psychological or societal impacts of threats are functions of cultural expectations of levels of order, predictability, security and prosperity, which can vary within and between different communities and polities (Douglas and Wildavsky 1982).

Crises furthermore induce a *sense of urgency*. If leaders ignore or downplay potential threats—for example, the Bush Administration's stance on al-Qaeda before 9/11, levee protection in southern Louisiana before Hurricane Katrina or climate change—the message is: 'there is no crisis.' While experts and activists might worry and attempt to push their concerns up the political agenda, many political leaders do not lose sleep over problems with a horizon that exceeds their political life expectancy. Conversely, public policymakers can feel a great sense of threat and time pressure when they or their organisations become the subject of intense and critical media or parliamentary scrutiny, even when the issues involved do not necessarily hold major importance for actors outside that policy arena. Sometimes, however, time pressure is hard, direct and non-negotiable. So, when former US President, George W. Bush, and Congressional leaders were told in 2008 that if they did not act immediately, 'we may not have an economy on Monday', they paid attention. The sense of time pressure can, however, also be self-generated: in cases of conflict and negotiation, every policymaker that seeks to pressure demonstrators, terrorists or states by setting a deadline or issuing an ultimatum also puts pressure on themselves to 'deliver' on time. When that deadline approaches with no solutions in sight, the sense of urgency may quickly become overwhelming—as is often the case with international trade negotiations or dispute-resolution summits.

In a full-blown crisis, the perception of threat is accompanied by a high degree of *uncertainty*. This uncertainty pertains to the nature and the potential consequences of the developing threat: what is happening? How did it happen? What's next? How bad will it be? More importantly, uncertainty clouds the search for solutions: what can we do? What happens if we select this option?

How will people—or markets—respond? Again, uncertainty can be inherent in the situation at hand but also in institutional responses to it. For example, when decision makers consult various radiation experts on the risks associated with an accident at a nuclear facility, such experts often disagree on the nature and depth of these risks or on the measures that need to be taken (Rosenthal and 't Hart 1991)—and they work with an exact science! Despite its modelling prowess and the unrelenting certitude conveyed by some of its best-known practitioners, the field of economics is anything but an exact science. So, by inference, in managing globalised national economies under conditions of unprecedented turbulence, expert disagreement is the norm and is, in fact, an additional source of uncertainty rather than a mechanism for helping policymakers cope with it.

In sum, crises are the combined products of unusual events and shared perceptions that something is seriously wrong. That said, it is vital to the perspective of this volume to remind ourselves that no set of events or developments is likely to be perceived in exactly the same way by members of a community. Perceptions of crisis are likely to vary, not just among communities—societies experience different types of disturbances and have different types and levels of vulnerability and resilience—but within them, reflecting the different biases of stakeholders as a result of their different values, positions and responsibilities (Rosenthal et al. 1989; 't Hart 1993; see further Chapter 2).

When perceptions of crisis are widespread, key public leadership challenges arise, regardless of the specific sector or context in which the events take place (Boin et al. 2005, 2008, 2009, 2010). The way in which these challenges are taken up, when and by whom greatly determines how crises will run their course in the systems in which they occur, and what sort of impact they will have on those systems. Prudent crisis leadership might not guarantee complete mitigation or total control of the problems. It is, however, a necessary condition for ensuring that the problems are addressed in a sensible, orderly fashion, which is understood and accepted by the maximum possible share of stakeholders, journalists and the general public. Moreover, effective crisis leadership is necessary to make sure that crises do not turn into messy blame games or give rise to ill-considered knee-jerk policy reforms (Boin and 't Hart 2003). The key challenges of crisis leadership are:

1. The challenge of *sense making*: diagnosing confusing, contested and often fast-moving situations correctly.
2. The challenge of *meaning making*: providing persuasive public accounts of what is happening, why it is happening, what can be done about it, how and by whom.

3. The challenge of *decision making*: making strategic policy judgments under conditions of time pressure, uncertainty and collective stress.

4. The challenge of *coordination*: forging effective communication and collaboration among pre-existing and ad hoc networks of public, private and sometimes international actors.

5. The challenge of *delimitation*: managing public expectations of the nature, scope and duration of crisis support that will be provided and determining principles for targeting and rationing such support among often ill-defined social and territorial 'victim' communities.

6. The challenge of *consolidation*: switching the gears of government and society back from crisis mode to recovery and 'business as usual', yet doing so without a loss of attention and momentum in delivering long-term services to those who are eligible.

7. The challenge of *accountability*: managing the process of expert, media, legislative and judicial inquiry and debate that tends to follow crises in such a way that responsibilities are clarified and accepted, destructive blame games are avoided and a degree of catharsis is achieved.

8. The challenge of *learning*: making sure that the organisations and systems involved in the crisis engage in critical, non-defensive modes of self-scrutiny and draw evidence-based and reflective lessons for their future performance rather politics-driven and knee-jerk ones.

9. The challenge of *remembering*: acknowledging that many crises are traumatic experiences for victims, responders and the organisations and communities involved and accommodating their desires that they and others should 'never forget'.

Most of these challenges are readily visible in the management of economic crises including the current global downturn. For example, the big *sense-making* challenge was obviously seeing it coming before it really happened. Very few policymakers, or economic forecasters for that matter, actually did. Once the problems had started to bite, the sense-making challenge was to gauge correctly what would happen next, which economic institutions and sectors were at greatest risk and how deep the eventual recession would flow. This was a daunting task. Those who were in the middle of it recall it as an experience that was bewildering, sobering and shattering all at the same time: absorbing a seemingly never-ending stream of indications (including rumours) that the problems were serious, bigger than before, bigger in fact that many could conceive of—and then going on to once again revise down one's own diagnosis and medium-term estimates.

Knowledge begets action. During the course of the crisis, national and international policymakers faced several critical *decision-making* junctures regarding interest rates, bailouts, the size and type of stimulus packages and,

7

early on, what to do after the Irish Government's announcement of bank deposit guarantees. These were big calls, often to be made in the course of days or even hours, when under less extreme circumstances decisions such as these would have been under consideration and scrutiny for weeks or months.

Because of the interconnected nature of financial markets and indeed the global economy as a whole, *coordination* challenges were manifold. The need for politicians and central bankers to carefully align their words and actions was highlighted. The crisis also saw remarkable features of transnational coordination, including concerted interest rate moves by national banks, an unprecedented EU-wide crisis-recovery plan and intensive G7/G8/G20 summitry. All these efforts were made in full awareness that, as political parties like to remind themselves periodically, 'disunity is death'. Even more so, in a fast-moving international financial crisis, lack of coordination in governmental signals to market actors can fatally undermine their effectiveness and risk wastage of billions of (borrowed) taxpayer dollars.

Once governments got into the business of bailing out banks and other corporations threatened with collapse, key challenges of *delimitation* arose. Which corporations were deemed 'too big to be allowed to fail', and on what grounds? Why give emergency aid to banks or car manufacturers and not to retailers or aircraft manufacturers? What if corporations receiving support kept coming back for more? Questions such as these generated robust public debate as well as significant disagreement among policymakers within and across different countries.

Issues of *consolidation* become poignant when the financial sector has stabilised and stock markets are buoyant again, but many sectors of the 'real economy' keep struggling and unemployment figures remain high. Does one accept that each recession leaves a residue of hundreds of thousands, if not more, people who will never make it back from the dole to a job? Or does one continue to define it as a crisis and treat it as such in terms of the commitment of political attention and government resources?

Meeting these challenges requires an approach to crisis response that is truly strategic, looking beyond the here and now of the operational challenges that can seem all consuming at the time and that dominate the daily news stories. In this volume, we focus on one particularly pivotal leadership task in the response to economic crises: the challenge of *meaning making*—how to communicate an unprecedented economic downturn to the public. This focus on crisis communication hardly exhausts the possibilities for analysing leadership responses to the global economic crisis, particularly regarding sense making ('why did they not see it coming?'), decision making and learning. Some accounts are already available, mostly by economists advancing particular theses about why the crisis became as big as it did (for example, Morris 2008; Shiller 2008;

Taylor 2009). At present, however, much of this analysis is premature, as events are still unfolding and information about the inner workings of corporate and governmental crisis-response machineries remains inaccessible to researchers. Meaning making, on the other hand, by definition takes place in public, and the signals sent by leaders and their reception in the public sphere can be easily gauged from readily available sources. Let us explain more what meaning making in crises entails, why it matters and how we propose to study it in the context of the 2008–09 financial crisis.

3. Meaning making in economic crises: frames and counter-frames

Arguably, the way in which problems are defined publicly permeates most of the other crisis leadership challenges. For example, if a crisis is seen as a case of pure misfortune, triggered by factors that none of the relevant policymakers could realistically have been expected to foresee or control, the debates about accountability and learning will be shaped quite differently from instances in which the crisis is widely seen to have been predictable and avoidable (Bovens and 't Hart 1996). Past research suggests that when critical contingencies unfold, politicians and senior public policymakers (as distinct from operational incident managers, who face more hands-on questions) are expected to provide answers to the same recurrent questions:

- how bad is the situation?
- how did this occur?
- who or what is to be held responsible for it?
- what if any changes to our current ideas, policies and practices are required to deal with it?

Clearly, answering each of these questions in the public arena is bound to be a matter of judgment and, more often than not, controversy. As implied above, how these questions are being answered in any given crisis has political and policy consequences. Politically, the ways in which causes and responsibilities are framed can have a severe impact on the public support for key actors and institutions. When something bad happens in a society, someone or something will be held to account. Apportioning blame is an integral part of contemporary politics in times of crisis (Bovens and 't Hart 1996; Brändström and Kuipers 2003; Furedi 2005; Boin et al. 2008). In policy terms, the very occurrence of significant crises (rather than run-of-the-mill incidents or slow-burning problems) raises acute questions about the effectiveness and robustness of current policies and institutions. In doing so, crises are threatening to the proponents of the status quo and provide opportunities for those committed to change and innovation. All parties will therefore seek to mould and exploit emerging crises in ways that suit their interests.

With the stakes of crises so high, the very act of defining and interpreting them constitutes a crucial battleground for stakeholders in the political and policy struggles that crises invariably unleash. In this volume, we study how public leaders in nine jurisdictions engaged in such 'framing contests' and how their attempts to interpret the cascading events of the economic downturn were received in the media. The *central question* of this volume is: how did key heads of government, finance ministers and national bank presidents publicly interpret the severity, causes, responsibilities and policy implications of the emerging global economic downturn and how were their framing attempts received publicly?

In Australia, for example, Prime Minister Kevin Rudd was conspicuously engaged in this politics of crisis exploitation. In an essay published in February 2009 in the magazine *The Monthly*, Rudd (2009) took the view: that the global economic downturn amounted to the biggest economic collapse since the Great Depression of the 1930s; that it was caused in large part by speculation and greed, which were allowed to reign free by the laissez-faire approach to economic regulation propagated and institutionalised by proponents of 'neo-liberalism'; that responsibility for the downturn should therefore rest with governments who allowed this to happen on their watch, in particular governments of the neo-liberal ilk (such as the government led by Rudd's predecessor, John Howard) that actively aided and abetted a 'let the market rule' philosophy, the credibility of which had now entirely collapsed; and that Australia needed a paradigm shift away from neo-liberalism and towards a rejuvenated form of social democracy in which the State was no longer seen as part of the problem but rather as a pivotal part of the solution when it came to creating and sustaining prosperous and fair societies.

Rudd's essay was also published in *Le Monde* and distributed among the participants of the 2009 G20 summit on the crisis. Within Australia, it was sharply criticised by the Liberal opposition and hotly debated in newspapers, the 'blogosphere' and subsequent issues of *The Monthly*. Whatever the intellectual merits of Rudd's argument, his framing attempt no doubt shaped the terms of Australian public debate about the underlying causes and wider implications of the crisis (see further Chapter 9).

In this volume, we look at Rudd as well as many of his counterparts internationally. We also look at other key office-holders in economic crisis management, particularly treasurers/finance ministers and national bank governors. How did other heads of government and other key managers of the national economy frame the unfolding events? How did these frames seek to accomplish their political and policy aims in dealing with the crisis? How persuasive were their accounts believed to be by key media and public opinion at large?

Theoretically, this study sits at the intersection of the fields of political communication, leadership and crisis management. Understanding political elites through rhetorical analysis is a tried and tested genre in political science and has found itself a new lease on life in the age of television and the Internet (Edelman 1977; Tulis 1987; Hart 1989; Hinckley 1990; Gaffney 1991; Uhr 2002, 2003). We are also not the first to study the economic rhetoric of leaders—in times of crisis or otherwise (see Wood 2007). Many scholars of political rhetoric stress its significance in making or breaking leaders' careers, as well as in influencing their effectiveness as agenda setters, legislators and policymakers, although there are indications that this influence should not be overstated (Edwards 2003; Canes-Wrone 2006; Curran 2004; Wood 2007:10–13). As described, the field of crisis management studies is vast and interdisciplinary, but studies that take a rhetorical perspective on it are few and far between in political science, though more common in business studies (cf. Bostdorff 1994; Kiewe 1994; Kuypers 1997; Fearn-Banks 2002; Millar and Heath 2003). The present study is, however, unique in examining the economic crisis rhetoric of leaders in the context of a broader, political theory of crisis leadership, which will be outlined in Chapter 2.

4. Overview and acknowledgments

The centrepiece of this volume is a series of structured and focused case studies of leader rhetoric about the economic crisis during its critical escalation stage (April 2008 to March 2009) and media and public opinion responses to that rhetoric. The volume comprises five parts. *Part I* sets the stage of the research project as a whole and continues in Chapter 2 with the presentation of the analytical framework underpinning all the national case studies. *Part II* looks at North America and is a study of contrasts. The crisis originated in the US sub-prime mortgage market and eventually swept up that country's entire financial system as well as destroying significant parts of its 'real' economy. The challenge for US leaders was therefore to read the writing on the wall and somehow get on top of a mountain of bad tidings and offer a realistic pathway out of the crisis, without themselves being consumed by the widespread public despair and disenchantment that accompanied the downturn. In Canada meanwhile, the Harper Government long stuck to a story of optimism about that country's economic resilience even while its neighbour—with whose giant economy Canada's was intimately intertwined—was coming unstuck economically and psychologically. In both countries, the escalation of the financial crisis coincided with elections, shaping the way in which old and new incumbents talked about the issues. In the United States, the voters punished the Republican Party; in Canada, the incumbent government managed to consolidate its mandate.

Part III switches focus to Europe. It contains case studies of the crisis rhetoric of the leaders of the United Kingdom, France, Ireland and the European Commission and the European Central Bank. The crisis hit hard and fast in the United Kingdom and Ireland. In both countries, long-serving governments struggled to switch from an initial facade of optimism to acknowledging the depth of the problems, yet sidestepped questions about their own responsibilities in exposing their financial systems and national economies to the risks of 'irrational exuberance' (Shiller 2006). In France, the relatively new President, Nicolas Sarkozy, did not labour under that kind of pressure. His rhetoric suggested that he saw the crisis as an opportunity for financial and economic reform, while not denying the grave threat it posed to the French economy and the already tenuous employment figures. Sarkozy furthermore had to combine roles as national leader with that of (rotating) President of the European Council, and thus carefully balance French national and supranational perspectives in his crisis rhetoric. In the final chapter of this part, we look at the leaders of the European Commission and the European Central Bank. The leaders of the former knew they were facing a stern test given the chequered history of attempts at keeping member states united in the face of major emergencies and crises, including the conflict in the former Yugoslavia, the wars in Iraq and Afghanistan and major veterinary emergencies including the outbreak of *Bovine spongiform encephalopathy* (BSE, or mad cow disease) (Van Selm-Thorburn and Verbeek 1998; Gronvall 2001). The global economic crisis thus became an exercise in demonstrating European crisis management capacity (cf. Boin et al. 2006)—one that EC President, José Manuel Barroso, seemed to embrace wholeheartedly in an oft-repeated public mantra that stressed European unity, opportunity and strength.

Part IV goes on to examine the leaders of three countries in the Asia-Pacific region: Singapore, Australia and New Zealand. The first is of special interest for three reasons: it is the only country in the set that had relatively recent experience of responding to a financial meltdown (the 1997–98 East Asian crisis); it is the only country without a free media (although the European Union does not as yet have its own public sphere either, but for a different set of reasons); and it has an extremely open economy highly dependent on foreign investment (like Ireland's). During the period studied here, Singaporean leaders consistently stressed their country's sound fiscal and monetary policies and pointed their fingers towards 'the West' as the cause of all the problems. Australia and New Zealand make for an interesting pair-wise comparison. In late 2007, Rudd's Labor government assumed office in less than ideal circumstances, taking charge of the national economy at the very moment when the financial crisis gained momentum. For that very reason, however, the crisis also presented the government with major opportunities for heroic posturing, sweeping policy packages and heaping blame on predecessors. Helen Clarke's three-term New

Zealand Labour government, in contrast, was facing a much more difficult political situation: a more vulnerable national economy, a strong and vocal opposition challenging its economic policy competence and a looming election deadline. This proved too much to handle; Labour lost the election. With the economy in ever more dire straits, the new National Party coalition government led by newcomer John Key faced severe policy predicaments but fertile political ground for advocating reforms.

Finally, *Part V* places the case studies in a broader perspective. It contains a number of thematic reflections by invited experts. Taking the focus away from executive government, Brendan McCaffrie looks at the role of opposition leaders during the crisis. Arjen Boin reflects on the limits of rhetoric and considers other critical challenges for leaders when faced with an economic crisis. Allan McConnell offers some thoughts on the place of framing and meaning making in leaders' broader strategies for remaining politically competitive and achieving the policy outcomes they seek to attain. Finally, Bengt Sundelius's chapter takes the form of a prescriptive memo to a government leader, reminding him/her of the broad array of challenges as well as opportunities that contemporary trans-boundary crises tend to present.

In the concluding editorial chapter, we review the fruits of this volume and offer some reflections triggered by the similarities and differences that can be observed in the ways in which leaders within and across the different jurisdictions go about the work of framing the global meltdown. We identify a number of contextual factors that we suggest shape their perceptions of the crisis and make them prefer some framing tactics to others. We also show that much of the rhetoric of the leaders followed a pattern of 'staged retreat': from denying the magnitude of the crisis, through acknowledgment, through various forms of blame deflection and, occasionally, some forms of contrition or at least public self-reflection. Finally, we review the public reception and political effects of leader rhetoric in this crisis. While it is clearly too early to produce a final assessment, one thing we note and reflect on is the remarkable absence of anything remotely resembling a 'rally around the flag effect' in the media or public opinion at large. The financial meltdown and the recession that followed it were, by and large, divisive issues that tended to play out along the lines of government versus opposition. Despite the magnitude and universal nature of the threat, no leader or government in the countries studied managed to construct a truly national coalition in tackling the crisis.

This volume is an exercise in quick-response research: a concerted effort to employ tools of social science research to shed light on key issues of politics and public policy and publish the results at the time when the events in question are still unfolding. The idea for devoting a volume to leader rhetoric on the financial crisis was born when the participants in Paul 't Hart and Karen Tindall's honours course on crisis leadership showed extraordinary ambition and application in conducting their empirical research assignments. Their sustained efforts form the backbones of parts II–IV of this volume, and they deserve our thanks for their first-class work. An auditor to that same course, experienced journalist Garry Sturgess, kindly commented in detail on all the papers that later became the chapters in this volume. His input was highly valued. The senior scholars featured in Part V responded quickly and positively to our call for them to contribute a thematic essay to this volume—and to do so fast. Fitting this into their busy schedules was an act of exemplary collegiality that we gratefully acknowledge. The Dean of the Australia and New Zealand School of Government, Professor Allan Fels, kindly provided instantaneous financial support for this exercise, without which we could never have produced a volume of this kind within three months. Finally, John Butcher of the Political Science Program at The Australian National University's Research School of Social Sciences was the ever-reliable conduit between us and ANU E Press, which kindly fitted us into their already tight production schedule. We thank John and the press for their assistance and flexibility.

Box 1.1 Global shockwaves and global initiatives, July 2007 – April 2009 [1]

July 2007: After rival banks decide not to bail out Bear Stearns, investors are told that they will get back little of the money invested in two hedge funds. Federal Reserve Chairman, Ben Bernanke, warns that the US sub-prime crisis could result in losses of $100 billion.

9 August: Investment bank BNP Paribas announces liquidity problems. The next week sees the European Union inject €200 billion into the banking market and the beginning of intervention by the US Federal Reserve and the Bank of Canada.

14 September: A BBC report that Northern Rock has requested emergency assistance from the Bank of England sparks the largest run on a British bank in more than a century.

October: Citigroup, Swiss bank UBS and Merrill Lynch all announce massive losses ($5.9 billion, $3.4 billion and $7.9 billion, respectively) from sub-prime related investments.

13 December: Five major central banks offer banks loans worth billions of dollars in a move coordinated by the US Federal Reserve.

9 January 2008: The World Bank predicts a slowdown in global economic growth during 2008.

---

21 January: Global stock markets experience their most significant falls since 9/11.

22 January: Global stock markets recover from massive falls the day before. In an attempt to avoid a recession in the United States, the Federal Reserve makes its largest rate cut in a quarter of a century.

10 February: Leaders of the G7 put the potential losses from the US sub-prime crisis at $400 billion.

17 March: JP Morgan Chase acquires Bear Stearns in a deal backed by $30 billion of central bank loans.

8 April: The International Monetary Fund (IMF) puts the figure for potential losses from the crisis at $1 trillion and warns the sub-prime crisis will likely affect other sectors of society.

14 July: Financial authorities in the United States intervene to assist the two largest lenders, Fannie Mae and Freddie Mac, after their share prices freefell the previous week.

4 August: HSBC, a major European bank, records a profit fall of nearly one-third.

7 September: After determining that the downfall of Fannie Mae and Freddie Mac poses a systemic risk to the stability of the US economy, the government rescues the two mortgage lenders in one of the largest bailouts in the country's history.

15 September: Lehman Brothers becomes the first major bank to collapse since the crisis began.

16 September: With an $85 billion rescue package, the US Federal Reserve attempts to save AIG, America's largest insurance company, from bankruptcy.

28 September: Fortis, a major European banking and insurance company, is partly nationalised. Lawmakers agree on the $700 billion rescue plan for the US financial sector, which is to be put forward for approval by Congress.

29 September: The US House of Representatives rejects the $700 billion rescue plan. The decision has major negative repercussions on Wall Street.

30 September: The Belgian, French and Luxembourg governments bail out European bank Dexia.

3 October: The US House of Representatives passes the $700 billion rescue package.

8 October: An emergency interest rate cut of 0.5 of a percentage point is made by the US Federal Reserve, the European Central Bank, Bank of England and the central banks of Canada, Sweden and Switzerland.

11 October: Washington, DC, hosts a meeting of the G7 finance ministers, who issue a plan of 'decisive action' to reinvigorate the frozen credit markets.

6 November: The IMF approves a $16.2 billion loan to the Ukraine.

14 November: The eurozone is officially in recession after a third-quarter contraction of 0.2 per cent. Washington, DC, hosts a meeting of the G20 leaders to discuss the global financial crisis, short-term solutions and possible long-term reforms.

20 November: After Iceland's entire banking system collapsed in October 2008, the IMF approves its first loan since 1976 to a Western European nation.

25 November: The IMF approves a $7.6 billion loan to Pakistan. The Federal Reserve plans to inject another $800 billion into the US economy.

26 November: The European Commission announces a €200 billion economic recovery plan.

31 December: In 2008, the FTSE 100 dropped 31.13 per cent, the Dax in Frankfurt fell 40.4 per cent and the Cac in Paris lost 42.7 per cent.

28 January 2009: The IMF warns that world economic growth is likely to decrease to 0.5 per cent in 2009. The International Labour Organisation (ILO) warns that up to 51 million jobs could be lost worldwide in 2009.

17 February: US President, Barack Obama, signs into law 'the most sweeping recovery package in our history'—a $787 billion economic stimulus plan.

14 March: G20 finance ministers announce that they will work together to bring the world out of recession.

2 April: London hosts a summit of G20 leaders, who agree on $1.1 trillion worth of measures to deal with the global financial crisis.

References

Boin, A. and 't Hart, P. 2003, 'Public leadership in times of crisis: mission impossible?', *Public Administration Review*, vol. 63, no. 5, pp. 544–53.

Boin, A., 't Hart, P., Stern, E. and Sundelius, B. 2005, *The Politics of Crisis Management: Public leadership under pressure*, Cambridge University Press, Cambridge.

Boin, A., Ekengren, M. and Rhinard, M. (eds) 2006, 'Protecting the union: the emergence of a new policy space', *Journal of European Integration*, vol. 28, no. 5 (Special issue), pp. 405–21.

Boin, A., McConnell, A. and 't Hart, P. (eds) 2008, *Governing After Crisis: The politics of investigation, accountability and learning*, Cambridge University Press, Cambridge.

Boin, A., McConnell, A. and 't Hart, P. 2009, 'Crisis exploitation: political and policy impacts of framing contests', *Journal of European Public Policy*, vol. 16, no. 1, pp. 81–106.

Boin, A., McConnell, A. and 't Hart, P. (forthcoming), 'Coping with unscheduled events: the challenges of crisis leadership', in R. A. Couto (ed.) *Political and Civil Leadership: A reference handbook*, Sage.

Bostdorff, D. 1994, *The Presidency and the Rhetoric of Foreign Crisis*, University of South Carolina Press, Durham.

Bovens, M. and 't Hart, P. 1996, *Understanding Policy Fiascoes*, Transaction Publishers, New Brunswick.

Brändström, A. and Kuipers, S. L. 2003, 'From "normal incidents" to political crises: understanding the selective politicization of policy failures', *Government and Opposition*, vol. 38, no. 3, pp. 279–305.

Canes-Wrone, B. 2006, *Who Leads Whom? Presidents, policy, and the public*, University of Chicago Press, Chicago.

Curran, J. 2004, *The Power of Speech: Australian prime ministers defining the national image*, Melbourne University Press, Melbourne.

Douglas, M. and Wildavsky, A. 1982, *Risk and Culture*, University of California Press, Berkeley.

Edelman, M. 1977, *Political Language: Words that succeed and policies that fail*, Academic Press, New York.

Edwards III, G. C. 2003, *On Deaf Ears: The Limits of the Bully Pulpit*, Yale University Press: New Haven.

Fearn-Banks, K. 2002, *Crisis Communication: A case book approach*, Erlbaum, Mahwah.

Furedi, F. 2005, *Politics of Fear*, Continuum, London.

Gaffney, J. 1991, *The Language of Political Leadership in Contemporary Britain*, St Martin's Press, New York.

Gronvall, J. 2001, 'Mad cow disease: the role of experts and European crisis management', in U. Rosenthal, A. Boin and L. K. Comfort (eds), *Managing Crises: Threats, dilemmas, opportunities*, Thomas, Springfield, pp. 155–74.

't Hart, P. 1993, 'Symbols, rituals and power: the lost dimension in crisis management', *Journal of Contingencies and Crisis Management*, vol. 1, no. 1, pp. 36–50.

Hart, R. P. 1989, *The Sound of Leadership: Presidential communication in the modern age*, University of Chicago Press, Chicago.

Hinckley, B. 1990, *The Symbolic Presidency: How presidents portray themselves*, Routledge, New York.

Kiewe, A. 1994, *The Modern Presidency and Crisis Rhetoric*, Praeger, New York.

Kuypers, J. A. 1997, *Presidential Crisis Rhetoric and the Press in the Post Cold War World*, Praeger, New York.

Millar, D. P. and Heath, R. L. 2003, *Responding to Crises: A rhetorical approach to crisis communication*, Erlbaum, Mahwah.

Morris, C. R. 2008, *The Trillion Dollar Meltdown: Easy money, high rollers, and the great credit crash*, Public Affairs Press, New York.

Rosenthal, U. and 't Hart, P. 1991, 'Experts and decision makers in crisis situations', *Knowledge, Diffusion, Utilization*, vol. 12, no. 4, pp. 350–72.

Rosenthal, U., Charles, M. T. and 't Hart, P. 1989, *Coping With Crises*, Thomas, Springfield.

Rudd, K. 2009, 'Essay: the global financial crisis', *The Monthly*, February, pp. 26–38.

Shiller, R. J. 2006, *Irrational Exuberance*, Doubleday, New York.

Shiller, R. J. 2008, *The Subprime Solution: How today's global financial crisis happened, and what to do about it*, Princeton University Press, Princeton.

Taylor, J. B. 2009, *Getting off Track: How government actions and interventions caused, prolonged, and worsened the financial crisis*, Hoover Institution, Stanford.

Tulis J. K. 1987, *The Rhetorical Presidency*, Princeton University Press, Princeton, NJ.

Uhr, J. 2002, 'Political leadership and rhetoric', in H. G. Brennan and F. G. Castles (eds), *Australia Reshaped: 200 years of institutional transformation*, Cambridge University Press, Cambridge, pp. 261–94.

Uhr, J. 2003, 'Just rhetoric? Exploring the language of leadership', in P. Bishop, C. Connors and C. Sampford (eds), *Management, Organisation and Ethics in the Public Sector*, Routledge, London, pp. 123–44.

Van Selm-Thorburn, J. and Verbeek, B. 1998, 'The chance of a lifetime? The European Community's foreign and refugee policies towards the conflict in Yugoslavia, 1991–95', in P. Gray and P. 't Hart (eds), *Public Policy Disasters in Western Europe*, Routledge, London, pp. 175–92.

Wood, B. D. 2007, *The Politics of Economic Leadership: The causes and consequences of presidential rhetoric*, Princeton University Press, Princeton.

Endnotes

1 The chronology is based on several sources but is drawn primarily from the BBC timeline ('Credit crunch to downturn', *BBC*, viewed 20 June 2009, http://news.bbc.co.uk/2/hi/business/7521250.stm). Unless otherwise stated, dollar values refer to US dollars. Thanks to Michael Jones for compiling the global chronology.

2. Understanding crisis exploitation: leadership, rhetoric and framing contests in response to the economic meltdown

Paul 't Hart and Karen Tindall

1. Crises as political battlegrounds

Dramatic episodes in the life of a polity such as financial crises and major recessions can cast long shadows on the polities in which they occur (Birkland 1997, 2006; Baumgartner and Jones 1993, 2002; Lomborg 2004; Posner 2004).[1] The sense of threat and uncertainty they induce can profoundly impact people's understanding of the world around them. The occurrence of a large-scale emergency or the widespread use of the emotive labels such as 'crisis', 'scandal' or 'fiasco' to denote a particular state of affairs or trend in the public domain implies a 'dislocation' of hitherto dominant social, political or administrative discourses (Wagner-Pacifici 1986, 1994; Howarth et al. 2000). When a crisis de-legitimises the power and authority relationships that these discourses underpin, structural change is desired and expected by many ('t Hart 1993).

Such change can happen, but not necessarily so. In fact, the dynamics and outcomes of crisis episodes are hard to predict. For example, former German Chancellor Gerhard Schröder miraculously emerged as the winner of the national elections after his well-performed role as the nation's symbolic 'crisis manager' during the riverine floods in 2002, yet the Spanish Prime Minister suffered a stunning electoral loss in the immediate aftermath of the Madrid train bombings of 2004. Former US President George W. Bush saw his hitherto modest approval ratings soar in the wake of the 9/11 attacks, but an already unpopular Bush Administration lost further prestige in the aftermath of Hurricane Katrina.

Likewise, public institutions can be affected quite differently in the aftermath of critical events: some take a public beating and are forced to reform (the National Aeronautics and Space Administration [NASA] after the *Challenger* and *Columbia* shuttle disasters); some weather the political storm (the Belgian gendarmerie after its spectacular failure to effectively police the 1985 European Cup Final at the Heysel Stadium in Brussels); others become symbolic of heroic public service (the New York City Fire Department after 9/11).

The same goes for public policies and programs. Gun-control policy in Australia was rapidly and drastically tightened after the 1996 Port Arthur massacre in Tasmania. Legislation banning 'dangerous dogs' was rapidly enacted in the United Kingdom after a few fatal biting incidents (Lodge and Hood 2002). And 9/11 produced a worldwide cascade of national policy reforms in areas such as policing, immigration, data protection and criminal law—for good or bad (cf. Klein 2007; Wolf 2007). In other cases, however, big emergencies can trigger big investigations and temporarily jolt political agendas but in the end do not result in major policy changes.

What explains these different outcomes? Most scholars writing about the nexus between crises, disasters and public policy note their potential agenda-setting effects, but have not developed explanations for their contingent nature and their variable impacts (Primo and Cobb 2003; Birkland 2006). The emerging literature on blame management has only just begun to address the mechanisms determining the fate of office-holders in the wake of major disturbances and scandals (Hood et al. 2007).

This literature suggests that the process of crisis exploitation could help to explain the variance in outcomes. Disruptions of societal routines and expectations open up two types of space for actors inside and outside government. First, *crises can be used as political weapons*. Crises mobilise the mass media, which will put an intense spotlight on the issues and actors involved. To the extent that they generate victims, damage and/or community stress, the government of the day is challenged to step in and show it can muster an effective, compassionate, sensible response. At the same time, it might face critical questions about its role in the very occurrence of the crisis. Why did it not prevent the crisis from happening? How well prepared was it for this type of contingency? Was it asleep at the wheel or simply overpowered by overwhelming forces outside its sphere of influence? In political terms, crises challenge actors inside and outside government to weave persuasive narratives about what is happening and what is at stake, why it is happening, how they have acted in the lead-up to the present crisis and how they propose we should deal with and learn from the crisis moving forward. Those whose narratives are considered persuasive stand to gain prestige and support; those who are found wanting can end up as scapegoats.

Second, *crises help 'de-institutionalise' hitherto taken-for-granted policy beliefs and practices* (Boin and 't Hart 2003). The more severe a current crisis is perceived to be, and the more it appears to be caused by foreseeable and avoidable problems in the design or implementation of the policy itself, the bigger is the opportunity space for critical reconsideration of current policies and the successful advancement of (radical) reform proposals (Keeler 1993; Birkland 2006; Klein 2007). By their very occurrence (provided they are widely felt and labelled as such), crises tend to benefit critics of the status quo: experts, ideologues and advocacy groups already on record as challenging established but now compromised policies. They also present particular opportunities to newly incumbent office-holders, who cannot be blamed for present 'messes' but who can use these messes to highlight the need for policy changes they might have been seeking to pursue anyway.

The key currency of crisis management in the political and policy arenas is persuasion. More specifically, this study presumes that crises can be usefully understood in terms of *framing contests*—battles between competing definitions of the situation—between the various actors that seek to contain or exploit crisis-induced opportunity space for political posturing and policy change (cf. Alink et al. 2001). [2]

Crises invite four types of framing efforts, concerning 1) the nature and severity of a crisis, 2) its causes, 3) the responsibility for its occurrence or escalation, and 4) its policy implications. Actors inside and outside government will strive to have their particular interpretations of the crisis accepted in the media and by the public as the authoritative account ('t Hart 1993; Tarrow 1994; Brändström and Kuipers 2003; De Vries 2004; see also Stone 2001). In other words, they seek to 'exploit' the disruption of 'governance as usual' that emergencies and disturbances entail: to defend and strengthen their positions and authority, to attract or deflect public attention, to get rid of old policies and sow the seeds of new ones (Keeler 1993). When a particular 'crisis narrative' takes hold, it can be an important force for non-incremental changes in policy fields that are normally stabilised by the forces of path dependence, inheritance and veto-playing (Hay 2002; Kay 2006; Kuipers 2006).

This chapter provides the analytical framework that has guided this comparative study of leader rhetoric and media responses to that rhetoric during the escalation stage of the global economic downturn. We place this rhetoric within the broader context of what we have elsewhere referred to as *crisis exploitation* (Boin et al. 2009). We define crisis exploitation as the purposeful utilisation of crisis-type rhetoric to significantly alter levels of political support for incumbent public office-holders and existing public policies and their alternatives. By studying and interpreting leaders' crisis rhetoric through this lens, we seek to open the 'black box' of politico-strategic crisis management (rather than its operational management, which is the focus of the bulk of existing research on emergencies and crises).

In formal terms, the ultimate explanandum of the study of the rhetoric of crisis exploitation is twofold: the nature and depth of changes in political support for key public office-holders and/or agencies; and the nature and degree of policy change in the wake of an emergency/disturbance. [3] Its triggering condition is the occurrence of non-routine, disruptive incidents or trends: the cascade of 'bad news' about the state of US financial institutions, the housing markets and its national economy, eventually spilling over into financial institutions and macroeconomic indicators worldwide. The focus of our analytical attention, however, lies with what happens in between; how these adverse events are 'framed' (that is, given meaning) by key public leaders.

2. Dissecting framing contests

To a considerable extent, emergencies, economic downturns and other forms of social crisis are all in the eye of the beholder. Following the classic Thomas theorem ('if men define their situations as real, they are real in their consequences'), it is not the events on the ground, but their public perception and interpretation that determine their potential impact on political office-holders and public policy. As many have remarked in the context of the emerging recession: much of it has evolved from perceptual, psychological factors such as confidence, trust and fear. Accordingly, we define crises as events or developments widely perceived by members of relevant communities to constitute urgent threats to core community values and structures. Notwithstanding that, it is essential to note no set of events or developments is likely to be perceived entirely uniformly by the members of a community. Perceptions of crisis are likely to vary not just among communities—societies experience different types of disturbances and have different types and levels of vulnerability and resilience—but within them, reflecting the different biases of stakeholders as a result of their different values, positions and responsibilities. These differential perceptions and indeed accounts of a crisis constitute the stuff of crisis exploitation, as will be detailed below.

Figure 2.1 offers a stylised representation of the constructed nature of 'crises'. Actors confronted with the same situation (for example, an earthquake, a case of collective corruption in the public service, a shooting spree or a child dying of parental abuse) might adopt fundamentally different types of frames. We distinguish here between three types.

- Type-1. Business-as-usual frame: denial that the events in question represent more than an *unfortunate incident*, and thus a predisposition to downplay the idea that they should have any political or policy repercussions whatsoever.
- Type-2. Crisis as threat frame: deeming the events to be a *critical threat* to the collective good embodied in the status quo before these events came to light, and thus a predisposition to defend the agents (incumbent office-holders) and tools (existing policies and organisational practices) of that status quo against criticism.
- Type-3. Crisis as opportunity frame: deeming the events to be a *critical opportunity* to expose deficiencies in the status quo ex ante, and hence a

predisposition to pinpoint blameworthy behaviour by status quo agents and dysfunctional policies and organisations in order to mobilise support for their removal or substantive alteration.

Figure 2.1 Severity and causality: the first two crisis-framing contests

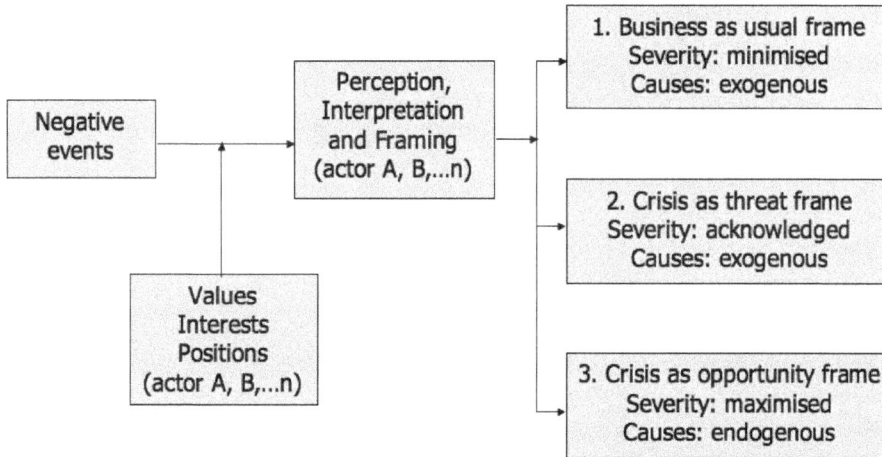

Not so long ago, type-1 or type-2 representations of incidents and disasters were likely to dominate and scholarly interest focused on the 'solidarity impulses' and 'altruistic communities' these events tended to generate (Barton 1969). Most disasters entered collective memory as an 'act of God', defying explanation, redress and guilt (Rosenthal 1998). They were treated as incomprehensible events that tested and defeated available administrative and political repertoires of prevention and response. After these events, which few people (if any) were able to fathom (let alone plan for), bewilderment and sorrow gave rise to an urgent need to move on and rebuild a state of order (see, for instance, Rozario 2005).

Even natural disaster experts agree that times have changed (Quarantelli 1998; Steinberg 2000; Quarantelli and Perry 2005). In today's risk society, disasters typically evoke nagging questions that spell trouble for incumbent leaders: why did they not see this coming? We have seen this before, so why did they not know what to do this time? Almost invariably, post-mortem activities bring to light that there had been multiple, albeit scattered and sometimes ambiguous hunches, signals and warnings about growing vulnerabilities and threats along the lines of the scenario that actually transpired. These were evidently not acted on effectively, and much of the political controversy in the aftermath of the once 'incomprehensible' crisis focuses on the question of why no action was taken. So type-3 ways of perceiving and framing the events have gained potential currency.

The first framing contest: severity—ripple or crisis?

Figure 2.1 presents two of four types of framing contests that occur in the event of any set of unscheduled, negative events. The first contest centres on the *significance* of the events: are they within or outside the community's 'zone of indifference' (Barnard 1938; cf. Romzek and Dubnick 1987) and its standard collective coping repertoires? Are they both 'big' and 'bad' for the community at hand (for example, the Al Gore view of climate change); bad but not really big (the nuclear industry's view of the nuclear-waste problem); only big but not really all that bad (the *Stern Report* view of global warming); or neither (the Dutch view of recreational soft drug consumption)? At stake in this significance contest is the agenda status of the issues raised by the events: will they be seen as top priority (however temporary that might turn out to be) or can they be ignored altogether or dealt with in routine, piecemeal fashion?

Clearly, proponents of type-1 frames argue to *minimise* event significance, proponents of type-2 frames are more likely to *acknowledge* event significance and proponents of type-3 frames are most likely to *maximise* event significance. The political risk of adhering to a type-1 frame is to be accused of 'blindness', 'passivity' and 'rigidity'; the political risk of type-3 frames is to come across as 'alarmist' or 'opportunistic'. Both can be accused of being divorced from reality, if not of outright lying. Equally clearly, a true sense of crisis can be said to exist in a political and policy sense only when there are sufficiently credible, audible voices and seemingly self-evident facts and images underpinning the idea that what is going on is indeed *big, bad* and moreover *urgent* (Rosenthal et al. 1989). If this is not the case, denials or otherwise comparatively benign and complacent definitions of the situation are likely to prevail.

Crisis framing in cases other than major disasters, huge outbursts of violence and the like is therefore a political challenge of considerable magnitude. Many unscheduled events and latent risks are fundamentally ambiguous, leaving considerable space for type-1 denials. Companies that see their share prices fall have no reason to claim that these depreciations reflect underlying problems in corporate strategy and/or management. In fact, many big companies as well as public organisations are on record as systematically neglecting and genuinely underestimating their own latent vulnerabilities (Slatter 1984; Mitroff and Pauchant 1990; Turner and Pidgeon 1997).

Take an example. A director of a child protection agency will not self-evidently treat the violent death of one of her agency's young clients as a major event. In her business, child-protection professionals have to live with the reality that not every endangered child can be saved. Even if two die within one week, this could still be explained away as a statistical aberration—as coincidence. There is a point, however, at which a type-1 reaction, however well entrenched, becomes cognitively or politically unsustainable—for example, if an unusually high number of children die in a given short time, or even if only one child dies in particularly gruesome circumstances, or if reports emerge about one hitherto unnoticed fatality that contain facts or allegations compromising the child protection agency's performance of its custodial role.

This tipping point, however, is never fixed or readily recognisable, because it is a function of a constellation of variable situational, historical, cultural and political forces (cf. Axelrod and Cohen 2000). Rosenthal (1988) has captured the only generalisation that might apply, arguing that the greater the sense of invulnerability in a society, the more likely it is that relatively minor disturbances will have major destabilising effects. In contrast, societies with a well-developed 'disaster subculture' or organisations with a resilient 'safety culture' have learned to live with adversity and have developed cultural and organisational coping resources.

In instances where denial is no longer a credible option, debates about responsibility, blame and policy implications take a different turn depending on which causal story about the nature and genesis of unscheduled events comes to prevail: the type-2 notion of well-meaning policymakers not being informed of looming vulnerabilities and threats (in which case blame goes down the hierarchy and outside the organisation); or the type-1 notion of senior executives unwilling to address the growing risk brought to their attention (in which case blame attribution moves upward and to the centre). The same applies to cases where the official response to a clearly exogenous incident or development is widely perceived as being slow, disorganised or insensitive to the needs of the stricken community.

For example, after Hurricane Katrina, the US Federal Emergency Management Agency and the White House took a terrible public beating—not so much because they had failed to prevent the levee break (although the Federal Government was certainly blamed by state and local authorities for having long neglected the flood defences in the region), but primarily because the disaster evoked an image of total disarray at the very heart of the government's much vaunted post-9/11 crisis-management machinery (cf. Garnett and Kouzmin 2007). Likewise, its tardy and seemingly indifferent response to the fate of thousands of its citizens victimised by the 2004 tsunami created political problems for the Swedish cabinet (Brändström et al. 2008). An official investigation revealed clear evidence that the need to build and maintain crisis-response capacity at the cabinet level had not been given the priority it deserved. Moreover, clumsy attempts by the prime minister and the foreign minister to deflect blame for the slow response compounded their problems. Not only did they fail to instigate quick and effective crisis operations, their limited grasp of the symbolic dimensions of the tsunami predicament was painfully exposed.

The second framing contest: causality—incident or symptom?

When type-1 crisis denial is not or no longer an option, the main emphasis in the framing contest centres on causality: who or what drives the course of events? At stake in the causality contest are the political fortunes of office-holders and their challengers, as well as the future of the current and existing set of policies, programs and organisations in the domain in which the crisis has materialised.

In their study of policy fiascos, Bovens and 't Hart (1996:129) argue that 'to explain is to blame'. As Figure 2.1 shows, type-3 causal frames that emphasise factors deemed to be foreseeable and controllable by a particular set of policymakers serve to 'endogenise' accountability; such frames focus blame on identifiable individuals and the policies they embody. Type-1/2 frames that 'exogenise' accountability serve to get policymakers 'off the hook' and leave the fundamental premises of existing policies in tact. These frames typically refer to forces of nature or 'out-groups' of various kinds (Islamic radicals; hard-core 'anarchists' in otherwise peaceful protest movements; greedy or fraudulent corporate managers; human errors of technical designers or low-level operators). They point to either unforeseeability (the Indian Ocean tsunami from the perspective of state and local officials in Indonesia, Thailand or Sri Lanka) or uncontrollability (an economic recession allegedly brought about by a global slump pervading an otherwise well-managed national economy). In the latter case, for example, some might argue that the central bank did not loosen monetary policy soon enough or that the government was complacent in riding a boom period based on a limited and therefore vulnerable mix of export assets. More often than not, however, they provide enough loopholes for blame diffusion across the 'many hands' that usually make up complex contemporary governance arrangements (Bovens 1998).

The third framing contest: the political game—blameworthy or not?

In the third framing contest (Table 2.1) the crucial issue at stake is where blame for the occurrence or escalation of the crisis lands. Anti-establishment actors—for example, opposition leaders, advocacy groups, but potentially also newly incumbent executive office-holders themselves—will have to decide whether they can convincingly blame (past) incumbents. If they find they have a case to make, they will have to decide whether they want to use it to call for sanctions against those office-holders or whether to stop short of that and merely use the crisis to undermine their authority by damaging their reputations. In contrast, (past or incumbent) office-holders must choose between rejecting, deflecting or diffusing responsibility for the crisis or accepting it wholly or partially. As said, newly incumbent leaders, such as some of the heads of government to be discussed in the case study chapters in this volume, can try and pinpoint blame on their predecessors. Blame deflection occurs when leader rhetoric points to exogenous factors ('market forces') or failures of subordinates (that is, the public service). Blame diffusion is the logical outcome of a 'many hands' argument: if people are persuaded that the causes of the crisis are multiple and complex then blaming a single leader or a small subset of leaders feels arbitrary. Such arguments seek to substitute a 'forensic' logic of responsibility for the 'political' logic of responsibility that can be found in doctrines of collective or ministerial responsibility. If the many-hands view prevails, the buck stops nowhere.

Critics Incumbents	Absolve blame	Focus blame
Accept responsibility	I. Blame minimisation: elite escape likely	II. Blame acceptance: elite damage likely
Deny responsibility	III. Blame avoidance: elite escape likely	IV. Blame showdown: elite damage, escape, rejuvenation all possible

Table 2.1 Who's to blame? The third crisis-framing contest

Table 2.1 depicts this third framing contest as a simple game matrix, juxtaposing the strategic choices office-holders and their critics will encounter in the politics of the post-crisis phase. It predicts the outcomes of the debate about accountability and blame that follows from particular configurations of political strategies.

All other things being equal, box II is the clearly preferred outcome for anti-establishment forces. They will, however, have to consider that the likelihood of incumbents simply absorbing responsibility for crises appears to be small. So they have to weigh the odds in the lower half of the figure. They can stop short of seeking wholesale removal of office-holders and push for a tactical victory (box III), but at the risk of ending up in their least favourable box I: letting the government off the hook entirely (this happens when incumbents opt for pre-emptive blame absorption and get away with ritual promises to do better next time around). Box IV depicts an indeterminate scenario, which is most likely to evolve into a protracted and intensely politicised process of crisis investigation, reinvestigation, spin and counter-spin. It is impossible to tell who will prevail in such a—potentially epic—struggle.

The calculus for (long) incumbent office-holders involves a similar political trade-off: fighting to come away unscathed (or even gain credit, for example, for allegedly wise or heroic crisis-response leadership) or pragmatically accepting whole or partial responsibility for alleged errors of omission or commission in the run-up to the crisis or during the response to it. If we assume government leaders first and foremost value their own political survival, boxes I and III are clearly their preferred outcome. They too, however, have to consider the likelihood of their opponents assuming the conciliatory posture that these two boxes presuppose. Depending on their assessment of the opposition's determination and ability to inflict major damage on them, they might consider proactively accepting responsibility and come out looking strong, fair and self-reflective. If, however, they make the much more likely assessment that the opposition is going to scream and holler, they are better off opting for a blame-avoidance strategy, if only to avoid their worst-case scenario (box II). They could still lose at the end of the protracted blame struggle that is then most likely to ensue (box IV). As incumbent government, however, they might have confidence in their heresthetic abilities (cf. Riker 1986) to manipulate (delay, speed up, displace, reframe) 'diversionary' mechanisms such as crisis inquiries. In sum, this matrix exercise suggests that, *ceteris paribus*, box IV is the most likely battleground where the third framing contest will end up.

The fourth framing contest: the policy game—maintain or change policy commitments?

The final part of crisis framing focuses on the lessons to be learned from the crisis of the day: does the crisis suggest that 'the system' (that is, the existing cluster of public policy beliefs, institutions and programs) is broken beyond repair or is essentially sound and merely needs some fixing up at the edges? Table 2.2 depicts the structure of the main conflicts over policy that crises induce. The key struggle here is between status quo and change-oriented players. Aspiring reformers can exploit crises rhetorically to engage in what Schumpeter called 'creative destruction': discrediting and deconstructing the status quo and proposing an alternative set of ideas and commitments. Reformers have to decide whether they feel the crisis of the day offers them the opportunity, through crisis rhetoric, to press persuasively for a wholesale overturning of the policy's ideological and/or intellectual underpinnings (Hall 1993), or whether to momentarily content themselves with advocating more incremental changes. For example, the bid by Australian Prime Minister Kevin Rudd (2009; see further Chapter 9, this volume), in a much-debated essay he wrote about the global financial crisis in early 2009 was to nudge the Australian public debate towards a paradigm shift, encompassing not one particular area of public policy but rather an entire philosophy of governance.

Status quo players have to gauge the degree of destabilisation and de-legitimisation of existing policies that the crisis narratives floating around have evoked among experts, stakeholders and the mass public alike. Based on that assessment, they might ask themselves whether they have the arguments and the clout to openly resist any change of policy advocated by inquiries or change advocates or whether some form of accommodating gesture ('learning the lessons') is necessary. In the case of the Rudd essay, two Liberal leaders (an aspiring prime minister and a former treasurer) who publicly responded to the essay Malcolm Turnbull (2009) and Peter Costello (*Lateline* 2009), decided that Rudd's case for paradigm change could be demolished, since both their responses flatly denied the need for a fundamental change of course.

That is nothing unusual. As Hall (1993) and Sabatier (1999) have argued, policymakers who have been instrumental in creating a particular status quo might be well prepared to change their beliefs and practices with regard to technical, instrumental, 'non-core' aspects of a policy, but they are much less likely to 'surrender' their core beliefs—for example, the heart of the policy paradigm.

Change advocates Status quo players	Press for policy paradigm shift	Press for incremental reform
Resist policy change	I. Policy stalemate or majority-imposed paradigm shift	II. Policy stalemate or majority-imposed incremental adjustment
Contain policy change	III. Major and swift symbolic gestures; incremental substantive policy change	IV. Negotiated incremental adjustment

Table 2.2 Maintain or change policy? The fourth crisis-framing contest

Depending on these two sets of actors' calculations and the power balance that emerges between them in the course of the crisis episode, the fourth framing contest can take different forms. When both parties play hardball, a protracted stalemate or a major paradigm shift is most likely, depending on each party's ability to form a winning coalition (box I). Incremental change is, not surprisingly, the most likely outcome in most of the other configurations. There are, however, important nuances between them that might bear on the long-term stability of the outcome: a set of incremental adjustments that is imposed by a more powerful change coalition (box II) is less likely to persist than a negotiated package between parties both of whom are prepared to settle pragmatically (box IV). In box III, the way out of a potential conundrum is found in an inherently unstable mixture of rhetoric and symbols suggesting major shifts (to placate change advocates) and a reality of much less far-reaching substantive changes (to satisfy the status quo players).

3. Crisis rhetoric and framing contests in the media arena

The mass media plays a crucial role in reporting elites' crisis rhetoric (cf. Seeger et al. 2003; Ulmer et al. 2007). The media is not just a backdrop against which crisis actors operate, it constitutes a prime arena in which incumbents and critics, status quo players and change advocates have to 'perform' to obtain or preserve political clout. Leaders need to convince news-makers to pay attention to their particular crisis frame and, if possible, support it.

Prior research (Boin et al. 2008, 2009) suggests that—as Edelman (1977) predicted—incumbent elites can be quite effective at 'selling' their frame to the media. They also show, however, that office-holders can fail miserably in this regard or succumb under the pressure of suitably dramatised counter-frames advanced by well-organised oppositional coalitions. The most interesting example of this contrast is US President Bush's differential framing performance during the aftermaths of 9/11 and Hurricane Katrina. During the first, Bush succeeded magnificently (in hindsight, many would argue he succeeded all too well, making any criticisms of his 'war on terrorism' seem unpatriotic), but he lost badly after Katrina hit Louisiana and Mississippi (Preston 2008; 't Hart et al. 2009). Note that in the former, Bush took the stance of a change advocate, whereas in the latter he acted as a status quo player.

Another interesting case was the fight between Spanish Prime Minister José Maria Aznar and opposition leader José Luis Rodríguez Zapatero, who tried to impose their diametrically opposing views of the causes of the 2004 Madrid bombings on the Spanish public, which was readying itself to vote several days later. Again, the status quo player lost; the change advocate won. Aznar lost (while leading in the polls up to the day of the bombings), mostly because he could not convince the public that Basque separatists had perpetrated the bombings and consequently was open to charges of deliberately misleading the public as to the real—to him, politically inconvenient—culprit, namely, al-Qaeda (Olmeda 2008).

The crisis communication literature argues that a proactive, professional media performance enhances an actor's credibility; reactive and disorganised crisis communication can do the reverse (Seeger et al. 2003; Fearn-Banks 2007). Lying, understating or denying obvious problems, and promising relief without delivering, undermine an actor's credibility (Boin et al. 2005). In this perspective, the degree to which the media's crisis reporting and commentary align with the frames put forward by a particular political actor depends on the credibility of that actor's crisis communication.

The rival interpretation is that the media pursues its own agenda in crisis reporting (see, for instance, Streitmatter 1997) and that the crisis communication performance by any of the actors matters less than the degree to which their rhetoric fits with the pre-existing biases of the main media outlets. The content analysis of media coverage in three countries (Finland, Norway and Sweden) that saw their nationals victimised by the Indian Ocean tsunami provides some support for the idea that the selection and tone of media reporting can also matter (Brändström et al. 2008). It appears especially relevant how willing the media is to apportion blame directly to individual office-holders, even if the direct causes are (in this case quite literally) far removed from them (Hearit 2006). The more the media's crisis reporting and commentary emphasise exogenous interpretations of a crisis, the less likely it is that government actors will suffer negative political consequences in its aftermath; the more it emphasises endogenous ones, the more likely it is that they will.

4. Studying framing contests during the economic meltdown: design and methods

So far, we have argued that skilful office-holders can manage to politically 'contain' crises and thereby insulate themselves and their colleagues from sanctions and reputation losses. Likewise, skilful status quo players can weather the storm of deinstitutionalisation that crisis inquiries unleash on existing polices and institutions and effectively protect their policy commitments from pressures for radical change. Oppositional forces, however, sometimes successfully attempt to politicise crises in their efforts to weaken or remove their office-holding rivals. Finally, change advocates might manage to exploit crises to discredit and dismantle well-entrenched policies and institutions.

In the chapters that follow, we track leader rhetoric and media responses to that rhetoric during the unfolding of the global economic meltdown, up to April 2009. We aim to detect if and when the kind of framing contests depicted here occurred in each of the nine jurisdictions studied here. We focus in particular on the verbal behaviour of three key managers of the national economy: the head of government, the minister of finance (or treasurer) and the president of the central bank. Specifically, we aim to answer the following questions:

- How, in their key speech acts, did each of the three actors name (severity), explain (causality), account for (responsibility/blame) and propose to manage (policy) the national manifestations of the global economic meltdown?
- How did these framing attempts evolve over time in response to the cascading events of the meltdown worldwide and nationally?
- To what extent were the meaning-making efforts of these three actors consistent with one another?
- To what extent did these framing efforts 'succeed' in terms of eliciting media support for their claims about the severity and causes of the crisis, for their own handling of the crisis and for their proposed policy stances going into the future?

In each case study, the author:

- reconstructed the local chronology of the economic meltdown in the period between late 2007 and March 2009 (with different local emphases as appropriate): key events, key government decisions, key public debates/controversies.

- studied the broader political context in the country to understand the backdrop against which key political actors operated, and took into account in their approach to the global economic meltdown—for instance, in Canada, New Zealand and the United States, the study period coincided with parliamentary or presidential elections; in the latter two, the crisis became a key election issue, and in both of them political transitions ensued.
- identified and analysed two to four key speech acts of the head of government, finance minister and national bank's president—for example, in parliament, direct addresses, press conferences and interviews or public lectures to key stakeholder audiences (the individual chapters will account for the selection of the speeches). The qualitative content analyses were aimed at tracing the speaker's claims regarding severity, causality, responsibility/blame and policy. Each speech was coded in a qualitative coding grid. The full extent of the coding work can be found in the online appendix at <http://globalfinancialcrisis.wetpaint.com/>.
- content analysed three major newspapers for their coverage and commentary regarding each speech act, categorising articles in terms of (implicitly or explicitly) supportive, neutral or critical, on each of the four critical dimensions of rhetoric discerned above (the individual chapters will account for the selection of newspapers used).
- finally, for each actor, the evolution of their rhetoric (through the series of speech acts) as well as the evolution of public responses to their speech acts were tracked.

The case studies were performed following the method of structured, focused comparison advocated by George and Bennett (2005). Data gathering and analysis were guided by a joint analytical protocol. In addition to the national case studies, we invited separate studies of the crisis rhetoric of the European Union's leaders (the President of the European Commission, the Finance Commissioner and the President of the European Central Bank), a comparative piece on the crisis rhetoric of opposition leaders and a series of short responses to the case study findings by senior scholars in the fields of leadership, crisis management and political communication. All these chapters can be found in Part V.

As pointed out in Chapter 1, this study does not aspire to be the definitive account of crisis management (or even crisis rhetoric) during the global financial crisis. As a form of 'quick-response research', it has limited scope in the time, numbers of actors and speeches and the types of mass media covered. Its limited depth cannot compete with the methodological rigour of Wood's (2007) comprehensive study of the economic rhetoric of US presidents. Having said that, our study looks at more than just presidents and other heads of government, which opens up analytical issues and possibilities not covered by Wood. Finally, our study does not fully cover all components of the crisis-exploitation framework sketched above, since it focuses exclusively on the rhetoric of incumbent elites (and its reception by the media and the public). A fully rounded crisis-exploitation analysis needs three further components: a) systematic analysis of opposition and other non-executive leaders' rhetoric; b) an analysis of the interaction between government and oppositional forces in the third and fourth framing contests applying the game matrices presented in Tables 2.1 and 2.2; and c) a systematic assessment of the political and policy outcomes of the crises studied. The last is impossible to do given that the crisis is continuing at the time of writing. The other two tasks were beyond the scope of the present study.

Having said all that, we are confident that this study presents a worthwhile 'first stab' at studying crisis leadership in what will surely become one of the most intensely scrutinised episodes of modern world history. In the final chapter of this volume, we shall compare the case study findings and interpret the patterns of similarities and difference in crisis framing that emerge from this comparison. We shall furthermore review the perspectives offered by the thematic chapters and the expert essays. All of this will feed into a set of—necessarily preliminary—conclusions about the possibilities and limits of crisis rhetoric in shaping politics and public policy.

References

Alink, F., Boin, A. and 't Hart, P. 2001, 'Institutional crises and reforms in policy sectors: the case of refugee policy in Europe', *Journal of European Public Policy*, vol. 8, no. 2, pp. 286–306.

Axelrod, R. and Cohen, M. D. 2000, *Harnessing Complexity: Organizational implications of a scientific frontier*, Free Press, New York.

Barnard, C. I. 1938, *The Functions of the Executive*, Harvard University Press, Cambridge, Mass.

Barrett, W. and Collins, D. 2006, *Grand Illusion: The untold story of Rudy Giuliani and 9/11*, HarperCollins, New York.

Barton, A. 1969, *Communities in Disaster: A Sociological Analysis of Collective Stress Situations,* Doubleday and Company, New York, pp. 203-79.

Baumgartner, F. R. and Jones, B. D. 1993, *Agendas and Instability in American Politics*, University of Chicago Press, Chicago.

Baumgartner, F. R. and Jones, B. D. (eds) 2002, *Policy Dynamics*, University of Chicago Press, Chicago.

Birkland, T. A. 1997, *After Disaster: Agenda setting, public policy and focusing events*, Georgetown University Press, Washington, DC.

Birkland, T. A. 2006, *Lessons of Disaster: Policy change after catastrophic events*, Georgetown University Press, Washington, DC.

Boin, A. and 't Hart, P. 2003, 'Public leadership in times of crisis: mission impossible?', *Public Administration Review*, vol. 63, no. 5, pp. 544–53.

Boin, A., 't Hart, P., Stern, E. and Sundelius, B. 2005, *The Politics of Crisis Management: Public leadership under pressure*, Cambridge University Press, Cambridge.

Boin, A., McConnell, A. and 't Hart, P. (eds) 2008, *Governing After Crisis: The politics of investigation, accountability and learning*, Cambridge University Press, Cambridge.

Boin, A., McConnell, A. and 't Hart, P. 2009, 'Crisis exploitation: political and policy impacts of framing contests', *Journal of European Public Policy*, vol. 16, no. 1, pp. 81–106.

Bovens, M. 1998, *The Quest for Responsibility: Accountability and citizenship in complex organizations*, Cambridge University Press, Cambridge.

Bovens, M. and 't Hart, P. 1996, *Understanding Policy Fiascos*, Transaction, New Brunswick.

Bovens, M., Peters, B. G. and 't Hart, P. (eds) 2001, *Success and Failure in Pubic Governance: A comparative analysis*, Edward Elgar, Cheltenham.

Brändström, A. and Kuipers, S. 2003, 'From "normal incidents" to political crises: understanding the selective politicization of policy failures', *Government and Opposition*, vol. 38, no. 3, pp. 279–305.

Brändström, A., Kuipers, S. and Daleus, P. 2008, 'The politics of tsunami responses: comparing patterns of blame management in Scandinavia', in A. Boin, A. McConnell and P. 't Hart (eds), *Governing After Crisis: The politics of investigation, accountability and learning*, Cambridge University Press, Cambridge, pp. 114–47.

De Vries, M. 2004, 'Framing crises: response patterns to explosions in fireworks factories', *Administration and Society*, vol. 36, no. 5, pp. 594–614.

Drennan, L. T. and McConnell, A. 2007, *Risk and Crisis Management in the Public Sector*, Routledge, Abingdon.

Edelman, M. 1977, *Political Language: Words that succeed and policies that fail*, Academic Press, New York.

Ellis, R. J. 1994, *Presidential Lightning Rods: The politics of blame avoidance*, University of Kansas Press, Lawrence, Kans.

Entman, R. 1993, 'Framing: toward clarification of a fractured paradigm', *Journal of Communication*, vol. 43, no. 4, pp. 51–8.

Fearn-Banks, K. 2007, *Crisis Communications: A case book approach*, 3rd edition, Lawrence Erlbaum, Mahwaw, NJ.

Garnett, J. L. and Kouzmin, A. 2007, 'Communicating throughout Katrina: competing and complementary conceptual lenses on crisis communication', *Public Administration Review*, vol. 67, no. 1, pp. 171–88.

George, A. L. and Bennett, A. 2005, *Case Studies and Theory Development in the Social Sciences*, The MIT Press: Cambridge, MA.

Hall, P. A. 1993, 'Policy paradigms, social learning and the state: the case of economic policymaking in Britain', *Comparative Politics*, vol. 35, no. 3, pp. 275–96.

't Hart, P. 1993, 'Symbols, rituals and power: the lost dimensions of crisis management', *Journal of Contingencies and Crisis Management*, vol. 1, no. 1, pp. 36–50.

't Hart, P. and Boin, A. 2001, 'Between crisis and normalcy: the long shadow of post-crisis politics', in U. Rosenthal, A. Boin and L. K. Comfort (eds), *Managing Crises: Threats, challenges, opportunities*, Charles C. Thomas, Springfield, pp. 28–46.

't Hart, P., Tindall, K. and Brown, C. 2009, 'Crisis leadership of the Bush presidency: advisory capacity and presidential performance in the acute stages of the 9/11 and Katrina crises', *Presidential Studies Quarterly*, vol. 39, no. 3, pp. 472–91.

Hay, C. 2002, *Political Analysis*, Palgrave Macmillan, Basingstoke.

Hearit, K. M. 2006, *Crisis Management by Apology*, Lawrence Erlbaum, Mahwah, NJ.

Heyse, L., Resodihardjo, S., Lantink, T. and Lettinga, B. (eds) 2006, *Reform in Europe: Breaking the barriers in government*, Ashgate, Aldershot.

Hood, C., Jennings, W., Hogwood, B. and Beeston, C. 2007, *Fighting fires in testing times: exploring a staged response hypothesis for blame management in two exam fiasco cases*, CARR Discussion Paper 42, Centre for Analysis of Risk and Regulation, London School of Economics, London.

Howarth, D., Norval, A. J. and Stavrakakis, Y. (eds) 2000, *Discourse Theory and Political Analysis: Identities, hegemonies and social change*, Manchester University Press, Manchester.

Jones, B. D. and Baumgartner, F. R. 2005, *The Politics of Attention: How government prioritizes problems*, University of Chicago Press, Chicago.

Kay, A. 2006, *The Dynamics of Public Policy*, Edward Elgar, Cheltenham.

Keeler, J. 1993, 'Opening the window for reform: mandates, crises, and extraordinary policy-making', *Comparative Political Studies*, vol. 25, no. 1, pp. 433–86.

Kingdon, J. 2003, *Agendas, Alternatives and Public Policies*, 2nd edition, Longman, New York.

Klein, N. 2007, *The Shock Doctrine: The rise of disaster capitalism*, Metropolitan Books, New York.

Kuipers, S. 2006, *The Crisis Imperative: Crisis rhetoric and welfare state reform in Belgium and the Netherlands in the early 1990s*, Amsterdam University Press, Amsterdam.

Lateline 2009, 'Transcript: Peter Costello joins *Lateline*', *Lateline* ABC TV, 3 February.

Lodge, M. and Hood, C. 2002, 'Pavlovian policy responses to media feeding frenzies? Dangerous dogs regulation in comparative perspective', *Journal of Contingencies and Crisis Management*, vol. 10, no. 1, pp. 1–13.

Lomborg, B. (ed.) 2004, *Global Crises, Global Solutions*, Cambridge University Press, Cambridge.

Mitroff, I. I. and Pauchant, T. C. 1990, *We're so Big and Powerful that Nothing Bad Can Happen to Us*, Carol Publishing, New York.

Mumford, L. 1934, *Technics and Civilization*, Harcourt Brace, New York.

Olmeda, J. 2008, 'A reversal of fortune: blame games and framing contests after the 3/11 terrorist attacks in Madrid', in A. Boin, A. McConnell and P. 't Hart (eds), *Governing After Crisis: The politics of investigation, accountability and learning*, Cambridge University Press, Cambridge, pp. 62–84.

Parker, C. F. and Dekker, S. 2008, 'September 11 and post-crisis investigation: exploring the role and impact of the 9/11 Commission', in A. Boin, A. McConnell and P. 't Hart (eds), *Governing After Crisis: The politics of investigation, accountability and learning*, Cambridge University Press, Cambridge, pp. 255–84.

Posner, R. A. 2004, *Catastrophe: Risk and response*, Oxford University Press, New York.

Preston, T. 2008, 'Weathering the politics of responsibility and blame: the Bush administration and its response to Hurricane Katrina', in A. Boin, A. McConnell and P. 't Hart (eds) *Governing After Crisis: the politics of investigation, accountability and learning, Cambridge University Press: Cambridge*, pp. 33-61.

Primo, D. M. and Cobb, R. W. 2003, *The Plane Truth*, Brookings Institution Press, Washington, DC.

Quarantelli, E. L. (ed.) 1998, *What is a Disaster? Perspectives on the question*, Routledge, London.

Quarantelli, E. L. and R. W. Perry (eds) 2005, *What is a Disaster? New answers to old questions*, Xlibris Press, Philadelphia.

Resodihardjo, S. 2006, *Crisis and Change: Understanding crisis-reform processes in Dutch and British prison services*, Free University, Amsterdam.

Riker, W. H. 1986, *The Art of Political Manipulation*, Yale University Press, New Haven.

Romzek, B. S. and Dubnick, M. J. 1987, 'Accountability in the public sector: lessons from the challenger tragedy', *Public Administration Review*, vol. 47, no. 3, pp. 227–38.

Rose, R. and Davies, P. 1994, *Inheritance in Public Policy: Change without choice in Britain*, Yale University Press, New Haven.

Rosenthal, U. 1988, 'The vulnerability of the city', in L. J. Roborgh, R. Stough and A. J. Toonen (eds), *Public Infrastructure Revisited*, Indiana University Press, Ind., pp. 1–21.

Rosenthal, U. 1998, 'Future disasters, future definitions', in E. L. Quarantelli (ed.), *What is a Disaster: Perspectives on the question*, Routledge, London, pp. 146–60.

Rosenthal, U., Charles, M. T. and 't Hart, P. (eds) 1989, *Coping with Crisis: The management of disasters, riots and terrorism*, Charles C. Thomas, Springfield.

Rozario, K. 2005, 'Making progress: disaster narratives and the art of optimism in modern America', in L. J. Vale and T. J. Campanella (eds), *The Resilient City: How modern cities recover from disaster*, Oxford University Press, Oxford, pp. 27–54.

Rudd, K. 2009, 'Essay: The global financial crisis', *The Monthly*, February, pp. 26–38.

Sabatier, P. A. (ed.) 1999, *Theories of the Policy Process*, Westview Press, Boulder.

Scharpf, F. 1997, *Games Real Actors Play*, Westview Press, Boulder.

Seeger, M. W., Sellnow, T. L. and Ulmer, R. R. 2003, *Communication and Organizational Crisis*, Praeger, Westport.

Slatter, S. 1984, *Corporate Recovery: Successful turnaround strategies and their implementation*, Penguin Books, London.

Snider, L. 2004, 'Resisting neo-liberalism: the poisoned water disaster in Walkerton Ontario', *Socio & Legal Studies*, vol. 13, no. 2, pp. 265–89.

Steinberg, T. 2000, *Acts of God: The history of unnatural disasters in America*, Oxford University Press, New York.

Stone, D. 2001, *Policy Paradox: The art of political decision making*, 2nd edition, W. W. Norton & Company, New York.

Streitmatter, R. 1997, *Mightier than the Sword: How the news media have shaped American history*, Westview Press, Boulder.

Tarrow S. 1994, *Power in Movement*, Cambridge University Press, Cambridge.

Thelen, K. 2004, *How Institutions Evolve: The political economy of skills in Germany, Britain, the United States, and Japan*, Cambridge University Press, New York.

Turnbull, M. 2009, 'PM's cheap money shot', *The Australian*, 7 March 2009, viewed 10 June 2009, <http://www.theaustralian.news.com.au/story/0,25197,25148674-7583,00.html>

Turner, B. A. and Pidgeon, N. 1997, *Man-Made Disasters*, 2nd edition, Butterworth Heinemann, London.

Ulmer, R. R., Sellnow, T. L. and Seeker, M. W. 2007, *Effective Crisis Communication: Moving from crisis to opportunity*, Sage, Thousand Oaks, Calif.

Wagner-Pacifici, R. 1986, *The Moro Morality Play: Terrorism as social drama*, University of Chicago Press, Chicago.

Wagner-Pacifici, R. 1994, *Discourse and Destruction: The City of Philadelphia versus MOVE*, University of Chicago Press, Chicago.

Wilkins, L. 1987, *Shared Vulnerability: The media and American perceptions of the Bhopal disaster*, Greenwood Press, New York.

Wilkins, L., Walters, T. and Walters, L. M. (eds) 1989, *Bad Tidings: Communication and catastrophe*, Lawrence Erlbaum, Mahwah, NJ.

Wolf, N. 2007, *The End of America: Letter of warning to a young patriot*, Scribe, Melbourne.

Wood, B. D. 2007, *The Politics of Economic Leadership: The causes and consequences of presidential rhetoric*, Princeton University Press, Princeton.

Endnotes

[1] This chapter is based on Boin et al. (2009), but is significantly abridged, adapted and expanded on here.

[2] Our notion of frames follows that of Entman (1993:52), who argues that 'to frame is to select some aspects of a perceived reality and make them more salient in a communicating text, in such a way as to promote a particular problem definition, causal interpretation, moral evaluation, and/or treatment recommendation'.

[3] These dimensions can be tightly connected, as when the political demise of key office-holders removes the main champion of a particular policy from the political scene. In many cases, however, the 'programmatic' (policy-focused) and 'political' (office-holders-focused) dimensions of policy evaluation and political accountability episodes appear to be completely unrelated. See Bovens et al. (2001).

Part II. One crisis, different worlds: the United States and Canada

3. The United States: crisis leadership in times of transition

Isaac Ijjo Donato

1. Going down: the escalation of the sub-prime mortgage crisis

The US financial crisis, which has since become global, originated in 2007 when the US mortgage industry began to perform poorly (Kregel 2008). For the past decade, the United States has pursued aggressive supply-side economic policymaking, emphasising low interest rates, low taxes and highly deregulated financial markets (Uchitelle 2008). This created a boom in which money became cheap, and positive forecasts on the housing market encouraged financial institutions and prospective homeowners, respectively, to lend and borrow exceedingly (Obama 2009b). Altogether, this gave rise to sub-prime lending, whereby banks lent money to even those with poor credit histories (Chomsisengphet and Pennington-Cross 2006). When the housing bubble finally burst in 2007, sub-prime mortgage loans, which by this time had grown substantially and had given rise to a lucrative secondary mortgage market (mortgage hedge market), were the most adversely affected (Kregel 2008).

The mortgage crash kicked off a market wind-down beginning, prominently, with Bear Stearns (Bear), a Wall Street investment bank. Earlier the previous year, Bear had implicated itself in the sub-prime mortgage market by committing more than $3 billion dollars to bail out one of its hedge funds that had bet heavily on the sub-prime loans (Burrough 2008). On the morning of 10 March 2008, a rumour about Bear's liquidity problems began to spread in the financial market (*PBS Frontline* 2009). An unprecedented stock sell-off ensued, driving the bank's stock down 47 per cent (Irwin and Tse 2008). Six days later, despite Federal Reserve and Treasury attempts to save the eighty-five-year-old investment bank, Bear ran out of its $18 billion cash reserve and collapsed (Irwin and Tse 2008).

Months later, in September 2008, Fannie Mae and Freddie Mac, the two federally backed mortgage lending firms that had also speculated heavily on the returns from their various mortgage investments, began to falter due to rising defaults on home mortgage repayments (Irwin and Tse 2008). The Bush Administration reacted to this by firing their managements and nationalising the banks (*KDKA-TV* 2008). In the same month, three other major US financial institutions—Lehman Brothers, Washington Mutual Inc. and American International Group—had either filed for bankruptcy or failed (*KDKA-TV* 2008).

This series of bank collapses was a strident manifestation of an economy in full-blown crisis, threatening the foundations and lifeblood—the financial and credit markets—of the US and world economies. On Thursday, 18 September 2008, Treasury Secretary, Henry Paulson, and Federal Reserve Chairman, Ben Bernanke, painted a bleak picture of the cascading crisis in a hastily convened emergency meeting involving the heads of key US financial institutions and political figures. Respectively, they warned, 'unless you act, the financial system of this country and the world will melt down in a matter of days' and 'if we don't act tomorrow, we won't have an economy on Monday' (*PBS Frontline* 2009).

Boin et al. (2009) observe from the Thomas theorem that it is not the events on the ground, but their public perception and interpretation that will determine their potential impact. In the case of the United States in September 2008, however, the country was in crisis at all levels: reality, perception, emotion and rhetoric. While the downturn presented policymakers with huge challenges to manage, it also opened political opportunities to exploit—at least for some of them. Drawing on the crisis-framing model of Chapter 2, this chapter studies how US Presidents George W. Bush and later Barack Obama, Treasury Secretaries Henry Paulson and his successor, Timothy Geithner, and the Federal Reserve Chairman, Ben Bernanke, framed the unfolding crisis and its policy and political implications. Some of these actors were predominantly in 'damage-control' mode; others were at times perhaps drawn towards 'opportunity exploitation'. In keeping with the analytical approach of this volume, this chapter also examines how these framing efforts were publicly received by the media and the public, and, thus, to what extent the various elite framing efforts resonated with (parts of) their intended audiences.

It is important to understand the context in which the leaders under study operated. As the meltdown was transforming financial markets, regime change was transforming politics in the United States. President Bush's tenure was due to end in early 2009 and Democrat candidate, Barack Obama, and Republican John McCain were contending for the presidency in the election due in November 2008. For the two candidates, and the incumbent president, the crisis played into their political manoeuvring. Although the scope of this volume excludes non-executive leaders, occasional reference will be made to the continuing election struggle, especially given that the policy debate between the two contestants reflected a strong partisan—Republican and Democrat—theme, which greatly influenced the political context in which Bush and later Obama operated as presidents when talking about the crisis.

2. Methodological considerations

This chapter is structured in fours parts. Parts one to three will analyse speech acts of the President, the Treasury Secretary and the Federal Reserve Chairman.

For each leadership position, four speech acts made by office-holders between April 2008 and March 2009 will be analysed. Given that there was a change of administration during this period, the analysis will reflect this by covering two speeches each by the former and current presidents and treasury secretaries.

Each of these speeches has been selected on the basis of it being delivered in response to a key development in the unfolding of the crisis in the United States. Time lapses have also been factored into the selection of the speech acts, in order to measure the evolution of the framing attempts by these leaders. To place these speeches in context and gain a sense of the public opinion at the time of these speeches, public opinion poll data published by *Gallup Poll* alone or in association with *USA Today* have been collected. In addition to the public opinion data, three US newspapers of national and international stature form the basis of the media response: *The Wall Street Journal*, *The New York Times* and *The Washington Post*. The ideological bent of the first is more towards the conservative end, whereas the other two are more towards the progressive end. *The New York Times* has a daily circulation of more than million readers, *The Wall Street Journal* has more than two million and *The Washington Post* more than 600 000 (Audit Bureau of Circulations 2009). For each speech act, a sample of articles was examined, including news reports, editorials and op-ed pieces relevant to the financial crisis published one or two days after the speech.

How the relevant leaders' framing attempts evolved over time in response to the unfolding events of the crisis—nationally and globally—is discussed in relation to each leadership position, based on an examination of the key speech acts. Four speech acts are analysed for each leadership position. As such, the analysis of this evolution was limited to only two speeches for each office-holder, bar Bernanke. Finally, part four of the chapter interprets the findings. At this point, the extent to which the meaning-making efforts of these actors relate to one another is examined, and the main 'battlegrounds' of the 'framing contests' surrounding the crisis are pinpointed.

Box 3.1 The United States' financial crisis trajectory, March 2008 – March 2009

10 March 2008: Bears Stearns' liquidity problems start, putting the bank on course to collapse seven days later.

14 March: Federal Reserve officials find Bear is 'systemically' connected with the wider financial markets, meaning its failure could risk the collapse of the whole financial system. Federal Government rescue efforts begin.

2 April: Federal Reserve Chairman, Ben Bernanke, testifies before Congress, warning that recession in the United States is possible.

10 April: The Senate passes a bipartisan measure aimed at boosting the housing market.

30 April: The Federal Reserve cuts interest rates to the lowest point in nearly four years.

11 July: IndyMac Bank fails.

12 July: Treasury Secretary, Henry Paulson, successfully seeks power to take over Fannie Mae and Freddie Mac, the two government-sponsored mortgage-lending entities.

30 July: President Bush signs a housing bill, allowing homeowners who cannot afford repayments to refinance access to more affordable government-backed loans.

7 September: The Bush Administration nationalises Fannie Mae and Freddie Mac.

12 September: Lehman Brothers requests a bailout, but Paulson decides not to bail the firm out, citing moral hazard.

14 September: Merrill Lynch sells itself to Bank of America and Lehman Brothers files for bankruptcy, after it fails to find a buyer in an increasingly nervous market.

16 September: The Federal Reserve changes course and spends $84 billion to bail out American International Group (AIG), the largest insurance firm in America.

18 September: Paulson proposes a $700 billion plan to buy toxic assets from America's biggest banks.

25 September: Washington Mutual Bank fails.

29 September: Congress rejects Paulson's proposal.

3 October: Congress approves Paulson's revised plan.

28 October: The Federal Reserve cuts its lending rate to 1 per cent.

4 November: Barack Obama is elected President.

14 November: Leaders of 20 major economies gather in Washington, DC, to discuss coordinated emergency action to address the financial crisis.

16 December: The Federal Reserve cuts its interest rates again—to nearly zero.

20 January 2009: Barack Obama is sworn in as the forty-forth President of the United States.

26 January: The Senate confirms Timothy Geithner as Treasury Secretary, succeeding Paulson.

10 February: Geithner outlines a new, sweeping overhaul and expansion of the government's rescue effort.

17 February: Obama signs a $787 billion package to revive the economy.

18 February: Obama announces a $275 billion plan to help financially struggling families to refinance their mortgages.

19 February: Obama orders the nation's 19 largest banks to undergo a 'stress test' to help bolster confidence in the bailout plan.

23 March: Geithner lays out a detailed version of his 10 February rescue plan.

24 March: Obama and the Federal Reserve seek to expand the Federal Government's power to seize control of troubled financial institutions deemed too big to fail.

3. Crisis development and elite rhetoric in the United States

From crisis to opportunity: Presidents Bush and Obama

The financial and economic meltdown that took place in 2008–09 affected Presidents Bush and Obama very differently. Bush was serving his last term in office and, by mid 2008, he was well and truly a lame-duck president. His steadily declining approval rating had hit a new low of 32 per cent by 14 March 2008, and never really recovered (Gallup Organization 2008). On the other hand, by the end of 2008, Obama had been voted into office on a popular platform of change. His approval rating was as high as 69 per cent at the time he assumed office (Jones 2009). What for Bush was yet another nasty crisis eating away at his political capital, and possibly his place in history, to Obama became a window of opportunity to dramatise his ability to bring a fresh approach and renewed vigour to the presidency at a time of national despair. Bush's challenge was to avoid being labelled as a modern-day Herbert Hoover (whose presidency was destroyed by the impact of the 1929 Wall Street crash); Obama's bid was to become a modern-day Franklin D. Roosevelt (whose 'New Deal' gave Americans hope and pioneered Keynesian economic policies that would become the norm after World War II).

14 March 2008: President Bush's 'business as usual'

By 14 March 2008, the financial crisis had taken a critical turn; banks on Wall Street were fear-stricken after Bear Stearns' liquidity problems (*PBS Frontline* 2009). In a speech he delivered to the Economic Club of New York four days after Bear's liquidity troubles began and two days before the bank collapsed, the President steered clear of using the word 'crisis' to describe the gathering storm. The closest he came to doing so was by describing the situation as a 'rough time' for the economy—an economic downturn and a slowdown, which he explained were inherent periodic features of the free-market system. In a free market, he claimed, 'there is going to be good and bad times...ups and downs, [which is] how markets work'. For Bush, there was no crisis; it was business as usual and his purpose in the speech was to downplay the problem and its extent.

The President was intent on alleviating public anxiety and rekindling faith in the American economy. 'I am coming to you as an optimistic fellow,' he told the club members, adding that he believed America's was a resilient economy, which would continue to grow, because its foundations were solid. He added that the government had recognised the market slowdown early and had taken action in the form of policies designed to spur growth and strengthen oversight of the mortgage industry. These policies included a tax package targeting 130 million households to boost consumer spending through a newly created Federal Housing Administration (FHA Secure) to help facilitate the prevention of unnecessary foreclosures.

Despite these assurances and initiatives, Bush's speech did not resonate in the media. The three newspapers surveyed for this article mostly disagreed with his claims regarding the origins and the severity of the situation and his proposed policy package (see the online appendix at <http://global financialcrisis.wetpaint.com/>). The few who welcomed the President's speech expressed a sigh of relief for Bush having at least acknowledged, though not fully, that there were problems with the economy (Thomas 2008). The main thrust, however, was criticism of Bush's alleged lack of leadership and his deliberately steering clear of the word 'recession', which by this time the United States was already in, according to key economists (Baker 2008; Thomas 2008). In none of the press reactions to the speech surveyed was there any statement of support for the President (Table 3.1). A host of reasons contributed to the lack of positive public response to the President's speech, but perhaps the overarching one was Bush's record low popularity on the wings of the nasty war in Iraq and his failure as national crisis manager during Hurricane Katrina. By 2008, crisis-management competence had long ceased to be a political selling point for a president who had once enjoyed a strong and comparatively long boost in popularity after the 9/11 crisis (Gallup Organization 2008; see 't Hart et al. 2009).

	Causality	Proposed policy	Support for speaker
Agrees		2	
Disagrees	5	3	
No comment/ neutral	3	3	8

Table 3.1 Media response to President Bush's 14 March 2008 speech

Clearly, President Bush had pre-existing credibility deficits in the face of the American public, even before the global financial crisis started to unfold (Boin et al. 2009:78). His understated admission that the American economy was going through a rough time served only to confirm this, certainly among media outlets long critical of his record. For example, in an editorial entitled 'George speaks, badly', a *New York Times* columnist derided Bush's poor articulation, inept understanding of the subject matter, lateness and, above all, incapacity to perform as a leader in crisis (Collins 2008).

24 September 2008: Bush's acknowledgment of deep problems

By September, President Bush had changed his tone. He delivered a prime-time address to the nation on the American economy and the proposed bailout on 24 September 2008. The speech came after it had become exceedingly clear that the American economy was in deep crisis. Three particular moments were noteworthy. In addition to Bear Stearns, seven other major banks had collapsed (FIDC 2009). The crisis was going global fast, and reached well beyond the financial and housing sectors alone. It became apparent that the US Government's (Paulson's and Bernanke's in particular) hitherto piecemeal efforts of bailing out one bank at a time had failed. So the Treasury Secretary and the Federal Reserve Chairman went to the President to ask Congress to release money for a wholesale rescue of the country's financial market (*PBS Frontline* 2009).

At this time, denial was no longer a credible option. In terms of the crisis-exploitation model of Chapter 2, Bush therefore shifted from type-1 to type-2 rhetoric, acknowledging that the entire economy, not just the housing market and the financial sectors, was in trouble. He admitted that America's economy was 'in the midst of a serious financial crisis', which he depicted as 'a moment of great challenge'.

His account of the causes of the crisis emphasised exogenous factors, particularly market forces (mortgage defaults, excessive risk taking and the influx of foreign capital) and unscrupulous financial trading practices. He said that many lenders approved loans for borrowers without carefully examining their ability to pay and many borrowers took out loans larger than they could afford.

In terms of his proposed response to the crisis, Bush invoked the same 'can-do' crisis-management rhetoric he had used successfully after 9/11, but which had backfired badly after Katrina, to reassure Americans that the government was in control. He asserted that Americans had good reasons to be confident of their economic strength, insisting that despite 'market corrections' and instances of abuse, democratic capitalism remained the best system ever devised—because it had given the American economy the flexibility to absorb shocks, adjust and bounce back.

This time, the media was somewhat more attentive and its opinions were more mixed. The acknowledgment of severity was welcomed, and a few voices agreed with the President's causality claims, but most did not. Of the press articles surveyed, a significant majority disagreed with Bush's proposed policies (Table 3.2). Notwithstanding that, a Gallup Poll conducted a week later showed that the $700 billion bailout Bush had proposed in the speech was well received by the public (Saad 2008). Paradoxically, the President's overall job approval rating plunged towards its lowest level—27 per cent—since his first speech in March (Jones 2008).

	Causality	Proposed policy	Support for speaker
Agrees	2	4	
Disagrees	4	8	
No comment/ neutral	6		12

Table 3.2 Media response to Bush's 24 September 2008 speech

4 February 2009: President Obama blames Wall Street

Having assumed office with all the energy of a new president enjoying an extraordinary political honeymoon, Obama arguably took the crisis as an opportunity to drive the last nail in the coffin of Bush's legacy. In his first key speech on the economy and executive pay, delivered on 4 February 2009, Obama took a type-3 stance, describing the situation as 'an economic crisis unlike any other we have faced in our lifetime...a crisis of falling confidence and rising debt'. Before becoming president, Obama had strongly focused blame for the meltdown and its persistence on the Bush Administration's fiscal and regulatory policies, which he had promised to change (Obama 2008). Now that he was in office, his blame focus had changed somewhat. The President's main targets were the executives in the financial institutions that had received government rescue funds.

The President remained in the offensive type-3 mode, with his aim now to change the remuneration regime that had helped trigger the crisis. He explained that the crisis had been years in the making and was brought about by a corporate culture that disregarded risk, cost and consequences by offering perverse incentives structures to traders and executives. Obama focused blame on Wall Street and utilised the opportunity to introduce his policy, the American Recovery and Reinvestment Plan, one aspect of which was reforming executive remuneration regimes. Through that, the President aimed to cap at $500 000 the pay of executives in firms receiving support from the government's rescue fund.

Media reaction to the President's speech was mixed (Table 3.3). The bulk of the press coverage sampled made no comment about the President's causality claims. More than half agreed with the salary cap aspect of the policy; and nearly all made no comment about support for the President. A Gallup Poll taken four days after the speech, however, put Obama's approval rating at 63 per cent (Jones 2009).

	Causality	Proposed policy	Support for speaker
Agrees	2	7	
Disagrees		6	
No comment/ neutral	12	1	14

Table 3.3 Media response to Obama's 4 February 2008 speech

24 February 2009: Obama's address to Congress

Obama showed his most strident type-3 posture in an address to the Joint Houses of Congress on the 24 February 2009. Acknowledging the recession up front, the President told the nation that 'the state of our economy is a concern that rises above all others…you do not need a long list of statistics to know that our economy is in a crisis'. He explained that the American economy had not fallen into decline over night and the problems had not started when the share and stock markets collapsed. The problems, Obama claimed, had roots in expensive health care, poor education and dependence on foreign energy sources—the challenges that went unmet while Americans spent more money and piled up more debt.

In accounting for the crisis, Obama implicitly attributed a significant portion of blame to the previous administration, although, as politicians often do, he explicitly denied doing so. Apart from the few lines of therapeutic rhetoric such as 'we will rebuild', 'we will recover and the USA will emerge stronger than before'—lines somewhat reminiscent of Bush's—Obama prescribed major reforms of health care, education and energy as a way out of the crisis. Constituting the thrust of the American Recovery and Reinvestment Plan, these reforms were to jump-start job creation, save existing ones, restart lending, bring the government deficit down and grow the economy.

Obama underlined his policy appeal with a sweeping use of historical analogies; he told Americans:

> History reminds us that, at every moment of economic upheaval and transformation, this nation has responded with bold action and big ideas…In the midst of civil war, we laid railroad tracks from one coast to the other that spurred commerce and industry…From the turmoil of the Industrial Revolution came a system of public high schools that prepared our citizens for a new age…In the wake of war and depression, the GI Bill sent a generation to college and created the largest middle-class in history.

Obama's rhetoric proved popular with the papers and the public. Most of the press coverage studied here supported the President's causality claims. The overwhelming majority agreed with his policy propositions and an equal amount expressed support for the President (Table 3.4). After his approval rating had dropped to 59 per cent two days earlier, a Gallup Poll taken on the day of the speech found the President's approval rating had spiked back up to 67 per cent (Jones 2009).

The result must be interpreted with some caution. Obama was elected to the presidency on a strong platform of change in the three key areas of energy, education and health care (Obama 2008). The positive response was arguably being expressed at least in part for Obama having acted on his election promises rather than his articulation of novel measures addressing the economic crisis. Indeed, only 41 per cent of people interviewed said they now had more confidence in Obama's plan to fix the economy (Morales 2009).

In comparison, Obama's crisis-framing effort in this subsequent speech changed quite significantly from that in his first. Given that no significantly seismic development in the unfolding crisis happened between his two speeches studied here, the change in his rhetorical pitch could be attributed to the particular policy aspect he sought to introduce through each speech. Obama's framing, especially his naming and explaining of the crisis in the first speech, bore a semblance to his predecessor's. This was mainly because his main targets were the corporate executives, whose pay-outs were a hot topic in the news at that time. The 24 February speech had a wider explanatory scope, setting up the audience for a much wider suite of policy measures.

	Causality	Proposed policy	Support for speaker
Agrees	3	7	7
Disagrees		1	
No comment/ neutral	4		1

Table 3.4 Media response to Obama's 24 February 2009 speech

From reassurance to repair: Treasury Secretaries Paulson and Geithner

Henry Paulson, a former chief executive officer of Goldman Sachs, had come to the Treasury job in the Bush Administration with intimate knowledge of the working of the financial markets outside government and the trading behaviours of those on Wall Street. His successor, Timothy Geithner, had been the president of the Federal Reserve of New York during the Bush Administration. He had worked with Bernanke and Paulson—albeit in vain—to avert Bear Stearns' demise in March 2008, and all the way thereafter until Obama appointed him to head the Treasury. Geithner had intimately experienced the crisis from a senior policymaker's perspective. He had observed Paulson respond to the crisis and saw part of it backfire—not in the least on Paulson himself. With these contexts in mind, this part of the chapter looks at how the two secretaries named, explained, accounted for and proposed to manage the unfolding crisis.

26 March 2008: Secretary Paulson's innuendo

Paulson delivered his first major speech of the period under study barely two weeks after he had witnessed the collapse of a nearly one-century-old financial institution, Bear Stearns. Even though the speech was about the problems in financial and housing markets, the Treasury Secretary steered clear of calling a spade a spade. He described the events as 'financial market stress', 'turbulence' and 'bumps', which he explained were a result of de-leveraging and re-pricing of risk (Paulson 2008a). Precipitated by unsustainable home price appreciation, these reduced access to short-term funding and liquidity and created turmoil in the American capital markets.

Like Bush at the time, Paulson was painting an image of the American economy as being essentially sound, albeit experiencing short-term 'market upheaval'. For Paulson, it was business as usual; hence, there was no need to account for the problem, apart from making clear the causes of the current turbulence, which, again, he sought within the market, not in government regulation or policy. In the speech, Paulson did not announce specific measures to address the market turbulence, though he noted that efforts were being made to limit the impact of the turbulence on the real economy, which was the highest priority.

He said such efforts to insulate the economy would be achieved through increasing the availability of affordable mortgage financing through the Federal Reserve's temporary lending facility.

Media commentators and the American public remained largely indifferent to Paulson's rhetoric (Table 3.5). Most articles expressed no agreement or disagreement with his causality claims and none expressed support or lack thereof for the secretary. The lack of a more marked response was perhaps due to the highly technical content of the speech, combined with the fact that in times of crisis it is the President, and not the Treasury Secretary, who is the chief economic storyteller in the country (Wood 2007:63–108). Some writers, however, did agree with the Treasury's policy proposition, especially the establishment of the FHA Secure initiative. Those who expressed support thought FHA Secure would revitalise the housing market and prevent foreclosures (Paletta 2008).

	Causality	Proposed policy	Support for speaker
Agrees		2	
Disagrees			
No comment/ neutral	8	6	8

Table 3.5 Media response to Paulson's 26 March 2008 speech

18 November 2008: Paulson's switch to crisis mode

Seven months after Paulson made his speech to the US Chamber of Commerce, and with more banks having collapsed, it had become clear that the problems were escalating well beyond the mortgage market and financial services sector. This was an economy-wide crisis that was rapidly going global. At the time, Paulson requested and was granted $700 billion to execute a full-scale rescue operation for the financial services sector. It was therefore inevitable that Paulson's framing had shifted from business as usual to acknowledging the threat for what it was. He acknowledged that the US economy was in crisis (Paulson 2008c). In fact, in his testimony to Congress on the implementation of the *Emergency Economic Stabilisation Act*, on 18 November 2008, Paulson mentioned the word 'crisis' at least nine times. He described the financial crisis as one of a magnitude and unpredictability that he and his peers in the sector had never dealt with—in their lifetimes.

Apart from describing the manifestation of the extent of the damage the crisis had done already in statistical terms, Paulson acknowledged that the financial system had gone belly-up and now the economy was in a system-wide crisis. In his testimony, he provided no causal explanation for the crisis and he did not accept or deny responsibility for its escalation. Rather like President Bush, he continued to assure Americans that he had confidence in the economy's regulators and markets. At the same time, he made it clear that there was no set script for responding to a level of turmoil they had never faced before. Referring to the bailout, he added that the administration would adjust its strategy to reflect the dynamics of the crisis, and he urged Congress to work with it to stabilise the financial system.

Media reaction to the Treasury Secretary's speech was more negative than positive. No-one voiced agreement with the secretary's causal claims or his proposed stimulus package. Some commentators thought the package was fundamentally misguided (for example, *Washington Post* 2008). While most were neutral about Paulson himself, one journalist criticised the 'erratic performance' of the secretary in the crisis (*New York Times* 2008).

	Causality	Proposed policy	Support for speaker
Agrees			
Disagrees	3	3	1
No comment/ neutral		6	8

Table 3.6 Media response to Paulson's 18 November 2008 testimony

10 February 2009: Secretary Geithner's historical analogy

On succeeding Paulson as Treasury Secretary, Geithner's view of the crisis departed significantly from that of his predecessor. In introducing the Obama Administration's Financial Stability Plan, Geithner was more candid, taking the offensive type-3 posture. He called the state of the economy the worst economic crisis in generations—more complex than any the American financial system had ever faced. The crisis, he explained, had many and complex causes, which had accumulated over time. These included: policies that caused a huge global boom in credit; imprudent lending and borrowing; excessive executive remuneration; and poor regulation and oversight.

To make matters worse, he stated, when the crisis began governments had been too slow to act. Policy was always behind the curve and always chasing the escalating crisis. The force of government support had not been comprehensive or quick enough to withstand the deepening pressure brought on by the weakening economy. Further, the lack of clear criteria and conditions applied to government interventions caused investors to pull back from taking risks. The crisis in housing had had devastating consequences and the US Government should have moved more forcefully to limit the damage.

Although Geithner did not explicitly mention the Bush Administration, he clearly apportioned blame to it for the causes and the deterioration of the crisis. Implicitly, he charged it with having acted too late, applied misguided policies and failed in its oversight and proper regulation of the financial markets.

His presentation of the new administration's crisis-management efforts took the form of a key announcement: that of the *Economic Recovery Act*—the Financial Stability Plan, which among other things, was aimed at restarting the flow of credit and imposing higher standards for transparency and accountability in the financial market. Geithner made a strong historical analogy in support of the plan. He referred to the Great Depression in the 1930s and to the Japanese experience in the 1990s to explain why government (implicitly, the Bush Administration) had failed to stem this crisis and what the Obama Administration intended to do differently. The secretary told Americans that the Obama Administration's efforts would be guided by the lessons of the preceding few months and by lessons of financial crises throughout history. In the United States in the 1930s and Japan in the 1990s, Geithner observed, crises lasted longer and caused greater damage because governments applied the brakes too early. For this reason, the administration's policy response would be comprehensive, forceful and might be sustained until recovery was firmly established.

Although the Treasury Secretary's rhetoric sounded forceful, it failed to elicit a positive public response. Six out of 10 of the articles reporting the speech disagreed with his policy proposal, although the main concerns were about how the administration would implement it rather than its content (Table 3.7). Much of the disagreement was directed at the Financial Stability Plan—an outgrowth of the Bush Government's Troubled Asset Relief Program (TARP), which was controversial. Geithner's involvement with the previous administration, however indirect, played into this sentiment.

	Causality	Proposed policy	Support for speaker
Agrees		6	
Disagrees		10	
No comment/ neutral	6	1	17

Table 3.7 Media response to Geithner's 10 February 2009 speech

No support for the secretary was expressed in the press coverage surveyed. Public opinion polls taken about a month later found Americans were divided on him, largely owing to his handling of the crisis when he was a senior Federal Reserve executive in the Bush Administration (Newport 2009). No comment was made about his version of the causality claims. Once again, this might be because a dominant framing of the causes of the crisis had already settled in the public mind.

26 March 2009: Geithner's testimony to the House of Representatives

Geithner's type-3 framing largely continued in written testimony to the House Financial Services Committee Hearing a month later. Geithner described the crisis as the most severe global financial crisis in generations. The financial system, he explained, had failed in basic and fundamental ways. Geithner saw the crisis in light of the fragility and instability of the whole financial system—and in light of the lack of proper government checks and balances, which resulted in compensation practices that rewarded short-term profits over long-term returns (for the whole catalogue of causation factors and his explanation, see the online appendix).

Again, Geithner endogenised the causes of the crisis, holding the Bush Administration to account for what he saw as government failure to regulate the markets. His management efforts concentrated on initiating a comprehensive reform: not modest repairs on the margins, but new rules of the game, which among other things would subject financial institutions that were critical to the functioning of the financial system to strong government oversight. The government's regulatory reform would cover four broad areas: systemic risk; consumer and investor protection; eliminating gaps in the regulatory structures; and international coordination (see the online appendix for a full list). Clearly, the bulk of Geithner's framing effort in this statement was focused on rallying support for the Obama Administration's reform agenda. Geithner failed, however, to convince the commentariat and the public once again. Only two out of 10 news stories that covered it in our sample supported the financial system reform plan. A range of sentiments and doubts was expressed—for example, the plan would not work, it was complicated and obscure, it certainly would not prevent the next crisis (Wessel 2009). One commentator put it colourfully:

> One of the cool things about being Treasury Secretary is that you get your signature on dollar bills, giving them authority, defending their honor. Timothy Geithner's plan to save the struggling banking system probably does the opposite, throwing good money after bad to a banking system struggling under the weight of its own mistakes. The markets don't like it. The Dow dropped 382 points while bonds rallied as a port in a continuing storm. (Kessler 2009)

And he continued:

> The Treasury Secretary seems stuck on keeping the banks we have in place. But we don't need zombie banks overstuffed with nonperforming loans—ask the Japanese. Mr Geithner wants to 'stress test' banks to see which are worth saving. The market already has. Despite over a trillion in assets, Citigroup is worth a meager $18 billion, Bank of America only $28 billion. The market has already figured out that the banks and their accountants haven't fessed up to bad loans and that their shareholders are toast.

None of the press coverage engaged with Geithner's causality claims or expressed support or lack thereof for the Treasury Secretary. At this time, however, as mentioned above, public opinion was divided over him (Newport 2009). In a Gallup Poll taken on 27–29 March 2008 about American opinion of Treasury Secretary Geithner, 42 per cent approved of the way Geithner was doing his job, 40 per cent disapproved and 18 per cent had no opinion.

When compared, Geithner's two speech acts bear close similarity. His naming, explaining, accounting for and management of the crisis remained the same. This is because, perhaps, the speeches were only a few weeks apart, during which the crisis took no dramatic new turns. The differences of emphasis between the two speeches were due to the development of the administration's crisis-response repertoire, not to any change of view or stance in relation to the crisis.

	Causality	Proposed policy	Support for speaker
Agrees		2	
Disagrees		6	
No comment/ neutral	12	4	12

Table 3.8 Media response to Geithner's 26 March 2009 testimony

Back to the Depression? Federal Reserve Chairman, Ben Bernanke

Ben Bernanke had made a career as a scholar of the Great Depression before coming to the Federal Reserve. For Bernanke, the current crisis—a 'once-in-a-century' crisis, as his predecessor, Alan Greenspan, described it—offered an unique opportunity to put into practice what he had taught all his academic life: invoking a Depression-era law to lend money from the central bank to non-depository institutions (Bernanke 2008a). At the same time, in his running of the Fed, he had stayed within the 'Greenspan paradigm', which was now clearly discredited—as even Greenspan himself eventually admitted. This section attempts to analyse how the Federal Reserve Chairman framed the unfolding crisis and how his framing effort evolved with the change of administration.

14 March 2008: Bernanke's response to Bear Stearns' collapse

Geithner (who was then the President of the New York Federal Reserve) told Bernanke at 4am on 14 March 2008 of Bear's precarious position and the potential risk posed to the US financial system if it collapsed. Even after this dire prediction, however, in his speech that day on fostering sustainable homeownership, Bernanke did not name the financial troubles (*PBS Frontline* 2009). The closest he came to that was in a general statement about mortgage delinquency and foreclosure rates that had been rising substantially during the preceding year and a half. In terms of the crisis-exploitation model, at this time, Bernanke's stance in relation to the financial crisis was a firm type-1: believing that the financial system itself was not in crisis. His framing and management efforts focused on the mortgage market only. The high rate of delinquencies and foreclosures, he explained, was owed to the sharp deterioration in the performance of sub-prime mortgages, particularly those with adjustable-rate features. This, he continued, had its origins in the past quarter-century's advances in information technology, the development of credit-scoring techniques and the emergence of a large secondary market, which had significantly increased access to the mortgage market.

Bernanke defended existing mortgage market policies. Although much of his mortgage-related explanations of the crisis pointed to imprudent sub-prime lending practices, he insisted that sub-prime lending was responsible—except that it expanded credit to borrowers with less than perfect credit histories. His account of the troubles emphasised exogenous—market dynamics—factors, increased access to mortgages, amid irresponsible borrowing on the part of homeowners. His proposed responses focused on devising a comprehensive rule to protect consumers from unfair lending practices; to ensure that borrowers could afford their repayments; banning loan repayment penalties; and tight regulation of the practices of brokers.

Public reaction to the Bernanke speech was minimal. Of the press articles surveyed, most made no comment about the causality claim of the chairman. While five agreed with his policy proposal, seven did not, and most expressed no support for Bernanke. The majority of the commentators criticised the chairman for interfering with the working of the market—more especially, encouraging excessive risk taking among bankers by guaranteeing a federal bailout of collapsing banks (Irwin and Tse 2008). The lack of diverse reaction to the chairman's speech was perhaps due to the attention dedicated to Bear's liquidity issues and Bernanke's role in it.

	Causality	Proposed policy	Support for speaker
Agrees		5	3
Disagrees	5	7	2
No comment/ neutral	8	1	8

Table 3.9 Media response to Bernanke's 14 March 2008 speech

1 December 2008: Bernanke's acknowledgment of crisis

In this second speech, on 1 December 2008, Bernanke's posture had shifted significantly after it had become clear that the nation's financial system was in full-blown crisis (and a change of administration was imminent). At that time, more major banks had collapsed and the speed at which the crisis was unfolding had overwhelmed the Federal Reserve and Treasury's capacity to cope; he and Paulson had asked for money to bail out the system and the crisis had gone global. Besides the speech's title now containing the phrase 'financial crisis', Bernanke described the troubles as economic and financial challenges and an extraordinary period of financial turbulence. Of all Bush-era officials analysed here, Bernanke came closest to endogenising the causes of the crisis, by admitting that there was a serious internal weakness in the American financial system: the absence of well-defined procedures and authorities for dealing with the potential failure of systematically important non-bank financial institutions.

His proposed policy responses to the crisis concentrated on directing the Federal Reserve's efforts to offsetting its effects on credit conditions and the broader economy. Ironically, however, at this stage, Bernanke might have not fully come to terms with the fact that the crisis had already affected the broader economy. The chairman outlined interest rate cuts, the *Emergency Economic Stabilisation Act* and systemic risk minimisation as the few tools at the disposal of the Federal Reserve to fight the crisis.

Bernanke acknowledged weaknesses in the US financial system, but at the same time, he insisted that by way of historical comparison, the Federal Reserve's action stood out as exceptionally rapid and proactive. That effort was not particularly successful. As Table 3.10 reveals, the speech received comparatively little coverage and the tone of the commentaries it did receive was either neutral or negative.

	Causality	Proposed policy	Support for speaker
Agrees			
Disagrees	1	2	
No comment/ neutral	4	3	5

Table 3.10 Media response to Bernanke's 1 December 2008 speech

18 February 2009: Bernanke after the presidential transition

Bernanke's third speech analysed in this chapter was chosen from the series he delivered after Obama had been sworn in as president. Obama took office with a series of policy proposals and measures focused on the crisis and other issues. Despite these, Bernanke's type-2 posture prevailed. He fully acknowledged that the economy was in crisis and recession, describing the time as extraordinarily challenging for the global economy and for economic policymakers—not least for central banks such as the Federal Reserve. Bernanke stopped short of explaining or accounting for the crisis and shifted to assuring Americans of the steps the Federal Reserve would take to restore financial stability and economic prosperity. Such efforts, he stated, would be directed towards easing credit through improving the functioning of credit markets and increasing the supply of credit to households and markets. He said that these measures would break with previous efforts that had been geared towards influencing short-term interest rates, which proved insufficient to overcome the effects of the crisis on credit conditions and the broader economy.

	Causality	Proposed policy	Support for speaker
Agrees			
Disagrees		1	
No comment/ neutral	7	6	7

Table 3.11 Media response to Bernanke's 18 February 2009 speech

10 March 2009: Bernanke acknowledges internal factors

In March 2009, as Federal Reserve chief in the new Obama Administration, Bernanke remained in the type-2 position. He described the crisis as the worst since the 1930s. While acknowledging that the fundamental causes of the crisis remained in dispute, the chairman explained that the crisis was a result of the 1990s' global imbalances in trade and capital flows. According to Bernanke, these had been caused by the chronic lack of savings relative to investment in the United States and other industrial economies, combined with extraordinary increases in savings relative to investment in many emerging-market nations. As a result, he maintained, the United States had experienced large capital inflows for more than a decade even as real interest rates remained low.

The risk-management system of the private sector and government oversight of the financial sector in the United States, Bernanke said, failed to ensure that the inrush of capital was prudently invested. This resulted in the powerful reversal in investor sentiment and seizing up of credit markets, hence precipitating a sharp downturn in the global economy. By way of explanation, Bernanke showed some degree of consistency with Obama's and Geithner's framing attempts in accounting for the crisis. As well as acknowledging the role of endogenous factors, he pointed to the failures of government in harnessing the inflow of capital—a failure that caused the crisis.

Media reaction remained consistently indifferent to Bernanke's third and fourth framing attempts analysed here (Tables 3.10 and 3.11). Of the 16 press articles surveyed, the overwhelming majority made no comment about the chairman's causality claim. All but one made no comment about continued support for him. Opinion about his proposed policy was equally divided. Public opinion polls, however, found that the chairman's approval rating averaged 71 per cent—better than the President's and his Treasury Secretary's (Izzo 2009).

4. Conclusions: the limits of crisis management by speech

For the Bush Administration, the political and policy implications of the framing contest regarding the financial crisis were disastrous. The administration's handling of the crisis was widely depicted as failing to grasp the nature and severity of the problems in time. President Bush's rhetoric failed to stem this tide, perhaps owing as much to his pre-existing credibility deficit as to his words and deeds in the current crisis. Bush, Paulson and Bernanke all took a type-1 stance at the early stage of the crisis, denying that the economic woes were more than incidental and self-correcting. Even after they switched to a type-2 posture, which implied acknowledgment of the crisis, they never regained control of the discourse.

Because the administration had initially insisted that there was no crisis, it did not see the need for a wholesale policy paradigm shift. Rather, it focused on ad-hoc, reactive measures such as the invocation of the Great Depression-style law that allowed the Federal Reserve to lend to non-banks and the bailout of one bank after another. These moves were aimed at aiding the process of market stabilisation. As we saw, this proved unpopular in the media and among the American public.

Until September 2008, Bush's rhetoric focused on talking up the economy and talking down the crisis. This stood in marked contrast with the pattern in his economic rhetoric during most of his first term, when he systematically talked down the economy in order to mobilise support for a series of unprecedented tax cuts, which he defended as a much-needed economic stimulus (Wood 2007). Bush's consistent stance during this period was one of 'it ain't broke, so why fix it'. For example, in his March 2008 address to the Economic Club of New York, the President said he disagreed with the idea of massive government intervention in the event of periodic instances of market 'stress' (Bush 2008a). When later in the year he bowed to the inevitable and started acknowledging the severity of the crisis, Bush's preference for minimal government intervention in the economy had to give way. The limited extent of his stimulus policy, however, betrayed his continued aversion to a more interventionist stance.

The administration came closer than ever to making a deeper policy change after shifting posture to type-2 when it pushed for the enactment of the *Emergency Economic Stabilization Act* (an economic stimulus package), which authorised Treasury to spend $700 billion to undertake a system-wide rescue of the American financial markets—to buy toxic assets, especially the mortgage-backed securities (Paulson 2008b). The scope of the stimulus plan, which covered mainly the private sector, especially the financial markets, signalled the administration's willingness to relax its beliefs in government non-interference in, and deregulation of, the financial markets. It also demonstrated, however, its unwillingness to make a real policy paradigm shift—for example, by adopting a new regulatory regime for financial markets. This was especially true for Bush and Paulson, as both strongly believed in market discipline and freedom and were anti-regulation (*PBS Frontline* 2009).

Obama's economic policy philosophy departed from Bush's. In his State of the Nation Address to a Joint Session of Congress in February 2009, Obama rejected the neo-classical economic doctrine concerning the need for small government (Obama 2009b). Before his election, Obama had already emphasised his belief that a radical shift in policy was called for—one that featured stronger government regulation and oversight of key financial and economic institutions, as well as more direct public investment (Obama 2008). Once president, Obama ironically followed in Bush's rhetorical footsteps by talking down the economy (more specifically, talking up the magnitude and institutional depth of the crisis) in order to mobilise support for his economic reform agenda—only the American Recovery and Reinvestment Plan, which became law in February 2009, was a quite different reform agenda from the one pursued by Bush during 2001–05. Combining economic stimulus with policy innovation, the plan's scope was broad based and far reaching, including major investments in the areas of energy, health care, education and infrastructure and heightening government regulation of the economy.

The extent to which Obama succeeded, as measured by the public opinion surveyed in the earlier part of the chapter, should not be overstated. First, President Bush was totally beleaguered as he prepared to exit office, whereas Obama had come to office with the energy of a new leader, not least on the promise of change in areas such as health care, education and energy, which large segments of the electorate had wanted 'fixed'. To some degree, the escalation of the financial crisis during the campaign was a political windfall for Obama, as it enabled him to develop an additional rationale for policy claims that had already struck a positive chord in the public anyway. Taking the offensive type-3 stance on the financial crisis from the outset, President Obama's crisis rhetoric acknowledged not just the role of unscrupulous financial trading on Wall Street, it put the emphasis on his predecessor's economic philosophies. Bush's attempt at defending his administration's record came late and was fatally flawed because of his declining popularity and the relentless avalanche of bad tidings about the economy.

There was a significant level of consistency between Obama's and Geithner's framing efforts during the early months of 2009. The two appeared to talk in unison in order to 'sell' the Obama Administration's change agenda. The differences were only of degree, not of kind. Once in office, Obama refrained from direct attacks on his predecessor's record, yet Geithner's framing directed blame squarely on the Bush Administration—not only for causing the crisis, but for failing to act early and decisively. His claims were blunt: the crisis accumulated over time through government policies that encouraged a global credit boom; and when the crisis began, the government response had been reactive, slow and incomprehensive.

The only one among the three office-holders to hold his position throughout, Bernanke charted his own rhetorical course during the crisis. His speeches did not betray any attempt to explicitly align his rhetoric with that of the Bush and later the Obama Administrations. Nor should such attempts be expected, given Bernanke's statutory independence. As observed earlier, Bernanke changed stance only once, from type-1 to type-2, nearly halfway through the unfolding of the global financial crisis in the period under study. Thereafter, the Federal Reserve chief consistently maintained the type-2 frame. After he had convinced himself that the current crisis was real and bigger than he had originally imagined, Bernanke, the scholar of the Great Depression, brought to bear his knowledge of its (mis-)management on his ideas about the unfolding financial crisis. It provided him with a wry opportunity: to test his hitherto untested academic belief that financial crises of this magnitude were manageable by capital injections from central banks.

Overall, this study lends some support to the notion that when major disruptive events such as the global financial crisis occur, public leaders are presented with an opportunity to reconsider their policy stances, and with a 'framing contest' that has potentially far-reaching political consequences. In the case of the United States in 2008 and 2009, the unfolding economic crisis significantly changed the economic policy and political landscapes, which started with the campaign rhetoric of John McCain and Barack Obama, graduated to partisan politicking between the Democrats and the Republicans and ended with the United States adopting major policy reforms that broke completely with the past.

The path to reform was paved by Obama and Geithner's crisis rhetoric, but not just theirs: there was an avalanche of media diagnosis of this crisis that was supporting their dire characterisations of the crisis and its causes. When it came to selling the idea that one—and only one—set of policies was best suited to combat the crisis, however, opinion was much more divided, and the public pronouncements of the new administration went only so far in carrying the day. In the end, it was probably the pressure-cooker effect of the escalating crisis itself that contributed as much as any other factor to the relatively quick success of Obama's arm-twisting of Congress to get his stimulus plan passed.

References

Audit Bureau of Circulations 2009, *US Newspaper*, 31 March, Audit Bureau of Circulations, viewed 28 April 2009, <http://www.accessabc.com/index.html>

Baker, P. 2008, 'On Wall Street, the President steers clear of recession', *The Washington Post*, 15 March, viewed 12 April 2009, <http://www.washingtonpost.com/wp-dyn/content/article/2008/03/14/AR2008031401537.html>

Bernanke, B. 2008a, Fostering sustainable homeownership, Speech to Community Reinvestment Coalition Annual Meeting, United States Federal Reserve, Washington, DC, 14 March, viewed 30 April 2009, <http://www.federalreserve.gov/newsevents/speech/bernanke/20080314a.htm>

Bernanke, B. 2008b, Federal Reserve policies in the financial crisis, Speech, United States Federal Reserve, 1 December, viewed 30 April 2009, <http://www.federalreserve.gov/newsevents/speech/bernanke/20081201a.htm>

Bernanke, B. 2009a, Federal Reserve policies to ease credit and their implications for the Fed's balance sheet, Speech, United States Federal Reserve, 18 February, viewed 29 April 2009, <http://www.federalreserve.gov/newsevents/speech/bernanke20090218a.htm>

Bernanke, B. 2009b, Financial reform to address systemic risk, Speech to the Council on Foreign Relations, United States Federal Reserve, Washington, DC, 10 March, viewed 29 April 2009, <http://www.federalreserve.gov/newsevents/speech/bernanke20090310a.htm>

Boin, A., 't Hart, P. and McConnell, A. 2009, 'Crisis exploitation: political and policy impacts of framing contests', *European Journal of Public Policy*, vol. 16, no. 1, pp. 81–106.

Burrough, B. 2008, 'Bringing down Bear Stearns', *Vanity Fair*, August, viewed 20 April 2009, <http://www.vanityfair.com/politics/features/2008/08/bear_stearns200808?printable.htm>

Bush, G. W. 2008a, 'Address to the Economic Club of New York, New York', *Presidential Rhetoric*, 14 March, viewed 30 April 2009, <http://www.presidentialrhetoric.com/speeches/03.14.08.print.html>

Bush, G. W. 2008b, 'The economy and the bailout: primetime address to the nation', *Presidential Rhetoric*, 24 September, viewed 29 April 2009, <http://www.presidentialrhetoric.com/speeches/09.24.08.print.html>

Chomsisengphet, S. and Pennington-Cross, A. 2006, 'The evolution of the subprime mortgage market', *Federal Reserve of St Louis Review*, vol. 88, no. 1, pp. 31–56.

Collins, G. 2008, 'George speaks, badly', *New York Times*, 15 March, viewed 12 April 2009, <http://www.nytimes.com/2008/03/15/opinion/15collins.html>

Federal Insurance Deposit Corporation (FIDC) 2009, *Failed Bank List*, Federal Insurance Deposit Corporation, viewed 30 May 2009, <http://www.fdic.gov/bank/individual/failed/banklist.html>

Gallup Organization 2008, *Gallup Poll*, 14 March, Gallup Organization, viewed 20 May 2009, <http://www.gallup.com/video/104983/Bush-Approval-Static-Congress-Sinks-Further.aspx>

Geithner, T. 2009a, Secretary Geithner introduces financial stability plan, Press release, United States Treasury, 10 February, viewed 29 April 2009, <http://www.treas.gov/press/releases/tg18.htm>

Geithner, T. 2009b, Written testimony to the House Financial Services Committee Hearing, United States Treasury, 26 March, viewed 29 April 2009, <http://www.treas.gov/press/releases/tg71.htm>

't Hart, P., Tindall, K. and Brown, C. 2009, 'Crisis leadership of the Bush presidency: advisory capacity and presidential performance in the acute stages of the 9/11 and Katrina crises', *Presidential Studies Quarterly*, vol. 39, no. 3, pp. 472–91.

Irwin, N. and Tse, T. M. 2008, 'Fed comes to rescue as Wall St giant slips; Bear Stearns gets emergency funds via JP Morgan', *The Washington Post*, 15 March, viewed 26 April 2009, <http://www.washingtonpost.com/wp-dyn/content/article/2008/03/14/AR2008031401617.html>

Izzo, P. 2009, 'Economists give Obama and Geithner low grades', *The Wall Street Journal*, 12 March, viewed 26 April 2009, <http://online.wsj.com/article/SB123671107124286261.html>

Jones, J. 2008, 'Bush's approval rating drops to new low of 27%', *Gallup Poll*, 30 September, Gallup Organization, viewed 9 May 2009, <http://www.gallup.com/poll/110806/ Bushs-Approval-Rating-Drops-New-Low-27.aspx?version=print.html>

Jones, J. 2009, 'Obama approval rating increases to 67%', *Gallup Poll*, 27 February, Gallup Organization, viewed 30 May 2009, <http://www.gallup.com/poll/116224/Obama-Approval-Rating-Increases.aspx>

KDKA-TV 2008, 'Timeline: "US credit crunch and financial failures"', *KDKA-TV CBS*, 15 September, viewed 9 May 2009, <http://kdka.com/business/credit.crisis.timeline.2.818699.html>

Kessler, A. 2009, 'Why markets dissed the Geithner plan', *The Wall Street Journal*, 11 February, viewed 12 April 2009, <http://online.wsj.com/article/SB123431465155370931.html>

Kregel, J. 2008, *Changes in the US financial system and the sub-prime crisis*, Working Paper, no. 530 (August), The Levy Economic Institute of Bard College.

Morales, L. 2009, 'Obama speech bolsters confidence for many Americans', *Gallup Poll*, 26 February, Gallup Organization, viewed 25 April 2009, <http://www.gallup.com/poll/116125/ obama-speech-bolsters-confidence-americans.aspx>

New York Times 2008, 'Getting to yes – readers' comments', *The New York Times*, 19 November, viewed 12 April 2009, <http://community.nytimes.com/comments/www.nytimes.com/ 2008/11/19/opinion/19wed1.html>

Newport, F. 2009, 'Americans divided on Treasury Secretary Geithner', *Gallup Poll*, 30 March, Gallup Organization, viewed 12 April 2009, <http://www.gallup.com/poll/117175/ Americans-Divided-Treasury-Secretary-Geithner>

Obama, B. 2008, 'An economic proposal', *Presidential Rhetoric*, 16 September, viewed 30 April 2009, <http://www.presidentialrhetoric.com/campaign2008/obama/09.16.08.html>

Obama, B. 2009a, 'Remarks on the economy and executive pay', *Presidential Rhetoric*, 4 February, viewed 29 April 2009, <http://www.presidentialrhetoric.com/speeches/02.04.09.print.html>

Obama, B. 2009b, 'The state of the nation: address to the Joint Session of Congress', *Presidential Rhetoric*, 24 February, viewed 30 April 2009, <http://www.presidentialrhetoric.com/speeches/02.24.09.html>

Paletta, D. 2008, 'Politics & economics: FHA may aid those "underwater" on loans', *The Wall Street Journal*, 31 March, viewed 30 April 2009, <http://www.realestatejournal.com/buysell/mortgages/20080331-paletta.html>

Paulson, H. 2008a, Remarks by Secretary Henry M. Paulson, jr, on financial and housing markets, Press release, United States Treasury, 26 March, viewed 30 April 2009, <http://www.treas.gov/press/releases/hp887.htm>

Paulson, H. 2008b, Paulson statement on *Emergency Economic Stabilization Act*, Press release, United States Treasury, 3 October, viewed 26 April 2009, <http://www.treas.gov/press/releases/hp1175.htm>

Paulson, H. 2008c, On the implementation of the *Emergency Economic Stabilization Act*, Press release, United States Treasury, 18 November, viewed 12 April 2009, <http://www.treas.gov/press/releases/hp1279.htm>

PBS Frontline 2009, 'Inside the meltdown', *PBS Frontline*, 17 February, viewed 12 April 2009, <http://www.pbs.org/wgbh/pages/frontline/meltdown/view/>

Saad, L. 2008, 'US financial rescue plan wins slim public support', *Gallup Poll*, 6 October, Gallup Organization, viewed 9 May 2009, <http:www.gallup.com/poll/110977/US-Financial-Rescue-Plan-Wins-Slim-Public-Support.aspx?version.htm>

Thomas, L. 2008, 'Run on Wall St bank spurs US-backed rescue', *The New York Times*, 15 March, viewed 12 April 2009, <http://www.nytimes.com/2008/03/15/business/15bear.html>

Uchitelle, L. 2008, 'A political comeback: supply-side economics', *The New York Times*, 26 March, viewed 24 May 2009, <http://www.nytimes.com/2008/03/26/business/26supply.html?_r=1>

Washington Post 2008, 'Troubled TARP, keep the bailout focused on job one: restoring bank solvency', *The Washington Post*, 19 November, viewed 12 April 2009, <http://www.washingtonpost.com/wp-dyn/content/article/2008/11/18/AR2008111803021.html>

Wessel, D. 2009, 'US new capital: Geithner's plan carries a new set of risks', *The Wall Street Journal*, 26 March, viewed 26 April 2009, <http://online.wsj.com/article/SB123800845407840625.html>

Wood, B. D. 2007, *The Politics of Economic Leadership: The causes and consequences of presidential rhetoric*, Princeton University Press, Princeton.

4. Canada: the politics of optimism

Anastasia Glushko

1. Warranted optimism or an illusion of invulnerability?

In late 2008, billionaire investor Warren Buffet called the financial crisis a 'financial Pearl Harbor' (Clark 2008) and former US Federal Reserve Chairman Alan Greenspan described it as a 'once-in-a-century event' (Stein 2008). Like the problem itself, however, Canada's experience of, and its government's response to, the financial meltdown have been more ambiguous. Canada entered the economic turbulence from a position of relative strength and suffered far less than would be expected of a country whose economy was so dependent on its southern neighbour. At the time of writing, Canada's financial system has been less affected by the global financial crisis than those of other industrialised countries such as the United States and the United Kingdom, and its banks have not required an injection of government capital. In fact, in October 2008, the World Economic Forum ranked Canada first in the world for the soundness of its banking system and, in March 2009, Canada's banks were expected to report another profitable quarter, defying global trends (Hopkins 2009).

On the other hand, no one major country in the world is as dependent on another nation for its economic wellbeing as Canada is on the United States. Canada ships almost four-fifths of its exports to the United States (Statistics Canada 2008), and all of Canada's recent surpluses in its current account are attributable to the United States' buying power (Fry 2009:35–6). In addition, investors in the United States account for about 58 per cent of the foreign direct investment stock in Canada and these investments have provided more than one million jobs for Canadian workers. Canada's tourism and hospitality sectors have also been seriously dependent on the United States since Americans account for about 80 per cent of all foreign visitors to Canada (Fry 2009:35–6).

As a result, the effects of the global financial crisis on the Canadian economy did not begin to be felt until late in 2008 and early 2009, when the reduction in American consumption began to translate into difficulties for Canada's export, service, auto and primary sectors. Rising unemployment, reduction in foreign investment and the falling value of the local currency were particularly significant manifestations of the financial crisis in Canada. Indeed, the full extent of its impact was being fully understood—and suffered—by ordinary Canadians only as of early 2009.

The three people responsible for leading Canada through this crisis and therefore subject to analysis in this study are Prime Minister Stephen Harper, Minister for Finance Jim Flaherty, and the Governor of the Bank of Canada Mark Carney. Harper and Flaherty are members of the Conservative Party, which has been a minority government since 2006. Carney's post is not political, since the Bank of Canada's Board of Directors appoints the governor. As this study will show, however, it was precisely the apolitical nature of his office that conferred significant importance and legitimacy on his public pronouncements—and meant Carney was a significant figure in shaping public opinion about the events.

Because the real extent of the effects of the crisis on the Canadian economy was not revealed until the end of 2008, for most of that year, the Conservative Government was able to exploit its position of incumbency and Harper's reputation as a respected economist—specifically, that Harper, who held an MA in economics, was Canada's first Prime Minister to be a professional economist. Emboldened by an economy that seemed largely unaffected by the crisis that was engulfing the rest of the world, and by a weak and divided opposition, the usually cautious Harper called an early election in October 2008. He asked Canadians for a mandate to lead the country through the financial storm (though it was widely accepted that he was also hoping to secure a parliamentary majority the Conservatives had hitherto lacked). Although the Harper Government was comfortably returned (albeit without a majority), the September election campaign, coupled with the simultaneous rapid fall on Wall Street, facilitated public discussion and awareness of the severity of the meltdown and revealed considerable flaws in the Conservatives' public framing of the crisis. After the election, the government's optimistic outlook proved to be increasingly fragile, as the reverberations of the global crisis steadily permeated the Canadian economy. The government was forced to rescind on its assurances that Canada's economy was so sound that it would even produce a surplus in the subsequent fiscal year. In fact, the government had to concede that Canada's economy was officially in recession and that the country would be forced to produce a deficit, the projected amount of which inflated from $30 billion in January 2009 to $50 billion at the time of writing in June (Jones 2009).

The continuous policy backtracking since December 2008 saw the government's credibility erode significantly. Its apparent reluctance to admit the severity of the crisis created a perception that the Conservative Government lacked empathy for ordinary Canadians hit by the crisis. Despite these setbacks, the government remained in a position of relative strength in June 2009. It was enabled by politically weak opposition parties, who had been riddled with their own leadership difficulties and who, despite the opportunity the crisis presented, were unable to put aside their divisions to effectively challenge the government on the basis of economic competency. A telling example was the parliamentary crisis in December 2008 when the Harper Government found itself facing the prospect of defeat in the House of Commons on a motion of confidence brought by the three opposition parties. In addition, the three parties signed a formal coalition agreement providing for a Liberal–NDP coalition government (supported by Bloc Quebecois) to assume power if the government was defeated. The government was forced to prorogue Parliament for two months, but the coalition fell apart almost as soon as Parliament returned, unable to agree on an appropriate response to the budget, thus ending the parliamentary crisis.

Box 4.1 Canada's financial crisis trajectory, April 2008 – April 2009

24 April 2008: Finance Minister, Jim Flaherty, announces that the government will tighten securities regulation to force more disclosure by financial institutions about their investments.

21 August: According to Statistics Canada, 15 of 22 industry groups reported higher profits, led by oil and gas extraction and manufacturing. Canadian corporations earned $69.4 billion in operating profits in the second quarter—up 2.5 per cent from the first quarter.

22 August: Flaherty uses his department's monthly fiscal update to announce that the Federal Government has revised its working estimate for growth to 1.1 per cent from the 1.7 per cent forecast in the February budget.

28 August: The Harris/Decima Investors Group Survey indicates that pessimism about the economy in the coming year fell 6 per cent since the previous survey in May, to 32 per cent.

6 September: Findings show Canadian employers hired 161,000 people in August, maintaining the unemployment rate at 6.1 per cent.

7 September: Prime Minister Stephen Harper, calls an early election for 14 October.

11 September: Labour productivity falls for the third consecutive quarter, highlighting a marked deterioration in Canada's competitiveness and a signal that growth is slowing.

15 September: As the Toronto Stock Exchange (TSX) closes down 515.55 points, Harper warns against economic pessimism about the unfolding US financial crisis, saying that if an economic crash was coming, it would have happened already.

19 September: Harper says Canadian financial institutions have not been hit hard by the US financial crisis; therefore, there is no need for a bailout of Canada's chartered banks.

---

23 September: Statistics Canada says Canada's consumer price index is at its highest point since March 2003 due to thriving food and gas inflation.

24 September: The Bank of Canada pledges $4 billion to unfreeze credit markets; Statistics Canada says inflation jumped to 3.5 per cent in August—the highest rate since early 2003.

25 September: The Bank of Canada pledges a further $6 billion in emergency short-term lending to help lenders deal with tighter credit markets.

29 September: The TSX closes 841 points down—the biggest one-day point drop ever—as the US Congress votes down the bailout package; Scotiabank Commodity Index drops 8.9 per cent.

30 September: The Bank of Canada injects an additional $4 billion into short-term money markets as a means to increase the flow of credit.

1 October: Volvo closes its Ontario plant, with a loss of 500 jobs; Statistics Canada says Canada's economy boomed in July, growing 0.7 per cent on the strength of surging energy output—the fastest pace of growth since March 2004.

8 October: Central banks announce coordinated rate reductions and the Bank of Canada lowers its interest rate by 0.5 of a percentage point to 2.5 per cent.

10 October: The Canadian dollar experiences its biggest one-day drop since 1971.

14 October: Harper's government is re-elected.

19 October: Flaherty predicts a 'modest' surplus for the current fiscal year.

21 October: The Bank of Canada lowers its interest rate by 0.25 of a percentage point to 2.25 per cent.

24 October: The government guarantees bank loans.

30 October: Harper announces a new cabinet, enlarging it to 38 members and increasing Ontario's representation. Three of the most heavyweight portfolios (finance, industry and transport) remain unchanged; the opposition criticises the retention of Flaherty.

31 October: The Harper Government announces it will limit the growth of equalisation payments to poorer provinces in light of the global financial crisis.

1 November: Bank of Montreal and Bank of Nova Scotia say Canada is entering a recession; the government denies it.

10 November: General Motors' shares drop to a 60-year low. The auto industry is Canada's largest industrial sector by employment, accounting for 12 per cent of manufacturing gross domestic product (GDP) and employing more than 500,000 Canadians.

12 November: Canadian stocks fall below 9000 points, as investors ignore a new Canadian Government pledge to better stimulate lending by the banks.

20 November: Harper makes his reply to the 'Speech from the Throne', emphasising that he will act quickly to protect Canadians in a time of global instability.

24 November: Flaherty concedes that Canada is in recession; the Canadian dollar is up 3.5 per cent, buoyed by the bailout of Citigroup.

30 November: Flaherty announces a five-year economic action plan to stimulate the economy.

9 December: The Bank of Canada lowers its interest rate by 0.75 of a percentage point to 1.5 per cent.

20 January 2009: The Bank of Canada lowers its interest rate by 0.5 of a percentage point to 1 per cent.

24 February: Parliament passes the Economic Action Plan, which seeks to provide almost $64 billion over two years to support the Canadian economy, including money for infrastructure, tax cuts and changes to the employment insurance scheme. The government predicts a deficit of $34 billion in the next financial year, and $30 billion in the year after that.

2 March: The Canadian dollar hits a three-month low against the US dollar, exacerbated by renewed risk aversion and the declining price of crude oil. A Statistics Canada report reveals that Canada's GDP shrank by 3.4 per cent in the fourth quarter—one of the lightest declines among the major global economies. On an annual basis, GDP fell by 0.7 per cent—the first decline in the annual rate since 1991.

3 March: The Bank of Canada lowers its rate by 0.5 per cent to 0.5 per cent.

11 March: The International Monetary Fund (IMF) announces that Canada is 'better placed than most' to weather the global recession due to a strong fiscal package announced in January and a healthy financial sector.

6 April: A study by the Canadian Centre for Policy Alternatives finds that rapid contractions of the economy and the job market eclipsed the Harper Government's stimulus package before any money was even dispensed. The study reports that the package laid out in the 27 January budget was too small, too late and 'out of proportion to the threat that Canadians are currently facing'.

9 April: The Statistics Canada Labour Force Survey shows employment declined by 61,000 places in March 2009, pushing the unemployment rate up 0.3 of a percentage point to 8 per cent—the highest rate in seven years.

2. Methodological considerations

This chapter follows the overall research design of this volume, so no detailed account of key concepts, propositions and study design principles is provided here. A few observations are in order, however, on the specifics of the speeches and newspapers selected for further analysis. The selection of key speeches was determined by the amount of media coverage they received. This was because the initial process of compiling a timeline of the crisis in Canada revealed a notable lack of general media interest (as manifest in the lack of coverage) in the manner in which the Canadian Government was handling the crisis, despite its magnitude. In addition, particular events that received considerable international coverage and could reasonably be assumed to have been of significance to Canadians—such as the biggest one-day drop in the Canadian dollar's value, the government's guarantee of banks loans and the proroguing of Parliament—curiously did not attract very much coverage. This indicated that to determine which events and consequently which particular speech acts registered on the Canadian public's radar (and therefore presented opportunities to frame the crisis), a comprehensive search of the chosen media outlets was necessary.

Thus, every article containing a reference to the economic crisis in chosen publications within the specified time frame was examined in chronological order. Speech acts that related to events that received significant media attention generally received significant coverage themselves and were selected for this merit. A secondary search of references to the selected speech acts and events was also conducted to ensure no coverage was missed. This method, although painstaking and time consuming, meant that the process of selection of relevant newspaper articles was almost simultaneous with the selection of the speeches.

The newspapers chosen for analysis in this study were *The Globe and Mail* and the *National Post*, as well as its business section, the *Financial Post*—two national newspapers with high circulation. It is worth noting that the *Toronto Star* has the highest circulation of all newspapers in Canada and was initially considered. A closer examination, however, revealed that the *Toronto Star* could be classified more accurately as a provincial newspaper, due to its preoccupation with Ontario-based issues. The high levels of circulation can likely be attributed to the fact that Ontario is by far the most populated province, with almost 13 million residents, compared with the 4.5 million in British Columbia, for example (Canadian Newspaper Association 2008:4–5).

The choice of national newspapers is admittedly limiting. Both newspapers are fairly conservative in their journalistic ethos and mostly endeavour to avoid particular bias (or attempts to influence public opinion) compared with some of their more colourful provincial counterparts. Moreover, given the strength of historical and economic divides between the provinces, regional (mostly tabloid) newspapers such as the *Vancouver Sun*, *The Calgary Herald* or *Le Devoir* are often read more widely in their respective localities than are the national broadsheet papers (Canadian Newspaper Association 2008:6–9). The crisis, however, affected different Canadian provinces in different ways; central Canada was by far the worst hit because of its reliance on service and auto manufacturing industries and the crisis was most painfully manifested in high levels of unemployment. On the other hand, the wealthier oil and gas-producing provinces of British Columbia and Alberta were far less affected, and the main issues for people there were fluctuating commodity prices that generated high levels of anxiety but, by early 2009, no significant job losses.

Provincial newspapers reveal a perennial preoccupation with their provincial interests rather than national issues, which presents a significant obstacle when attempting to measure popular and media opinion in Canada. With this in mind, the study does on occasion consider a small cross-section of provincial coverage, particularly where there were wide discrepancies between the views conveyed in national and provincial papers.

The selected articles were summarised and then coded using a three-point scale of agreement (agreement, disagreement or neutral/no comment) against four analytical categories, which referred to the leaders' framing of the severity and the causality of the crisis, proposed policy implications and overall support for the leader. This method was useful in demonstrating the amount of coverage each speech act received and provided a useful basis when analysing media interest (or lack thereof) in the government's framing of the crisis. These findings were, where possible, supplemented with relevant national public opinion polling statistics, reflecting the government's popularity and credibility. The findings were interpreted through the lens of the crisis exploitation framework described in Chapter 2.

3. Crisis development and elite rhetoric in Canada

12 May 2008: the Finance Minister's assertion of Canadian resilience

Jim Flaherty used his address to the Economic Club of Toronto to assure Canadian voters that Canada's economy would prove to be resilient. He acknowledged a number of challenges facing the Canadian economy: the US housing market, volatile financial markets, the strong Canadian dollar (in the face of waning demand for exports), energy prices and an ageing population. He used upbeat rhetoric, however, to argue that Canadian banks were well capitalised, the local housing market was solid and more Canadians were working than before. He also made a number of historical references to Sir John A. Macdonald, the first Prime Minister of Canada, whose tenure spanned 18 years and who was the only Canadian prime minister to win eight majority governments. He drew parallels between Macdonald's preference to 'always look a little ahead' and his own government's preference for grounding broader economic policies in the long term, rather than 'band-aid, ad hoc solutions'.

Given the extent to which Canadians were exposed to the US media (and what would have already been a daily drumbeat of dire economic news), this speech served a vital function in shaping Canadian public opinion of the domestic manifestations of the global financial crisis and its causes. This was particularly significant given the incumbency of the Harper Government—and therefore its vulnerability to blame for the impact of the crisis on Canada.

	Severity	Causality	Policy implications	Support for speaker
Agrees	1		1	1
Disagrees				
No comment/ neutral	1	2	1	1

Table 4.1 Media response to Flaherty's 12 May 2008 speech

The global financial crisis did not start to affect Canada seriously until about October 2008 and the Canadian public did not fully accept the fact even a number of months after that. At this stage of the crisis, media agreement with proposed policy implications was closely tied to support for the national leaders, since the Canadian Government had not proposed any new measures to deal with the crisis, instead emphasising the importance of 'staying the course'. While a lack of media interest in Flaherty's subsequent public pronouncements might have indicated a level of public despondency with the Harper Government, the fact that this speech attracted very minimal coverage in May 2008 was a big positive for the Conservative Government. A Strategic Counsel opinion poll conducted shortly after Flaherty's speech showed that the Conservatives enjoyed the support of 38 per cent of decided voters—down only 1 per cent from a high of 39 per cent in February 2006 (Strategic Counsel, CTV and Globe and Mail 2008a) and, a month later, the same poll showed that 38 per cent of people felt the Conservative Party was best able to manage the economy in the case of a downturn—compared with the Liberal Party's 27 per cent (Strategic Counsel, CTV and Globe and Mail 2008b). It can therefore be concluded that the reason why Flaherty's 12 May speech received little public attention was because the global economic crisis was not yet a major issue for the Canadian media and public. Flaherty's choice of using consistently positive rhetoric and downplaying the interdependence of the US and Canadian economies, however, proved an effective meaning-making strategy for the time being.

25 September 2008: bank governor Carney's crisis narrative

Mark Carney used his address to the Canadian Club of Montreal to outline how the upheaval in global financial markets and the slowdown in the US economy were important international factors affecting the Canadian economy. Using blunter language than Canadians had come to expect from their government, Carney said that global markets were now at a critical juncture and the nature of the slowdown in the US economy—with weakness in the housing and auto sectors—posed particular problems for Canadian exports. He also argued, however, that the turmoil might be cathartic in restructuring markets, prompting decisive policy responses and speeding up the reordering of the financial system to make the world more stable. He concluded that Canada's financial system was well positioned to weather the financial storm because it had been prudent and soundly capitalised. He added that the Bank of Canada would continue to monitor economic and financial developments carefully and would 'continue to set monetary policy consistent with achieving the two per cent inflation target over the medium term'.

From the outset, it is worth noting that beyond announcements affecting interest rates, public pronouncements from the Bank of Canada have rarely attracted much media attention. This could probably be attributed to the level of detail provided by Carney and the Bank of Canada, which was uninteresting or difficult for ordinary Canadians to understand (Financial Consumer Agency of Canada 2008). It was also for this reason that the media often oversimplified Carney's speech acts. Of the five articles analysed, four essentially disagreed with Carney's positive assessment of Canada's economy and portrayed the severity of the economic crisis as very acute (Table 4.2). All five left out Carney's assurances that Canada's financial system was well placed and that high commodity prices could even benefit the Canadian economy, and they expressed very pessimistic observations about the prospects for the Canadian economy.

	Severity	Causality	Policy implications	Support for speaker
Agrees		5		2
Disagrees	4		1	
No comment/ neutral	1		4	3

Table 4.2 Media responses to Carney's 25 September 2008 speech

Unlike Harper and Flaherty, who preferred to avoid any discussion of causality in their public pronouncements, Carney appeared to view explaining what had happened as part of his job as the Governor of the Bank of Canada. All five articles agreed with Carney's assessment of the causes of the crisis. Perhaps because Canadians realised that Carney had nothing to gain politically by exploiting the crisis, and perhaps because they did not realise that it was in his professional interest to keep public confidence buoyant, none of the articles expressed criticism of him. In covering this speech, however, three articles showed disapproval of the Harper Government and portrayed Flaherty and Harper as dishonest, clueless and uninformed.

It is also worth noting that Carney's speech attracted significant attention in media sources not used in this study, particularly regional newspapers. Local media sources such as the *Prince George Citizen* and *The Montreal Gazette* produced very positive accounts of his pronouncements and focused on his assertion that Canada could weather the US storm. In the midst of all the gloom coming from national and US media sources, regional Canadians clearly craved some positive news.

7 October 2008: Prime Minister Harper's bid for re-election

This speech, the release of his party's election platform, marked a deliberate attempt by Harper to reverse the downward trend in support for the Conservative Party. Hitherto in the election campaign, Harper had taken advantage of his position as the frontrunner and as leader of the incumbent party. He had refrained from presenting a comprehensive package. Although acknowledging that 'Canada is heading into a period of economic uncertainty and slower growth', Harper used this speech to urge Canadians not to panic because Canada was well placed to weather the financial storm. Responding to criticisms that the government had not responded quickly enough to the global financial crisis, Harper said his opponents were panicking and he vowed to stay the course: 'prudent leadership does not set out economic strategy for the nightly news or re-write plans for the morning papers...you don't shift long term plans for short-term considerations.' The speech emphasised previous achievements: variations on the phrase 'we will continue to' and 'the Conservative government has already' recurred in the text. In contrast with Harper's usually very reserved and formal communication style, this speech made a memorable pseudo-biblical reference ('the plan on which we have been acting is the plan...as the saying goes, it wasn't raining when Noah built the Ark'), which was ridiculed by some commentators.

The policy proposals were modest, probably in order to complement the government's mantra that Canada's banks were insulated from the building storm in global markets. This logic had seemed like a winning one in early September when the Conservative Party called the snap election hoping to secure the majority 'before the tidal wave sweeping the global financial system breached Canada's levies' (Callan 2008). As the global financial crisis deepened, however—the Toronto Stock Exchange dropped 3942 points or 28.6 per cent between 1 September and 8 October (*The Economist* 2008)—and media discussion and awareness about its causality and severity increased, this 'happy-go-lucky' message (*The Globe and Mail* 2008) proved to be fragile and increasingly irrelevant as it was largely abandoned by many of Canada's top banks.

	Severity	Causality	Policy implications	Support for the speaker
Agrees	2	4	3	1
Disagrees	6		6	8
No comment/ neutral	5	9	4	4

Table 4.3 Media responses to Harper's 7 October 2008 speech

The media analysis reported in Table 4.3 demonstrates a substantial lack of support for the national leader as well as the proposed policy implications. There was marked disagreement about the severity of the global financial crisis, with six out of the 13 articles analysed refuting Harper's argument that Canada's financial system was sound and criticising his resistance to introduce special measures to deal with the crisis. The research clearly indicated that the familiar meaning-making script aimed at convincing voters that the government anticipated the current problems back in August 2007 had failed. Of the 13 articles analysed, nine questioned Harper's proposed policy implications and expressed concerns about the government's understanding of the global financial crisis. This was significant given that Harper, a professional economist, had traditionally been able to control the domestic economic debate.

Having said that, despite Harper's incumbency, little mention (and no disagreement with the government) was made of the causes of the crisis. The coverage implied agreement with Harper's diagnosis of the causes of the crisis being exogenous. At least in part, this was testament to the strength of the reputation he built throughout his tenure as a competent, sensible and pragmatic economist.

A major criticism of Harper was his perceived inability to communicate empathy for the anxieties of the Canadian people or to reach out with convincing reassurance to those who reasonably continued to fear losing their jobs, losing their savings and deferring their hopes of retirement. Eight of 13 articles surveyed berated Harper for his lack of sensitivity. Harper's suggestion that stock market bargain hunters could benefit from the economic panic became a particular target. There were also some concerns that the lack of sensitivity was a portent of future inflexibility, particularly if the Conservatives were delivered a majority at the election. The fact that he delivered the speech to the Empire Club of Canada (as opposed to a group of factory workers, for example) only exacerbated the perception that Harper's response to the global financial crisis was cerebral and out of touch. The voters appeared to share the scepticism of some of the media. According to a Harris/Decima opinion poll taken one day after the speech (and eight days out from the election), only 31 per cent of decided voters supported the Conservative Party—down from a high of 41 per cent one month earlier (Heard 2008). All of this probably accounted for the fact that the title of the speech was amended from 'True north strong and free: Stephen Harper's plan for Canada' to something less self-congratulating before it was placed on the Prime Ministerial web site.

17 October 2008: a re-elected Harper opens the new Parliament

Opening the new Parliament, this speech was a broad-strokes outline of the government's agenda. The Throne Speech is traditionally a vague statement of priorities for the new government. It did not contain any details of the economic stimuli (the government did not release these until the budget announcement at the end of January 2009). For the most part, Harper stuck to pledges he and his Conservative Party made in the election campaign, but warned that the country could be headed back into deficit because it would be 'misguided' to inflict economic pain to avoid it. The speech was a sober one, evoking great battles of World War I and the subsequent generation that 'overcame the Depression and again confronted the devastation of war'. In all, it was a clear attempt by Harper to manage public expectations by acknowledging the severity of the situation, yet at the same time highlighting that no matter how serious the economic downturn might be, far greater challenges had been met and overcome in Canadian history.

	Severity	Causality	Policy implications	Support for speaker
Agrees	4		2	2
Disagrees			3	3
No comment/ neutral	2	6	1	1

Table 4.4 Media responses to Harper's 17 October 2008 speech

The speech enjoyed a low-key, but mixed reception in the press (Table 4.4). Of the six articles analysed, three expressed disagreement with the speaker and his policy proposals. Although most articles agreed with Harper's perception of the severity of the crisis (as conveyed in the speech), a major point of concern appeared to be the suggestion that Canada could return to deficit spending. This might have been an unintended consequence of Harper's reluctance to publicly convey the real severity of the economic crisis and manage public expectations accordingly (and consistently) during the preceding election campaign.

Interestingly, it appears that Harper's adherence to tradition in avoiding using the Throne Speech to exploit the economic crisis politically backfired on him. The New Democratic Party's leader, Jack Layton, criticised Harper's address for lacking any bold or significant action with regard to the economic crisis. He argued that this was another illustration of Harper's lack of empathy for ordinary Canadians—a criticism that was readily picked up by five out of six articles analysed. This highlights one of two things: either Harper's inability to interpret the national mood (a common criticism of his leadership) or his sound judgment in preferring to be criticised for sticking to tradition in times of crisis rather than inappropriate exploitation (and potentially, partisanship). To Harper's credit, the Throne Speech was not one that usually received significant amounts of coverage, so while the former criticism might have been common, unless especially controversial, this particular speech was never likely to be brought up against him by his critics in the future.

Given how general the speech was, how little coverage it received and how few policy announcements it contained, it was surprising that it was met with such relative disapproval. This could be attributed to the widespread feeling of disillusionment after the election. A national qualitative study conducted by Ensight Canada the day after the election found that there was widespread consensus that the election was 'a waste of time and money' and 'prevented meaningful action being taken to protect Canada's economy amidst the financial crisis' (Watt 2008:2–4). The study showed that the voters were disappointed with Harper's vision and program for the economy during the election, but chose him 'as the best of an unhappy set of choices' (Watt 2008:1–2). As such, this speech illustrates that the capacity of a leader's rhetoric to influence public debate is always limited by the broader context of public mood.

27 January 2009: Finance Minister Flaherty's budget speech

Flaherty characterised his budget as necessary to protect jobs and businesses from the ravages of the financial crisis. The financial plan devoted about half of the new spending to construction projects that Flaherty hoped would revive the economy by creating new jobs and stoking demand for lumber and other Canadian-made goods. In what was his fourth budget in three years, Flaherty offered consumers a tax break on home renovations and pledged to expand employment-insurance benefits for two years. Flaherty also stated that the Conservative Government would make available another $70 billion in credit to businesses that were struggling to find affordable loans as a result of the global financial crisis. Although Flaherty used powerful language to introduce and conclude this lengthy speech, the urgency he hoped to convey did not really capture the media's imagination. Not unusually for a budget speech, the majority of the coverage focused on policy rather than sentiment.

	Severity	Causality	Policy implications	Support for speaker
Agrees	12	5	7	7
Disagrees	4	2	13	9
No comment/ neutral	8	17	4	8

Table 4.5 Media response to Flaherty's 27 January 2009 speech

The major point of concern in media reception of the speech was that the policies and measures proposed by the Harper Government were inappropriate to the national needs (Table 4.5). While the majority of the coverage expressed agreement with Flaherty about the severity of the crisis, there was a strong view that the budget's lack of a single compelling direction—'the whole leaves the impression of miscellany' (*The Globe and Mail* 2009)—was evidence of it having fallen prey to political engineering. This led many to disagree with the proposed policy implications—and, therefore, with the necessity of the debt they brought with them.

Most articles, however, agreed that the government had to step up in times of crisis and did not refute the need for stimulus. This support was also reflected in a research poll, conducted in early February, which indicated that 56.6 per cent of Canadians at least somewhat supported deficit spending to stimulate the economy (Nanos 2009). The research also revealed, however, that a common sentiment was that the recession should be seen as an opportunity 'to do what needs to be done anyway' (Ivison 2009a) so that Canada could emerge from it 'leaner and meaner' (Corcoran 2009) than before. Instead, the overwhelming opinion was that the budget needlessly pandered to the masses at the expense of Canada's future economic prosperity.

Of the 24 articles analysed, 13 argued in some way that the budget lacked foresight and was based on wishful thinking that revenues would recover and grow more quickly than spending by the next election. Inarguably, this would have been exacerbated by the still-lingering criticisms that the Harper Government saw the economy through rose-coloured glasses and therefore did not realise the gravity of going into deficit. The research indicated that while there was a belief that the government might have been well intentioned, the overwhelming suspicion was that help for the Canadian economy would arrive too late, in the wrong place and hang around longer than expected.

These concerns did not, however, translate into strong public disapproval of Flaherty as a leader. Overall, he was seen as beholden to Harper, whose imposing leadership style and public presence were well documented. Flaherty's own merits were overtly criticised in only one article; the rest were critical of him only by the virtue of being Harper's Finance Minister. This also translated into assessments of Flaherty's performance: only those who agreed with the Harper Government more broadly tended to be complimentary of Flaherty.

Coverage of the budget three months after it was introduced was far more positive, despite the massive and growing gap between the number of Canadian job losses and the jobs target in the budget (Akin 2009). This suggested the government's attempts to convince the Canadian public that benefits of stimulus measures would take some time to filter through the economy had been successful.

10 February 2009: bank governor Carney's 'realism'

Carney used this address to reiterate his forecast that after a challenging first half, 'the economy will rebound at the fastest pace in decades'. This was almost twice the pace forecast by the International Monetary Fund (IMF) and most private-sector economists (Schoffield 2009). Carney confidently spoke of the Bank of Canada's economic outlook, but said that it would materialise only if the United States and other major economies took 'exceptional' measures to end the crisis in financial markets. In reply to a suggestion by John McCallum, the Liberal's finance critic, that the bank was going 'out on something of an optimistic limb', Carney replied, 'We don't do optimism. We do realism at the Bank of Canada. We don't do spin.' He added that the Bank of Canada would continue to monitor economic and financial developments carefully and 'will continue to set monetary policy consistent with achieving the two per cent inflation target over the medium term'.

	Severity	Causality	Policy implications	Support for speaker
Agrees	5	2	4	5
Disagrees	1		1	1
No comment/ neutral		4	2	

Table 4.6 Media responses to bank governor Carney's 10 February 2009 speech

While Carney's positive outlook had hitherto been met with considerable scepticism, his plain assertion that the Bank of Canada did not 'do spin' appeared to resonate well. This lent his latest crisis assessment considerable legitimacy and in turn enabled greater control of the message (Table 4.6). Four of the six analysed articles emphasised in some way that the predictions of the Bank of Canada were based on economic models and data and therefore should not be dismissed as mere rhetoric or personal grandstanding (like that of political leaders). In other words, Carney could be trusted. This accounted for the broad support for the policy implications Carney recommended, as well as the agreement with his assessment of the severity of the crisis.

In addition, five out of six surveyed articles lent their support to Carney's leadership. This was in marked contrast with previous coverage, which tended to stay neutral on this issue. Portrayal of Carney as a credible leader did not change even when he adjusted his outlook two weeks later by cutting the Bank of Canada's interest rate in half to just 0.5 of a percentage point and admitting that there would be 'a sharper decline in Canadian economic activity' in the next couple of months 'and a larger-than-expected erosion of business and consumer confidence could mean the economy will not begin to bounce back until early 2010' (Bank of Canada 2009). Despite the fact that this essentially proved Carney's earlier critics right, the media attack focused on Harper's personal leadership instead, and again gave rise to suggestions that Harper and Flaherty were not prepared for the recession, did not understand what was going on and were ill equipped to deal with the economic crisis.

23 February 2009: Flaherty attempts to rally the public

Flaherty's piece in the opinion section of the *National Post* sought to reassure Canadian families and businesses that the new federal budget would help cushion the impacts of the downturn and support those hit hardest by the global financial crisis. He reasserted the Harper Government's line about the causes of the crisis (exogenous) and that of the virtues and near-invulnerability of the Canadian financial system. While acknowledging that 'there is not [a] magic bullet to return the world economy back to previous heights' and that the United States' recovery was essential to Canada's, he assured his readers that the Conservative Government had acted swiftly to 'keep our edge'. And, like Harper, he reiterated once again that most countries were far worse off than Canada. He went on to recapitulate the key points of the 2009 budget and ended by urging his fellow parliamentarians to 'set games aside' and put his plan to work, arguing that delay and 'obstructionism' were no longer appropriate in such difficult times.

It is quite unusual for a Canadian Finance Minister to write a column in a major national newspaper, so one could conclude that by this virtue alone the piece might have attracted some attention. Flaherty's article, however, received very few reader comments (four) and even less media coverage. There was only one short article, also in the *National Post*, and it focused mainly on Flaherty's point that the United States' recovery would be essential for Canada to pull itself out of the economic quagmire. In media terms, this framing attempt went down like a lead balloon (Table 4.7).

	Severity	Causality	Policy implications	Support for speaker
Agrees				
Disagrees				
No comment/ neutral	1	1	1	1

Table 4.7 Media responses to Flaherty's 23 February 2009 article

A thorough search of other media outlets not included in this study (including regional newspapers in Flaherty's native Ontario) also failed to produce any findings. This lack of national interest points to a number of things. First, that Flaherty's rhetoric simply failed to kindle public interest. If Harper was frequently portrayed as dull and uncharismatic by the Canadian media (for example, Martin 2008), Flaherty seldom said anything that Harper had not already said in almost exactly the same way. There was never any disagreement or disparity between the two leaders, so for journalists there was little incentive to cover Flaherty's utterances. Second, in most countries, the Minister for Finance (Canada's equivalent of Treasurer) tends to be viewed as the expert on most macroeconomic questions. Harper's extensive background as an economist, however, and the fact that his credibility as a prime minister was built almost entirely on his reputation as a great economic tactician and manager, meant that as far as public opinion was concerned, Flaherty's views and statements were redundant. Moreover, Harper's dominance of cabinet—some commentators referred to his alleged 'controlling' and 'secretive' leadership style (Travers 2007)—left little room for Flaherty to make his own mark in the public eye, despite his central position in the Harper Government. Finally, this lack of media interest could indicate that Canadians were growing tired of hearing the same thing from their government since its re-election.

Indeed, the government's messaging was highly consistent throughout the period under study, enabled by a weak and fractured opposition, which had helped develop the budget in the first place. On one level, all of this might suggest that the Harper Government had some success in controlling the meaning-making script of the global financial crisis in Canada. Indeed, the United States casts a long shadow on Canada and few would disagree that any Canadian recovery was not feasible without a US recovery. On another level, however, this lack of engagement might be a marker of public despondency and apathy regarding the government and its limited ability to do anything about the global financial crisis at home. The lukewarm opinion polls provide some support for such an interpretation (Strategic Counsel, CTV and Globe and Mail 2009).

10 March 2009: Harper's continued optimism

Although this particular address appeared to be an attempt by Harper to promote his government's action to reduce red tape to ensure the efficient delivery of stimulus measures, media coverage of the speech largely ignored the intended message. Instead, it focused squarely on Harper's optimistic outlook for the Canadian economy. 'Typically a politician who likes to under-promise and over-deliver' (Laghi 2009), Harper asserted that Canada would be the first major country to come out of the recession, that Canada had been hurt by it much less than other countries and that Canada's banking system was the soundest in the world. He reminded the audience about some of the budget measures designed to stimulate the economy, such as the home renovation tax credit. In addition, Harper announced his frustration 'with the opposition since the election' and encouraged his audience to tell the Liberal Party to 'stop the political games'. The overall tone was one of boosting morale, with Harper going as far as saying that 'if ever there was a time to put away that legendary Canadian modesty, it is now'.

It is important to note that Harper chose to deliver this speech in Brampton, Ontario. Ontario is sometimes called 'car country' because its economy relies so greatly on automobile manufacturing. General Motors, Ford and Chrysler had been producing more cars and light trucks in Ontario than Michigan—due in part to the generous health care available in Ontario (Fry 2009:37). With all three companies suffering deep financial setbacks, Ontario's manufacturing sector had been devastated almost to the same extent as Michigan's (Hamilton Chamber of Commerce 2009). Of all Canadian provinces, Ontario had been the most severely affected by the global financial crisis. The largest employers in Brampton were Chrysler and General Motors and the city had experienced a dramatic increase in unemployment; figures from Statistics Canada show that Brampton's unemployment in March was 10.9 per cent, 2 percentage points higher than the rest of Ontario (8.9 per cent) and higher still than the national rate (8.3 per cent) (Statistics Canada 2009a).

Harper's choice of venue and upbeat rhetoric suggested a deliberate attempt to reassure the most-affected Canadians of his government's competency. In addition, his attack on the opposition presented an attempt to exploit the crisis to his party's advantage. This alleged inability to curb his partisan instincts was perceived by some commentators as antagonistic and irrational (given that Harper did not enjoy a majority government and that, without the opposition's cooperation, the government's vaunted economic plan would not have been produced with so few adjustments).

	Severity	Causality	Policy implications	Support for speaker
Agrees	1		2	1
Disagrees	5		2	4
No comment/ neutral	2	8	4	3

Table 4.8 Media responses to Harper's 10 March 2009 speech

The media analysis shows a preponderance of disagreement with Harper about the severity of the crisis (Table 4.8). Of eight articles analysed, five were critical of Harper's 'rose-tinted' (Ivison 2009b) view of the Canadian economy. Seven gave a platform to the Liberal leader, Michael Ignatieff's, condemnation of Harper as being 'on a Conservative planet, off in outer space'. A number of articles implied that Harper's boisterous outlook rang hollow with the Canadian public. One captured the mood by observing 'yes, Canada is in good shape relative to everyone else, but that doesn't mean we're in good shape relative to our own expectations and our own standards' (Cowan 2009). A closely related criticism was that Harper's 'boasting' was tactless and completely out of touch with the reality of the difficulties many Canadians faced as a result of the crisis (Radwanski 2009).

With Harper's assessment of the severity of the crisis clearly contested (in contrast with the question of causation, which was widely ignored, reflecting a broad consensus about this being overwhelmingly exogenous), there were some concerns about the policy direction the government was taking to deal with it. Overall, however, the coverage of policy implications was mostly neutral, probably enabled by the opposition's focus on criticising Harper's lack of sensitivity rather than his policy trajectory (quite probably because the opposition approved the economic plan with very few adjustments and little debate). Clearly, at this point, crisis politics and crisis policy had become divorced in the rhetoric of all the major parties. It is worth mentioning that reader comments (not included in the quantitative assessment) did express concerns about Harper's policy decisions, particularly the proposed tax reform. When coupled with the low-level coverage this speech received, this suggested that the extent of public disapproval of Harper could have been greater than these findings implied. Indeed, a Harris Decima election tracing opinion poll shows that public approval for the Conservative Party fell to 29 per cent between 8 March and 29 March—down from 33 per cent in late February and early March (Harris Decima 2009).

1 April 2009: the bank governor sees light at the end of the tunnel

With the US and global economies plunging deeper and deeper into recession, Carney used his address in Yellowknife to reassure Canadians that they could be confident that unprecedented policy measures would—eventually—restore growth. Using the most powerful language to date (far stronger than any of Harper's or Flaherty's public utterances), Carney acknowledged that these were 'very challenging times' for an economy 'in the most severe financial meltdown since the Great Depression'. He also remarked that the current crisis was more challenging than previous downturns because it represented more than a cyclical shock. He said that Canadians were understandably more concerned about their economic future than they had been in decades, but he added that 'there is a plan to restore confidence and growth, we are implementing it, and it will work'.

	Severity	Causality	Policy implications	Support for speaker
Agrees	4	2	4	4
Disagrees			1	
No comment/ neutral	1	3	1	2

Table 4.9 Media responses to Carney's 1 April 2009 speech

This speech, although optimistic in parts, was a marked departure from Carney's usually positive outlook. It was met with considerable agitation by the media. None of the media commentators questioned his assessment of the severity of the crisis, but most tended to amplify it by declaring the central bank's hitherto bullish outlook officially buried. Carney's personal leadership also went unquestioned, but his pessimism gave rise to criticisms of Flaherty and Harper's refusal to increase the size of the government's stimulus program. Three out of the five articles called for the increase, despite the fact that in the same speech Carney warned about the dangers of overshooting the target with stimuli.

The criticisms of Harper were particularly interesting since, as one of the articles noted, he had indicated in a series of recent interviews with foreign media that policymakers must do 'everything necessary' to pull the global economy out of the crisis—a sentiment clearly at odds with Carney's reservations (Vieira 2009). While a disparity of views between the Prime Minister and the Bank of Canada Governor would theoretically make for interesting coverage (particularly given the vastly different reputations the two enjoyed), in this instance, it failed to capture public imagination. Nor did it seem to get the attention of the opposition.

4. Framing the financial crisis in Canada: analysis and conclusions

Because the real extent of the effects of the global financial crisis on the Canadian economy was not revealed until late in 2008, the government was able to frame the crisis in optimistic terms for most of the year. In this, they were greatly enabled by their incumbency and Harper's reputation as a competent economic manager. His credentials as an 'economist by training' and his government's perceived competence at managing the national economy had been readily circulated by the Canadian media for a long time. These were his major electoral strengths before the economic downturn began in earnest. In contrast, during 2008, the major opposition party, the Liberal Party (which had held government for 12 years before Harper's victory in 2006), was led by the highly unpopular Stephane Dion. A former political science academic, Dion was widely perceived as 'a thinker rather than a doer...a pie-in-the-sky intellectual' who was frequently unable to explain basic economic realities (McLean 2008:12). Harper recognised this weakness and frequently sought to exploit it. In fact, it was commonly accepted that Harper's surprising decision to call an early election in September was motivated largely by his recognition of the public perception that the Liberal Party (and especially Dion) was ill equipped to lead Canada through perilous times. Michael Ignatieff, another intellectual, replaced Dion in December. Dion's disastrous period of leadership, however, had an enduring impact on the credibility of the party and continued to compromise the public perception of the party's economic management credentials throughout 2009.

As the findings of this study indicate, however, Harper overestimated his ability to shape public opinion and exploit the crisis to his advantage. By the time the election campaign started in September and the Wall Street collapse began in earnest, Canadians began to question his persistently rosy outlook on the state of the economy. Although Harper's previous policies were not blamed for causing the crisis, significant portions of the commentariat as well as most ordinary Canadians did not believe that problems south of the border would not eventually affect the Canadian economy. Harper's unwillingness to concede the severity of the crisis created an impression that he was putting his political interests ahead of his economic knowledge. This eventually raised concerns about the policy direction the government was taking to deal with the crisis.

The government's credibility could in theory have been assisted by the fact that Flaherty's messaging was consistent with Harper's throughout the crisis. Harper's dominant leadership style, however, and his tendency to speak for the government on all matters regarding the economy throughout the Conservatives' tenure had long ago compromised the capacity of the Minister for Finance to shape public debate. Consequently, Flaherty's pronouncements were ignored at best and, at worst, were seen as politically motivated and thus were cynically received.

It might have been helpful for Harper to emphasise the similarities between his outlook and that of Bank of Canada Governor, Mark Carney, since the latter's apolitical office meant that the public did not question his agenda. Given Harper's vested interest in avoiding implicating his government in the causes of the domestic manifestations of the global financial crisis, however, it is not surprising that he should want to distance himself from the Bank of Canada's past (and for that matter, future) fiscal policy decisions. By the same token, it is reasonable to assume that if Harper were to publicly align himself with Carney, the credibility of the Governor of the Bank of Canada would be compromised in more ways than one.

Moreover (and somewhat ironically), Harper's unwillingness to resort to explicit crisis rhetoric fed into pre-existing perceptions of him as a cold, uncaring leader who lacked sympathy for the plight of everyday Canadians. This was exacerbated as the effects of the global financial crisis on the Canadian economy became increasingly obvious. Instead of convincing voters that his government anticipated the problems long before they became apparent, Harper's continuous resistance to introducing special measures to deal with the crisis led Canadians to question whether the government realised the gravity of the global financial crisis—and consequently, whether it was equipped to deal with the crisis appropriately and effectively.

By clinging to a positive outlook that was increasingly portrayed as overoptimistic, Harper painted himself into a corner. When he and his government were eventually forced to admit that the country was in recession, this was widely perceived as backtracking. It seemed to confirm growing fears that perhaps Harper was not the amazing economic manager Canadians had come to believe he was. It was no surprise then that the Canadian public received the 2009 budget—which projected a huge deficit—with considerable suspicion.

It is worth questioning why this erosion of credibility under the weight of the escalating economic problems failed to pose any significant political threat to the Harper Government. One of the answers lies with the weak and politically divided opposition parties, which failed to challenge the Conservatives in any meaningful way. An international observer might intercede here and note that surely the December 2008 parliamentary crisis constituted one such memorable challenge. If anything, however, the parliamentary crisis served to affirm the position of the Harper Government. National polls conducted during and after the impasse suggested that although Canadians were beginning to have more doubts about the Harper Government's economic competence, they were even more cynical about the opposition parties' ability to form a fungible coalition (reservations that were amplified by their very colourful public disagreements during the election period). To some extent, Canadians even seemed to blame the opposition parties for the crisis (Reuters 2008). As a matter of fact, the proposed alternative coalition government fell apart during its very first test—the 2009 budget—thus ending the parliamentary crisis.

One of the main reasons why the opposition parties failed to present a threat to the government was their unwillingness to challenge it on the very issue of economic management until well into 2009. The main opposition parties consistently echoed Harper's optimistic outlook; they all initially downplayed the economic crisis. Even during the election campaign, as the markets went into free fall, average Canadians watched their investments begin to evaporate and the economic crisis was obviously spiralling out of Harper's control, Dion and his opposition counterparts, Jack Layton (of NDP) and Gilles Duceppe (of Bloc Quebecois), did not question his mantra of 'the fundamentals of the Canadian banking system remain strong' and 'Canada is well placed to weather the economic storm'. The budget presented another obvious opportunity for the opposition to effectively challenge the government's credibility in addressing the global financial crisis. Indeed, it committed Canada to a $38 billion deficit just two months after Harper asserted that Canada was doing fine and would even produce a surplus in the next financial year. The opposition parties, however, spent so much time attacking one another's stances on the budget that the infighting attracted almost as much media coverage as the budget itself.

All of this considered, it is important to conclude with a reflection on what is perhaps the most interesting finding of this study: the notable lack of media interest in the manner in which the Canadian Government was handling the domestic manifestations of the global financial crisis. The reasons for this lack of interest are very difficult to pin down, but two speculations can be offered. First, Canada is saturated with US media outlets so it is possible that Canadians' view of the crisis was shaped more by the bombardment of alarmist crisis rhetoric and imagery beamed into their homes from south of the border than by the public pronouncements of their own leaders. Canadians might therefore have viewed the economic downturn as far too colossal for their government to halt at home, and consequently might have held low expectations of their leaders' capacity to affect change. In this case, it would have been in the interests of Harper and Flaherty to stick with their usual bland rhetoric so as not to attract further media attention.

It is also possible that the lack of media interest in the government's efforts to frame the crisis was a symptom of a general sense of disillusionment, cynicism and distrust of the government and the opposition among Canadians—that is, a sign of general disengagement from the political process. It might have been the case that Canadians were deeply sceptical of their government's handling of the crisis, but sensed that things could be much worse if the squabbling opposition parties held the reins. A telltale indicator of this alternative interpretation was that voter turnout at the October 2008 election was the lowest in Canadian history (CBC News 2008). Regardless of the reasons, this notable absence of media interest and serious pushback helped keep the Conservative Government firmly in the saddle: it was exercising crisis leadership by default.

References

Akin, D. 2009, 'Interview: Flaherty says he's sticking with budget', *National Post*, 11 April.

Bank of Canada 2009, Bank of Canada lowers overnight rate by 0.5 percentage point to 0.5 per cent, Press release, 3 March, viewed 1 July 2009, <http://www.bankofcanada.ca/en/fixed-dates/2009/rate_030309.html>

Callan, E. 2008, 'Tory adaptation of bank PR even surprises banks', *Financial Post*, 15 October.

Canadian Newspaper Association 2008, *Daily Newspaper Circulation Data: 2008*, Canadian Newspaper Association, viewed 1 July 2009, <http://www.cna-acj.ca/en/aboutnewspapers/circulation>

CBC News 2008, 'Voter turnout drops to record low', *CBC News*, 15 October, viewed 1 July 2009, <http://www.cbc.ca/news/canadavotes/story/2008/10/15/voter-turnout.html>

Clark, A. 2008, 'Buffett says: act or face 'economic Pearl Harbor', *The Guardian*, 25 September, viewed 20 May, <http://www.guardian.co.uk/business/2008/sep/25/banking.wallstreet1>

Corcoran, T. 2009, 'Flaherty digs himself a deep, dark hole', *National Post*, 27 January.

Cowan, J. 2009, 'Harper boasts of Canada's recession plan', *Financial Post*, 10 March.

Economist 2008, 'Editorial: please have the decency to panic: economic fears ambush Harper's hopes of a majority', *The Economist*, 9 October.

EKOS and Associates Poll 2008, 'Outlook on the current situation: preferred solution for current political impasse', 4 December, EKOS and Associates Poll, viewed 1 July 2009,

<http://www.ekoselection.com/wp-content/uploads/
1069-cbc-results-dec-4-final-with-analysis1.pdf>

Financial Consumer Agency of Canada 2008, *Moving forward with financial literacy: synthesis report on reaching higher*, Canadian Conference on Financial Literacy, September.

Fry, E. H. 2009, 'Canada's economic relationship with the United States', *Policy Options*, April.

Globe and Mail 2008, 'Editorial: Harper stays true to form', *The Globe and Mail*, 8 October.

Globe and Mail 2009, 'A missed chance to build toward Canada's future', *The Globe and Mail*, 28 January.

Hamilton Chamber of Commerce 2009, *Manufacturing Job Losses*, March, Hamilton Chamber of Commerce.

Harris Decima 2009, Liberals maintain edge nationally, National vote intention table, Press release, 21 April, Harris Decima, viewed 1 July 2009, <http://www.harrisdecima.com/en/downloads/pdf/news_releases/042309E.pdf>

Heard, A. 2008, Canadian election opinion polls, Political Science Department, Simon Fraser University, viewed 1 July 2009, <http://www.sfu.ca/~aheard/elections/polls.html>

Hopkins, A. 2009, 'Canada's Banks seen profiting from stronger markets', *The Globe and Mail*, 25 May, viewed 20 June, <http://www.globeinvestor.com/servlet/story/ROC.20090525.2009-05-25T135520Z_01_TRE54O2L2_RTROPTT_0_CBUSINESS-US-BANKS/GIStory>

Ivison, J. 2009a, 'A budget for the wishful thinker in everyone', *National Post*, 27 January.

Ivison, J. 2009b, 'Don't worry, be Harper', *National Post*, 3 April.

Jones, K. 2009, 'Canada: furore over soaring federal budget deficit', *The Globe and Mail*, 29 May.

Laghi, B. 2009, 'Why Stephen Harper is suddenly an optimist', *The Globe and Mail*, 10 April, viewed 10 July 2009, <http://www.theglobeandmail.com/news/politics/article975962.ece#article>

McLean, J. 2008, 'The messenger is the message', *Options Politiques*, November.

Martin, L. 2008, 'Stephen Harper: the tactics, the leadership (Part 1)', *The Globe and Mail*, 15 September, viewed 10 July 2009, <http://www.theglobeandmail.com/servlet/story/
RTGAM.20080912.wcomartin15/BNStory/politics/home>

Nanos, N. 2009, 'Nanos research poll', *Policy Options*, February.

Radwanski, A. 2009, 'He just can't help himself', *The Globe and Mail*, 10 March.

Reuters 2008, 'Harper has crushing poll lead on crisis', *Reuters*, 5 December, viewed 1 July 2009,
<http://ca.reuters.com/article/topNews/idCATRE4B42X520081205/>

Schoffield, H. 2009, 'Recovery hinges on U.S. stimulus: Carney', *The Globe and Mail*, 10 February.

Statistics Canada 2008, *Imports, Exports and Trade Balance of Goods on a Balance-of-Payments Basis, by Country or Country Grouping*, Statistics Canada, viewed 1 July 2009,
<http://www40.statcan.gc.ca/l01/cst01/gblec02a-eng.htm>

Statistics Canada 2009a, *Labour Force Survey*, 8 May, Statistics Canada, viewed 1 July 2009,
<http://www.statcan.gc.ca/subjects-sujets/labour-travail/lfs-epa/lfs-epa-eng.htm>

Statistics Canada 2009b, *Imports, Exports and Trade Balance of Goods on a Balance-of-Payments Basis, by Country or Country Grouping*, 10 June, Statistics Canada, viewed 1 July 2009,
<http://www40.statcan.gc.ca/l01/cst01/gblec02a-eng.htm>

Strategic Counsel, CTV and Globe and Mail 2008a, 'Vote intention poll', *The Strategic Counsel*, 12 May, viewed 1 July 2009,
<http://www.thestrategiccounsel.com/our_news/polls/2008-05-12%20GMCTV%20--%20FINAL2.pdf>

Strategic Counsel, CTV and Globe and Mail 2008b, 'Vote intention poll', *The Strategic Counsel*, 10 June, viewed 1 July 2009,
<http://www.thestrategiccounsel.com/our_news/polls/2008-06-10%20GMCTV%20--%20final.pdf>

Strategic Counsel, CTV and Globe and Mail 2009, 'Vote intention poll', *The Strategic Counsel*, 9 March, viewed 1 July 2009,
<http://www.thestrategiccounsel.com/our_news/polls/2009-03-09%20-%20Vote%20Intention.pdf>

Stein, S. 2008, 'Greenspan: this is worst economy I've ever seen', *The Huffington Post*, 14 September, viewed 20 May,
<http://www.huffingtonpost.com/2008/09/14/greenspan-this-is-the-wor_n_126274.html>

Travers, J. 2007, 'Harper's leadership style mimics Chretien's, to a point', *The Record*, 27 November, viewed 1 July 2009,
<http://news.therecord.com/article/274938>

Vieira, P. 2009, 'Carney warns of too much stimulus', *Financial Post*, 2 April.

Watt, J. 2008, 'The morning after: now for the hard part', *Options Politique*, November.

Part III. Dark clouds and turbulence in Europe

5. United Kingdom: the politics of government survival

Justin Pritchard

1. From Northern Rock to a global financial crisis

For the United Kingdom in early 2007, the US credit crisis seemed to be a foreign concern. By August, however, the French bank BNP Paribas, one of the largest banks in the eurozone, announced to investors that they would be unable to withdraw funds from two of the bank's hedge funds; and by September 2007, when British bank Northern Rock requested emergency financial support from the Bank of England, the credit crisis had hit home. The significance of this development was magnified by the fact that Northern Rock's troubles were first brought to public attention not by the government, but by the media. On 14 September, the day after the BBC Economics Editor Robert Peston had broken the Northern Rock story, depositors withdrew £1 billion from the bank—the largest run on a British bank for more than a century. So, from the first very public manifestation of the credit crisis in the United Kingdom, the media had set the agenda and the government was on the back foot. In 2008, more British institutions announced multi-billion-pound exposures to the US credit crisis, including the Royal Bank of Scotland (RBS) in April, Barclay's and Halifax Bank of Scotland (HBOS) in July and Bradford & Bingley in August. In response to these developments, the British Government nationalised Northern Rock in February 2008 and partly nationalised Bradford & Bingley in September 2008 and HBOS, Lloyd's and RBS in October 2008.

This chapter focuses on three key actors responsible for managing the global financial crisis in the United Kingdom: Prime Minister Gordon Brown, Chancellor of the Exchequer Alistair Darling, and Bank of England Governor Mervyn King. As well as buying up risky assets and nationalising financial institutions, these three implemented a number of fiscal and monetary responses to the crisis. Brown and Darling cut the value-added tax (VAT) from 17.5 per cent to 15 per cent, raised the aged pension and offered new tax breaks. Together with King, they injected £300 billion into the financial system. King, who before 2007 was a fairly low-profile technocrat, presided over a slash in the official bank interest rate from 5.75 per cent in August 2007 to a historic low of 0.5 per cent in March 2009 (Kollewe 2009b). By this time, King had become a prominent public figure.

From 2007 into 2009, the British political landscape was dominated by economic turmoil. Contextual factors of this period are, however, worth noting. Brown's succession to the prime ministership in June 2007 failed to have much of an impact on the low approval ratings the 10-year-old Labour Government had endured since late 2005 (UK Polling Report 2009). Brown's failure to reinvigorate Labour's support base can be attributed in part to his role as Chancellor of the Exchequer throughout the entirety of the reign of former Prime Minister, Tony Blair. As one pundit phrased it particularly colourfully, Brown and Blair appeared 'as two cheeks of the same arse' (Galloway 2006). Despite a brief increase in Brown's popularity after the Northern Rock crisis, in July 2008, it was widely reported in the British press that Secretary of State for Foreign and Commonwealth Affairs David Miliband, would challenge Brown for the leadership. Miliband, however, made a tactical blunder and the challenge did not materialise. Throughout 2008, however, Brown's popularity steadily declined, sitting consistently 12–16 points behind the Conservative Party leader David Cameron, as preferred prime minister (UK Polling Report 2009).

Since replacing Brown as Chancellor of the Exchequer in June 2007, Alistair Darling was scrutinised for more than just his handling of the financial crisis. In November 2007, Darling announced that the Revenue and Customs Department had lost two data discs containing the records of 25 million citizens claiming child-benefit assistance (*BBC* 2007). This incident damaged confidence in the Chancellor just as the financial crisis was taking hold (see *Times* 2007). Just as it had for Brown, the media reported that Darling would be challenged for the Chancellorship by the Secretary of State for Children, Schools and Families Ed Balls, after the 2008 local UK elections (Mulholland 2008). While this challenge also failed to materialise, the intra-party division and the spectre of leadership challenges are important contextual factors when investigating Brown's and Darling's responses to the financial crisis.

Box 5.1 The United Kingdom's financial crisis trajectory, September 2007 – March 2009

13 September 2007: BBC Business Editor Robert Peston, breaks the story that Northern Rock has secured emergency financial support from the Bank of England (BOE). Northern Rock had relied on market investments, rather than savers' deposits, to fund its mortgage lending.

14 September: Northern Bank depositors withdraw £1 billion—the biggest run on a British bank for more than a century.

17 September: Northern Rock's shares have fallen precipitously since 14 September. The government announces that it will guarantee all savings of Northern Rock depositors.

19 September: The BOE breaks with its previous position not to inject any funding into financial markets and pumps £10 billion into the system.

15 November: Barclay's Bank announces a £1.3 billion exposure to the US sub-prime mortgage collapse.

29 November: The BOE announces that the number of mortgage approvals has fallen to a three-year low.

6 December: The BOE slashes interest rates by 0.25 per cent to 5.5 per cent.

12 December: The world's five largest central banks announce an unprecedented $110 billion lifeline to commercialise banks over Christmas, of which £10 billion is given to the British banks.

21 January 2008: Global stock markets, including London's FTSE 100 index, experience their worst falls since 11 September 2001.

7 February: The BOE slashes interest rates by 0.25 per cent to 5.25 per cent.

17 February: The government announces that it has knocked back the bid of Richard Branson's Virgin Group to take over Northern Rock, and nationalises the bank.

3 March: The amount in sub-prime loans being written off by HSBC rises to £51 million a day—a sign of trouble to come for the London-based bank.

10 April: The BOE slashes interest rates by 0.25 per cent to 5 per cent.

22 April: The RBS announces the biggest rights issue in UK corporate history: £12 billion. It also writes off £5.9 billion of assets.

22 April: HBOS announces a £4 billion rights issue.

14 May: Bradford & Bingley announces a £300 million rights issue.

25 June: Barclay's Bank announces for sale a round of discounted shares, intended to raise £4.5 billion.

1 July: UK annual house prices suffer their biggest fall since 1992.

21 July: The HBOS rights issue receives little enthusiasm from shareholders, forcing the company's underwriters to purchase the remaining shares for £4 billion.

17 September: Lloyd's Banking Group offers £12 billion to acquire HBOS.

29 September: Bradford & Bingley is nationalised, although its savings operations and branches are sold to Spain's Santander Bank.

30 September: The government announces that it will raise the limit of guaranteed bank deposits from £35,000 to £50,000.

6 October: The Icelandic Government announces a rescue package to save its banking sector and forces its banks to sell off its foreign assets.

8 October: The UK Government threatens legal action against the Icelandic Government to retrieve UK citizens' savings tied up in Iceland's banking sector. The UK Government announces a £50 billion rescue package of the UK banking system.

9 October: The UK Government announces plans to freeze assets of Icelandic companies in the United Kingdom under anti-terrorism legislation.

13 October: The UK Government provides £37 billion to HBOS, the RBS and Lloyd's Banking Group, beginning a takeover of the former two by Lloyd's that concludes in January 2009.

15 October: UK jobless figures experience their biggest rise in 17 years.

16 October: The FTSE hits a five-year low: 3850.

24 October: The UK Office of National Statistics announces that the United Kingdom is on the brink of a recession, revealing that the economy contracted in the third quarter of 2008.

6 November: The BOE radically slashes the official bank rate from 4.5 per cent to 3 per cent—the lowest interest rate level since 1955.

24 November: Alistair Darling announces in his pre-budget report that the VAT will be cut from 17.5 per cent to 15 per cent, while the UK Government's borrowing will increase. The government also announces plans to inject £20 billion into the economy in 2010—representing 1 per cent of gross domestic product (GDP).

4 December: The BOE slashes the official interest rate by another full percentage point to 2 per cent—the lowest level in 57 years.

17 December: The UK Office of National Statistics announces that there are now 1.86 million Britons without work, making the jobless figure—6 per cent—the highest in more than a decade.

31 December: The FTSE 100 closes down 31.3 per cent since the beginning of 2008—the biggest annual fall since the index began in 1984.

8 January 2009: Having existed for 315 years, the BOE slashes interest rates to an all-time low of 1.5 per cent.

19 January: The government announces a second bank rescue package worth £50 billion.

5 February: The BOE slashes interest rates once again to another record low of 1 per cent.

6 February: The BOE announces a plan to lend directly to credit-starved companies, aimed at bypassing the banks altogether.

18 March: The International Monetary Fund (IMF) announces that it expects the UK economy to continue to contract in 2010 even as other economies begin growing again. It predicts that the UK economy will contract by 3.8 per cent in 2009.

19 March: Adair Turner, head of Britain's Financial Services Authority (FSA), releases his report on Britain's regulatory structure and the global financial crisis. In it he says that, with hindsight, the FSA and the national regulatory system had a number of key shortcomings.

24 March: Figures show that the United Kingdom's jobless figure is rising above two million for the first time since 1997.

2. Methodological considerations

The focus of this chapter is the period of April 2008 to March 2009, when the 'credit crunch' turned into what has been widely described as the worst global financial crisis since the Great Depression. Since the United Kingdom experienced the first effects of the global financial crisis in September 2007, this chapter summarises the early rhetoric of each actor. Exploring their early crisis framing establishes how much room each actor left himself to manoeuvre when the crisis worsened through 2008. The speeches analysed within this chapter were sourced from the official web sites of the individual or their institution. The speeches were identified as being significant because of their heavy use of crisis-exploitation rhetoric, but also because most of them received considerable media coverage. It is worth noting that Darling's and King's web sites did not provide a wide range of their speeches and were missing some speeches that had been mentioned in the media. This meant that not only was the choice of speeches somewhat limited, the Chancellor and the bank governor had, by omitting some speeches from their web sites, signalled that others were the ones intended for public consumption.

The chapter attempts to gauge the media and public response to the crisis exploitation of the three actors through a survey of three newspapers that represent a fair spectrum of British society: *The Guardian/Observer*, *The Times* and the *Financial Times*. *The Guardian* (circulated Monday to Saturday) and its sister paper, *The Observer* (circulated on Sundays), owned by the public non-profit Scott Trust, currently have circulations of about 400,000 (*Guardian* 2009). They are typically seen as left leaning. Whereas 80 per cent of *The Guardian/Observer* readership voted Labour in 2000, a 2005 survey showed that only 48 per cent voted Labour. This figure was likely to be even lower by 2008 given the further slide in Labour's popularity (Ipsos Mori Poll 2005).

The Times, owned by News Corporation and historically the best-known UK paper, has a circulation of 617,000. Its Sunday edition momentarily has a circulation of 1.2 million (*Guardian* 2009). For decades, it took a centre-right political stance, but in the 2001 and 2005 elections, it supported the Labour Party. *The Daily Telegraph*, a paper with a political stance further right than *The Times* and a slightly larger overall readership, was not selected for analysis because of its limited coverage of the global financial crisis. The *Financial Times* has a lower circulation than the aforementioned papers, but offers a deeper level of economic insight to the crisis. It is owned by the education and media conglomerate Pearson PLC and generally adopts free-market stances (*Financial Times* 2009b). All three selected papers are published in London. When attempting to track the media and public response to the three key actors' crisis rhetoric, however, the cross-section of ideological views was deemed to be more important than a regional interpretation of the crisis.

3. Crisis development and elite rhetoric in the United Kingdom

1 October 2007: Prime Minister Brown's 'age of turbulence' speech

In the weeks after the 14 September run on Northern Rock, all major British polls (UK Polling Report 2009) calculated that Labour had extended its 3–5-point lead to 6–13 points despite some considerable media criticism of its handling of the crisis (Pratley 2007). Brown's, and Labour's, surge in the polls, however, proved to be remarkably short-lived; by October 2007, the Conservative Party had become the preferred government (UK Polling Report 2009). It was against this backdrop that Brown delivered his earliest keynote speech on the downturn in world financial markets.

Certainly, it would be unreasonable to expect that Brown could have known of the scale of the global financial crisis that was to emerge one year later. Nonetheless, his speech was noteworthy insofar as Brown clearly gave his British audience some expectations about the strength of Britain's economy and its ability to confront future turmoil. This early speech was significant because it affected his room to manoeuvre in subsequently framing the global financial crisis as it entered a more severe phase in September 2008. Brown acknowledged that the downturn in financial markets throughout 2007 was a concerning sign and imputed responsibility for this downturn primarily to global economic factors and partially to the irresponsibility of 'those who own and run banks' in Britain. He also emphasised the need to make 'changes in the financial system globally as well as nationally'.

Brown attempted to normalise the Northern Rock crisis in what he described as the modern 'age of turbulence', in which 'turbulence is the essence of the financial system'. This was an early attempt to defend the economic approach based on free markets taken by 'New Labour' since its election victory in 1997. Brown's speech lauded former US Federal Reserve Chairman Alan Greenspan (whom Brown was introducing at the Reuters Building) and he agreed with Greenspan's statement that the market was now 'more...self-correcting...than it was even a quarter of a century earlier', and claimed that this approach had given Britain 'greater flexibility...to adjust when events threaten our [Britain's] growth'. Brown warned of the dangers of governments around the world 'responding with heavy-handed regulation' and thereby defended the economic status quo. In denouncing protectionism, he furnished the historical analogy of the Enron and WorldCom crashes in the United States, to which the United Kingdom 'did not respond with heavy-handed regulation'.

One notable assessment of Brown's speech came from a *Guardian* journalist who acknowledged that Northern Rock's directors were at fault, but criticised Brown's complete denial of responsibility for the crisis. 'Gordon Brown, a man who claims to be a master of prudent financial management while presiding over a debt-addicted and unbalanced economy, must bear a share of the responsibility' (Sunderland 2007). Despite Brown's intent to have this speech seen as a major statement on the economy, it did not receive significant press coverage. Much of the media concentrated instead on Brown's lead in the polls and the possibility that he would call an early election.

September 2007 – February 2008: Chancellor Darling's early rhetoric

After just three months as Chancellor of the Exchequer Alistair Darling was confronted with the largest run on a British bank in more than a century. Public confidence in the nascent Chancellor was dented by the fact that the British Broadcasting Corporation (BBC), not the government, had broken the story to the public. Furthermore, after the withdrawal of £1 billion in savings from Northern Rock, it took Darling three days to announce that the government would guarantee all deposits up to £35,000.

After the Northern Rock crisis and announcements in late 2007 by more British banks of multi-billion-pound exposures to the US sub-prime mortgage market, Darling averred that the United Kingdom was in 'uncertain' and 'turbulent times' (Darling 2007b). Nevertheless, he emphasised that the British economy was fundamentally strong and that the public could be confident that the economy would continue to grow. Darling blamed the recent downturn in world financial markets on institutions that had based their growth on risky business models, but also on factors far from British shores that damaged the globalised UK economy. Despite conceding that globalisation and free-marketism had presented challenges to the United Kingdom, the Chancellor declared that the UK economy had been overwhelmingly strengthened by an open and globalised approach since 1997. He also portrayed a potential retreat into protectionism as a dangerous alternative, utilising the exact historical analogy as the Prime Minister—that of the Enron and WorldCom collapses—to demonstrate that financial crises need not be met with a hyper-reactive move away from the sound fundamentals of globalisation and free markets (Darling 2007a). Darling defended the political-economic status quo and prescribed an open and globalised economic orientation as the way for Britain to make it through the financial turmoil.

Through 2007, Darling blamed the crisis on reckless British banks and global factors in equal measure, but in early 2008 he began to emphasise the latter as the predominant cause of Britain's economic downturn. By this time, Darling was also depicting the crisis in less sanguine tones. In January 2008, he stated that 'we operate in far more turbulent times' (Darling 2008a) and claimed that 'the global economy is facing its biggest test for more than a decade' (Darling 2008b). His previous predictions that economic growth would remain high were now conspicuously absent. He did, however, maintain that the strong fundamentals of the UK economy—which were created by the Labour Government—meant that 'Britain is well placed, indeed better placed than almost any other, to see through this uncertainty' (Darling 2008a).

Overall, the press was more disapproving than supportive of Darling in this period. The three newspapers analysed in this chapter unanimously declared that the Chancellor and the Labour Government had misjudged the severity of Northern Rock's predicament and had been slow to act when depositors withdrew their savings en masse. In terms of the Chancellor's severity narrative, *The Guardian* wrote that Darling was underplaying the turmoil but that this was 'fair enough' considering he did not want to 'spread doom and despondency' (Elliot 2008a). *The Times* wrote that Darling had offered only a 'crossed-fingers' approach that the slowdown would not be too severe' (Riddell 2008a:28).

Darling's causality narrative divided opinion. *The Guardian* supported Darling, saying that 'neither he nor the government is the source of the Northern Rock crisis in any way' (Kettle 2008). The *Financial Times*, however, declared that the seed of the credit crisis was the Labour Government's ill-considered centralisation of British financial regulation in 1999 (Morley 2007:11). Darling's policy proposals prompted little media response, although *The Times* stated that Darling had 'little sense…[about] how in the long-term public finances will be restored to health' (Riddell 2008a:28).

September 2007 – April 2008: bank governor King's early rhetoric

Before the North Rock crisis, Mervyn King was a technocrat known mainly to people within the financial industry and newspaper economics correspondents. His name was periodically mentioned in the general press when he announced interest rate adjustments. His profile rose exponentially, however, after the Northern Rock crisis and he became a key figure in imparting meaning to Britain's financial turmoil.

King's early pronouncements on the financial turmoil were more sober than those of the Chancellor and the Prime Minister. Immediately after the run on Northern Rock, King publicly stated that to bail out the bank would be a 'moral hazard'. Simply put, to rescue the bank with an injection of public funds would discourage responsible financial management among British companies and set a standard for bailing out a raft of irresponsible companies. This indicated King had cause to believe that Northern Rock's predicament was not an isolated one. Indeed, the Bank of England (BOE) was aware that HSBC had £10.5 billion of exposure to the US sub-prime mortgage market in February 2007 (Seager 2009). Regulatory authorities in the United Kingdom had been aware of other British banks having to write off billions of pounds worth of bad debt throughout 2007. King's rhetoric in this early period was serious, but perhaps not quite as pessimistic as he might have been behind closed doors. He used measured phrases to acknowledge the significance of the crisis while not denting consumer confidence. He explained that 'conditions were not yet back to normal and remain[ed] fragile', and that the intention of financial institutions 'to tighten conditions further' was 'unlikely to be short-lived' (King 2008a).

King's early speeches identified the sub-prime mortgage market in the United States as being the focal point of financial turmoil. King stated, 'The challenges facing us…many of them originate from outside our shores' and 'Northern Rock [was] not the epicentre of the current crisis' (King 2008a) In November 2007, King admitted that, if he had his time again, he would have done several things differently in handling the Northern Rock crisis. This acceptance of partial responsibility was oddly conspicuous compared with the complete denial of blame by Brown and Darling, and later placed less pressure on King to admit blame for not recognising the oncoming British recession (Seager 2009).

The commentary in the three papers expressed some moderate concern that King was underplaying the severity of the crisis, but the main focus was on his causality narrative and policy proposals. *The Guardian* argued that the Northern Rock crisis was not at all the fault of King or the BOE. *The Times* agreed that King did not cause the Northern Rock crisis, but pilloried his volte-face on the issue of government bailouts and claimed that the BOE significantly exacerbated the Northern Rock crisis. The *Financial Times* also pardoned King and the BOE from the charge that they were to blame for not recognising the poor business model of Northern Rock and other British banks, instead blaming the FSA. The *Financial Times* did, however, indirectly blame King as part of a group of influential central bankers in the developed world, whose monetary policy between 2002 and 2004 was so irresponsible that it was a key source of the present financial turmoil.

12 March 2008: the Chancellor's budget statement

There was much gloomy economic news in Britain at the beginning of 2008. January had seen the biggest one-day fall of the FTSE 100 and in February there had been the last-resort nationalisation of Northern Rock and HSBC's announcement of massive exposure to the US sub-prime mortgage market. Nonetheless, the Chancellor's keynote budget speech did not alter his late-2007 description of the severity of the crisis, declaring that 'these were times of global economic uncertainty'. He reiterated the role of global factors in causing the crisis and defended the globalised, free-market orientation of the British economy.

Darling continued to predict growth for the UK economy, although the forecasts were slightly less optimistic than before. One major difference to his previous speeches, however, was that he emphasised economic 'stability' more than 'growth'. Nonetheless, Darling asserted that Britain was 'uniquely placed to succeed in the global economy' and 'enter[s] this period of uncertainty better placed than any other major economy'.

The budget was the dominant issue in the media in the week after its release, with the three major papers largely disagreeing with Darling's severity narrative. *The Times* called it a recklessly courageous act to continue to predict growth, while the *Financial Times* stated that 'like the rest of us, Alistair Darling is navigating the global economic storms without a compass' (Stephens 2008:5). The newspaper critiques of Darling's policy proposals, however, remained vague. The *Financial Times* argued that the budget was highly imprudent and that the 'higher borrowing figures were an embarrassment' (Stephens 2008:5). *The Times* stated that Darling's budget was a 'fingers-crossed' budget, but qualified this by saying that 'there is…nothing new about fingers-crossed budgets' and that this approach 'was about as good as could have been expected' in such a challenging economic climate (Kaletsky 2008:1). These newspapers indicate the scepticism and negativity surrounding the policy proposals outlined in Darling's budget speech.

10 June 2008: King's 'normalisation' of turmoil

Consistent with the increase in the severity of the crisis since early 2008, King described the financial milieu as 'the most prolonged period of financial turmoil that most of us can remember'—a remarkable statement given King's 40-year career as an economist. This austere statement came before the credit crisis evolved into the global financial crisis after the September 2008 collapse of Lehman Brothers. While this statement did maximise the severity of the crisis, it did not convey the possibility of dire systemic turmoil of which King appeared to be aware at this time.

As if to downplay the possibility that his serious description of the financial turmoil might be received with panic, King normalised the financial crisis in the context of economic history. Rather than calling the crisis 'unprecedented', as he, Darling and Brown would do in later months, he stated that 'financial crises [had] been a regular, and disturbing, feature of our and other developed economies'. He stressed that at this time there should not be a reactionary move back to the pre-1997 regulatory framework, adding that 'no framework can avoid shocks, so we must think carefully about reform'. King also insisted that 'there is no point blaming anyone for the outcomes'.

King's reluctance to identify specific actors for their culpability in the crisis might be explained by the critical scrutiny he was receiving in the press for his and the BOE's handling of the financial crisis, particularly their performance during the Northern Rock crisis. The three newspapers analysed in this chapter focused not on his causality narrative but on his policy proposals. The papers were critical of the fact that the inflation rate had overshot King's inflation target by a full 1 per cent, and were sceptical about his policy outlook for the continuing credit crisis.

13 October 2008: the Prime Minister's 'unprecedented times'

Brown's October 2008 speech was markedly different in tone to his October 2007 address. By this time, the small UK banking crisis and worldwide credit crunch had morphed into the global financial crisis. Northern Rock required full nationalisation in January 2008 after the unsuitability of takeover bids. In the subsequent months, six more banks—HSBC, HBOS, RBS, Bradford & Bingley, Lloyd's and Barclay's—had announced monumental losses (*BBC* 2009). Moreover, just a few days before Brown's speech, the Icelandic economy had begun to collapse, and Brown had threatened Reykjavik with legal action in a bid to retrieve savings of UK citizens tied up in Icelandic banks. The domestic political backdrop had also changed from a year before. Brown was consistently between 8 and 15 points behind Conservative leader, David Cameron, in the polls for preferred prime minister (UK Polling Report 2009).

Brown declared that 'these [are] unprecedented times'. He maximised the severity of the crisis, claiming that 'the stakes are higher than ever before'. Continuing on from his October 2007 speech, in which he had identified global financial forces as the primary cause of the Northern Rock crisis, Brown proclaimed that 'this is first and foremost a global crisis'. Furthermore, Brown defended himself, his government, the BOE and the FSA from charges of negligent financial regulation, stating that 'no one country alone can resolve what is truly a global problem'. Brown declared that this global crisis required a global solution, one in which there would be increased international cooperation to regulate global capital flow. Brown utilised the historical analogy of Franklin D. Roosevelt and Winston Churchill planning the revolutionary post-1945 Bretton Woods regulatory structure in the midst of World War II as a means of affirming the possibility of a new global regulatory system to be achieved by modern-day leaders in the thick of the global financial crisis.

More significantly, Brown emphasised the global causes of the United Kingdom's financial troubles and thereby shifted what in Chapter 2 of this volume was termed the 'policy game' to an international battlefield in which the Conservative Party could not effectively compete (Boin et al. 2009:90–1). In doing so, Brown not only defended the status quo approach to British financial regulation, he cast himself as a 'change-oriented' player on global regulatory reform. Brown was at pains in his speech to emphasise his global financial regulation credentials, stating: 'Almost exactly 10 years ago in a speech at Harvard University I made detailed policy proposals to reshape the international financial system for the new world.'

Brown's first major speech since the collapse of Lehman Brothers and the subsequent freefall in world financial markets received a lot of media coverage. Brown's severity narrative encountered some disagreement in *The Guardian* and *The Times* and he was criticised for failing to mention that Britain was heading towards recession. Brown's causality narrative, in which he exogenised blame and failed to accept that he or the British regulatory structure had a role in causing the crisis, was refuted by all three major papers. Despite this, in all three papers Brown was praised for taking a leading role in the Europe-wide fiscal stimulus and reports were cautiously optimistic about Brown's ability to lead on global regulatory reform—which they all agreed was the key to preventing another major global financial crisis.

29 October 2008: Darling's focus on global economic governance

The Mais Lecture is an annual speech delivered by the Chancellor of the Exchequer about the current state and future prospects of the UK economy. The 2008 Mais Lecture was delivered after the precipitous fall in world financial markets in September 2008 triggered by the US financial services firm Lehman Brothers filing the largest bankruptcy claim in US history. Domestically, the FTSE 100 had hit a five-year low and the UK Office of National Statistics had announced that Britain was on the brink of a recession.

Unsurprisingly, Darling portrayed the severity of the crisis in starker terms than he had before September 2008. He continually emphasised the speed at which the global financial crisis had manifested and declared that 'the UK, as well as other countries, is moving into recession'. Despite Darling's portrayal of a more severe crisis, however, and economic commentators' increasingly gloomy predictions of the future, Darling neither accepted any personal responsibility for the crisis nor attributed any blame to endogenous actors. Rather, he continued to exogenise blame—focused predominately on global factors but also on the British banking industry. Darling also diminished the regulatory record of previous governments: 'looking back over 30 years of Mais lectures, I see many attempts to find solutions to domestic problems. But one aspect of modern policymaking which seems to have been understated is the impact of global events.'

Darling criticised the global economic governance system led by the major international financial institutions (IFIs), and even accepted blame, albeit very indirectly, as he claimed that the world's major nations had 'for too long...acted as an elite'. This criticism of the 'world's major nations', which undoubtedly included Britain, was noteworthy in so much as it was an angle completely absent from Brown's crisis-exploitation narrative. It appeared that Darling was diffusing blame across the major economies, thereby accepting slightly more blame on the Labour Government's behalf than the Prime Minister, although indirectly and still very little. Darling claimed that the radical fiscal stimulus was not an admission of the failure of the 'marketist' economic paradigm that the government had adhered to since 1997. Rather, Darling portrayed it as a logical development and renewed his commitment to open markets, referencing economist J. M. Keynes: 'it is right that the conduct of policy should evolve. Just as markets change, so should policy. As Keynes said, "when the facts change, I change my mind".' Ultimately, Darling asserted that a global solution to worldwide regulatory failure was the most important policy that must be achieved in years to come.

Darling's address received a fair amount of press coverage. *The Times* pilloried Darling's severity narrative, describing the Mais Lecture as 'a Panglossian exercise in making the best of where we are now. It should have been subtitled a study in ambiguity' (Riddell 2008b). Darling's exogenisation of the causality of the crisis came under similarly heavy attack from the *Financial Times*: 'Alistair Darling tried hard last night to deflect the blame from his immediate predecessor for scrapping the rules on which Gordon Brown once rested the government's economic credibility' (Eaglesham 2008). For his policy proposals, however, Darling received sympathetic criticism from *The Guardian*, which claimed that the Mais Lecture was a mediocre performance constrained by the rotten legacy of Brown's chancellorship (see *Guardian* 2008). *The Times*, too, condemned Darling's address for 'its vagueness in indicating a way forward' and its failure on all three aspects of economic policy: fiscal, monetary and regulation (*Times* 2008). Overall, then, each aspect of Darling's crisis exploitation in his Mais Lecture was negatively received.

20 January 2009: governor King's 'political' edge

By the beginning of 2009, an interesting contextual change in the relationship between King, Darling and Brown had occurred. The crisis-exploitation narrative that had been fairly unified was becoming discordant. Amid a spiralling decline in the British economy—high joblessness, low consumer demand (reflected by record low interest rates) and a plummeting currency value—King had begun intimating that he, Brown and Darling had all been partly responsible for the emergence of the United Kingdom's financial turmoil. After Brown's announcement of a second stimulus package the day before King's speech, the press reported that King disapproved of any potential further fiscal stimulus by the government. This put Brown in a defensive position because, without the fiscal tools of handouts and tax breaks, he would have to rely more on the monetary policy of the BOE. Hence, King's statements during this period became not only discordant from Brown's, but more overtly political.

Some parts of King's crisis rhetoric remained conventional: he declared that '2009 will be a difficult year for all of us', he maintained that global factors were primarily responsible for the crisis and he portrayed the crisis as a leviathan beyond the control of any single national regulatory system. The speech was, however, in some key aspects a distinct break from King's past crisis-framing efforts. Perhaps the most salient discontinuity was King's admission that before the Northern Rock crisis there had been some failings in the UK regulatory system—a system that might have contributed to the emergence of financial strife in Britain and in which he played an integral role. King stated that 'it is clear that policy did not succeed in preventing the development of an unsustainable position' in which the United Kingdom now found itself. Although this was only a guarded acceptance of partial responsibility for the crisis, it stood in stark contrast with the unwavering denial of culpability that Brown and Darling had maintained since September 2007. Hence, while the earlier part of King's speech characterised the global financial crisis as being too serious for any single national regulatory authority to prevent, his admission indicated that the UK response to the global financial crisis had not been as rapid or effective as it could have been.

The speech received a considerable amount of coverage in the major newspapers. The opinion of King's severity narrative was mostly negative. All papers agreed with the now widespread public view that the crisis was the most severe in more than half a century, but disagreed with King's rose-tinted portrayal of unemployment and credit easing. In the week or so after the speech, King's causality narrative received little attention, probably because King had mentioned that there were flaws in the UK regulatory system during a number of doorstop interviews and press releases in the weeks before the speech. Taking into consideration the press coverage of these minor speech acts, the papers overwhelmingly agreed with what they considered a long-overdue admission of responsibility from the governor. There was not much coverage of King's policy proposals, but the *Financial Times* was in agreement with King that wages had to be restrained in order to combat inflation.

26 January 2009: Brown's continued global crisis narrative

Brown's speech of 26 January was delivered at a time when the public was becoming increasingly aware that the foundations of the UK economy were not as strong as Brown and his government had initially portrayed. The European Commission had forecast on 19 January that the UK economy would not only enter recession, it would contract significantly—by 2.8 per cent in 2009—and would then recover only marginally in 2010 (Gow 2009). Also on 19 January, Brown had announced a second stimulus package of £50 billion.

Brown's speech reflected the increasingly gloomy state of the UK economy and further maximised the severity of the global financial crisis. Brown conjured florid metaphors of 'storms' and 'hurricanes' to describe the forces battering the UK economy. Brown stated that 'the sheer scale and speed of recent events makes this no ordinary crisis'. Brown also reiterated his previous statements that promoted the UK economy as among the best equipped to endure financial turmoil, by stating that 'Britain is better placed to benefit as the storm passes'.

Brown continued to deny that the government's regulatory regime was responsible for the crisis. He witheringly described the financial regulatory regime before 1997 as archaic and asserted that only Labour's revolutionary post-1997 reforms had made British financial regulation effective. Brown declared, however, that no national regulatory framework—not even one as effective as Britain's—could have prevented the unprecedented global financial crisis. Only through an international system of financial regulation could the global financial crisis have been forestalled. The Prime Minister's policy solutions remained focused on achieving the 'radical reform of our global financial system' (Webster and Duncan 2009).

Surprisingly, the speech did not receive much press coverage; only *The Times* published articles relating to the Prime Minister's crisis framing in the days after the speech. The paper quoted polls showing that '58 per cent…of people…believe he [Brown] is refusing to acknowledge the full depth of the crisis' (Webster and Duncan 2009), and further expressed criticism for Brown's causality narrative: 'Gordon Brown is fond of emphasising that the recession is global, and that it was made in America. But as massive deleveraging takes place around the world, it has become clear that the UK economy was one of the most overleveraged in the world' (*Times* 2009a).

It is hard to gauge from the limited newspaper coverage the overall support for Brown, although the few available articles were not very supportive of him. This comports with the polls at the time, which indicated that Brown's deficit to Cameron in the polls had increased to 9–14 points, from 1–7 points just one month earlier, in December 2008 (UK Polling Report 2009).

10 February 2009: Brown under increasing pressure

Coming only two weeks after Brown's previous major speech act, this address was important, not for any specific shift in the framing of the UK and global financial crises, but because it provoked a significant media reaction. There were two significant contextual developments in the two weeks between speeches. First, the International Monetary Fund (IMF) had declared on 28 January that the United Kingdom would be among the countries worst affected by the global financial crisis, revising its previous forecast of a 1.3 per cent contraction to 2.8 per cent (Kollewe 2009a). Second, the BOE Governor, Mervyn King, had, since late 2008, been noticeably less critical of British banks and other financial intuitions. Instead, he had started to describe, albeit in vague terms, that the banks were not alone in their failure to prevent the crisis. This led to much media speculation that there was a rift between King and Brown.

In this speech, Brown continued to make the most of the global financial crisis and exogenise its causes. Additionally, like all of his speeches since 2007, this speech again advertised Brown's strong credentials for achieving global financial reform and made use of the same historical analogy—the creation of the Bretton Woods institutions. In fact, in this speech, he expanded the analogy of the postwar economic reconstruction by referencing the Marshall Plan and describing it as a revolutionary fiscal stimulus package that brought the European and world economies back from the brink of ruin to the longest boom in modern economic history, from 1945 until the 1973–74 global recession. Thus, the analogy could be seen as a defence of the large fiscal stimulus Brown had injected into the UK economy and also a pre-emptive justification of future fiscal stimulus by the government, which was widely believed to be forthcoming despite the injection of a second round of £50 billion stimulus into the UK financial system just weeks earlier.

In his speech to the Brookings Institution, Brown also blamed British banks for promoting a culture that rewarded short-term risk over long-term sustainability. Perhaps the most interesting aspect of this speech, however, was that for the first time Brown emerged from his hitherto position of denial to admit that there were flaws in the domestic regulatory structure. He then qualified this, however, with the ameliorating line that no country's regulatory system could have prevented the leviathan global financial crisis.

The three papers all agreed with Brown's appreciation that the crisis was at this point egregious. *The Guardian*, however, noted that Brown's realisation of the severity of the crisis was overdue, saying that his claim that Britain 'was the victim of international, specifically US, banking problems' had become a 'threadbare tale' (Kettle 2009). The *Financial Times* also criticised Brown's causality narrative after recent negative publicity about 'how the City of London [the hub of the financial sector] was run during Mr Brown's tenure at the Treasury' (*Financial Times* 2009a). The aspect of Brown's speech on which all three papers critically focused was, however, his plan to cut bonus payments from the banks that had been fully or partly nationalised. All three papers vehemently disagreed with this proposal for various reasons, ranging from *The Guardian*'s contention that it would punish genuinely creative entrepreneurs to the *Financial Times*' opinion that it was a tawdry populist policy that did not address the major problems at the heart of the economy in recession. Overall, then, there was little to no support in the major newspapers for Brown's severity narrative or causality narratives, or for his policy proposals.

11 March 2009: Darling's G20 finance ministers' meeting

Since Darling's October 2008 speech, British economic news had been increasingly bleak. At the turn of 2009, the pound had fallen to a historic low against the euro, the jobless figure of 6 per cent was the worst in a decade, the FTSE 100 continued to fall dramatically and the BOE had cut interest rates to the lowest figure in the bank's 315-year history.

Darling had admitted in his October speech that the United Kingdom was headed for recession. In his address to the Foreign Press Association at the G20 Finance Ministers' Summit, however, he too put a twist on his old rhetoric of growth, saying that 'we mustn't lose sight of [the fact that] the global economy is expected to double, so there's a huge prize to be won'. This speech is notable because of its heavy use of crisis-exploitation rhetoric. It was particularly strident in identifying global factors as the primary cause of Britain's financial crisis and global re-regulation as the most important policy to achieve. Again, Darling attempted to shift debate away from the domestic battleground, where the government was being staunchly challenged by the Conservative Party, to an international arena in which the opposition, with no internationally recognised mandate to speak for the UK electorate, could not compete.

Somewhat surprisingly, there was almost no media coverage of Darling's address to the press contingent at the meeting of G20 finance ministers. As the President of the G20 in 2009, Britain had clearly embraced the G20 as a body that could effectively combat the crisis and effect global financial re-regulation. In the only article that dealt with Britain's role in the G20, however, *The Times* was dubious about the government's embrace of the G20 after ignoring the body for a number of years. 'Gordon Brown will be chairman of the summit and his enthusiasm for remaking supranational organisations almost invites mockery because the ambitions so far outstrip the amount of work that has been invested in realising them' (*Times* 2009b). It was noteworthy that there was a complete absence of specific coverage of Darling's speech. This suggests that his concerted crisis-exploitation efforts went largely unrecognised by the public.

17 March 2009: King's caution against rash action

Amid an escalation in the tension between King and Brown, visible in their media comments since January, the BOE Governor delivered his most significant speech on the continually worsening effects of the global financial crisis. Newspapers had widely reported that UK unemployment had reached a 12-year high of two million people (Hopkins 2009a) and the BOE had again slashed interest rates to another historic low, of 0.5 per cent. This speech, again, represented another shift away from the crisis-exploitation rhetoric of Brown to which King had closely adhered between September 2007 and late 2008.

As in his previous speeches, King maximised the severity of the crisis. At the same time, however, King downplayed the urgency required for the next response to the stagnating—if not worsening—financial situation and instead advised that all key leaders take time to choose the right course of action. This could have been directed at Brown, who had already approved a number of fiscal stimulus packages, as just one week later, on 24 March, King sensationally announced that further fiscal stimulus by the government was inadvisable (Duncan and King 2009; Hopkins 2009b; Wintour 2009).

King's causality narrative became more nuanced in this speech. King again identified global forces as the primary cause of the crisis—particularly the poor performance of IFIs and the absence of a global regulatory order. King added another layer, however, to his imputation of blame to global forces by criticising the role of creditor and debtor nations in the crisis. He criticised creditor nations for loaning money without pressuring debtor nations to repay and pilloried debtor nations for naively borrowing massive amounts of money, prolonging their repayments and racking up significant public debt. From this criticism, he did not exempt the United Kingdom, which, in Organisation for Economic Cooperation and Development (OECD) terms, had neither high nor low public debt (CIA 2009b).

There was no media coverage of King's severity narrative or the new strand about creditor and debtor nations in his causality narrative. Only the *Financial Times* addressed King's causality narrative in any detail, taking issue with King's excuse that his inflation targets had not worked because he did not have adequate power to achieve them. Instead, the paper accused King of being a key part of a short-sighted hierarchy that had not adequately prepared for a financial downturn when the economy was booming (Giles 2009). 'In reality, all three institutions in the so-called tripartite arrangements for financial supervision were culpable in failing to recognise the toxic combination of rapid credit expansion and financial innovation' (Stephens 2009).

There was, conversely, a plethora of coverage of King's policy proposals. The papers were unified in their praise for King's proposals to abolish the banks' 'casino' lending and gambling practices as well as his subtle suggestions for the Prime Minister to avoid further fiscal stimulus. The majority of articles in these three papers, however, criticised King for his pessimism and for talking down the UK economy. King was also criticised for failing to admit that the BOE—not just the FSA and the Treasury—needed to undergo reform to prevent future crises.

4. Framing the financial crisis in the United Kingdom: analysis and conclusions

It was not until the precipitous falls in financial markets through mid 2008 that the global financial crisis manifested in the United Kingdom. Since September 2007, however, the financial turmoil in Britain has been a historic affair. The British public, more so than the populaces of countries whose economies began visibly struggling only in mid 2008 after the collapse of Lehman Brothers, had become more attuned to news of the worsening financial turmoil.

Naming, explaining and accounting for the crisis

At first sight, Brown's, Darling's and King's labelling and explanation of the financial turmoil of 2007–09 followed similar paths. The *severity* narratives of Brown and Darling were so similar in their progression towards ever-starker characterisations as to suggest a high level of coordination between the two. There was, however, a noteworthy inconsistency among the three actors' severity narratives. Brown and Darling initially engaged in minimisation, stating from late 2007 and throughout 2008 that the United Kingdom was in a distinctly strong economic position to confront the financial crisis. King, on the other hand, did not engage in any such minimisation.

The three actors' *causality* narratives, and the attendant task of accepting or denying blame, were fairly consistent. From the outset, they all emphasised global factors as the primary cause of the United Kingdom's financial turmoil. Again, the causality narratives of Brown and Darling were similar to one another while King's account diverged in a few small, but key ways. First, whereas Brown and Darling initially failed to admit flaws in their handling of the Northern Rock crisis, King in November 2007 absorbed minimal blame, claiming that, if he had his time again, he would have responded differently to Northern Rock's

117

predicament. Second, in late 2008, King began to eschew specifically identifying global factors or British financial institutions as causing the crisis. Instead, he described in vague tones that they were not alone in acting irresponsibly during the pre-2007 period of high world economic growth. This suggests that King was admitting, albeit indirectly, that he and other regulators—but more significantly, the Prime Minister and the Chancellor—had played a part in the escalation of the crisis. Third, King added another unique strand to his causality narrative by blaming not just international financial institutions or a lack of global financial regulation, but debtor economies such as the United Kingdom, which had complacently relied on easy credit.

It appeared that King's blunt criticism prompted Brown and Darling to admit in February 2009 that there had been flaws in the regulatory system before the global financial crisis. The press, however, interpreted these admissions as cynical 'road-to-Damascus' conversions that were a reaction to King and a pre-emption of the late-March release of the Turner Review, an official government review on the state of the UK financial regulatory system before September 2007 and those most responsible for its creation. King's late-2008 departure from the causality and blame narratives of Brown and Darling presented an interesting intra-regime framing contest. This contest contributed to the greater framing contest between the three actors: the Labour Government (along with the supposedly apolitical BOE Governor, who was likely to cooperate with the incumbent government), the opposition Conservative Party and the media.

Framing contests: political survival and policy reform

To examine the larger framing contest, it is broken down into two distinct contests that have most influenced the political game over issues of *responsibility*: between the government and the opposition (parliamentary and extra-parliamentary); and the policy game over *reform*: between proponents of the status quo and change advocates (cf. Table 2.2 in Chapter 2).

Contests over policy framing can be separated into the domestic and international battlegrounds. Both stemmed from the causality narrative of the political actors Brown and Darling—and to a lesser extent the non-partisan technocrat King—who argued that the United Kingdom's financial turmoil was caused primarily by global factors. The domestic policy-framing contest was over the injection of £300 billion into the financial system—Brown and Darling's response to the global financial crisis. Brown and Darling depicted this sizeable and highly statist fiscal stimulus as absolutely necessary. More significantly, the framing contest centred on implications for existing British financial regulation policies. Brown and Darling had argued that the British regulatory structure was world class and revolutionary by British standards; that even this could not prevent the leviathan global financial crisis hitting British shores; and that policy implications should be minimal because Britain's crisis was caused predominately by global problems. In terms of the crisis-framing typology of Chapter 2, Brown and Darling clearly adopted on the domestic battleground a type-2 frame in which the crisis was viewed as a 'critical threat to the collective good embodied in the status quo' and as such the status quo must be defended against critics.

As argued in Chapter 2, such a type-2 defence is typical of incumbents. For Brown and Darling, it was a logical frame to adopt. Labour, a long-serving government, was unpopular in the electorate and, like many long-serving governments, it appeared to aspire to short-term regime survival. By denying responsibility for the crisis for so long, however, the two political actors set up a 'blame showdown' in which they might escape political repercussions, but are more likely to suffer political damage (see Table 2.1, Chapter 2). In the international policy reform game, however, the government sidestepped the role of status quo defender and cast itself decisively as a change-oriented player.

Brown and Darling seized the political opportunity afforded to them by the exogenous-causality narrative and declared that the most important policy outcome of the global financial crisis should be the complete restructuring of the global regulation of finances. They unified and strengthened their type-3 rhetoric (focusing blame and attacking the status quo) by deploying historical analogies that affirmed the benefits of global financial re-regulation, notably the reference to the creation of the Bretton Woods system. In their declaration to the public that they and their Labour cabinet colleagues were best credentialled to achieve such global regulatory reform, Brown and Darling adopted, on the international battleground, type-3 frames, which regarded the crisis as 'a critical opportunity to expose deficiencies in the status quo ex ante' (see Chapter 2).

Adding to this intricate combination of type-2 and type-3 frames, the defence of the government's open and globalised economic approach by each of the three main UK actors placed the Conservative opposition in a difficult political position. As *The Guardian*'s Economics Editor Larry Elliot suggested, the government's defence of its marketist approach, combined with its calls to re-regulate the global economy, put the Conservative Party in an awkward position because the 'Conservative Party [has] obviously much more of a [marketist] deregulatory bent than Labour in historic terms' (Elliot 2008b). Labour used its centrist 'third way' ideology as a means of wedging the Conservative Party on its key policy proposals—maintaining open and globalised markets and re-regulating the global economy.

Brown and Darling's multilayered framing strategy—a type-2 frame defending the domestic status quo; a type-3 frame portraying the government as a change-oriented player; and a defence of marketism and global re-regulation—seemed set for success. The fact that the press and public largely agreed with Brown and Darling's claims that global factors were the primary cause of Britain's financial turmoil appeared to have made the international framing contest one that put the incumbents in an advantageous political position.

Nonetheless, the framing contest most important for the political fortunes of the government and their parliamentary opposition was the domestic one. While the press agreed that global factors were primarily responsible for the United Kingdom's financial turmoil, they reacted vehemently against Brown and Darling's long-time denial of responsibility for the crisis. The later concessions by the Prime Minister and the Chancellor that they were responsible for some flaws in the British regulatory structure further damaged their government's popularity (UK Polling Report 2009). This development fits with the claims of Boin et al. (2005:86–7) that actors who belatedly admit responsibility for a crisis suffer far more damage than those who absorb minimal blame early in the crisis. While the three actors' assertions that the domestic financial turmoil was caused primarily by global factors was supported by the press and public, Brown and Darling's long-time denial of culpability for the emergence of the crisis and their defence of the status quo domestic financial regulation was overwhelmingly rejected by the electorate. This left them in March 2009 far behind in the polls with just more than a year before the compulsory date for the next national election.

For King, it appears as though he suffered only minor damage to his credibility. This appears to be a result of two factors: his acceptance of minimal blame for the Northern Rock and the British financial crisis in general; and the general view that he is not technically a political player. King was not required to engage as much as Brown or Darling in the key task of managing the public's expectations about the crisis; as such, he could instead focus on providing technical explanations and solutions for Britain's financial crisis. This is not to say that King is apolitical. The Governor of the BOE became politicised by his own doing—specifically, by implying that endogenous actors were responsible for the crisis and, more significantly, by publicly halting the government's plans for a further fiscal stimulus. King's divergence from his previous line of crisis rhetoric—which had been fairly concordant with that of the Prime Minister and the Chancellor—was hardly inspired by political motives. He was up for reappointment to the second of a maximum two-term tenure in January 2008, which he duly received regardless of his 'inconvenient' stance on the issue of responsibility for the financial crisis.

A general observation that can be drawn from the UK case study, and that might even apply to all case studies in this volume, is that financial crises, by nature, appear to require governments to talk up and support the national economy in the incubation period of the crisis, at the expense of locking themselves into a specific frame. If key government actors are aware that financial turmoil is likely to hit their nation's economy, they are likely to downplay the severity in an attempt to maintain consumer confidence and curb the damage of a potential crisis. If they do not do this, they can easily be blamed for exacerbating any financial crisis that hits the nation.

The response to the British manifestation of the global financial crisis comports with the proposition that long-serving governments find it difficult to convince the public that they are fit to make the changes necessary to prevent another crisis in the future. The findings from this chapter, however, suggest that the chances of long-serving governments flourishing in a financial crisis are made even more remote by their necessary but risky obligation to talk up the national economy in the incubation period of the crisis.

References

BBC 2007, 'UK families put on fraud alert', *BBC News*, 20 November, viewed 4 April 2009,
<http://news.bbc.co.uk/2/hi/uk_news/politics/7103566.stm>

BBC 2009, 'Timeline: global credit crunch: a quick guide to the origins of the global financial crisis', *BBC News*, 3 April, viewed 20 April 2009,
<http://news.bbc.co.uk/2/hi/business/7521250.stm>

Boin, A., 't Hart, P., Stern, E. and Sundelius, B. 2005, *The Politics of Crisis Management: public leadership under pressure*, Cambridge University Press, Cambridge.

Boin, A., 't Hart, P. and McConnell, A. 2009, 'Crisis exploitation: political and policy impacts of framing contests', *Journal of European Public Policy*, vol. 16, no. 1, pp. 81–106.

Brown, G. 2007, Speech on the global economy at the Reuters Building, 1 October, viewed 28 March 2009, <http://www.number10.gov.uk/Page13355>

Brown, G. 2008, Speech on the global economy at the Reuters Building, 13 October, viewed 28 March 2009,
<http://www.number10.gov.uk/Page17161>

Brown, G. 2009a, Speech on global economic crisis, 26 January, viewed 30 March 2009, <http://www.number10.gov.uk/Page18153>

Brown, G. 2009b, Q&A session on the global economy with the Brookings Institution, 9 February, viewed 30 March 2009,
<http://www.number10.gov.uk/Page18266>

Central Intelligence Agency (CIA) 2009a, *Country Comparisons: GDP (purchasing power parity)*, Central Intelligence Agency, 14 May, viewed 29 May 2009, <https://www.cia.gov/library/publications/the-world-factbook/rankorder/2001rank.html>

Central Intelligence Agency (CIA) 2009b, *Rank Order—Public debt*, Central Intelligence Agency, 14 May, viewed 30 May 2009, <https://www.cia.gov/library/publications/the-world-factbook/rankorder/2186rank.html>

Darling, A. 2007a, Speech at the Reuters Building, 1 October, UK Treasury, viewed 1 April 2009, <http://www.hm-treasury.gov.uk/speech_chex_011007.htm>

Darling, A. 2007b, Speech to the CBI Conference, 27 November, UK Treasury, viewed 1 April 2009, <http://www.hm-treasury.gov.uk/speech_chex_271107.htm>

Darling, A. 2008a, Speech to the Royal Society for the Encouragement of the Arts, Manufacturers and Commerce, 15 January, UK Treasury, viewed 2 April 2009, <http://www.hm-treasury.gov.uk/press_03_08.htm>

Darling, A. 2008b, Speech to the Worshipful Society of International Bankers, 4 February, UK Treasury, viewed 2 April 2009, <http://www.hm-treasury.gov.uk/speech_chex_040208.htm>

Darling, A. 2008c, Chancellor of the Exchequer's budget statement, 12 March, UK Treasury, viewed 12 May 2009, <http://www.hm-treasury.gov.uk/bud_bud08_speech.htm>

Darling, A. 2008d, The Mais Lecture on maintaining stability in a global economy, 12 October, UK Treasury, viewed 3 April 2009, <http://www.hm-treasury.gov.uk/press_110_08.htm>

Darling, A. 2009, Address to the Foreign Press Association at the G20 Finance Ministers' Summit, 11 March, UK Treasury, viewed 2 April 2009, <http://www.hm-treasury.gov.uk/speech_chex_110309.htm>

Duncan, G. and King, I. 2009, 'Mervyn King: UK can't afford any more stimulus plans', *Times Online*, 24 March, viewed 26 March 2009, <http://business.timesonline.co.uk/tol/business/economics/article5966450.ece>

Eaglesham, J. 2008, 'Chancellor tries hard to deflect blame', *Financial Times*, 30 October, p. 2.

Elliot, L. 2007, 'Let's not rush to enter Virgin territory', *The Guardian*, 27 November, viewed 27 March 2009, <http://www.guardian.co.uk/business/2007/nov/27/northernrock.creditcrunch1>

Elliot, L. 2008a, 'Brown mannerisms, rose-tinted forecasts but few green measures', *The Guardian*, 13 March, viewed 27 March 2009, <http://www.guardian.co.uk/commentisfree/2008/mar/13/budget.alistairdarling/print>

Elliot, L. 2008b, 'Video commentary on Alistair Darling's speech to Labour Party conference', *The Guardian*, 22 September, viewed 27 March 2009, <http://www.guardian.co.uk/politics/video/2008/sep/22/darling>

Financial Times 2009a, 'Brown's chance to save himself', *Financial Times*, 13 February, viewed 19 May 2009, <http://www.ft.com/cms/s/8e4b3ac2-fa09-11dd-9daa-000077b07658>

Financial Times 2009b, 'About us', *Financial Times*, 17 June 2009, viewed 17 June 2009, <http://www.ft.com/aboutus>

Galloway, G. 2006, 'Interview by Kieran Meeke', *Metro UK*, 28 April, viewed 4 April 2009, <http://www.metro.co.uk/fame/interviews/article.html?in_article_id=12486&in_page_id=11>

Giles, C. 2009, 'King back in his castle', *Financial Times*, 28 March, p. 9.

Gow, D. 2009, 'European Commission predicts UK economy will shrink by 2.8%', *The Guardian*, 19 January, viewed 21 May 2009, <http://www.guardian.co.uk/business/2009/jan/19/european-economic-forecast>

Guardian 2008, 'Throwing out the rulebook', *The Guardian*, 30 October, viewed 5 April 2009, <http://www.guardian.co.uk/commentisfree/2008/oct/30/economy-darling-crunch-government-borrowing>

Guardian 2009, 'ABCs: national daily newspaper circulation January 2009', *The Guardian*, 6 February, viewed 28 May 2009, <http://www.guardian.co.uk/media/table/2009/feb/06/abcs-january-national-newspapers>

Hopkins, K. 2009a, 'UK unemployment nears 2 million', *The Guardian*, 11 February, viewed 6 May 2009, <http://www.guardian.co.uk/business/2009/feb/11/uk-unemployment-job-losses>

Hopkins, K. 2009b, 'Britain cannot afford any further fiscal stimulus, King warns', *The Guardian*, 24 March, viewed 26 March 2009, <http://www.guardian.co.uk/business/2009/mar/24/bankofenglandgovernor-banking/print>

Ipsos Mori Poll 2005, 'Voting intention by newspaper readership quarter 1', *Ipsos Mori Poll*, 21 April, viewed 28 May 2009, <http://www.ipsos-mori.com/content/polls-05/voting-intention-by-newspaper-readership-quarter-1.ashx>

Kaletsky, A. 2008, 'Fingers crossed, Darling: budget 2008', *The Times*, 13 March, p. 1.

Kettle, M. 2008, 'In defence of Darling', *The Guardian*, 18 February, viewed 27 March 2009,

<http://www.guardian.co.uk/commentisfree/2008/feb/18/ indefenceofdarling/print>

Kettle, M. 2009, 'Now Brown has to accept his share of guilt for the mess', *The Guardian*, 13 February, viewed 26 March 2009, <http://www.guardian.co.uk/commentisfree/2009/feb/13/ gordon-brown-financial-crisis/print>

King, M. 2008a, Speech at the dinner hosted by the CBI and the IoD South West, 22 January, Bank of England, viewed 4 April 2009, <http://www.bankofengland.co.uk/publications/speeches/2008/speech333.pdf>

King, M. 2008b, Speech to the British Bankers Association, 10 June, Bank of England, viewed 5 April 2009, <http://www.bankofengland.co.uk/publications/speeches/2008/speech347.pdf>

King, M. 2009a, Speech to the CBI dinner, 20 January, Bank of England, viewed 5 April 2009, <http://www.bankofengland.co.uk/publications/speeches/2009/speech372.pdf>

King, M. 2009b, A return from risk, Speech to the Worshipful Society of International Bankers, 17 March 2009, Bank of England, viewed 6 April 2009, <http://www.bankofengland.co.uk/publications/speeches/2009/speech381.pdf>

Kollewe, J. 2009a, 'IMF: UK economy will be hardest hit in the worst recession since second world war', *The Guardian*, 28 January, viewed 23 May 2009, <http://www.guardian.co.uk/business/2009/jan/28/ ilo-global-unemployment-to-soar>

Kollewe, J. 2009b, 'Bank of England cuts rates to 0.5% and starts quantitative easing', *The Guardian*, 5 March, viewed 6 April 2009, <http://www.guardian.co.uk/business/2009/mar/05/ interest-rates-quantitative-easing>

Morley, I. 2007, 'Darling is throwing out baby, water and bathtub', *Financial Times*, 26 November, p. 11.

Mulholland, H. 2008, 'Ed Balls issues veiled threat to David Miliband over Labour leadership', *The Guardian*, 1 September, viewed 4 April 2009, <http://www.guardian.co.uk/politics/2008/sep/01/labourleadership.labour>

Pratley, N. 2007, 'Rock run finds Bank and Darling off the pace', *The Guardian*, 18 September, viewed 2 April 2009, <http://www.guardian.co.uk/business/2007/sep/18/politics.money>

Riddell, P. 2008a, 'With the public in such a gloom, could this be Labour's point of no return', *The Times*, 20 March, p. 28.

Riddell, P. 2008b, 'Chancellor is glossing over the crucial questions', *Times Online*, 30 October, viewed 27 April 2009, <http://www.timesonline.co.uk/tol/comment/columnists/peter_riddell/article5042498.ece>

Seager, A. 2009, 'Mervyn King refuses to apologise for not spotting recession', *The Guardian*, 11 February, viewed 24 April 2009, <http://www.guardian.co.uk/business/2009/feb/11/bank-of-england-inflation-report>

Stephens, P. 2008, 'The bad news Darling can't banish', *Financial Times*, 12 March, p. 5.

Stephens, P. 2009, 'Autocratic leadership has failed the Bank of England', *Financial Times*, 30 March, viewed 21 April 2009, <http://www.ft.com/cms/s/0/1a885002-1d59-11de-9eb3-00144feabdc0.html>

Sunderland, R. 2007, 'Gordon needs to parcel up the Rock before Christmas', *The Guardian*, 18 November, viewed 27 March 2009, <http://www.guardian.co.uk/business/2007/nov/18/comment.businessandmedia/print>

Times 2007, 'Poll tracks anger over data loss', *The Times*, 23 November, viewed 30 May 2009, <http://www.timesonline.co.uk/tol/news/politics/article2926574.ece>

Times 2008, 'Lost in the Mais', *The Times*, 30 October, viewed 27 April 2009, <http://www.timesonline.co.uk/tol/comment/leading_article/article5042273.ece>

Times 2009a, 'The pounding of the pound', *The Times*, 21 January, viewed 24 April 2009, <http://www.timesonline.co.uk/tol/comment/leading_article/article5556168.ece>

Times 2009b, 'A summit for stimulus', *The Times*, 14 March, p. 2.

UK Polling Report 2009, 'Voting intention since 2005', *UK Polling Report*, 20 May, viewed 29 May 2009, <http://ukpollingreport.co.uk/blog/voting-intention>

Webster, P. and Duncan, G. 2009, 'D-Day for Brown as he says world is already in a depression', *The Times*, 5 February, p. 7.

Wintour, P. 2009, 'Mervyn King's economic assessment will infuriate Downing Street—but will be warmly welcomed by Treasury', *The Guardian*, 25 March, viewed 26 March 2009, <http://www.guardian.co.uk/politics/2009/mar/25/treasury-borrowing-mervyn-king/print>

6. Republic of Ireland: from Celtic tiger to recession victim

Adam Masters

1. Boom to bust

> Ireland is being battered by international storms the like of which this generation has never seen. But I am saying this to the Irish people—if we work together as a team we can ensure that we have a prosperous future for ourselves, our children and future generations on this island. (Cowen 2009a)

The case of Ireland presents a distinctive experience of a nation's response to the financial crisis. There are, of course, marked similarities with other countries covered in this volume, such as Ireland having a small open economy like New Zealand or membership of the European Union like the United Kingdom. The contextual similarities are, however, far outweighed by differences. Ireland's economy had been built up in the 'Celtic tiger' years on foreign investment and high-tech industry. On the back of these external inputs, the boom years generated bloated domestic finance and real-estate markets. The good times also resulted in a disproportionate expansion of the public sector and an expectation by government that the financial cornucopia would always bestow its manna on the Emerald Isle.

The Irish political leadership first acknowledged the impact of the global financial crisis on Ireland after a sharp fall in government revenue in July 2008. The revenue drop was linked to a downturn in the building industry and housing market, higher food and fuel prices and 'international financial market turbulence' (Hurley 2008b). Before July, Irish authorities had viewed the turbulence in financial markets as a problem linked to the sub-prime crisis in the United States and the toxic debt instruments associated with poor lending practices by US banks (O'Brien 2008:18). During the next nine months, the impact of the crisis on Ireland became increasingly pronounced as it manifested within the domestic economy.

The key manifestations of the financial crisis in the Irish economy were driven by external and internal factors. External factors included the liquidity crisis triggered by the financial turmoil, which in turn severely impacted on the domestic banking sector. The Irish banks, although not directly exposed to the US sub-prime mortgage market, had lent heavily to property developers, thereby inflating values and creating Ireland's own real-estate bubble. Some of these causal factors had been years in the making; others emerged as a result of the crisis, driven by the economic downturn.

Three key public figures responsible for leading Ireland during this period were the Taoiseach (Prime Minister) Brian Cowen, his Minister for Finance Brian Lenihan, and John Hurley Governor of the Central Bank and Financial Services Authority (CBFSA). Cowen and Lenihan came to these roles in May 2008 after the former Taoiseach Bertie Ahern, stood down. Cowen had been Ahern's Minister for Finance and Lenihan previously held the position of Justice Minister. Hurley had held the position of CBFSA Governor since 2002 (Mitchell 2008). This chapter examines, through the lens of the crisis exploitation framework presented in Chapter 2, these three leaders' attempts to manage and frame the global financial crisis as it manifested within Ireland.

Box 6.1 Ireland's financial crisis trajectory, July 2008 – March 2009

8 July 2008: After the Exchequer reports an expected shortfall in government revenue of €3 billion, the new Taoiseach (and former Finance Minister), Brian Cowen, announces a number of new budgetary measures decided on by the government in response to the 'emerging financial pressures'. The measures trigger their own crisis, with a backlash against proposed cuts to pensioners' medical benefits.

19–20 September: *The Irish Times* reports that Minister for Finance, Brian Lenihan, is prepared to review the government system of guaranteeing 90 per cent of deposits up to a limit of €20,000 amid calls for this limit to be raised. The next day, the Irish Government moves to secure the deposits in Irish banks to prevent a run on them. The €20,000 guarantee is increased to €100,000.

25 September: Ireland is officially the first EU member state to slip into recession.

30 September: Finance Minister Lenihan presents the Credit Institutions (Protection) Bill 2008 to the Dáil (the Irish national parliament). The bill enables the government to take a stake in any financial institution that receives financial support. It also incorporates an 'insurance premium' of 0.2 per cent of deposits over the two years it is in effect. This could amount to €1 billion in additional revenue to the government in return for a guarantee of more than €400 billion. The institutions being offered the protection of the guarantee are Allied Irish Bank, Bank of Ireland, Anglo Irish Bank, Irish Life & Permanent, Irish Nationwide Building Society and Educational Building Society.

---

8 October: The CBFSA reduces the interest rate by 50 basis points.

15 October: The budget is brought forward. Cowen outlines the measures to achieve savings, including additional government borrowing, reduction in public services and raising taxes. Cowen also incorporates an agenda of public service reform.

26 November: The Taoiseach announces measures of reform within the public sector.

5 December: The open, export and service-driven economy of Ireland has nosedived, pushing the government's five-year projected deficit up to about €12.5 billion. The Finance Minister, indicating the budget position is worse than expected, announces stimulus borrowings, further review of public sector spending and the establishment of the Special Group on Public Service Numbers and Expenditure Programmes. Much of this is overshadowed by a separate crisis related to an outbreak of foot and mouth disease in Irish swine, which occurred just before the Christmas season when hams were in high demand.

18 December: The Taoiseach announces and releases *Building Ireland's Smart Economy: A framework for sustainable economic renewal*. The announcement and release of the framework appear to be the result of a long process predating the global financial crisis. The framework is, however, absorbed into the government's reaction to the global financial crisis and linked to the future policy direction for development in Ireland.

19 December: Seán FitzPatrick, chairman of the Anglo Irish Bank (AIB), resigns. He had been temporarily transferring €87 million in loans to another institution before the fiscal year's end to avoid disclosure of their existence to shareholders—a practice that had been occurring for eight years. The other institution is believed to be the Irish Nationwide Building Society. The chief executive of AIB resigns several hours later. In response, Finance Minister Lenihan announces plans to recapitalise AIB and the Bank of Ireland, take effective control of AIB and clear out the remaining board members.

9 January 2009: Patrick Neary, chief executive of the Irish Financial Services Regulatory Authority, resigns after allegations that his staff first learned in January 2008 that FitzPatrick had been transferring loans.

28 January: Cowen, speaking in the Dáil, indicates the crisis in Ireland has developed further. A five-year shortfall of €15 billion has been identified. Cowen says measures, further to those already announced, will be necessary. A new policy is also announced: A Pact for Solidarity and Economic Renewal. This is intended to involve social partners (unions, employers) in the solutions and garner political support for future measures.

3 February: The Taoiseach delivers a statement to the Dáil detailing the fiscal and budgetary measures to be taken in 2009/10 to rein in borrowing and reduce expenditure. The unions (social partners) do not agree with the plan, but the government intends to go ahead regardless. The measures include cuts to child care, reduction in overseas aid, reduction in public service pay and delays in agreed pay rises.

19 February: Finance Minister Lenihan presents the second stage reading of the Financial Emergency Measures in the Public Interest Bill 2009.

10 March: CBFSA Governor Hurley, who has agreed to stay on in his role post-retirement age, claims in response to questions from the Committee on Economic Regulatory Affairs that the government had ignored his many warnings about the state of the Irish economy.

24 March: The Minister for Finance meets with two government-appointed board members for the Irish Nationwide Building Society (INBS) over recent disclosures in relation to the remuneration of the CEO of INBS, which requires further investigation.

2. Methodological considerations

It is safe to say in Ireland there is no shortage of speech material from the Taoiseach or the Minister for Finance relating directly or indirectly to the financial crisis. Four key speech acts of each leader were therefore selected for their relationship to key events or the level of public response, rather than the amount of content relating to the case at hand. Examples of key speeches not analysed were Finance Minister Lenihan's speeches in the Dáil introducing the Financial Emergency Measures Bill (Lenihan 2009b). Although rich in crisis rhetoric, the speeches did not introduce new key measures or draw significant media response.

Selection of key speech acts was also limited to those available on the official web sites of the leaders. Although there were media references to speech acts that were not on the web sites, these were discounted from analysis for three reasons. First, the references in the media could be interpreted as vague, referring to what 'the Taoiseach said this week' with no pinpoint reference. Second, the volume of speech material available via the media, even limited to three outlets, was prohibitively large. Finally, leaders must take full ownership of what was posted on an official web site and its provenance should not be disputed.

In analysing the domestic media's response to the Irish leadership with respect to the global financial crisis, two daily newspapers, the *Irish Independent* and the *Irish Times*, and one weekly, the *Sunday Business Post*, were selected. Selection of the daily newspapers was based primarily on their position as leading Irish dailies, with the highest and second-highest circulation, respectively. The *Sunday Business Post* was selected on the basis of the quality of analysis and depth of the articles it published. Although the *Sunday Business Post* did not have the highest circulation for Irish Sunday papers, its focus on financial and economic activity was considered relevant for this case study.

After the selection of the speeches for analysis, searches were conducted in the chosen newspapers for the week after the speech act. Articles were scanned for relevance to the speech act or the related event. Articles selected for analysis were coded using a three-level scale (agreement, disagreement, neutral/no comment) in relation to four analytical categories: leaders' framing of the severity and the causality of the crisis and support for proposed policies and for the leader. These results were then considered in relation to the crisis-exploitation framework of Chapter 2 to determine the manner with which, and how successfully, these three leaders were able to frame and manage the crisis in Ireland.

3. Crisis development and elite rhetoric in Ireland

18 April 2008: Governor Hurley's trouble-on-the-horizon speech

Governor Hurley's address to the Institute of Auditors on 18 April 2008 was a measured speech designed to provide reassurances that there was nothing wrong with the fundamentals of the Irish economy, but that trouble was on the horizon. Entitled 'Recent issues in financial stability', the speech explained the developing crisis in terms of the turbulence in the international financial markets, which had persisted longer than many had predicted. Hurley spoke of future outcomes that could 'manifest itself in terms of banking crises and recessions and can be very costly for any economy'. He also noted the greater than anticipated challenges ahead for the Irish economy in 2008. In a more positive vein, however, he listed the 'skilled workforce, flexible labour market, moderate taxation, business friendly regulatory environment and [Ireland's] sound fiscal position' along with the economy's ability to 'absorb adverse shocks' as reasons for confidence in the future.

Blame for the turbulence in global financial markets was attributed to the effects of the US sub-prime crisis and the toxic debt instruments backed by US mortgages. The CBFSA Governor believed that there was little direct exposure by Irish banks to these instruments—once again underpinning the overall strength of the Irish economy. The only domestic factor cited was attributed to a 'marked decline in house-building'. All of these were exogenous to the CBFSA and there was no acceptance of responsibility in this speech. Hurley limited the management role of the CBFSA, in terms of its response, to 'monitor[ing] the situation very closely' and participation in international attempts at the EU level to understand the origin of the events in the global markets.

As if to underscore the lack of interest in the doings of the CBFSA Governor, only a single article was published in the three main newspapers referring to Hurley's speech. The article reported that Citigroup (which at the time had 2000 employees in Ireland) was sacking 9000 employees globally. No job losses were announced in Ireland and the journalist duly noted Hurley's comment that the CBFSA and the financial regulator 'regularly stress-tested the Irish banking sector and found that it can weather a significant slowdown' (Carswell 2008a).

8 July 2008: Finance Minister Lenihan's mixed message

In July 2008, Irish political leaders did not acknowledge any significant impact of the global financial crisis on the Irish economy. 'Our remarkable economic progress has not been reversed overnight,' the Finance Minister asserted in his budget speech. As his statement evolved, however, he did signal the need for change in the government's fiscal approach. 'If we do not act now, the situation facing us for 2009 will be more difficult and the action needed more urgent'. The urgency that he conveyed was explained by a shortfall in government revenue of €3 billion resulting from expenditure running 11 per cent ahead and due to higher unemployment.

To manage the shortfall, Lenihan announced the government's intent not to implement planned pay increases for ministers and senior public servants. In doing this, the Finance Minister acknowledged a responsibility for government to act and lead the way in making sacrifices without taking any blame for developments in the economy. The expected savings from the cutbacks were to total €440 million in 2008 and €1 billion in 2009. Towards the end of his statement, Lenihan asserted that the government would stand by its choices in regard to the programs and investments of the previous 11 years in which his party had been in power.

	Severity	Causality	Proposed policy	Support for speaker
Agrees	18	13	9	7
Disagrees	1	2	19	18
No comment/ neutral	12	16	3	6

Table 6.1 Media response to Lenihan's 8 July 2008 speech

The response to Lenihan's announcement of budget cuts was mixed (Table 6.1). Of the articles analysed, only one disputed the severity of the situation, arguing that 'it isn't Armageddon' as this announcement allegedly had implied (*Irish Times* 2008a:15). Lenihan successfully conveyed the causality, which was reflected by only two articles disagreeing with him and pointing instead to past policies of Lenihan's government. While there was general agreement on severity and causality, there was greater opposition to the proposed policies (that is, cuts to spending) and little support for the government that was driving them.

10 July 2008: Governor Hurley's moderation

The timing of the launch of the CBFSA *Annual Report* coincided with speeches by the Taoiseach (not analysed) and the Finance Minister (see above). Governor Hurley remained restrained. In explaining the Irish economic situation, Hurley again pointed to the slowdown in the housing sector as a causal factor. He added a new factor: the fall in the share price of the Irish banks. Hurley repeated reassurances that the Irish banks had little to no direct exposure to the US sub-prime crisis, which was still perceived as the main threat to Ireland's economy.

For Hurley, international turbulence in the financial markets was attributed to downturns in real estate in major economies as well the steep rise in food and fuel prices. In turn, higher commodity prices were both cause and effect of the escalation of the financial problems. The devaluation of the pound against the euro had caused consumers to cross to Northern Ireland or the United Kingdom to take advantage of better exchange rates, resulting in an outflow of capital from the Irish economy. With so many exogenous factors available, there was no acceptance of blame. The only management strategy offered by Hurley was the slight increase in interest rates—a matter for the European Central Bank (ECB), not the CBFSA.

	Severity	Causality	Proposed policy	Support for speaker
Agrees	5	7	5	1
Disagrees	2		1	
No comment/ neutral			1	6

Table 6.2 Media response to Hurley's 10 July 2008 speech

The reserved language of the CBFSA Governor did not resonate with all journalists reporting on the launch of the *Annual Report*. Some argued the severity of the downturn was higher than Hurley was letting on. In the *Sunday Business Post*, there was an acknowledgment that the CBFSA often forecast market contractions, however, this was often buried in the fine print of the *Annual Report* rather than as part of the public statement from the governor (Curran 2008). The *Irish Independent* listed many of the global indicators that had impacted on Ireland and noted that Hurley, and the CBFSA, 'were not nearly as pessimistic' (*Irish Independent* 2008a). Nonetheless, all analysed reports agreed with the causes Hurley had identified as producing the darker economic outlook.

With respect to his recommendations on inflationary and fiscal control, commentary was heavily in Hurley's favour. His warnings of too much interference in the markets were accepted, along with the broader government objective of spending cuts announced by the Minister for Finance. Comparing this speech with Lenihan's above, Hurley received approval from the financial press whereas Lenihan did not (cf. Table 6.1). A possible explanation might be found in the authorship of the policy being attributed more to the politicians than to the CBFSA Governor, who was seen to be acting as an instrument of the government's policy.

2 October 2008: Taoiseach Cowen offering deposit guarantees

In a speech to the CBI-IBEC Joint Business Council Dinner at Trinity College, the Taoiseach left his audience in little doubt about the scale and seriousness of the global financial crisis in Ireland: 'We live in perilous times...if we do not make the right [choices] it will have catastrophic consequences for the future prospects of our economy...nobody will be immune from the pain'. Through the use of unequivocal language, Cowen set the crisis in terms that were by this time familiar to his audience and had been for a number of months.

The speech followed a number of meetings and an announcement that the government would guarantee deposits in Irish banks up to €100,000. While that decision had been well received in the banking sector, at the time of Cowen's speech at Trinity College, legislation had just been passed to give substance to the announcement. Cowen needed a degree of popular support to shore up support for the new measure, taken unilaterally by the government, the shock waves of which had reverberated through the rest of Europe and beyond. His crisis rhetoric of 'right choices' as opposed to 'catastrophic consequences' was a reference to this recent legislative action.

In accounting for the impact of the crisis on Ireland, Cowen was brief: 'we are an open economy'. This followed a more detailed coverage of what had happened: a collapse in the housing market, 'turbulence in international financial markets, exchange rate shifts and rapidly rising oil prices', which combined to result in a €6.5 billion shortfall in government revenue. There was no acknowledgment of any responsibility, even though Cowen had been Finance Minister for a number of years before his elevation to Taoiseach. Blame was attributed to the vaguely exogenous factor of greed, although greed 'has not been absent in Ireland'.

	Severity	Causality	Proposed policy	Support for speaker
Agrees	45	35	24	26
Disagrees		5	13	12
No comment/ neutral	4	9	12	11

Table 6.3 Media response to Cowen's 2 October 2008 speech

As Table 6.3 illustrates, the majority of articles from the week after Cowen's Trinity College address supported his assertion that the root cause of the local banking crisis had been greed, the collapse in the housing market and the global financial turmoil. There was a higher level of agreement on the severity of the crisis. The proposal to protect depositors up to €100,000 was supported in just less than half the commentary, with one-quarter disagreeing and a similar number making no commitment either way. Those who disagreed were concerned primarily with the risk to the national economy posed by the guarantee (Kelly 2008:16) or whether it was in line with EU arrangements (Smyth 2008:8).

The Taoiseach's efforts to frame the banking crisis in a way that supported his Fianna Fáil Government were relatively successful. Only one-quarter of the articles analysed reflected a lack of support for the national leader. The strongest support came from other European news media. Germany's *Frankfurter Allgemeine Zeitung* praised the Irish Government: 'By calming citizens and securing bank financing, the guarantee should achieve its aim of avoiding forced bank nationalisation' (*Irish Times* 2008b). Media praise was leavened, however, by criticism of the guarantee by EU leaders such as Germany's Angela Merkel and UK Prime Minister, Gordon Brown (Collins and Carswell 2008:1). The strongest criticism was directed against Cowen in the letters to the editor of the *Irish Times*, questioning the fiscal and economic policies from when he had been the Finance Minister (*Irish Times* 2008c).

3 October 2008: Governor Hurley's support for the deposit guarantee

By October 2008, the continuing drama in Ireland's banks finally drove the CBFSA Governor to use crisis rhetoric. Nonetheless, in his statement to support government moves to guarantee bank deposits for the six major domestic banks, Hurley maintained his reserved manner and used the specific word 'crisis' only once. He was more explicit when describing the urgency of 'events [which] came to a head last Monday evening when the supply of funding…was seriously threatened' and as a result 'decisive action to protect the stability of the economy…was needed'. The reason the crisis had manifested in such an acute manner for Hurley was the 'unprecedented shortage of liquidity in financial markets', and any solution needed to target that problem directly.

Hurley 'had to inform the Minister that the risks to financial stability were becoming unacceptably high with knock-on effects for the wider economy'. As a result of this advice, the government had decided to guarantee depositors and lenders to Irish banks, thereby protecting the stability of the Irish financial system. The legislation for the guarantee had passed the day before Hurley's speech. While not accepting responsibility for causing the crisis, Hurley and the government accepted the responsibility for making key and critical decisions to meet the crisis head-on.

	Severity	Causality	Proposed policy	Support for speaker
Agrees	9	8	8	6
Disagrees				
No comment/ neutral	1	2	2	4

Table 6.4 Media response to Hurley's 3 October 2008 speech

Response to Hurley's speech was found within the major media coverage of the banking guarantee (Table 6.4). As with Cowen's speech at the same time (see above), his assessment of the severity and causes of the crisis leading up to the guarantee was not questioned. There was, however, a major difference in the responses to the politician and to the banker. Hurley received proportionally much greater support for himself and the policy proposals than did Cowen. This was because articles that mentioned Hurley analysed the economic and fiscal ramifications of the guarantee in greater detail, rather than focusing on the political results. Four of the 10 articles analysed in response to this speech were also used to analyse response to Cowen's first speech act (Carswell 2008b:8; Carswell et al. 2008:1; Hennessy 2008:9; *Irish Independent* 2008c).

Hurley's popularity also stemmed from his rapid response to one bank's attempt to exploit the guarantee. After a rapid investigation, the CBFSA and financial regulator issued a €50,000 fine to the Irish Nationwide Building Society (INBS) for 'touting'. A senior employee of INBS (who was also the son of the chief executive) had sent an email to potential customers. The email claimed the INBS was 'the safest place in Europe for deposits and money in INBS bond accounts was guaranteed regardless of the size of the deposit' (*Irish Independent* 2008b, 2008e). The positive windfall for the governor from the swift action by the CBFSA and the financial regulator was reinforced by a biographical piece on Hurley reflecting on his long public service career as he approached retirement (Mitchell 2008). Hurley's role as a statutorily independent public servant minimised his use of crisis rhetoric and buffered him somewhat from opinionated coverage.

15 October 2008: the Taoiseach's reform agenda

In his budget statement, Cowen utilised the crisis as a vehicle to push through public service, welfare and education reforms. Public sector reform had been high on Cowen's agenda since taking office as Taoiseach, when he announced the outcomes of an Organisation for Economic Cooperation and Development (OECD) review of the Irish Public Service. Using the language of crisis, Cowen framed the crisis as being 'on a scale last seen in the 1930s'. The proposed level of reform by his government was justified because 'unprecedented times call for unprecedented measures'. Direct action was necessary as 'it is tempting' during difficult times 'to batten down the hatches and wait until the storm is over'—a statement contrived to leave the audience morally obliged to follow the government's lead.

The reason given for the big impact of the global crisis in Ireland was once again its open economy, with decreasing exports hurting government revenue. In this budget, however, the Taoiseach announced measures to manage revenue shortfalls that, had it not been a 'crisis' situation, would have had little chance of being supported. Reductions to pensioners' medical benefits and child benefits were to be supplemented by restructuring of tax benefits for pension contributions. One of the major initiatives to manage the crisis would be the implementation of a public sector reform agenda. In an extension of his early strategy of leading by example, Cowen announced that government ministers and departmental heads would take a voluntary 10 per cent pay cut. The only responsibility Cowen acknowledged was not for the economic crisis, but for the previous high levels of growth.

	Severity	Causality	Proposed policy	Support for speaker
Agrees	21	7	4	6
Disagrees		4	39	38
No comment/ neutral	24	34	2	1

Table 6.5 Media response to Cowen's 15 October 2008 speech

Media reaction to the budget was very negative towards Cowen and the government. In the first week, the majority of media coverage focused on the changes to pensioners' medical benefits. Of the 45 articles analysed, 31 focused on the pensioner medical card debacle. While it made up a relatively small portion of the overall budget (€100 million out of a health budget of €15 billion), the backlash caused Cowen and his government to 'do a U-turn in respect of this measure' (*Irish Independent* 2008g). Less than half of the coverage acknowledged the severity of the crisis in their commentary; the remainder made no comment on it at all. Cowen's causality claims were also largely ignored. The four articles that disagreed on causality blamed the past policies of Cowen's Fianna Fáil Government.

Cowen was unable to fully exploit the global financial crisis and pass all his announced budget cuts. The relatively minor financial return from cutting pensioners' health benefits resulted in a political crisis within Fiánna Fail, with government members rebelling (*Irish Independent* 2008f) and ruptures with independent parliamentarians (McGee 2008:7). Overwhelmingly, the response was negative, with only one opinion piece offering any support to the government's actions (*Irish Times* 2008e).

5 December 2008: Lenihan's reform salesmanship

'We are in very difficult times' was a clear public acknowledgment made by the Finance Minister about the deteriorating condition of the government's fiscal position. In a statement on the economy delivered to the Seanad Éirann (The Senate) in early December, Lenihan explained that 'a major gap has emerged between spending levels and tax receipts' resulting in a projected government deficit of €3.5 billion for 2008 and €4.7 billion for 2009. The cause of the consistent slide in revenue rested with the downturn in the domestic housing sector and the 'major deterioration in the global economic environment…traced to…sub-prime mortgage debt'.

To manage the budget shortfall, Lenihan introduced a range of measures to review spending in the public sector. In doing so, he appeared to make a conscious and careful effort to use language that would not inflame resistance to the foreshadowed changes. Lenihan asserted that 'everybody in this room [the Séanad] is a public servant' and 'the kind of demonisation of the Public Service that has featured in public debate…including political parties' had been deplorable. This linguistic move shifted the blame for any perceived attack on the public sector to his political opponents. Reforms outlined by Lenihan also focused on job preservation and support for the unemployed through social services and access to education and training.

	Severity	Causality	Proposed policy	Support for speaker
Agrees	16	12	5	4
Disagrees		2	10	11
No comment/ neutral	2	4	3	3

Table 6.6 Media response to Lenihan's 5 December 2008 statement

Table 6.6 indicates that in December 2008 the government's framing of the severity of the crisis was widely accepted. The public, media, business and unions all shared Lenihan's view. There was also less debate about the causality of manifestations of the global crisis in Ireland. Dispute generally rested on criticism of past government policy, which some said had failed to insulate the Irish economy from the current financial trauma.

Lenihan's use of his 'Statement on the economy' to drive the policy outcomes required to address the global financial crisis was less than successful. The statement was made amid organised protest against government economic and fiscal policy. A demonstration of students organised by the teachers' union brought about 50,000 protesters to the streets of the capital in a strong show of dissatisfaction with the Finance Minister's policies, which translated into a much lower level of support for the government's leadership (Flynn 2008:17). Loss of respect within the Fianna Fáil was also generated by an apparent lack of consultation among party members and accusations of rule by a triumvirate that included Lenihan, Cowen and the Tanaiste (Deputy Prime Minister), Mary Coughlan (*Irish Independent* 2008i). The difficulties of balancing the budget and the use of the crisis to drive reform were soon to be overshadowed as the banking crisis re-emerged in the New Year.

15 January 2009: Lenihan's take on AIB nationalisation

There had been much speculation after the government's deposit guarantee in October 2008 about whether the marker would be called in by the banks as a result of the global financial crisis. In mid January, Lenihan announced that the funding position of the Anglo Irish Bank (AIB) had weakened and 'unacceptable practices that took place within it had caused serious reputational damage' (CBFSA 2009). As a result, the government moved beyond recapitalisation to the 'decisive step of public ownership'. The government decision was to 'safeguard the interests of depositors of Anglo, and the stability of the economy'.

The swift response by the government required a high level of management to ensure that the public purse would not be hit by a further loss. AIB shares were suspended from trade in Ireland and the United Kingdom. Information was made available to shareholders and the public in the form of a question and answer page on relevant government web sites and that of the AIB. With the move to nationalisation, the interests of shareholders became secondary to those of depositors. 'Shares in Anglo will be transferred to [the Minister of Finance, who] will appoint an independent assessor, who will decide the value of the shares and decide what level (if any) of compensation shareholders will get' (*It's Your Money* 2009).

The share value for AIB had fallen sharply since May 2007—from €17.50 to €0.22 (O'Halloran 2009:8).

The poor share performance had led to calls for the government to inject funds into AIB and hold an extraordinary general meeting (EGM) of shareholders. The government's decision not to bail out AIB and nationalise the bank came the day before the EGM. Nationalisation angered many of the attending shareholders, particularly when it became apparent their shares had become virtually worthless and were to be appropriated by the government (Beesley 2009:9).

	Severity	Causality	Proposed policy	Support for speaker
Agrees	33	29	10	8
Disagrees		3	23	22
No comment/ neutral	8	9	8	11

Table 6.7 Media response to Lenihan's 15 January 2009 speech

Reaction to the nationalisation of a major bank, as seen in Table 6.7, reflected societal awareness of the severity of the financial crisis facing Ireland and an acceptance of the causality. This did not, however, translate into an immediate policy victory for Lenihan in his framing of the crisis, nor did it engender political support. Tracking the tone of media articles through the week reflected an initial stunned media and public response, followed thereafter by a level of anger, particularly from shareholders and taxpayers—the former group likely to lose money in the arrangement and the latter likely to join them (*Irish Independent* 2009a). When grouped with the variety of opposition parties, there was nearly three times as much opposition to the government's decision to nationalise AIB as there was support. Media reports, however, did not blame the government for the collapse of AIB. Blame was directed at the AIB chairman and board of directors, who in the public's mind were guilty of criminal behaviour (O'Toole 2009:14).

Lenihan's credibility as a leader during the global financial crisis was undermined when he was caught out in a radio interview not knowing what the statement posted on the CBFSA web site actually said. According to one commentator, Lenihan 'did not know that the official government response to [the disgraced chairman of AIB] FitzPatrick's gigantic scam on his bank's shareholders was that it was "disappointing"' (O'Toole 2009:14). This was a massive understatement compared with the public and media opinion of the behaviour of the AIB chairman and board of directors. As one letter to the editor phrased it: 'which is the appropriate Government Department to approach for a no-strings-attached, interest-free and fully concealable loan of approximately €87 million?' (*Irish Times* 2009a:17).

28 January 2009: Cowen's crisis plan

In his statement to the Dáil Éireann, Cowen began by framing the situation as Ireland facing 'the most difficult global economic conditions in seventy years' and 'the most severe financial crisis since the Great Depression'. Once again, the Taoiseach attributed Ireland's economic problems to the openness of the economy, adding 'the sharp appreciation in the value of the Euro' and decline in the demand for Irish exports. Cowen's brevity in naming, explaining and accounting for the crisis was balanced by a detailed plan to manage it.

Cowen reminded his audience that the government had moved 'swiftly [to] introduce a banking guarantee' and had acted to provide support for mortgagees who had fallen behind in payments. The government also 'support[ed] efforts at [an] international level to establish regulatory mechanisms' and what was proportionally Europe's largest capital investment program. Cowen described these actions as having the main goal of 'return[ing] the economy to sustainable growth per [the] Framework for Sustainable Economic Renewal'. The framework was a 105-page plan focused on a 'smart economy' based on research and development, innovation, environmental balance, infrastructure investment and efficiency in the public sector (Department of the Taoiseach 2008). To implement the broader plan, Cowen called for a Pact for Stabilisation, Solidarity and Economic Renewal to be negotiated with the social partners.

Cowen used crisis rhetoric in an attempt to box in the social partners so they would endorse the government's policy agenda. The Taoiseach implied that any failure would rest with the social partners.

	Severity	Causality	Proposed policy	Support for speaker
Agrees	16	14	6	7
Disagrees		1	10	11
No comment/ neutral	4	5	4	2

Table 6.8 Media responses to Cowen's 28 January 2009 speech

There were two key factors influencing public reaction to the Taoiseach's speech. First, there were continuing negotiations to secure €2 billion in savings with the unions, in their role as social partners. After a long period of industrial harmony supported by economic growth, there was little chance that Cowen would garner the unconditional support of the union leadership for economic measures that directly impacted on union members. The lack of support for Cowen is attributable to the well-reported response of the unions. Second, there was Barack Obama. The American President-Elect's speeches calling for sacrifice in times of economic uncertainty were widely reported. To add to Cowen's woes, the media and public drew comparisons between the two leaders and the Irishman was found wanting (*Irish Times* 2009b:15).

There were calls for the Taoiseach to make a state of the nation address, similar to the US 'State of the Union' address (Devlin 2009). Further comparison found that 'unlike Obama, Cowen [had] no plan. He [had] not had a plan since he started, nor did he have one as Finance Minister' (Arnold 2009). This additional pressure made it increasingly difficult for the Taoiseach to exploit the crisis for policy or political gain.

3 February 2009: Cowen's break with the social partners

The breakdown of the social partnership between the government and the unions demonstrated the speed and depth of the impact of the crisis on Ireland. There was less than a week between Cowen's announcement on delivering sustainable economic renewal and securing public finances and his announcement of the Framework for Stabilisation, Social Solidarity and Economic Renewal. With a slight variation on his speech of a week before, Cowen described the situation as 'the most profound global economic crisis in seventy years'. In another push to manage the financial crisis, the government had spent the intervening period engaged in discussions with the social partners that had resulted in the framework. The framework took 'urgent and radical action to restore stability in public finances, to maximise short term economic activity and employment and to improve competitiveness'.

The Taoiseach had tried to manoeuvre the unions into providing support the previous week. As a result of the negotiations, the unions decided they could not agree to the framework, thereby giving Cowen's government a scapegoat should the framework fail. The government took a political risk by taking decisions without backing from one of the major social partners—a break with a key feature of Irish socioeconomic governance since 1987.

The plan to manage the financial crisis was to be a major economic undertaking. With an initial commitment to save €2 billion and a total of €18.5 billion in economic adjustments by 2013, it 'represent[ed] a huge political, economic and social challenge for every single person' in Ireland.

	Severity	Causality	Proposed policy	Support for speaker
Agrees	36	11	18	17
Disagrees		2	21	24
No comment/ neutral	10	33	7	5

Table 6.9 Media response to Cowen's 3 February 2009 speech

The reaction to the Taoiseach's announcement of the framework was from a population now feeling the effects of the crisis. While most media reporting agreed with the severity of the crisis in Ireland, there was no commentary on the causal factors. By this stage, however, nearly every speech act by the Taoiseach made reference to the global financial crisis, so there was no need for the media to reinforce what was well known. The two articles that disagreed with the causal factors attributed the blame to the past policies of Cowen's government.

The framework stimulated greater media coverage than the other speeches analysed in this chapter. This was largely due to it marking the collapse of the social partnership arrangement between unions, business and government that had dominated previous decades. The articles that disagreed with the fiscal policies in the framework focused mainly on the union movement's reaction and the foreshadowed industrial action protesting against a new pension levy for public servants (*Irish Independent* 2009d). Comparing Cowen's speeches (cf. Tables 6.3, 6.5 and 6.8), however, the negative reaction was not as overwhelming as previously experienced. Cowen received support from those who appreciated his direct style of communication and from business and private sector groups (*Irish Independent* 2009b, 2009c).

4 February 2009: Lenihan's blame management

Facing an 'ocean of advice out there about [what] to do', the Minister for Finance laid out a grim message to the Dáil when seeking its support in 'tackling the current economic and fiscal crisis'. Lenihan's statement on economic and spending measures forecast decline in growth, negative export growth and a significant increase in unemployment. These negative factors had resulted in growth in government borrowing to €18 billion for 2009. The result of these developments had blown out national debt to 45 per cent of gross national product (GNP), with an annual interest bill of '€4.5 Billion, or 12 per cent of total tax take'. The government's plan to address this was threefold: first, getting the cost base down; second, keeping 'up the real value of…investment in national productive capacity'; and finally, doing the first two in a fair manner.

A high level of blame management accompanied the tough measures. Lenihan addressed those who 'instead of advancing constructive policies…try to fix the blame and not the problem'. Lenihan then attempted to acknowledge his own culpability while simultaneously transferring it: 'perhaps as a government we were over-ambitious in trying to meet the…demands…for more and better public services when the resources were there'. This statement was immediately followed by the observation that the opposition had never called for 'less spending, lower social welfare increases, higher taxes, more levies' when the government had rolled out its agenda in the good times. Blame was also transferred to the unions, as the social partners could not agree to the government's savings regime in the middle of the 'worst crisis in international financial markets in 60 years'.

	Severity	Causality	Proposed policy	Support for speaker
Agrees	15	7	5	6
Disagrees			11	10
No comment/ neutral	3	11	2	2

Table 6.10 Media response to Lenihan's 4 February 2009 speech

Lenihan's statement on economic and spending measures was delivered a day after the Taoiseach announced the Framework for Stabilisation, Social Solidarity and Economic Renewal (see above). As a result, much of the commentary on the government's performance was in response to both these speech acts. A little more than half of the media reports reflected the lack of support for the government program—due mainly to the fallout from union opposition to spending cuts and pay reform in the public sector. As the bearer of bad economic tidings and social upheaval, the Finance Minister did not succeed in exploiting the crisis for political gain.

Letters to the editor of the *Irish Times* provided a snapshot of public opinion. Most reflected the anger within Ireland towards the situation at hand and much of that anger was directed towards the government. This anger went so far as to call for 'senior churchmen or religious leaders [to] come together and issue a joint condemnation of the Government's handling of the economic crisis' (*Irish Times* 2009c:17). Successful exploitation of the crisis in Ireland was an enormous challenge for the elected politicians, whether in government or opposition.

10 March 2009: Hurley's blame deflection

The final speech act analysed in this chapter presented an interesting turnaround for the otherwise staid Governor Hurley. Only two significant speech acts are located on the CBFSA web site after the banking guarantee. Both were to committees of the Oireachtas (Parliament), and it was the second on 10 March to the Committee on Economic Regulatory Affairs that highlighted the change in Hurley's rhetoric. The change was not only in the speech, but in the media response it garnered, particularly in relation to the questions asked of Hurley by committee members after the speech.

The opening of Hurley's statement was rich in the rhetoric of crisis. His economic assessment covered the recent history of the downturn and its development at global, EU and national levels. The global conditions were blamed for making the 'domestic economic situation much worse'. He outlined actions taken by the government and the CBFSA, including the provision of liquidity early in the crisis, involvement at EU level to ensure national regulatory action dovetailed with international plans and the actions to nationalise the AIB. After his opening statement, Hurley opened himself and his colleagues to questioning by the committee. The questions were not listed as part of the speech, however, the media reported a large amount of blame transference from the CBFSA Governor to the government for the severity of the crisis (Carswell 2009a:18, 2009b:2; *Irish Independent*, 2009f, 2009g, 2009h, 2009i, 2009j; McManus 2009:16).

	Severity	Causality	Proposed policy	Support for speaker
Agrees	2			2
Disagrees	1	1		3
No comment/ neutral	6	8	9	4

Table 6.11 Media response to Hurley's 10 March 2009 speech

Hurley's address to the Oireachtas initially appeared to bemuse the media. Two reasons for his change in rhetoric and entry into the blame game were immediately apparent. First, Hurley had remained on as governor beyond his retirement date to help get Ireland through the global financial crisis (*Irish Independent* 2009f). This 'post-retirement' sense of complete independence led him to be more 'forthright than is usual for central bankers' (*Irish Independent* 2009g). Second, Hurley appeared to be defending his own reputation through blame deflection (O'Malley and Duffy 2009:17).

Hurley claimed he had issued numerous warnings regarding the looming peril, which had been ignored by the government; however, this attempted deflection drew criticism from the media. The majority of the articles analysed tended to focus on the man, not the policy. He was variously described as 'gloomy', the 'Central Bank Cassandra' (*Irish Independent* 2009h) and 'downbeat' (*Irish Independent* 2009g). One piece described Hurley's attempt to deflect blame as 'handwashing of breathtaking proportions' (McManus 2009:16). Hurley's annual salary was also subjected to media scrutiny after his call for the Irish not to be paid more than their EU counterparts (Carswell 2009a:18). The negativity continued, as the only commentary that discussed Hurley's financial forecasts disagreed with his framing and predicted an even bleaker outlook than the one outlined by the CBFSA (*Irish Independent* 2009g).

4. Framing the financial crisis in Ireland: analysis and conclusions

Initial government attempts to exploit the financial crisis in Ireland were discernable in two key policy moves: reform of the public sector and a push to implement major structural change in the way the Irish economy was moving into the future. Within the analytical framework and time frame examined, there was little evidence that these attempts were successful. The broader context of Irish politics and history, however, must be taken into account to allow for a more nuanced view of the findings. The following discussion will examine public sector reform within a historical context and economic reform within a political context, as well as considering some of the unintended consequences of the government's response to the global financial crisis. The chapter will conclude with a comparative analysis of how these polices, in the context of the global financial crisis in Ireland, were framed by the Taoiseach, the Finance Minister and the bank governor.

Public sector reform

In April 2008, three months before the global financial crisis seriously manifested in Ireland, the Fianna Fáil Government led by Bertie Ahern and with Brian Cowen as Minister for Finance commissioned the OECD to review the operation of the Irish Public Service. A task force was appointed on the day Cowen became Taoiseach with the goal of preparing an implementation plan for the OECD recommendations (Cowen 2008c). The timing of the task force announcement illustrates the political imperative and the importance in Cowen's view of public sector reform. Within a historical context, the Irish public services had grown in the boom years of the 'Celtic tiger' economy. Quite literally, hundreds of departments, agencies and quangos (quasi-non-governmental organisations) developed in the good times and the State could no longer afford them. This growth in the public sector led to a corresponding growth in the level of service provided to and received by the Irish population. Ireland had struggled economically for many years and had been considered one of the 'poor four'—or, more unkindly, 'PIGS' (Portugal, Ireland, Greece and Spain)—of the European Union (Rumford 2002:154). This had changed with the boom economy and there was understandable resistance in the population and the unions to any government move to wind back spending, which would in turn impact on jobs and services. With the downturn in tax revenue, the larger public sector was no longer a sustainable proposition.

The push for public service reform by linking it to the financial crisis was a politically daring attempt to win popular support—as well as support from the social partners, or at least their acceptance of reduced government bureaucracy and service. The announcement to implement the task force reforms fell between the banking guarantee in October 2008 and the December 2008 budget. The timing was designed to foreshadow the cuts the Finance Minister would announce and to prepare the public and social partners—now cognisant of the downturn—for the belt-tightening changes ahead.

Reform of the Irish economy

The second major reform pushed by the Fianna Fáil Government was a modernisation of the Irish economy. After the budget in December, the Taoiseach launched the government's Framework for Economic Renewal. The 105-page plan opened with 'Ireland faces challenging economic circumstances but there are also great opportunities on the horizon' (Department of the Taoiseach 2008:Foreword). Economic reform in these circumstances was a case of a type-3 framing stance. The government was laying the groundwork needed to use the opportunity of the crisis to reform the economy. The plan repackaged existing policies with a vision to 're-prioritise the business of Government and to re-focus resources in a manner that will hasten economic renewal' (Department of the Taoiseach 2008:Foreword).

The framework was not well received, being variously described as 'stale reheats' (*Irish Independent* 2008i), a 'woolly document' (*Irish Times* 2008f:17), a 'patchwork document' (Lord 2008:9) and a 'lead balloon' (Lucey 2008:15). Most of the criticism focused on the government's attempt to map out a medium and long-term plan for the economy, based on previously announced strategies, while failing to address the immediate necessities of the financial crisis. The framework disappeared almost immediately into the background as the banking crisis resurfaced with the nationalisation of AIB. Furthermore, a different and more pressing crisis was leading public concern: a suspected break-out of foot and mouth disease in Irish piggeries (*Irish Independent* 2008h). This major export industry was deeply affected in the lead-up to Christmas. Visible in the media was the call for decisive leadership to see the Irish people through the combined crises. Such leadership was glaringly absent, according to the commentators.

The media and the opposition parties both criticised the lengths to which Cowen and Lenihan had gone in order to protect the social partnership while trying to save the economy. The speed with which the global financial crisis manifested in Ireland made the protracted negotiation process not only redundant in the eyes of some commentators, but an economic hazard (Collins 2008:16). Between the crisis in the piggeries and the broad range of political criticism, the economic reform agenda laid out in the framework failed to gain traction. What was not made clear in public statements or action until February 2009 was any acknowledgment that it would be impossible to introduce the necessary reforms or reduce spending levels to save the economy *and* meet all the needs of the social partners. Decisive, coherent and bold leadership was being called for (McDonough 2009:11). Bold leadership, however, had its own pitfalls.

Unintended consequences

The Irish Government's handling of the financial crisis triggered a series of unintended consequences with their own political and policy ramifications—for example, the backlash over the pensioner medical card discussed in the analysis of the Taoiseach's budget speech of 15 October 2008.

Also in October 2008, the banking guarantee generated its own crisis in the European Union. Questions were raised about whether the Irish Government's actions were strictly legal in terms of the financial arrangements between EU members. The question of legality was itself subjected to its own political intrigues. There had been pressure on Ireland to hold a second referendum on the Lisbon Treaty after the first referendum ended with a 'no' vote. Although concerned about the legality of the Irish banking guarantee, the European Union allegedly did not strongly oppose the move for fear of jeopardising chances of a new Irish referendum (*Irish Times* 2008b). The Irish Government was also aware that any move to bring the matter of bank guarantees before a European court would take nearly two years and it felt secure in its actions (*Irish Independent* 2008d; *Irish Times* 2008d). Nonetheless, the Irish economy and banking sector are inextricably linked to the euro currency and the ECB, and EU membership is an integral part of Irish politics. The opinions from EU member states' news media impacted on the domestic response to particularly the Taoiseach's speeches. As such, the Irish leaders still had to remain cognisant of their nation's position as part of the European Union.

Another unintended consequence of the October 2008 banking guarantee was the nationalisation of the AIB. All the government statements from the time of the guarantee declared that no bank would be nationalised as they were all financially sound. The guarantee was simply to underpin national economic security. This was disputed at the time AIB was nationalised; a prominent economist claimed the government had been warned not to include AIB in the guarantee because of its unstable circumstances (*Irish Independent* 2009e). This claim led to a political slanging match in the papers over who knew what when, and what was said to whom (*Irish Independent* 2009e).

Nationalisation of the AIB generated another political crisis over the 'golden circle'—a group of 10 high-level borrowers who were allegedly given loans of €450 million by AIB to buy shares in AIB. Details of this arrangement came out after the nationalisation of the bank. There were allegations that Cowen knew of the arrangement and the names of the borrowers and this led to substantial political pressure on Cowen and Lenihan to 'name names' (Collins and Hennessy 2008:1; O'Regan 2009:8).

Rhetorical consistency

The number of sub-crises generated in Ireland in the wake of the global financial crisis necessitated a level of unity among the political leadership, which will now be examined. With parliamentary elections not due until 2012, this chapter's period of analysis was situated within a relatively safe political period for Cowen and Lenihan. This safety translated into consistency between the political leaders in addressing the global financial crisis. When comparing the Taoiseach and Finance Minister with the Governor of the CBFSA, however, there were discernable differences in the type of rhetoric used in framing the global financial crisis. Whereas Cowen and Lenihan had a political game to play, the more secure Hurley stuck closer to the facts at hand without recourse to crisis language.

In marked contrast with the elected leaders, the Governor of the CBFSA was initially more reserved in his public statements. His role had been primarily to maintain a sense of calm and to prevent panic in the markets. It was only when the banking guarantee was announced that Hurley began to use crisis rhetoric, falling in line with Cowen and Lenihan at that time. As noted above, Hurley later attempted to avoid blame by claiming the government had ignored his warnings of financial dangers (Hurley 2009).

The economic drama that manifested in Ireland was primarily the result of exogenous factors that were beyond the control of the Irish Government. Attempts by the opposition to blame the government for the impact of the global financial crisis on the Irish economy were largely ineffectual. As indicated in the above discussion on public sector reform, Fianna Fáil had not been criticised when it was spending the boom-time revenues on public services and infrastructure (Lenihan 2008b). Short of a major revolt within the governing party, there was little chance of leadership change before the 2012 national elections. This left Cowen and Lenihan room to implement some of their medium-term strategies of reforming the public sector and economy.

In terms of the crisis-exploitation framework presented in Chapter 2, the long-time incumbent Fianna Fáil Government somewhat surprisingly emerged as a key advocate of radical policy change. The Taoiseach, Finance Minister and government were the main reformers (the parliamentary opposition were also advocates of changes, albeit different ones). The chief status quo players were found in the unions and among student, pensioner and other interest groups. This produced a stalemate in relation to the pensioner medical card issue and the break between the government and the social partners. As the financial resources of the State contracted, decisive leadership was privileged over political niceties. While the government conceded on the pension card in October 2008, by February 2009, it was prepared to introduce economic plans without the consent of the unions. The Irish Government had gone from policy stalemate to a politically imposed paradigm shift.

In the political game, the Irish Government was not forced to fend off blame for the *global* financial crisis, but it was subjected to criticism for past fiscal policies. There is little evidence to suggest that the continuing criticism had any serious traction. The majority of commentary accepted that the major causal factors were exogenous and had their roots in the global financial crisis. Critics of past policies had trouble concurrently attacking new proposals, as they would appear as mere nay-sayers. This, combined with the remoteness of elections, was a major factor curtailing potential blame games.

References

Arnold, B. 2009, 'I don't want to be governed by unions or this Taoiseach', *Irish Independent*, 31 January.

Beesley, A. 2009, 'Cabinet feared bank could soon become insolvent', *Irish Times*, 17 January, p. 9.

Carswell, S. 2008a, 'Citigroup announces 9,000 job cuts after €3.2bn loss', *Irish Times*, 19 April, viewed 28 March 2009, <http://www.irishtimes.com/newspaper/frontpage/2008/0419/1208468840934_pf.html>

Carswell, S. 2008b, 'Government keen to show strength as it decides on bank fees', *Irish Times*, 4 October, p. 8.

Carswell, S. 2009a, 'Banks "did not alter behaviour" despite central bank warnings', *Irish Times*, 11 March, p. 18.

Carswell, S. 2009b, 'EBS takes pain up front with loan write-off', *Irish Times*, 13 March, p. 2.

Carswell, S., McGee, H. and Beesley, A. 2008, 'Government seeks €2bn from banks for funding guarantees', *Irish Times*, 4 October, p. 1.

Central Bank and Financial Services Authority (CBFSA) 2009, Minister's statement—Anglo Irish Bank, Press release, 15 January, Central Bank and Financial Services Authority of Ireland, viewed 25 March 2009, <http://www.centralbank.ie/frame_main.asp?pg=nws_curr.asp&nv=nws_nav.asp>

Collins, S. 2008, 'Air of unreality as plan's long view ignores storm now raging', *Irish Times*, 19 December, p. 16.

Collins, S. and Carswell, S. 2008, 'Cabinet to finalise details of bank rescue scheme', *Irish Times*, 7 October, p. 1.

Collins, S. and Hennessy, M. 2008, 'Economic recovery programme to include tax stimulus', *Irish Times*, 18 December, p. 1

Cowen, B. 2008a, Address by the Taoiseach, Mr Brian Cowen TD, to the CBI-IBEC Joint Business Council Dinner in Trinity College, Dublin, 2 October, Department of the Taoiseach, viewed 28 March 2009, <http://193.178.1.117/index.asp?locID=582&docID=4031>

Cowen, B. 2008b, Statement on budget 2009, Speech by An Taoiseach, Mr Brian Cowen TD, 15 October, Dáil Éireann, Department of the Taoiseach,

viewed 27 March 2009,
<http://193.178.1.117/index.asp?locID=582&docID=4049>

Cowen, B. 2008c, Speech by An Taoiseach, Mr Brian Cowen TD, at the launch
of the government's statement on transforming public services, Dublin
Castle, 26 November, Department of the Taoiseach, viewed 27 March
2009, <http://193.178.1.117/index.asp?locID=582&docID=4114>

Cowen, B. 2009a, Delivering sustainable economic renewal and securing our
public finances, Statement by the Taoiseach, Mr Brian Cowen TD, Dáil
Éireann, 28 January, Department of the Taoiseach, viewed 27 March
2009, <http://www.taoiseach.gov.ie/index.asp?locID=605&docID=4223>

Cowen, B. 2009b, Taoiseach announces government decision on the
implementation of the Framework for Stabilisation, Social Solidarity and
Economic Renewal following negotiations with the social partners,
3 February, Department of the Taoiseach, viewed 27 March 2009,
<http://www.taoiseach.gov.ie/index.asp?locID=605&docID=4237>

Curran, R. 2008, 'The inquisitor: how foolproof is the central bank's stress test?',
Sunday Business Post, 13 July, viewed 19 April 2009,
<http://archives.tcm.ie/businesspost/2008/07/13/story34363.asp>

Department of the Taoiseach 2008, *Building Ireland's Smart Economy: A framework
for sustainable economic renewal*, 18 December, Department of the
Taoiseach, viewed 27 March 2009, <http://193.178.1.117/attached_files
/BuildingIrelandsSmartEconomy.pdf>

Devlin, M. 2009, 'Cowen needs a rallying call to unite the people', *Irish
Independent*, 29 January.

Flynn, S. 2008, 'The budget offended ordinary people and trampled on the
aspirations they hold for their own children', *Irish Times*, 9 December,
p. 17.

Hennessy, M. 2008, '24 hours that brought Irish banks back from the brink',
Irish Times, 4 October, p. 9.

Hurley, J. 2008a, Recent issues in financial stability, Address to the Institute of
Internal Auditors, 18 April, Central Bank and Financial Services
Authority of Ireland, viewed 25 March 2009,
<http://www.centralbank.ie/frame_main.asp?pg=abt_gove.asp&nv=
abt_nav.asp>

Hurley, J. 2008b, Opening statement of Governor John Hurley, Press briefing
to mark the publication of the *Annual Report* of the Central Bank and
Financial Services Authority of Ireland, 10 July, Central Bank and
Financial Services Authority of Ireland, viewed 25 March 2009,

<http://www.centralbank.ie/frame_main.asp?pg=abt_gove.asp&nv=abt_nav.asp>

Hurley, J. 2008c, Statement by Governor John Hurley, 3 October, Central Bank and Financial Services Authority of Ireland, viewed, 25 March 2009, <http://www.centralbank.ie/frame_main.asp?pg=abt_gove.asp&nv=abt_nav.asp>

Hurley, J. 2009, Opening statement by Governor John Hurley to the Joint Oireachtas Committee on Economic Regulatory Affairs, 10 March, Central Bank and Financial Services Authority of Ireland, viewed 18 May 2009, <http://www.centralbank.ie/frame_main.asp?pg=abt_gove.asp&nv=abt_nav.asp>

Irish Independent 2008a, 'Battered banks get key vote of confidence', *Irish Independent*, 11 July.

Irish Independent 2008b, 'Building society apologises for using guarantee to lure savers', *Irish Independent*, 4 October.

Irish Independent 2008c, 'Hoping for calm after the storm', *Irish Independent*, 4 October.

Irish Independent 2008d, 'Lenihan's destiny will be defined by next two weeks', *Irish Independent*, 6 October.

Irish Independent 2008e, 'Irish Nationwide fined €50,000 for "touting"', *Irish Independent*, 8 October.

Irish Independent 2008f, 'Cowen sought loyalty but got only open revolt', *Irish Independent*, 20 October.

Irish Independent 2008g, 'One shambles after another', *Irish Independent*, 20 October.

Irish Independent 2008h, 'Kitt hits out at Cowen over control by trio', *Irish Independent*, 8 December.

Irish Independent 2008i, 'Rescue blueprint is "100 pages of stale reheats"', *Irish Independent*, 19 December.

Irish Independent 2009a, 'Nervous taxpayers await the real bill for Anglo', *Irish Independent*, 17 January.

Irish Independent 2009b, 'Public sector pensions still the biggest perk of the job', *Irish Independent*, 6 February.

Irish Independent 2009c, 'Brian's mask slips to reveal glimpse of a better leader', *Irish Independent*, 7 February.

Irish Independent 2009d, 'Pension strikes threaten to cripple country', *Irish Independent*, 9 February.

Irish Independent 2009e, 'Neary to face new grilling over bank scandal', *Irish Independent*, 23 February.

Irish Independent 2009f, 'Banks ignored warnings on lending risks, says governor', *Irish Independent* 11 March.

Irish Independent 2009g, 'Economy to shrink by more than 6pc, TDs told', *Irish Independent*, 11 March.

Irish Independent 2009h, 'Shadow of a gunman leads to a sombre mood in House', *Irish Independent*, 11 March.

Irish Independent 2009i, 'EU may have to 'print' money to survive global crisis', *Irish Independent*, 11 March.

Irish Independent 2009j, 'How world banking salaries compare', *Irish Independent*, 12 March.

Irish Times 2008a, 'Real or imagined cutbacks?', *Irish Times*, 9 July, p. 15.

Irish Times 2008b, 'Eurogroup Chairman rejects European rescue fund', *Irish Times*, 2 October.

Irish Times 2008c, 'State guarantee to Irish banking system', *Irish Times*, 3 October, p. 15.

Irish Times 2008d, 'Handling of seismic events was good for Irish politics', *Irish Times*, 4 October, p. 15.

Irish Times 2008e, 'There must be a return on our trust in the Taoiseach', *Irish Times*, 21 October, p. 13.

Irish Times 2008f, 'Financial realities still to be faced', *Irish Times*, 19 December, p. 17.

Irish Times 2009a, 'State takeover of Anglo Irish Bank', *Irish Times*, 17 January, p. 17.

Irish Times 2009b, 'The need for leadership', *Irish Times*, 29 January, p. 15.

Irish Times 2009c, 'Facing up to crisis in the public finances', *Irish Times*, p. 10 February, p. 17.

It's Your Money 2009, 'Anglo Irish Bank Corporation Limited: information for consumers', *It's Your Money*, 15 January, viewed 25 March 2009, <http://itsyourmoney.ie/index.jsp?1nID=93&2nID=100&3nID=153&nID=569&aID=657 >

Kelly, M. 2008, 'Bailout inept and potentially dangerous', *Irish Times*, 2 October, p. 16.

Lenihan, B. 2008a, Statement by Brian Lenihan TD, Minister for Finance, 8 July, Department of Finance, viewed 28 March 2009,

<http://www.finance.gov.ie/viewdoc.asp?DocID=5370&CatID=54 &StartDate=01+January+2008&m>

Lenihan, B. 2008b, Statement on the economy to Seanad Éirann by Minister for Finance, Mr Brian Lenihan TD, 5 December, Department of Finance, viewed 28 March 2009, <http://www.finance.gov.ie/viewdoc.asp?DocID=5568&CatID=54 &StartDate=01+January+2008&m>

Lenihan, B. 2009a, Economic and spending measures, Statement by Minister for Finance, 4 February, Department of Finance, viewed 28 March 2009, <http://www.finance.gov.ie/viewdoc.asp?DocID=5659&CatID=54 &StartDate=1+January+2009&m =>

Lenihan, B. 2009b, Second stage reading: Financial Emergency Measures in the Public Interest Bill 2009, Minister for Finance, Brian Lenihan TD, Dáil Éireann, 19 February, Department of Finance, viewed 28 March 2009, <http://www.finance.gov.ie/viewdoc.asp?DocID=5681&CatID=54 &StartDate=1+January+2009&m=p >

Lord, M. 2008, 'Vision of a smart Ireland leaves most observers perplexed', *Irish Times*, 19 December, p. 9.

Lucey, B. 2008, 'The government that mistook a blueprint for a recovery plan', *Irish Times*, 20 December, p. 15.

McDonough, T. 2009, 'Stop bailing out bad banks and build good ones', *Irish Times*, 24 March, p. 11.

McGee, H. 2008, 'McGrath breaks off deal with Fianna Fáil', *Irish Times*, 21 October, p. 7.

McManus, J. 2009, 'Governor of Central Bank has raised a few eyebrows', *Irish Times*, 16 March, p. 16.

Mitchell, S. 2008, 'Bailout broker', *Sunday Business Post*, 5 October, viewed 19 April 2009, <http://archives.tcm.ie/businesspost/2008/10/05/story36459.asp>

O'Brien, C. 2008, 'US stocks fall on fears banks will be hit by new credit-market losses', *Irish Times*, 26 January, p. 18.

O'Halloran, B. 2009, 'Anglo board and auditors criticised at EGM, shareholders told Fitzpatrick owed bank a total of €129m in 2007', *Irish Times*, 17 January, p. 8.

O'Malley, E. and Duffy, M. 2009, 'Coping with crisis in public finances', *Irish Times*, 12 March, p. 17.

O'Regan, M. 2009, 'Cowen denies knowing who received Anglo loans', *Irish Times*, 18 February, p. 8.

O'Toole, F. 2009, 'Credibility shredded by mess of Anglo Irish', *Irish Times*, 20 January, p. 14.

Rumford, C. 2002, *The European Union: A political sociology*, Blackwell, Oxford.

Smyth, J. 2008, 'Commissioner wary of guarantee', *Irish Times*, 2 October, p. 8.

7. France: dominant leadership

Natalie Windle

1. Crisis as leadership opportunity

The issue of political leadership in France has drawn a great deal of media and public attention since Nicolas Sarkozy was elected President on 6 May 2007—not least during the French Presidency of the European Union during the second half of 2008. This period saw Sarkozy take the reins of European leadership and acquire the moniker 'Super-Sarko'. Sarkozy's confident and fast-paced leadership not only drove the broad political agenda of the European Union during those six months, it faced the challenge of the heightened severity of the global financial crisis, which initially surfaced in August 2007. Moreover, the catchphrase 'the European Union brings force'[1] rang very true for Sarkozy, whose message was heard more widely when he spoke on behalf of the European Union than when speaking for France alone (Missiroli 2009). The EU platform thus played a significant role in the framing of the global financial crisis in France, especially from Sarkozy's perspective.

On the domestic front, the crisis manifested itself in France most notably from September 2008, triggered by the collapse of the investment firm Lehman Brothers in the United States, which sent shockwaves around the globe. In France, Fortis stock collapsed on 26 September as confidence in its solvency fell and, four days later, the French, Belgian and Luxembourg governments committed €6.4 billion towards the rescue of the bank Dexia. In the 12 months before these events, the sub-prime crisis in the United States had already damaged the international financial sector. In this environment, France had been taking more precautionary measures such as 'the law for economic modernisation',[2] which was aimed primarily at simplifying French small and medium businesses (SMEs).[3] The crisis, however, put such initiatives on hold as more immediate measures were taken to ensure the continued financing of the economy. At the close of 2008, Sarkozy announced a stimulus plan totalling €26.4 billion, to be spent on public investment projects across many sectors within the next year.

In the following analysis of the French elite's rhetoric on the financial crisis, the focus remains on three key actors: the President Nicolas Sarkozy, the Minister for the Economy, Industry and Employment Christine Lagarde, and the Governor of the Banque de France Christian Noyer. All three actors held these offices throughout the period of analysis—April 2008 to March 2009—with Sarkozy and Lagarde taking their posts from the May 2007 election and Noyer being appointed the governor in November 2003. The period of analysis is situated in the early to mid-term of the French electoral cycle, with the next elections due in 2012. The *quinquennat* (five-year term) is relevant to this case study as the longer-term crisis management of the incumbent government will likely be a critical consideration in the 2012 election.

Sarkozy entered his presidency with high popularity ratings, reaching 65 per cent in the first month (*CNN* 2007), indicating confidence in his leadership during 'normal times'. This *phase-two* period is, however, indicative of his leadership capabilities in a time of crisis. The first of President Sarkozy's speeches analysed in this chapter, from 25 September 2008, was referred to by a journalist for *Le Figaro* as 'a speech which incontestably marks the start of the second phase of the five year term'[4] (Jeudy 2008). Sarkozy's leadership is a clear focus of this analysis, which aims to address the beginning of phase two and how it has impacted on public and media opinions.

Box 7.1 France's financial crisis trajectory, April 2008 – March 2009

28 April 2008: Minister for the Economy, Industry and Employment Christine Lagarde, holds a press conference to present a plan for the law of economic modernisation.

13 May: While travelling to Vienna, President Sarkozy reassures artisans and small shopkeepers that the law for economic modernisation will simplify the process of owning your own business. On the broader economic situation, rising prices are not a 'fatality', according to Sarkozy.

15 May: Lagarde congratulates the remarkable resistance of the French economy in the first quarter of 2008, especially the vigour of investments, which are up to 1.8 per cent from 1.2 per cent in the fourth quarter of 2007. The French *produit intérieur brut* (PIB, or gross domestic product [GDP]) progresses to 0.6 per cent in the first quarter of 2008, according to the National Institute of Statistical and Economic Studies (*l'Insee*), which also reviews a rise of 0.2 points on the growth of 2007, to 2.1 per cent.

27 May: A freeze is put on property sales.[5] According to recent figures from the Ministry for Development, sales dropped to 27.9 per cent in one year, between January and March.

29 May: Natixis, the French corporate and investment bank whose primary shareholders are Banque Populaire and Caisse d'Épargne, announces the suppression, in the next 18 months, of 1100 jobs, of which 850 are in France.

2 June: Presentation of the economic modernisation bill to the National Assembly by Finance Minister Lagarde.

11–12 September: EuroFin Conference in Nice, organised under the French EU Presidency and chaired by Lagarde.

26 September: Financial giant Fortis's stock collapses. Fortis is refloated on 29 September by Belgium, the Netherlands and Luxembourg (the Benelux states). BNP Paribas takes control of Fortis in Belgium and Luxembourg for €14.5 billion.

30 September: The governments of Belgium, France and Luxembourg underwrite the rescue of the top-tier retail bank Dexia by subscribing to an increase in capital of €6.4 billion to keep it afloat.

10 October: The French Government promises €320 billion in state-guaranteed lending to banks and €40 billion to recapitalise any bank in difficulty.

12 October: At the initiative of President Sarkozy, Paris adopts the European anti-crisis plan based on the protection of savings, financing the economy and avoiding financial institutions' bankruptcy.

18 October: Sarkozy and José Manuel Barroso, President of the European Commission, meet with US President, George W. Bush, to discuss the redesign of the world's financial structure.

23 October: In a speech at Argonay, Sarkozy announces a meeting of the G20 as well as a new strategic investment fund involving €26 billion of loans, in order to assure the financing of the French PME.

7 November: EU summit is held, at which a common set of principles for reform of the International Monetary Fund (IMF) is agreed on.

20 November: Between 163,000 and 220,000 French teachers and tertiary and high school students protest against the loss of jobs and education reforms.

4 December: Sarkozy announces a stimulus plan to boost the French economy with €26.4 billion (1.3 per cent of GDP) to be spent on public sector investments and loans for France's automotive industry.

6 December: A *Le Monde* opinion poll suggests that 71 per cent of respondents do not believe the Socialist Party has a 'vision' for France. The Socialist Party was struggling to mount an effective response to the crisis.

10 December: After the announcement of a fall in private consumption, a rise in unemployment and a commercial record deficit, Insee reveals a dive of 2.7 per cent in overall industrial production in October.

> **20 January 2009:** Prime Minister, Francois Fillon, announces the government's intention to provide €5–6 billion to aid struggling car manufacturers.
>
> **9 February:** German Chancellor, Angela Merkel, and Sarkozy propose a meeting of the 27 EU member states. Sarkozy announces that two French automobile manufacturers, Renault and PSA Peugeot-Citroen, will receive €6 billion in state loans, on the condition that they do not close factories in France.
>
> **10 February:** Fillon unveils a stimulus package involving 1000 projects across France; 75 per cent of the allotted €26 billion must be spent by the end of 2009.
>
> **24 March:** Sarkozy delivers an address at Saint-Quentin, defending his economic policy and promising to go even further.

2. Methodological considerations

This chapter is designed in line with three key approaches outlined in Chapter 2 of this volume. Specifically, it covers a 12-month period beginning in April 2008, and presents: an interpretation of leaders' speeches addressing the financial crisis; the public and media responses to these speeches; and a crisis-exploitation analysis of the elite actors' framing efforts. President Sarkozy, Minister for the Economy, Industry and Employment, Christine Lagarde, and Banque de France Governor Noyer were selected on the basis of their key roles in managing the crisis. The Prime Minister, Francois Fillon, though a key player in the French Government, was not included in this analysis because his visibility in the crisis was eclipsed by the dominant presence of Sarkozy. The actors' key speeches were then chosen according to the following criteria: focus, audience and response. Each of the key speeches analysed in this study maintained a focus on the financial crisis and was addressed to an audience for whom the crisis was an issue of high importance. They also received a significant amount of coverage in the media, though this was the most true for Sarkozy.

Second, this chapter provides an empirical analysis through media and public responses to the leaders using four daily newspapers and public opinion data. According to popularity and circulation numbers, the three major daily newspapers in France are *Le Monde*, *Le Figaro* and *Libération*, with respective circulations of 440,000, 330,000 and 135,000 (*The Connexion* 2009). A fourth daily newspaper, *Les Echos*, which could be likened to the *Financial Times* and the *Wall Street Journal*, was chosen for its position as a major financial and economics daily, with a circulation of 120,000 (About-France 2009). *Le Monde* was established in 1944 by General Charles de Gaulle and is viewed as a centre-left publication. *Le Figaro* has a much longer history, dating back to 1826, and is a relatively conservative newspaper. *Libération* was founded in 1973 by Jean-Paul Sartre for the 1968 generation, and holds a more socialist position (*The Connexion* 2009).

To measure media responses to the actors' speeches, daily newspapers were referenced and presented according to their (dis)agreement or neutrality towards each leader and how they framed the crisis in terms of causality, severity and policy proposals. In addition to the media response, *Le Figaro-LCI Politoscope*, which published weekly surveys regarding domestic and international political events, was utilised as a resource to gauge French public opinion. The surveys engage 900–1100 people each week, through an online system called Cawi (computer-assisted web interview), and compile the results along with quotas for age, sex, socio-professional category and residential region (*Le Figaro-LCI Politoscope* 2008). Last, by utilising the crisis-exploitation framework and considering contextual factors unique to the French case, this chapter aims to shed light on the unfolding of the French manifestation of the global financial crisis and the framing of the crisis by three key individuals: Nicolas Sarkozy, Christine Lagarde and Christian Noyer.

3. Crisis development and elite rhetoric in France

Nicolas Sarkozy, though originally trained as a barrister with a master's degree in private law, has had a long career in the French Public Service, beginning with his position as Mayor of Neuilly-sur-Seine from 1983 to 2002. During this time, he was also Minister for the Budget (1993–95) and Minister for Communications (1994–95). Sarkozy was elected to his current position as President of the French Republic with 53 per cent of the votes on 6 May 2007. He was the key government voice on the crisis for the French audience, as well as on the European stage while France held the rotational EU Presidency from July to December 2008.

Christine Lagarde rose to senior management positions at the international law firm Baker & McKenzie. In June 2005, she was asked by then French Prime Minister, Dominique de Villepin, to join his government as Minister of Foreign Trade. After a cabinet reshuffle, she became the first woman in a G7 country to hold the post of Finance and Economy Minister (EuroFin 2008). A former head of the French Treasury, Christian Noyer was appointed Vice-President of the European Central Bank (ECB) in 1998. His international experience included work with the European Monetary Committee, the Organisation for Economic Cooperation and Development (OECD), G7 and G10 and positions as alternating governor at the IMF and World Bank. In November 2003, he was appointed Governor of the Banque de France (Banque de France 2004).

25 June 2008: the bank governor's early diagnosis

Noyer's first key address in relation to the global financial crisis came in June 2008. The day before the Banque de France annual report was released, Noyer addressed the General Assembly of the Office of Bank and Financial Coordination. Contextually, this can still be considered the pre-crisis phase in the French economy. The symptoms of the sub-prime crisis had remained largely contained to the United States and the United Kingdom, although its effects had been seeping through the international financial sector.

Noyer defined the cause of the problems as mismanagement of the system. 'This situation originated in a general perception that investment opportunities in assets, apparently of good quality, were almost unlimited, and this altered the judgement of actors'[6] . In this speech, Noyer proposed 'an ensemble of good practices'[7] more than specific policy proposals. For example, he affirmed the importance of the role of governance in terms of managing risk, as well as conveying that the banks that were best equipped to respond to challenges were those that invested early in developing evaluation and control procedures and developed their knowledge of the risks inherent in complex products. The media response to this address was largely neutral towards Noyer's framing of the crisis and his leadership, although there was some disagreement with his portrayal of the severity of the crisis (Table 7.1). An article in *Le Figaro* expressed this disagreement, saying 'even though on the stock exchange, banks have been seriously mismanaged, the Bank Commission wants to be more optimistic'[8] (Bohineust 2008).

	Causality	Severity	Proposals	Support for speaker
Agrees	1		2	
Disagrees		2		
No comment/ neutral	5	4	4	6

Table 7.1 Media response to Noyer's 25 June 2008 speech

25 September 2008: Sarkozy's Toulon address

President Sarkozy's address at Toulon in September 2008 came on the heels of the collapse of Lehman Brothers in the United States. This event was a watershed event in the financial crisis. In France, this marked the escalation of the national crisis. Sarkozy's approach at Toulon was twofold: he highlighted the uniqueness of the crisis and he made a call for a new international financial order. From the outset, Sarkozy labelled the crisis 'a crisis of confidence without precedent'.[9] He did, however, make a reference to the depression of the 1930s, noting the current crisis had seen no equivalent since. The majority of the population—those under the age of seventy—had not experienced the 1930s depression, so Sarkozy effectively conveyed the uniqueness of this crisis as the first of its kind in most peoples' lifetimes. After this introduction, Sarkozy highlighted the pitfalls of the system that caused the crisis. 'The financial crisis is not the crisis of capitalism. It is the crisis of a system which did away with the most fundamental values of capitalism, which in some sense, betrayed the spirit of capitalism'.[10]

According to Sarkozy, capitalism had allowed the rise of the West throughout seven decades, but a betrayal of capitalist values had emerged. Having established its corruption as the fundamental cause of the crisis, Sarkozy proposed the reform of capitalism, because 'anticapitalism does not offer any solution to the actual crisis'[11]. Sarkozy's plan for a new equilibrium between the market and the State started with the regulation of the banks and controlled remuneration. He insisted that the severity of the crisis was substantial, labelling it the end of the post-Cold War capitalist world.

This address is vital to understanding Sarkozy's framing of the crisis because he illustrates the situation in terms of its exceptionality. Effectively, his message was that in an exceptional case, one called for an exceptional response. The media responded to this address with overall support for Sarkozy, but also with some concern about his policy proposals (Table 7.2). Most notably, the media acknowledged the significance of this speech. *Le Figaro* referred to it as 'the day when Sarkozy called for mobilisation against the crisis'[12] (Jeudy and Visot 2008). *Les Echos* mirrored this perspective, saying, 'Nicolas Sarkozy's discourse pronounced at Toulon on 25 September marks his entry into the war against the crisis'[13] (Cornudet 2008). The Toulon address was undoubtedly Sarkozy's first attempt at crisis exploitation in the face of a financial crisis that had worsened in the national economy.

Libération called Sarkozy's 'classic allocution' *messianique* in his wish to be heard by the French, who feared for their economy (Guiral 2008). This fear was real, as demonstrated by a poll conducted by Ifop on 18–19 September, which indicated that 81 per cent of French respondents were concerned about the French economy in the financial crisis (Angus Reid Global Monitor 2008). Sarkozy's attempt at crisis framing in the Toulon address failed to reassure the concerned French public, as evidenced by a CSA survey published in the newspaper *Le Parisien* on 28 September, which showed that 51 per cent of those surveyed did not have confidence in Sarkozy to reduce the impact of the crisis in France (*Les Echos* 2008).

	Causality	Severity	Policy proposals	Support for speaker
Agrees	1	7	2	6
Disagrees		1	5	3
No comment/ neutral	8	1	2	

Table 7.2 Media response to Sarkozy's 25 September 2008 speech

26 September 2008: Finance Minister Lagarde's budget speech

One of Lagarde's first public speeches after the manifestation of the crisis in France was delivered ahead of the upcoming budget for 2009. From the outset, Lagarde looked past the short term and framed the crisis beyond 2008–09. She noted that 'the plan for programming public finance effectively brings us to 2012'[14]. This foresight acknowledged the severity of the crisis at hand, which demonstrated that Lagarde's was not a type-1 'business-as-usual' frame, but rather a type-2 frame of crisis acknowledgment.

Lagarde maintained a matter-of-fact tone throughout this speech, conveying the grim financial projections but simultaneously reassuring that the eurozone was better situated than the US economy. With this comparison with the United States, Lagarde defined the crisis as one without precedent and also accounted for its origins in the US financial sector. 'The turbulences endured by international financial markets over the past year reflect the consequences of a deep purge of the American financial sector'[15]. Lagarde outlined the various proposals of the French Government for the five-year period to 2012, which included structural reforms for employment policy (targeted at employment candidates, seniors and youth), buying power, economic modernisation and a tripling of the research tax credit (CIR).

The media response to Lagarde's presentation of the 2009 budget was focused primarily on public deficit figures and proposed policy, and there was neither support nor opposition expressed towards Lagarde herself (Table 7.3). There was implicit agreement with the severity of the crisis and its impact on the budget. For example, an article in *Le Figaro* agreed that the financial crisis had weakened the French economy. 'The financial crisis which has raged for one year has finally impacted the global economy and provoked a net slowdown in France'[16] (Lachevre and Visot 2008a).

One particular policy proposal that was criticised in the representative media response was related to civil servants. *Le Monde* stated that '30 600 jobs would be done away with in the public service compared to 20 900 in 2008. This is a little less than the promise of not replacing one for every two civil servants who leave for retirement'[17] (Lachevre and Visot 2008a). This argument was well founded in the context of uncertainty about rising unemployment and it also brought to the fore the credibility of the government by questioning its commitment to its promises. On the whole, the media response to Lagarde's presentation of the budget was critical of the government's approach to the weakened economic conditions in France, but paid little attention to Lagarde herself.

	Causality	Severity	Policy proposals	Support for speaker
Agrees		4	1	
Disagrees			3	
No comment/ neutral	4			4

Table 7.3 Media response to Lagarde's 26 September 2008 speech

15 October 2008: Lagarde presenting a recovery plan

Lagarde's next key address was delivered to the Senate and was titled 'National plan for assuring the financing of the economy and restoring confidence'.[18] In the opening lines of this address, Lagarde defined the financial crisis in the following terms: 'the crisis through which we are living is excessive.'[19] This crisis of excess was explained by four factors: the excess of speculation, the excess of credit in the United States, the excess of complexity in which the financial profession lost control of the tools it created and the excess of irrationality and panic on the stock exchange.

Lagarde then proceeded to outline the government's proposal for management of the crisis. The proposal was threefold: first, the creation of a society of refinancing whereby funds would be raised with a state guarantee; second, the possibility of the State reinforcing the equity capital of French banks; and third, the Dexia guarantee in cooperation with Belgium and Luxembourg. On the first point, Lagarde made note of a marked contrast with the plan proposed by US Treasury Secretary, Henry Paulson, saying 'our proposal is completely opposite to the Paulson plan...the American state proposes to take control of the worst assets...in France, the state will not buy the assets. It will loan to the banks.'[20] This contrast was paramount in Lagarde's greater narrative, which insisted that France remained in a better financial position than many other nations, especially the United States.

The media response to Lagarde's 15 October speech was similar to that to her 26 September address in terms of the focus on government policy, rather than on Lagarde herself. Lagarde was effectively viewed as the representative or spokeswoman for a larger decision-making body. Most notable among the media responses illustrated in Table 7.4, *Le Figaro* conveyed agreement with the proposed policy because it would go a step further than other plans adopted in Europe and the United States: 'French measures can serve to achieve two purposes by helping business to refinance themselves in the mid-term'[21] (Lachevre 2008).

	Causality	Severity	Policy proposals	Support for speaker
Agrees		1	1	
Disagrees			2	
No comment/ neutral	3	2		3

Table 7.4 Media response to Lagarde's 15 October 2008 speech

21 October 2008: Noyer's struggle to be heard

Christian Noyer delivered a noteworthy address titled 'Reflections on the crisis' in October 2008. In the months since his address to the General Assembly of the Coordination Office, Noyer had been curiously absent from the public eye.

After this gap in public presence, Noyer continued his framing of the crisis at an address to the Crédit Agricole Congress on 21 October. According to Noyer, at this time, there were two certainties about the crisis: it would impact on the economy in the long term and it was defined as a crisis of liquidity. Noyer directed the focus away from the government's leadership, towards the role of central banks, which effectively stood 'in the front line'[22] during the combat. Noyer organised his speech around four themes: the nature of the crisis, the policies put in place to manage it, the macroeconomic perspectives and financial regulation perspectives. On the last two themes, he reinforced that the fall in confidence was not centred on France, and he promoted the value of a deep knowledge of the banking sector, not only at the microeconomic level but in terms of limiting risk across the entire global system. His overarching message maintained that French banks were solid and profitable and he demonstrated support for Sarkozy's push to organise Europe's crisis response.[23]

After his address at Nice, Noyer was presented by *Le Monde* as a timid figure in the shadow of Sarkozy, with the paper saying he was 'inaudible in a room of 100 people'[24] (Bacqué 2008). This was one of the very few articles that focused on the personality and leadership of Noyer himself, as most of the media and public attention was engaged with policies in the banking sector rather than its key actors (Table 7.5). Overall, there was more opinion on France's banking policy than on the governor himself (Ganiko 2009). The article in *Le Monde* on 24 October detailed Noyer's background and provided a very positive character reference as well as crediting Noyer with the plan for the bank guarantees.

	Causality	Severity	Policy proposals	Support for speaker
Agrees				1
Disagrees			2	1
No comment/ neutral	4	4	2	2

Table 7.5 Media response to Noyer's 21 October 2008 speech

23 October 2008: Sarkozy's Argonay address

One month after his Toulon address—and also subsequent to the Dexia rescue on 30 September 2008 by the French, Belgian and Luxembourg governments—Sarkozy delivered a key speech at Argonay. Conveying the truth to the French people was the dominant theme of his speech. Sarkozy reiterated the exceptional circumstances, also confirming that it was a global and not a French, or European, crisis. This effectively exogenised the cause and origin of the crisis. Building on his speech at Toulon in September, Sarkozy pinpointed responsibility for the crisis to the faults and errors of financial institutions. In advancing his declaration of the end of the post-Cold War capitalist world, which was introduced in his Toulon discourse, Sarkozy announced that 'without doubt, this crisis will mark the true start of the twenty-first century, the moment when everyone will understand that it was time to change'[25] . At Argonay, Sarkozy proposed the need for moralisation, transparency and protection. He announced a new strategic investment fund of €26 billion, the appointment of Réné Ricol to the position of National Credit Mediator and structural reforms such as opening businesses on Sundays.

In this speech, Sarkozy framed the responsibility for the crisis as lying outside France, but he accepted the responsibility of the French State to respond to it, and to act sooner rather than later. He continued to advocate the idea of a summit, in the form of a new Bretton Woods, thus reinforcing his commitment to fundamental changes to the global financial system. Table 7.6 demonstrates a similar media response to that of the speech at Toulon, with slightly more agreement with his policy proposals and a majority of overall support for Sarkozy. *Le Monde* illustrated such support for Sarkozy, saying that 'it remains that the style of Nicolas Sarkozy, sometimes disparaged, has played more in his favour' and quoted a German diplomat who said 'during a crisis, hyperactivity becomes energy, arrogance becomes tenacity, unpredictability becomes pragmatism'[26] (Ferenczi 2008). This demonstrated a sense of public support for Sarkozy's leadership in a time of crisis.

	Causality	Severity	Policy proposals	Support for speaker
Agrees		1	5	6
Disagrees			3	2
No comment/ neutral	10	9	2	2

Table 7.6 Media response to Sarkozy's 23 October 2008 speech

4 December 2008: Sarkozy's Douai address

Sarkozy's third key speech was delivered at Douai, where he affirmed that the crisis was not a passing phenomenon. In this address, he also envisaged a longer-term framing of the crisis and proposed how France would emerge from it. In explaining the protracted nature of the global financial crisis, Sarkozy acknowledged the looming problem of higher unemployment: 'it is unemployment that strikes up the crisis of confidence which precedes the economic crisis.'[27] This framed the crisis as a chain of events. The address focused on government measures, especially in the explanation of the €26 billion stimulus plan. The stimulus was to be spent on public sector investments and loans for the French automotive industry, which employed, directly or indirectly, 10 per cent of the working population. Sarkozy portrayed this 'massive investment plan'[28] as a historic responsibility to remake France in terms of infrastructure, universities and research.

The media response to the Douai address continues the pattern of the response to Sarkozy's other speeches. Table 7.7 demonstrates overall support for Sarkozy, but slightly higher disagreement with his policy proposals. Two journalists for *Le Figaro* called the policy proposal in this speech 'an arsenal of anti-crisis measures'[29] (Lachevre and Visot 2008b).

	Causality	Severity	Policy proposals	Support for speaker
Agrees		1	3	5
Disagrees		1	4	2
No comment/ neutral	8	6	1	1

Table 7.7 Media response to Sarkozy's 4 December 2008 speech

13 January 2009: Lagarde's optimism for the New Year

Lagarde's 2009 New Year address was more reflective than her previous speeches. It conveyed optimism for the year ahead. There appeared to be a deliberate absence of explanation and accounting for the crisis in this address in order to focus on asserting the success of crisis management to date, as well as on future plans. As such, with the early manifestation of the crisis behind her, Lagarde outlined four reasons for hope in 2009, including positive economic signs such as inflation coming down again to 1.6 per cent in November 2008, even though it had gone as high as 3.6 per cent in July 2008. Other reasons were the induction of a new administration in the United States led by President, Barack Obama, and Secretary of the Treasury, Timothy Geithner; Europe retaining the unity and international standing it had gained under the French presidency; and the government's actions, such as the stimulus plan. There was little discussion of Lagarde's New Year address in the papers analysed in this chapter, suggesting just how much of the media spotlight on this matter was focused on Sarkozy. Where reports were found, there was little disagreement with Lagarde's framing of the crisis (Table 7.8).

	Causality	Severity	Policy proposals	Support for speaker
Agrees		1		2
Disagrees			1 (implicitly)	
No comment/ neutral	2	1	1	

Table 7.8 Media response to Lagarde's 13 January 2009 speech

21 January 2009: Noyer's strategies for French and European finance

Noyer delivered his address 'Global financial crisis: public and private strategies in response to the crisis'[30] in the United Arab Emirates, on 21 January 2009. This was a key speech, as Noyer readdressed two key themes of the crisis—its nature and the policies in response to it—and delivered it in an international location. In this speech, Noyer simplified the definition of the crisis. He called it a crisis of liquidity that began in August 2007 and moved to affect the economy on a large scale. Noyer noted that, in addition to a crisis of liquidity, it was also a crisis of securitisation, where the packaging of debt into a financial product, for the purpose of rating and trading, did not discriminate against bad debt. After this, Noyer provided a further explanation of the crisis by describing how the instability of financial structures had been concealed and the chain reaction this had initiated. According to Noyer, there were two fundamental realities: first, responsibility for the crisis was concentrated in the hands of financial institutions; and second, in order to remedy the consequences of this, structural innovation was necessary. Having established the causes, and thereby the responsibility for the crisis in the financial sector, Noyer ushered in the role of the State. According to him, the State held the responsibility to modify the policy budget, which in turn would restart the economic machine. Noyer referred, in addition to the French domestic economy, to a wider plan for Europe, especially in light of the French EU Presidency. The media response to Noyer's address largely ignored his framing of the causes of the crisis and his overall leadership, although there was some disagreement about his severity framing and the policies that his speech put forward.

	Causality	Severity	Policy proposals	Support for speaker
Agrees		1 (implicitly)	2 (implicitly)	1
Disagrees		1	1	
No comment/ neutral	4	2	1	3

Table 7.9 Media response to Noyer's 21 January 2009 speech

24 March 2009: Sarkozy's Saint-Quentin address

At Saint-Quentin, Aisne, Sarkozy delivered the last key speech during this chapter's 12-month period of analysis. In this address, Sarkozy referred to values and morality while reiterating that this was an unprecedented crisis. A notable departure from his earlier speeches was evident in the explicit reference to public opinion, which had manifested in protests through early 2009. Sarkozy acknowledged this dissent, saying, 'my task is to listen to those who protest, but I also have the responsibility to listen to those who do not march in protest'.[31] It is in this speech that one can perceive the type-3 framing at play. Sarkozy claimed that the crisis gave new freedoms to think, to imagine, to act and to invent France's future. In even more straightforward terms, Sarkozy affirmed that 'it is necessary to benefit from the crisis'.[32] Sarkozy insisted, however, that in order to realise these freedoms and opportunities, everyone had a moral responsibility, including himself.

Table 7.10 demonstrates that, despite continuing public protests and declining popularity ratings, there was still overall support for Sarkozy in the media. In the context of the speech at Saint-Quentin, *Libération* posed the question: 'What to say to reassure a public opinion which repudiates him in the opinion polls? Speak of values and landmarks'[33] (Guiral 2009b).

In contrast with earlier media responses, some articles after this speech took electoral issues into consideration; 'to have his nose on the crisis does not prevent him having an eye on his campaign promises and the presidential election of 2012'[34] (Cornudet 2009). With the 2012 election in mind, other articles discussed the post-crisis era.

After Toulon in September at the start of the crisis, Douai in December on the stimulus plan, Saint-Quentin is supposed to open perspectives on the post-crisis. All of these speeches are small stones scattered on the path which will take Sarkozy back to the Elysée in 2012.[35] (Guiral 2009a)

	Causality	Severity	Policy proposals	Support for speaker
Agrees		4	4	10
Disagrees			1	
No comment/ neutral	10	6	5	

Table 7.10 Media response to Sarkozy's 24 March 2009 speech

4. Framing the financial crisis in France: analysis and discussion

The very central role of Sarkozy aside, the three actors assumed markedly different roles in the framing of the financial crisis. On the whole, however, there was little disagreement between their crisis rhetoric. The French leaders paid little attention to the cause of the crisis, which was explained by the consequences of the US sub-prime crisis in a highly globalised economy, and this explanation was questioned to a minimal extent, if at all, by the media and the public. Rather, the framing contest in France was centred on the severity of the crisis and the proposed measures and changes to policy.

Sarkozy's key speeches during the 12-month period of analysis until 31 March 2009 maintained the underlying themes of opportunism and a break with the past. The public response to Sarkozy's framing of the crisis fluctuated between support and opposition. While one could infer that the French population eagerly accepted Sarkozy's call for a new international financial order, it is necessary, however, to consider the socialist opposition to fully understand the public response to Sarkozy and his crisis framing. As one academic commented: 'A crisis in global capitalism provides the French political left with a blessed opportunity to rebuild its strength in a country traditionally uneasy about so many tenets of the free market ideology and always prone to revert to state-centred solutions' (Charnoz 2008:1). The political left in France, however, was not able to mount a convincing or popular response to Sarkozy, especially because the Parti Socialiste (PS) had recently been undergoing leadership changes.

Le Figaro-LCI survey for the week ending 27 November asked respondents: 'In your opinion, if she was in power would Martine Aubry [the newly elected leader of the PS] do better, worse or neither better nor worse than Nicolas Sarkozy?' Twenty-four per cent of respondents said Aubry would do better, 31 per cent thought she would do worse and 44 per cent said neither better nor worse (*Le Figaro-LCI Politoscope* 2008:15). In comparison with his nearest competitor, therefore, Sarkozy was viewed by some margin as doing a 'better job'. In a later *Le Figaro-LCI* survey, on 26 March 2009, respondents were questioned specifically about Sarkozy's crisis leadership. Only 46 per cent of respondents said they had confidence in Sarkozy in facing the crisis (*Le Figaro-LCI Politoscope* 2009:10).

The media response to Lagarde's framing of the global financial crisis was more difficult to determine compared with that of Sarkozy. Lagarde appeared to play more of a spokeswoman role than participating actively in framing or crisis exploitation. Her role was described as that of a 'back office executive' (de Buttet 2009). The limited visibility of Lagarde's rhetoric in the media places greater weight on public opinion data in order to analyse the response to her crisis framing. Although French public opinion of Lagarde was generally quite favourable, she won greater respect abroad than at home, where her reputation came under increasing attack. A key point of contention was her (with hindsight cavalier) suggestion that 'the big risk is behind us' (*The Economist* 2008), even though financial markets were continuing to fall at the time.

There was disparity, however, between the media response and public opinion data, because according to *Paris-Match* ratings in October 2008, Lagarde's popularity jumped by 5 points to 46 per cent, at a time when Sarkozy's rating remained at 44 per cent (*The Economist* 2008). Shortly after her key speech in early 2009, Lagarde's rating rose to 52 per cent in February, seemingly exempting her from the otherwise growing public dissatisfaction (*TF1* 2009).

Overall, the public's opinion of Christian Noyer was best exemplified by his presence, or lack thereof, in the French media. Tables 7.1, 7.5 and 7.9 demonstrate no comment or neutrality in most of the media responses after Noyer's key speeches. Noyer is for the most part not a visible public figure, especially in comparison with Sarkozy. This can be attributed to two main factors. There was the prominent presence of Sarkozy and the strong public interest in all aspects of his energetic leadership style, especially during the French EU Presidency. On the other hand, the role and visibility of Banque de France had diminished significantly after the creation of the ECB (de Buttet 2009). In effect, there was more public interest in French, and European, banking policy than in the central bank governor himself.

In France, the government's crisis-exploitation efforts were characterised largely by type-3 opportunism and a concerted attempt to combine short and long-term management strategies. During the global financial crisis, the attempt to alter levels of political support in France was focused primarily on public policies, situated in the bigger picture of policy reform. Effectively, a 'crisis as opportunity' approach prevailed in Sarkozy's rhetoric in particular. This crisis framing, however, must also be considered explicitly within the context of three key distinctive features of the French case: French public opinion and political culture; the lack of significant political opposition; and the wider context of the crisis on the European, even global, stage.

French political culture: public opinion and state structure

French political culture is unique in terms of its state–citizen relationship and has strong historical undertones that have continued to influence French politics throughout the crisis period. According to David Bell (2002:15), 'The French state plays a much larger part in civil society (in both economics and social life) than in some other countries. The state has provided a continuity in the life of the nation and that has not been seriously challenged in the past.' The national leaders' framing and utilisation of the crisis cannot be analysed in isolation from the deep-seated traditions of French political culture, particularly with regard to public opinion and the structure of the State. Policy proposals and state actions were publicly questioned early in 2009 by way of unseasonal protests as the crisis began to take hold at an increasingly individual level. The French tendency to protest is considered quite normal, but it follows a routine whereby the months that flank summer—May and September—tend to be the peak of the protest season (Ganiko 2009). Nicholas Bavarez, an economic commentator, gave a succinct explanation of this culture, referring historically to the Jacquerie uprising of 1358, and conclusively classifying recurrent revolts and violence as epitomising French exceptionalism[36] (*The Economist* 2009b).

In addition to protest, the structure of the French State was a crucial contextual factor, which influenced how the global financial crisis played out in France. France responds badly to economic shocks partly because of a lack of civic institutions below the State (*The Economist* 2009b). The highly centralised system of governance therefore did not translate into comprehensive crisis management.

Moreover, concern about unemployment, which prompted the winter protests (especially in the automotive industry, which at the time employed up to 10 per cent of the working population), was influenced by the pre-crisis labour structure. France's two-tier labour market overly protected permanent jobs and thus encouraged companies to hire most workers on flexible short-term contracts. Once the crisis hit, it was these non-permanent jobs that were being shed (*The Economist* 2009a). This labour structure sparked the public's concern about rising unemployment and the State's inability to alleviate this. In the context of French political culture and the history of protesting, the public response to the global financial crisis was manifested in public protests. Therefore, French political culture—particularly the relationship between public opinion and the structure of the State—was one of the major contextual factors that influenced leaders' framing of and the public response to the global financial crisis.

A lack of political opposition

Sarkozy's, and to a lesser extent Lagarde's, success in crisis framing was made possible by a chronic lack of politically credible counter-frames. This issue, although noticeable in the leaders' speeches, became evident through deeper analysis of the media response and public opinion data. The crisis-exploitation framework set out in Chapter 2 proposes that there are two spheres of a framing contest: the political sphere and the policy sphere. In the French case, however, a political contest was almost non-existent at the time. As a non-political actor, Noyer was by definition not part of the political crisis-exploitation game from the outset. On the other hand, Sarkozy and Lagarde had political careers potentially at stake. The Parti Socialiste, however, the key opposition party, failed to mount a response to the framing of the crisis by Sarkozy and Lagarde. Therefore, it is the policy crisis-exploitation matrix that is most relevant to the French case (cf. Table 2.2, Chapter 2).

According to 'the policy game' and taking into consideration the opportunism of the type-3 frame, French leadership projected an image of itself as an advocate for change, rhetorically pressing for a policy paradigm shift, but in fact implementing incremental change, at least in the short to mid-term. The crisis-exploitation framework also proposes that

> change-oriented players have to decide whether they feel that the crisis has created the need and the opportunity to press for a wholesale overturning of the policy's ideological and/or intellectual underpinnings…or whether to momentarily content themselves with advocating more incremental changes. (Boin et al. 2009:90)

Public opinion, especially visible in the unusually high number of protests in the winter months, forced Sarkozy and Lagarde to turn their attention towards the everyday difficulties increasingly faced by the French population. This, at least momentarily, made a 'policy paradigm shift' less desirable.

Consequently, the grand agenda for change, exemplified by the pre-crisis movement for the 'the law for economic modernisation'[37] as well as Sarkozy's call in September 2008 for a new international financial order, was contested by status quo players in particular change-averse, protest-minded segments of public opinion. The policy game in France can therefore be situated in box IV of 'the policy game'—negotiated incremental adjustment.

France in a truly global financial crisis

Following the crisis-exploitation framework, type-3 frames attempt to endogenise a crisis—to find fault in the present system and call for change (see Chapter 2, this volume). The French case study is consistent with this frame to the extent that the key players identified faults at the systemic level. At the same time, however, the key players exogenised the responsibility issue by using the crisis to establish that the French State was not to blame. In terms of causality and responsibility, there was little or no disagreement across the leaders' speeches and the public response. There was seamless consistency between Sarkozy, Lagarde and Noyer, each of whom named the origins of the crisis in the US sub-prime crisis. In effect, their narrative emphasised the global level, portraying the French economy as mired in a financial system that, as Sarkozy highlighted, had betrayed the values of capitalism.

With the benefit of holding the EU Presidency at a critical time, Sarkozy moved beyond his national platform in framing the crisis. He pushed the initiative for a global conference of the G20 nations, which was realised in November 2008 in Washington, DC, and followed up by the summit in London in early April 2009. His approach to leading the financial crisis at the regional European level did not, however, meet with great enthusiasm in other EU member states, as evidenced by the German Finance Minister, who 'clearly opposed the principle of "international macroeconomic regulation", a line that seemed to open the way for the French idea of a European economic government' (Charnoz 2008:2). This suggests that there was an underlying French agenda to push for greater economic integration in the European Union.

Once again, the political culture of France is highly relevant here—in particular, the French *dirigiste* tradition. 'The *dirigiste* outlook currently goes against the grain of globalisation and free market fashions everywhere else in the Western world. There has, as with other Western societies, been a withdrawal of the state since the 1980s but not to the same extent as elsewhere' (Bell 2002:15). The *dirigiste* tradition came to the fore in this crisis period. 'Despite calls from the Americans to do more to lift consumer demand, [the French] stimulus plan relies heavily on front-loading investment in infrastructure…in line with their *dirigiste* tradition' (*The Economist* 2009c). This tradition not only reinforces the uniqueness of the French State, it demonstrates the differences between the crisis responses in the major economies of the world.

Sarkozy's combined French and EU leadership during the early crisis invites an interesting analysis of his personal leadership style that can be touched on only briefly in this chapter. Sarkozy's framing of the crisis was wrought with wider policy and political implications. Moreover, Sarkozy projected an unfaltering confidence in his own persuasive abilities. Complementary to this, Lagarde maintained an optimistic demeanour across her key speeches and Noyer consistently maintained support for government policy proposals. According to McLennan (2009:2), one of the key rules in crisis leadership is confidence before realism; leaders who succeed in times of crisis outwardly radiate confidence, plan contingencies and 'push forward with their gut instinct'. Sarkozy certainly fit that bill during the period studied here.

The French case study suggests that national leaders' crisis framing, as well as the public response to this, cannot be viewed in isolation from its political context. French political culture, a lack of political opposition and the EU and global platforms provided a valuable complement to the crisis-exploitation analysis. In sum, national contextual factors, individual leadership style and crisis opportunism shaped French crisis management in a truly global financial crisis.

References

About-France 2009, 'The French press: the dailies', *About-France*, viewed 27 April 2009, <http://about-france.com/french-newspapers.htm>

Angus Reid Global Monitor 2008, 'French clearly worried about financial crisis', *Angus Reid Global Monitor*, 28 September, viewed 27 April 2009, <http://www.angus-reid.com/polls/view/french_clearly_worried_about_financial_crisis/>

Bacqué, R. 2008, 'Christian Noyer Banquier antistress', *Le Monde*, 24 October.

Banque de France 2004, *Organisational Structure: Christian Noyer's biography*, Banque de France, viewed 26 May 2009, <http://www.banque-france.fr/gb/instit/orga/noyer.htm>

Bell, D. S. 2002, *French Politics Today*, Manchester University Press, Manchester.

Bohineust, A. 2008, 'Le gendarme des banques appelle a la vigilance', *Le Figaro*, 27 June.

Boin, A., 't Hart, P. and McConnell, A. 2009, 'Crisis exploitation: political and policy impacts of framing contests', *Journal of European Public Policy*, vol. 16, no. 1, pp. 81–106.

Charnoz, O. 2008, 'A French perspective on the financial crisis', in J. Kirton (ed.), *The G20 Leaders Summit on Financial Markets and the Global Economy*, University of Toronto, Toronto, viewed 30 May 2009, <http://www.g20.utoronto.ca/g20leadersbook/index.html>

Chavigné, J.-J. 2008, 'Chronologie de la crise financière 2007–2008', *Democratie-Socialisme.org*, 6 October, viewed 30 April 2009, <http://www.democratie-socialisme.org/spip.php?article1643>

CNN 2007, 'French kiss, lunches hinder reform', *CNN*, 30 May, viewed 31 May 2009, <http://www.cnn.com/2007/WORLD/europe/05/30/france.lunches.reut/index.html>

Connexion 2009, 'French media read all about it', *The Connexion*, November, viewed 27 April 2009, <http://www.connexionfrance.com/expatriate-news-article.php?art=276>

Cornudet, C. 2008, 'Les dessous d'une préparation au cordeau', *Les Echos*, 4 December.

Cornudet, C. 2009, 'L'œil rivé sur 2012, Nicolas Sarkozy refuse de se laisser dévier par la crise', *Les Echos*, 24 March.

de Buttet, G. 2009, Telephone interview with author, 18 May.

Economist 2008, 'On Lagarde', *The Economist*, 23 October.

Economist 2009a, 'A time of troubles and protest', *The Economist*, 22 January.

Economist 2009b, 'Super-Sarko falls to earth', *The Economist*, 16 April.

Economist 2009c, 'Vive la difference!', *The Economist*, 7 May.

Economist Intelligence Unit 2009, 'Economist Intelligence Unit monthly reports on France', *The Economist*, September 2008 – March 2009, viewed 27 April 2009, <http://www.eiu.com>

EuroFin 2008, 'Speaker's CVs: Lagarde', *EuroFin*, EuroFin Conference, Nice, 11–12 September, viewed 26 May 2009, <http://www.emcnet.eu/doc/WEBSITE%20CVs/LAGARDE.pdf>

Ferenczi, T. 2008, 'Nicolas Sarkozy, un président pour temps de crise?', *Le Monde*, 24 October.

Ganiko, I. Telephone interview with author, 5 May 2009.

Guiral, A. 2008, 'Le laisser-faire, c'est fini', *Libération*, 26 September.

Guiral, A. 2009a, 'Sarkozy vend sa pilule du lendemain qui chante à Saint-Quentin', *Libération* , 24 March.

Guiral, A. 2009b, 'Reportage: Nicolas Sarkozy en mission diversion', *Libération*, 25 March.

Jeudy, B. 2008, 'Nicolas Sarkozy veut "refonder le capitalisme"', *Le Figaro*, 26 September.

Jeudy, B. and Visot, M. 2008, 'Relance: comment Sarkozy prépare son plan', *Le Figaro*, 2 December.

Lachevre, C. 2008, 'Le plan de soutien français bien reçu des économistes', *Le Figaro*, 16 October.

Lachevre, C. and Visot, M. 2008a, 'Un budget "de crise" pour 2009 marque par le creusement des déficits et l'austérité', *Le Figaro*, 27 September.

Lachevre, C. and Visot, M. 2008b, 'La relance massive de Nicolas Sarkozy', *Le Figaro*, 4 December.

Lagarde, C. 2008a, Projet de loi de finances pour 2009, Speech, 26 September, viewed 29 May 2009, <http://www.budget.gouv.fr/discours-presse/discours-communiques_budget.php?type=discours&id=619&rub=>

Lagarde, C. 2008b, Plan national pour assurer le financement de l'économie et restaurer la confiance, Speech, 15 October, viewed 29 May 2009, <http://www.budget.gouv.fr/discours-presse/ discours-communiques_budget.php?type=discours&id=623&rub=>

Lagarde, C. 2009, Voeux a la presse, Speech, 13 January, viewed 29 May 2009, <http://www.budget.gouv.fr/discours-presse/ discours-communiques_budget.php?type=discours&id=644&rub=>

Le Figaro-LCI Politoscope 2008, 'Season 3, wave 13', 27 November, viewed 9 May 2009, <www.lefigaro.fr/assets/pdf/oway27nov.pdf>

Le Figaro-LCI Politoscope 2009, 'Season 3, wave 27', 26 March, viewed 9 May 2009, <http://www.opinion-way.com/pdf/lefigaro-lci-politoscope-saison3vague27.pdf>

Les Echos 2008, 'Crise financière: Gueant légèrement plus rassurant que Sarkozy', *Les Echos*, 29 September.

McLennan, K. 2009, 'Neuroscience and evolutionary psychology assist our leadership minds as we respond to the global financial crisis', *Leadership Reflections*, February, Heidrick & Struggles Leadership Consulting, Sydney.

Missiroli, A. 2009, Europe: the state of the union, Address given at the National Europe Centre, The Australian National University, Canberra, 22 April.

Noyer, C. 2008a, Assemblée générale de l'Office de Coordination bancaire et financière, Speech, 25 June, viewed 29 May 2009, <http://www.banquedefrance.fr/fr/instit/telechar/discours/2008/ disc20080625.pdf>

Noyer, C. 2008b, Réflexions sur la crise, Speech, 21 October, viewed 9 May 2009, <http://www.banque-france.fr/fr/instit/telechar/discours/2008/ disc20081020.pdf>

Noyer, C. 2009, Crise financière mondiale: stratégies publiques et privées pour faire face à la crise, Speech, 21 January, viewed 9 May 2009, <http://www.banque-france.fr/fr/instit/telechar/discours/2009/ disc20090123.pdf>

Sarkozy, N. 2008a, Discours de M. le Président de la République au Zénith de Toulon, Speech, 25 September, viewed 9 May 2009, <www.elysee.fr/download/?mode=press&filename= 29.09_Discours_Toulon_du_30.pdf>

Sarkozy, N. 2008b, Discours de M. le Président de la République, Argonay, Haute-Savoie, Speech, 23 October, viewed 9 May 2009, <www.elysee.fr/download/?mode=press&filename=argonay.pdf>

Sarkozy, N. 2008c, Plan de relance de l'économie francaise, Speech, 4 December, viewed 9 May 2009,
    <www.elysee.fr/download/?mode=press&filename=04.12_DOUAI.pdf>

Sarkozy, N. 2009, Discours de M. le Président de la République à Saint-Quentin, Speech, 24 March, viewed 9 May 2009,
    <http://www.elysee.fr/documents/index.php?mode=view&lang=fr&cat_id=7&press_id=2463>

TF1 2009, 'Lagarde épargnée par la crise', *TF1*, 10 February, viewed 29 May 2009, <http://tf1.lci.fr/infos/france/politique/
0,,4253136,00-lagarde-epargnee-par-la-crise-.html>

Endnotes

[1] 'L'Union fait la force.'

[2] 'Le loi pour le modernisation de l'économie.'

[3] Petites et Moyennes Entreprises.

[4] 'Un discours qui marque incontestablement le début de la phase 2 du quinquennat.'

[5] 'Coup de froid.'

[6] 'Cette situation a été à l'origine d'une généralisation de la perception selon laquelle les opportunités d'investissement dans des actifs apparemment de bonne qualité étaient quasi illimitées et a altéré le jugement des acteurs.'

[7] 'Un ensemble de bonnes pratiques.'

[8] 'Alors qu'en Bourse les Banques étaient sérieusement malmenées hier, la Commission bancaire…se voulait plutôt optimiste.'

[9] 'Une crise de confiance sans précédent.'

[10] 'La crise financière…n'est pas la crise du capitalisme. C'est la crise d'un système qui s'est eloigné des valeurs les plus fondamentales du capitalisme, qui en quelque sorte, a trahi l'esprit du capitalisme.'

[11] 'L'anticapitalisme n'offre aucune solution à la crise actuelle.'

[12] 'Le jour où il avait sonné la mobilisation contre la crise.'

[13] 'Le discours que Nicolas Sarkozy a prononcé à Toulon, le 25 septembre, marque son entrée en guerre contre la crise.'

[14] 'Le projet de loi de programmation des finances publiques nous amène en effet jusqu'en 2012.'

[15] 'Les turbulences qui perdurent sur les marchés financiers internationaux depuis un an refletent les conséquences d'une purge profonde du secteur financier americain.'

[16] 'La crise financière qui sévit depuis un an a finalement impacté l'économie mondiale et provoque un net ralentissement en France.'

[17] '30 600 postes seront supprimés dans la fonction publique contre 22 900 en 2008. C'est un peu moins que la promesse de ne pas remplacer un fonctionnaire sur deux partant à la retraite.'

[18] 'Plan national pour assurer le financement de l'économie et restaurer la confiance.'

[19] 'La crise que nous vivons est excessive.'

[20] 'Ce que nous proposons c'est tout le contraire du plan Paulson…l'Etat americain propose de prendre à sa charge les actifs les plus mauvais…en France, l'Etat n'achetera pas d'actifs. Il pretera aux banques.'

[21] 'Elles peuvent aussi servir à faire d'une pierre deux coups en aidant à moyen terme les enterprises à se financer.'

[22] 'Au premier rang.'

[23] 'Grâce, notamment, au rôle leader de la France, l'Europe s'est organisée.'

[24] 'Inaudible dans une salle de 100 personnes.'

[25] 'Cette crise marqerua sans doute pour l'histoire le commencement veritable du XXIe siècle, le moment où tout le monde aura compris qu'il était temps de changer.'

26 'Reste que le style de Nicolas Sarkozy, parfois décrié, a plutôt joué en sa faveur. En période de crise, l'hyperactivité devient de l'énergie, l'arrogance de la ténacité, l'imprévisibilité du pragmatisme.'

27 'C'est autour du chômage que se noue la crise de confiance qui precipite la crise économique.'

28 'Plan d'investissement massif.'

29 'Un arsenal anticrise.'

30 'Crise financière mondiale: stratégies publiques et privées pour faire face à la crise.'

31 'J'ai le devoir d'entendre ceux qui manifestent, mais j'ai également la responsabilité de ceux qui ne défilent pas.'

32 'Il faut profiter de la crise.'

33 'Que dire pour rassurer une opinion publique qui le désavoue dans les sondages? Parler des "valeurs", donner des "repères".'

34 'Avoir le nez sur la crise ne l'empêche pas d'avoir un œil sur ses promesses de campagne et sur l'élection présidentielle de 2012.'

35 'Après Toulon en septembre, au début de la crise, Douai en décembre, sur le plan de relance, Saint-Quentin est censé ouvrir des perspectives sur l'après-crise. Tous ces discours sont des petits cailloux semés sur le chemin qui doit ramener Sarkozy à l'Elysée en 2012.'

36 'L'exception française.'

37 'Loi de modernisation de l'économie.'

8. The European Union: from impotence to opportunity?

Tully Fletcher

1. The European Union and the global financial crisis

The European Union is a curious and constantly evolving political institution and the way in which EU leaders have managed their responses to the global financial crisis draws out its unusual and at times opaque approach to crisis management. Economic decision-making power is divided between the leaders and finance ministers of the European member states through the European Council and the Council of Ministers, the European Commission (the central executive bureaucracy), the European Central Bank (ECB, which administers the common monetary policy) and the increasingly powerful European Parliament (McCormick 2005:79–91). It is often impossible to divorce the coordinated crisis-management response of the European Union from the actions of its constituent member states. It is also easy to underplay the significance of EU institutions and their actions once a common position has been adopted. As the global financial crisis struck Europe, its leaders eventually managed to overcome their initial paralysis and weld a stronger, more systematic Europe-wide response.

The EU member states initially dealt with the crisis on an individual basis, but by the end of 2008, the European Union's complex array of leaders was manoeuvring to adopt a common approach to the management of the crisis and coordinate a strong Europe-wide response through the commission and the Central Bank. By the end of October 2008, a 'European Framework for Action' had been adopted. By the end of November, a substantial multi-billion-euro stimulus plan had been announced. A record-breaking cut was made to interest rates in early December; and, at the G20 meeting of leading global economies in March 2009, coordinated EU pressure had provided much of the momentum for global agreements on new financial and banking regulation and economic stimuli. The crisis had demonstrated the combined power of the European institutions and provided an opportunity for Europe to develop a stronger common economic approach.

It is in that context that this chapter assesses the meaning making of three key actors in the European Union: the Commission President José Manuel Durão Barroso, the Commissioner for Economic and Financial Affairs Joaquín Almunia, and the President of the ECB Jean-Claude Trichet. Each of these actors was a significant decision maker and leader within the European Union's institutional framework vested with significant responsibility to respond to the economic changes across the European Union as a whole. Until the end of 2008, the Presidency of the European Council (often described as the EU Presidency) was held by France and exercised by French President, Nicolas Sarkozy. Despite the leadership potential of this latter office (Tallberg 2006), this chapter sets to one side the deliberations of member state and 'intergovernmental' (that is, the presidency) leaders and focuses on the roles of the 'supranational' leaders. The Commission President is a significant, influential and vocal EU leader in his own right (McCormick 2005:82–6; Verbeek forthcoming). This chapter found that the European Union's key leaders sought to frame the crisis in such a way as to avoid harmful political blame and achieve effective economic cooperation, substantial structural reforms in banking and finance regulation and a heightened sense of European unity. In the process, the institutional leaders of the European Union helped to drive a significant shift in macroeconomic ideology and policy to a more interventionist style.

Box 8.1 The European Union's financial crisis trajectory, July 2008 – March 2009

1 July 2008: French Presidency of the European Union begins.

3 September: The ECB cuts the growth forecast for 2009 from 1.5 per cent to 1.2 per cent.

8 October: Central banks around the world coordinate an interest rate cut in response to the credit crunch. The ECB cuts rates from 4.25 per cent to 3.75 per cent.

12 October: An emergency summit is held of national leaders of the eurozone countries. An agreement is reached regarding measures to repair confidence, promote cooperation among European leaders and ensure liquidity for financial institutions.

15–16 October: An EU summit is held and there are calls for reform of the international financial system.

18 October: Commission President Barroso and current EU President, Nicolas Sarkozy, meet with US President, George W. Bush, to discuss the global financial crisis. A series of meetings of international leaders to review national and international responses is established.

6 November: The ECB cuts rates from 3.75 per cent to 3.25 per cent.

7 November: EU Summit held (informal gathering of EU member state leaders) and agrees on a common set of reform principles for the International Monetary Fund (IMF).

---

9 November: São Paulo, Brazil, hosts G20 meeting of finance ministers and central bank governors, including EU member state representatives.

14 November: The eurozone officially enters recession after figures for the European Union show a 0.2 per cent contraction of the economy in the third quarter of 2008.

15 November: The EU-initiated G20 summit is held in Washington, DC, bringing together 19 of the largest national economies; includes EU representation as well as senior figures of the United Nations, the IMF, World Bank and the Financial Stability Forum.

19 November: Memorandum of understanding signed on financial assistance to Hungary—to provide up to €6.5 billion, with the first €2 billion instalment released before the year's end.

26 November: The European Commission releases the European Economic Recovery Plan, worth €200 billion, with the goal of boosting confidence in the financial systems and stimulating spending throughout the European Union.

28 November: Inflation in the eurozone had been at 3.2 per cent in October 2008, but falls to 2.1 per cent.

4 December: ECB cuts interest rate from 2.75 per cent to 2.5 per cent—the greatest reduction since the euro currency was introduced.

11–12 December: The European Council approves the European Economic Recovery Plan. The plan provides a common framework across the European Union and is worth approximately €2 billion or 1.5 per cent of the European Union's gross domestic product (GDP).

1 January 2009: Czech Presidency of the European Union begins.

15 January: The ECB cuts eurozone interest rates a further 0.5 per cent to 2 per cent.

26 January: Memorandum of understanding signed on financial assistance to Latvia—to provide up to €3.1 billion assistance.

9 February: EU Commissioner for Economic and Monetary Affairs Joaquín Almunia's article 'Solve the toxic asset problem' is published in the *Wall Street Journal*.

1 March: EU leaders attend an informal European Council meeting and establish an agreement on measures to deal with banks' toxic assets

5 March: ECB announces further cuts in the interest rate—to 1.5 per cent.

11 March: Supplemental memorandum of understanding with Hungary—announcing the second instalment of €2 billion (of up to €6.5 billion).

14 March: G20 finance ministers and central bank governors meet in the United Kingdom ahead of the 2 April London G20 summit.

25 March: European Union expresses its intention to provide up to €5 billion assistance to Romania.

2. Methodological considerations

Obtaining speeches made by the three key EU leaders during the period under study was simple, as EU institutions keep extensive online records and key speeches, and crisis updates were readily distinguishable from more mundane announcements, especially during the financial crisis. It proved much more difficult to conduct a study of media responses to those speeches that would be on a par with those conducted for the national case studies reported elsewhere in this volume. Perhaps reflecting the widely acknowledged knowledge deficit (and absence of a well-established 'public sphere') associated with EU institutions (McCormick 2005:135–6), the wide array of commentary and critique from established and accessible print media readily available for national leaders is less evident for EU institutional leaders.[1] Nevertheless, some consistent but limited press coverage of and responses to the key speeches were available in four of the world's most respected international English-language news sources: *The New York Times*, *The Financial Times*, *The Guardian* and *Reuters*. All four widely circulating sources carry large international sections and a commitment to observing the behaviour and news of the European institutions. With the exception of *The Guardian* (a noted British left-wing newspaper), all media sources used here are relatively centrist in political terms, although *The Financial Times* is skewed towards financial reporting and is pro-market. Despite their quality, the coverage of the crisis by these sources focused on national leaders in Europe and articles were sparse. One or two additional articles were used from the respected American paper *The Washington Post* and Germany's popular *Der Spiegel* (available online in English).

To supplement the media response, the responses and attitudes of the national leaders of the three largest European states have also been used to demonstrate the level of consensus achieved across the European Union. As such, this chapter includes an overview of the positions adopted by French President, Nicolas Sarkozy (who was also the EU President until the end of 2008), German Chancellor, Angela Merkel, and British Prime Minister, Gordon Brown. Their positions will be compared with those adopted by the key EU institutional leaders in order to assess the latter's success in the 'framing contests' that developed around the global financial crisis (see Chapter 2, this volume). The leaders of member states are as much a part of the audience for statements from EU institutional leaders as are the EU citizenry. Of course, the obvious limitation of this methodology is that it is entirely debatable who influences whom in the EU structure, particularly in terms of the relationship between the European Council and the commission. For the purposes of the analysis in this chapter, however, the extent of success for an EU institutional leader in the framing contest has been determined by the extent to which the views of the three key national leaders were in concert with the EU leaders.

3. The President of the European Commission

Barroso's key speech acts

29 October 2008: European 'Framework for Action'

On 29 October 2008, Commission President Barroso made a set of remarks after an extraordinary commission meeting called to provide an initial response to the global financial crisis. His speech marked one of the commission's first comprehensive statements on the crisis. Barroso firmly acknowledged the crisis and its risks and sought to portray it as an opportunity for increased European cooperation and solidarity, and a chance to implement complementary policies for growth and sustainability. He also flagged an upcoming and comprehensive EU recovery plan to be presented in November.

Barroso opened by telling reporters that 'the Commission has set out how we can move from financial crisis to sustainable recovery'. There was no explicit explanation of what was occurring (or why it was happening), though he briefly described the problem as a 'downturn' and a threat to European employment and economic stability. The speech dealt primarily with the management plan Barroso set out as part of the European response to the financial crisis. He pushed firmly for European coordination, solidarity and partnership and argued that the EU funds designed to assist members should now be put to use. He also reiterated the importance of the euro and suggested that the European Union would be much worse off without the single currency.

'We must swim together or sink together,' Barroso said, before setting the groundwork for the later stimulus plan:

> We must keep unemployment to the absolute minimum and support those who have lost their jobs. We will review how we can reinforce the effectiveness of the Globalisation Adjustment Fund. We will encourage Member States to re-programme funds under the European Social Fund, to support measures to quickly get unemployed people back into work. I also want to work with Member States to see if we can build on the progress already made under the Lisbon Strategy to help people, in

particular unemployed people, to start up new businesses quickly and cheaply.

The president also suggested that the European response to the crisis should take into account priorities in energy efficiency and climate change mitigation:

> There is scope to provide new opportunities for the economy, including for small and medium-sized enterprises [SMEs] while at the same time helping the EU to meet other objectives, like those I have mentioned on climate change…For example, investment in energy efficiency in buildings can provide opportunities for the construction sector while contributing to tackling climate change.

Though Barroso did not play the blame game in the statement, there was a clear inference that the crisis had exogenous causes. Barroso rhetorically accepted responsibility to act but not fault. The president framed the crisis as an exogenous event through which Europe might be further united: 'Europe will come through this economic storm and emerge stronger'.

26 November 2008: the stimulus plan

The themes of the European Framework for Action statement of the previous month were continued when President Barroso announced the €200 billion economic stimulus package in the European Economic Recovery Plan in Brussels on 26 November 2008. Barroso was more explicit this time in outlining his view of the risk presented by the financial crisis:

> Business as usual is not an option. That would lead to a vicious recessionary cycle. It would lead to falling purchasing power and falling tax revenues, to rising unemployment and the accompanying human misery, to ever wider budget deficits, ultimately to a risk of social instability. That is the lesson of the 1930s.

He also presented a qualification, however, on the nature of the stimulus package and warned that

> short-term spending without structural reform and without a smart strategy for investing and paying back the borrowing can fuel a downward spiral of debt and unemployment in the future. The cost of fighting this crisis must not be a worse crisis in the future as we struggle to deal with a hangover of debt.

Again, there was no particular apportionment of responsibility for causing the crisis, but there was a detailed plan for management of the crisis through various proposals for structural reform including measures to create labour demand, enhanced finance access for businesses, improved energy efficiency, high-speed internet and increased investment in research and development in the green manufacturing sector.

Again, Barroso attempted to frame the crisis as an opportunity for greater European integration and cooperation: 'The full extent of the benefits of individual Member States' fiscal measures will only be reaped if they are part of a co-ordinated European response'. The emerging theme in Barroso's commentary on the crisis was that the crisis was serious, but presented a significant opportunity to implement reforms that had been long considered. His tone was one of optimism and confidence and he sought to portray the European Union as an active player doing everything it could to address the crisis, in what Chapter 2 of this volume would characterise as a strong, type-3 framing statement:

> In all crises there lies also opportunity. And there is an opportunity now, for Member States and European institutions, indeed for European citizens, to understand that acting together, we can make the most of the instruments we have at national and Community level. We can succeed, not only for the good of Europe and European citizens, but also for the good of the world...There are no miracle solutions and it will not happen overnight. But I believe Europe will come through this economic storm and emerge stronger.

25 February 2009: banking regulation

After the commission meeting on 25 February 2009, Barroso emerged to announce that the commission would be seeking to strengthen banking supervision across the union and to develop new levels of European cooperation in finance generally. This time the president was less circumspect about the apportionment of blame and squarely laid the blame for the crisis at the feet of 'hubris' in the banking and finance sector:

> The crisis has shown why we must deepen our supervisory cooperation at EU level. Why we must have better crisis management systems. Why we must be able to have a basic core set of high level rules—both regulatory and supervisory—that are rigorously applied to all firms, by top class supervisors. Why we must avoid what Jacques de Larosière calls *chacun pour soi* solutions—everyman for himself—with no concern whatsoever about the neighbours. That is not good enough. It never was. And now it is totally unacceptable...Workers and families across Europe and the world have suffered the consequences of hubris in the financial markets. Citizens expect us to change the rules of the game and the way the game operates. We must not let citizens down.

Barroso reiterated his position that the correct approach to the management of the crisis was through increased European cooperation and noted that this was especially important in the lead-up to the approaching G20 summit. A consistent framing pattern had emerged in which Barroso either implied or explicitly deflected causal responsibility (though it could have been argued that the European Union had failed to adequately regulate and supervise the financial and banking sector before the emergence of the crisis), but portrayed an active and comprehensive European response designed to address and mitigate the effects of the crisis.

31 March 2009: the G20

Barroso's championing of European coherence reached new heights on 31 March 2009 just before the G20 meeting:

> The G20 will not end this crisis overnight. But it can, it must, it will, make a difference. For the first time ever in an economic crisis, the world is working together—and not against each other. The European Union is leading by example. There is convergence around the EU's common position. We have a unique opportunity to re-shape globalisation.

He argued that 'the EU was the first to act. For example on credit rating agencies, on capital requirements, on deposit guarantees. The Commission will very soon take action on hedge funds, private equity and remuneration'. This was grand (and likely hyperbolic) language, which rhetorically placed the European Union at the centre of things.

Again, the president was much less circumspect about attributing the blame for the financial crisis, highlighting a lack of market ethics and inadequate regulation of hedge funds, credit ratings agencies, accounting standards, remuneration, tax havens and 'uncooperative' jurisdictions. The proactivity of Barroso's proposals and the commission's position neatly sidestepped any question of prior failure to act on Europe's part.

Media responses to Barroso's framing

There was little coverage in the chosen media of the earlier 'framework for action' and Barroso's approach to the G20 summit; however, there was a substantial media response to the commission's European Economic Recovery Plan. *The New York Times* reported the stimulus package on 26 November 2008 with a relatively supportive tone, quoting Barroso extensively. *The New York Times* also quoted a leading economist who, approvingly, noted that the package was 'more ambitious' than had been expected. Some cynicism was expressed about German cooperation with the plan and the possibility of complete European cooperation (Castle and Jolly 2008).

In contrast, *The Guardian* took a more sceptical stance, noting that the commission's plan was designed to 'seize the initiative' after lagging behind the responses of other countries: 'Barroso and the Commission have come under criticism in recent weeks for being behind the curve on the financial meltdown and the depressing economic climate. Today's proposals appeared to be an attempt to catch up' (Traynor 2008) This contradicted Barroso's claim that the commission's response so far had been active and comprehensive. *The Guardian*'s report also criticised the stimulus package for being 'unclear' on everything from where the money was coming from to whether it would work at all. Finally, the report suggested that the plans were less an European Commission initiative and more of a repackaging of measures already announced by Germany and Spain.

The Guardian was also scathing of the European Union's proposals for an increase in banking regulation, noting on 24 February 2009 that 'the hedge fund and private equity industry will this week launch a last-ditch effort to head off EU moves to impose draconian regulation in the wake of the continuing financial crisis' (Gow 2009). The story drew attention to the significant divisions at the top of the commission's governance structure, driven by French, German and British disagreement about the reach and extent of proposed regulation. Though Barroso had called for cooperation generally, he had not alluded in his announcement to the existence of pervasive political divisions (Traynor 2008).

The key framing contest here seemed to be whether the European Commission had acted promptly or appropriately in response to the crisis. Though it did not appear to be strongly challenged by the media, Barroso himself certainly engaged in a consistent portrayal of the crisis as a key opportunity to implement a raft of structural economic reforms and bring forward planned investments and policy changes. Skirting over considerable disagreement among member states about the size and nature of stimuli packages as well the regulatory implications of the crisis that were in plain view, he tried—with some success—to muster political will and public support for concerted action at the European level.

4. EU Commissioner for Economic and Financial Affairs

Almunia's key speech acts

11 November 2008: a recipe for recovery

On 11 November 2008, Commissioner Almunia gave a speech to the second Brussels International Economic Forum titled 'A recipe for recovery: the European response to the financial crisis'. Almunia was explicit in identifying the crisis and its causes, arguing that

> after the period of excess and risk accumulation in the financial sector, we are now living through a painful market correction. The financial system is enduring a phase of severe deleveraging, characterised by dysfunctional credit markets, unprecedented write-downs in asset

valuations, generalised risk aversion, and threats to the stability of the banking sector.

He went on to state that 'from the beginning', Europe had taken 'decisive action' with an injection of capital into credit-starved banking institutions and cutting interest rates and the unprecedented level of coordination across Europe in the response. The commissioner also argued (and perhaps pre-empted comments about hindsight and lack of action) that 'the last months have exposed the weaknesses in our financial systems'.

In terms of the proposed management of the crisis, Almunia echoed many of the commission president's stated priorities and argued for long-term reforms in increased research and development, projects for a green economy, energy efficiency and a strong and coordinated European response. Almunia, however, also had another priority and argued for the preservation of the free-trade area in Europe and an aggressive international campaign against protectionism and barriers to global trade:

> We also need to work together to prevent protectionism from taking hold. In developed and developing countries alike, economic nationalism is on the rise and the benefits of globalisation are being questioned following the crisis. This is understandable. But history tells us that it is a dangerous tendency, one that can turn a downturn into a protracted and more severe problem...It is vital that we in Europe reaffirm our commitment to the principle of openness and lead by example. We must uphold the competition rules that underpin the Single Market and come out strongly against trade barriers.

In general, Almunia framed the crisis as one with exogenous causes (inadequately regulated international financial institutions), but accepted (as did Barroso) responsibility to address the underlying factors and treat the symptoms of the crisis. These were to be achieved with European cooperation and increased supervision, but avoiding protectionist measures.

25 February 2009: interview with The Financial Times

On 25 February, Commissioner Almunia granted a wide-ranging interview with *The Financial Times* (see Atkins and Barber 2009). He did not discuss the crisis or its causes specifically but rather assessed the European management of the crisis and some of the challenges it presented. He was more circumspect than the commission president on the effect of the European stimulus and noted that the 'degree of co-ordination could be seriously improved...I don't say the present fiscal stimulus is useless at all. But the efficiency of the stimulus will be increased if the degree of co-ordination is improved'.

Almunia made the inference that the poorly regulated finance and banking sector (including tax havens) was to blame and expressed his support for stronger and 'broader' financial regulation:

> The financial system will be more regulated. This will mean less leverage, less flexibility in the financial system, and less influence for the financial system in the aggregated results of our economy…Either we accept that our growth will be lower than in the past because the stimulus from the financial sector will be smaller.

He also noted, however, that the present level of direct state intervention in banks would be temporary and that, in time, 'capitalism' would return to business as usual: 'I don't think we'll go back to the high level of state intervention and public regulation in industry or other sectors'. The commissioner seemed to be striking an almost apologetic tone, clearly regretting the changes that were being made and the increased level of government intervention in the economy, but still supporting the necessity of the measures being put in place.

4 May 2009: spring forecast

On 4 May 2009, Almunia delivered his spring forecast on the economic and financial state of the union and its key institutions. The forecast opened with a 'nutshell' summary that provided a neat synopsis of the commissioner's frame of the crisis:

> Intensification of financial crisis and sharp contraction in world trade drove global and EU economies into recession; Financial markets gradually stabilising, but remain fragile; Ambitious EU and government action key to achieving stabilisation towards end 2009 and moderate growth in 2010; [and] Leading indicators provide some positive signals.

The commissioner called the financial crisis Europe's 'deepest and most widespread recession since World War II', but he attributed a gradual stabilisation to the 'swift and massive intervention' of the European Community through the European Economic Recovery Plan. Almunia noted that the projections were for a recovery in the coming quarters thanks to the fiscal stimulus measures, the bank rescue plans and monetary easing. He also argued that the fiscal stimuli should continue into the future in order to effectively manage the crisis over time. Essentially, the framing sought here was that the crisis had exogenous causes, but was being dealt with effectively by European authorities.

Media responses to Almunia's framing

Overall, explicit and systematic coverage of Almunia's speeches was poor; his public visibility when addressing the European Union's handling of the global financial crisis outside Brussels was largely eclipsed by that of Commission

President Barroso. In response to Almunia's 'recipe for recovery' speech on 11 November 2008, *The Financial Times* called into question the commission's claim to be pioneering the proposed measures. Though Almunia (like Barroso) claimed much of the credit for the European response, *The Financial Times* noted that:

> Economists said some governments were already proceeding along the lines suggested by Mr Almunia. The ruling coalition in Germany, for example, wants to offer tax incentives for the installation of energy-efficient home heating systems or the purchase of cars emitting lower levels of carbon dioxide. (Barber 2008)

The Financial Times journalist also suggested that the individual EU governments had taken the lead in drawing up the main emergency rescue measures for the banking sector, though the commission had been responsible for some of the subsequent specific details (Barber 2008). The contest here appeared to be over whether the commission had in fact been providing leadership in the crisis or whether it had just adopted measures already being undertaken and claimed them as its own.

5. The President of the European Central Bank

Trichet's key speech acts

4 December 2008: cutting interest rates

At the press conference after a meeting of the governors of the ECB, President Trichet announced a decision to cut interest rates by 75 basis points (the biggest cut the ECB had ever made) after two 50-point reductions in the previous two months. This was the direct response to what the ECB had identified as a significant reduction in inflation, attributed to the 'intensifying and broadening' financial crisis. Pointing to 'global economic weakness', Trichet told journalists:

> The economic outlook remains surrounded by an exceptionally high degree of uncertainty. Risks to economic growth lie on the downside. They relate mainly to the potential for a more significant impact on the real economy of the turmoil in financial markets, as well as concerns about protectionist pressures and possible disorderly developments owing to global imbalances.

Like the two commissioners, Trichet highlighted the need for disciplined and uniform policymaking across the European Union. The purpose of this was, Trichet said, to preserve fragile public confidence in the economy. Throughout his comments, Trichet too sought to outsource any blame for the crisis while adopting responsibility for addressing the symptoms of the problem and framing the European response as a policy success.

9 January 2009: paradigm change

In January 2009, Trichet went a lot further when he addressed a round table at the International Colloquium. In a reflective speech, he focused on what he portrayed as the underlying causes and key solutions to the crisis. He pointed to the responsibility of international financiers:

> The current crisis stands out because it is affecting the heart of the global financial system. Its root cause was a widespread undervaluation of risk in the global financial system, especially in the most advanced economies. This included an underestimation of the quantity of risk financial institutions took upon themselves and an underpricing of the unit of risk. Risk was underpriced because, among other things, financial market participants largely extrapolated ongoing trends and the very low levels of volatility in financial markets and in the real economies going forward.

The European Union had, in contrast (according to Trichet), 'reacted promptly' and in a coordinated manner to prevent 'contagion'. The ECB President further hammered financial firms and argued that short-term thinking and excessive risk taking were directly to blame for the crisis:

> Among financial market participants (traders, managers, risk committees and boards of directors alike) for a long time there has been an excessive focus on short-term profits to the detriment of longer-term business performance. This has resulted in excessive risk-taking and, particularly, an underestimation of low probability risks stemming from excessive leverage and concentration.

He also outlined his views about the appropriate response and called for increased transparency and regulation in the banking sector. Like his colleagues at the commission, Trichet praised the European institutions for their quick action:

> The swiftness and the magnitude of the decisions taken by central banks as regards the supply of liquidity and the decisive actions taken by governments and parliaments as regards recapitalisation in the financial sector and the provision of guarantees have proved effective in avoiding a meltdown of global finance.

He concluded by arguing that the necessary response to the present situation was to engage in a 'paradigm change' in the global economy, away from short-term thinking to an approach based on 'medium and long-term sustainability' (but was otherwise low on the specifics of such an alternative 'paradigm'). Again, the dominant framing sought was one of exogenous responsibility but a 'domestic' opportunity and responsibility to enact a new regulatory system and a success story so far for the European response.

27 April 2009: Chatham House speech

As the pressures of a collapsing European economy mounted, Trichet became even less circumspect when he addressed the Chatham House Global Financial Forum on 27 April 2009. He now blamed the crisis squarely on the finance and banking sector's 'unfettered speculation and financial gambling' instead of the management of 'genuine' economic risk. Though 'financial liberalisation and financial innovation had made a significant contribution to the economy', there had been a simultaneous weakening of the screening procedures for credit, which had resulted in a decline in underwriting standards and lending responsibility.

Trichet told his audience that the ECB's main response to the crisis was to lower interest rates, followed by a guarantee for European banks designed to back up liquidity. There was an imperative to manage the crisis and improve productivity by increasing and maintaining public confidence in the euro and the European economy. Trichet said that ensuring the continued viability of Europe's banks was his primary concern and a foundation for potential recovery. In all, this third speech was less of an exercise in self-praise than his previous 'paradigm change' speech and more of an apportionment of (exogenous) blame and plans for mitigation.

Media response to Trichet's framing

The New York Times lauded the 'historic pace' of the reduction in interest rates across the globe, but especially in Europe, in an article on 4 December 2008 (Dougherty 2008). The article also highlighted divisions between Trichet, the European Commission and European governments over the pace of change. It suggested that despite the unprecedented reduction in rates, 'The European Central Bank's reluctance to outline a more forceful strategy for the future exposes it to the charge that it is underestimating the severity of the downturn, and that it is passing on opportunities to get ahead of it, analysts said' (Dougherty 2008).

At the press conference for the reduction in ECB interest rates itself, Trichet faced questions about whether such a significant reduction might have a detrimental impact on market confidence (which he claimed was his primary concern), and whether his focus as the President of the ECB on rates alone was too narrow to appropriately address the crisis.

The primary framing contest over the ECB's interest rate cut (the only one of Trichet's three key statements analysed here to attract significant media attention in the sources used) was in regard to the reduction in rates and whether this represented an appropriate response. Furthermore, questions seemed to exist about whether the rate cut was substantial enough or even too substantial. More broadly, Trichet appeared to work hard to characterise the crisis as the result of excessive risk taking in the financial sector.

6. Member state leaders: the road to collaboration

As discussed earlier in this chapter, it is impossible to divorce decision making at the EU institutional level from the thoughts and actions of leaders of the member states, particularly the larger states such as France, Germany and the United Kingdom. The leaders of those three key EU member states are used here to shine additional light on the public and political impacts of Barroso's, Almunia's and Trichet's efforts to frame the severity, causes and implications of the crisis in particular ways.

French President Sarkozy, German Chancellor Merkel and British Prime Minister Brown demonstrated a remarkable consistency of views in the public arena once the initial 'cascade' of hasty national decisions to guarantee bank deposits had run its course. From late 2008 onwards, more coordination took place at the EU level, especially in the lead-up to the G20 summit. Initially, however, there was significant disagreement about the size and necessity of stimulus packages and the extent of new banking regulation, with Germany holding out for a more fiscally conservative line. As the New Year rolled over, however, the extent of agreement on the necessity for European cooperation on new regulation and stimulus and the need to rethink the commitment to unrestrained markets became remarkable. The statements of the various national leaders mirror that evolution.

As early as September 2008, *The Washington Post* had reported on a speech that Sarkozy had given in Toulon (see also Windle, this volume), in which the French President had

> joined a broad spectrum of European leaders and commentators who have interpreted the financial crisis as a death knell for the current financial markets and banking systems. Their comments sometimes have betrayed an 'I told you so' sentiment, after years during which US officials suggested that many of Europe's economic problems stemmed from an excess of regulation and government intervention. (Cody 2008)

As the crisis gathered pace in September, Merkel's rhetoric was strongly geared towards harsh criticism of policymaking in Washington. Her government rejected the need to provide a stimulus package or bailout for the German financial system (*Der Spiegel* 2008). And, in early December, while Brown, Sarkozy and Barroso all called for more cooperation between EU leaders to respond to the economic crisis, Merkel continued to resist the need for a stimulus package and refused to commit to funding the commission's stimulus plan. 'Merkel has said for the past 10 days that she would not join in a race to spend billions of taxpayers' euros as one way to stimulate the economy and instead would take her time and assess what short- and long-term measures to take' (Werdigier and Dempsey 2008).

By late January 2009, however, Germany had implemented a stimulus package of its own and was supporting the European stimulus plan. It was now in lockstep with France and Britain in calling for tighter regulation of financial markets and increased European cooperation (Connolly 2009; Fincher 2009). It was a major U-turn, and it was clear that Merkel's government had given in to economic reality and EU pressure. By the time the G20 summit rolled around towards the end of March 2009, Germany, France and Britain had all adopted the same policy response to the crisis, as separate states and as part of the EU institutions. It was clear that all three leaders had adopted a joint enthusiasm for government intervention in the economy, including intensive European cooperation. Their rhetoric began to reflect this. It appeared more likely that they had been convinced by each other, rather than by Barroso, but nonetheless it was clear that the key European leaders had come to accept the crisis framing and policy stances that had been adopted consistently by the EU institutional leaders early on.

7. Conclusions: the power of rhetoric or the power of interdependence?

The three key EU players attempted to mobilise support for major, closely coordinated policy change in response to the crisis. Barroso, Almunia and Trichet all identified the crisis as a profound event with exogenous causes. There was a consistent pattern of attempting to apportion blame for the crisis to excessive risk taking and the unrestrained capitalistic behaviour of private banks and financial institutions, studiously avoiding mention of any regulatory deficiencies either at the EU or the national level (for example, the allegedly 'soft' UK system of banking regulation, which had tolerated and even encouraged precisely that kind of behaviour). The assessment of the severity of the crisis was also consistent across the three EU protagonists: they identified and expressed the global financial crisis as a significant risk to the existing economic structure and to growth, productivity and employment. All three made credible statements about what the crisis meant for Europe, across the months sampled here.

In general, though some media coverage was critical of the success or timeliness of the European Union's decision making and policy program, it appears that the message of key opportunities for substantial structural change and increased European cooperation and coordination broke through, and gained traction among the media and the leaders of three key member states discussed above. The best proof of this came from the unified approach taken by the European Union at the G20 summit after successful cooperation before the event. The available coverage of the European response to the crisis revealed few complaints that the commission and the ECB had failed to act appropriately or that the

European Union's stated goals of increased regulation and European cooperation were not the universally favoured outcomes. Each of the European leaders had acted decisively, on a broad scale, and in tune with their EU colleagues and the commission.

The remarkable turnaround in German political opinion on how best to address the crisis and the consistent pattern of exogenous blame shifting and type-3 opportunity-seeking rhetoric from the EU institutional leaders and the three key member state leaders could be construed as evidence of how successful these actors were in framing the crisis and creating their desired meaning. It was someone else's fault (the United States, the financial sector) and the commitment to free markets had to be reconsidered where a clear need existed for the European Union and EU member states to directly intervene in their economies to address the crisis.

The most substantial gain achieved by the three EU actors during the period analysed by this chapter was an increased level of European cooperation on the functions of the banking and finance system. Each time a leader made a speech or a statement, the primary stated cause of the crisis was the various failures of the international banking and finance system, and each time a solution was proposed it was either a temporary stabilisation measure or a substantial and pan-European structural reform designed to reduce the potential for a repeat crisis. As the timeline moved forward, it became clear that a consensus had emerged that strong collective regulatory action was an appropriate response to the crisis. The rhetoric strongly suggested that a substantial paradigm shift had occurred in the political and policy realm: for the Europeans, there was a new mandate for government intervention in the economy and a new legitimacy for European Union-wide economic action. What is less clear, however, is whether these shifts occurred because of the inherent persuasiveness of the EU actors' discourse. Perhaps, in line with Lindberg and Scheingold's (1970) classic statement on the pivotal role of crises in forging European integration, member state leaders came to the party because the sheer pressure of economic realities left them with little room to manoeuvre.

References

Almunia, J. 2008, A recipe for recovery: the European response to the financial crisis, Speech to the second Brussels International Economic Forum, 11 November, viewed 30 May 2009, <http://europa.eu/rapid/pressReleasesAction.do?reference=SPEECH/08/601&format=HTML&aged=0&language=EN&guiLanguage=en >

Almunia, J. 2009, Spring forecast 2009, Speech, 4 May, viewed 30 May 2009, <http://ec.europa.eu/commission_barroso/almunia/iframes/conferences/2009/files/09_05_04_speakings.pdf >

Atkins, R. and Barber, T. 2009, 'Europe has sown seeds of slow recovery', *The Financial Times*, 25 February, viewed 30 May 2009, <http://www.ft.com/cms/s/de3b2af8-0371-11de-b405-000077b0765>

Barber, T. 2008, 'EU urged to accelerate reforms', *The Financial Times*, 11 November, viewed 30 May 2009, <http://www.ft.com/cms/s/0/9771bdba-afe0-11dd-a795-0000779fd18c.html?nclick_check=1 >

Barroso, J. 2008a, From financial crisis to recovery: a European framework for action, Remarks to the extraordinary European Commission meeting, Brussels, 29 October, viewed 29 May 2009, <http://europa.eu/rapid/pressReleasesAction.do?reference=SPEECH/08/566&format=HTML&aged=0&language=EN&guiLanguage=en>

Barroso, J. 2008b, A European economic recovery plan, Press conference, Brussels, 26 November, viewed 29 May 2009, <http://europa.eu/rapid/pressReleasesAction.do?reference=SPEECH/08/654&format=HTML&aged=0&language=EN&guiLanguage=en>

Barroso, J. 2009a, Opening remarks, European Commission meeting, Brussels, 25 February, viewed 29 May 2009, <http://europa.eu/rapid/pressReleasesAction.do?reference=SPEECH/09/76&format=HTML&aged=0&language=EN&guiLanguage=en>

Barroso, J. 2009b, The G20—a unique opportunity, Press conference, Brussels, 31 March, viewed 29 May 2009, <http://europa.eu/rapid/pressReleasesAction.do?reference=SPEECH/09/160&format=HTML&aged=0&language=EN&guiLanguage=en>

Boin, A., 't Hart, P. and McConnell, A. 2009, 'Crisis exploitation: political and policy impacts of framing contests', *Journal of European Public Policy*, vol. 16, no. 1, pp. 81–106.

Castle, S. and Jolly, D. 2008, 'Giant stimulus plan proposed for Europe', *The New York Times*, 26 November, viewed 30 May 2009, <http://www.nytimes.com/2008/11/27/business/worldbusiness/27euro.html?_r=1&scp=12&sq=EU%20and%20%22financial%20crisis%22%20and%20%22barroso%22&st=cse>

Cody, E. 2008, 'Sarkozy advocates systemic change after crisis', *The Washington Post*, 26 September, viewed 25 May 2009, <http://www.washingtonpost.com/wp-dyn/content/article/2008/09/25/AR2008092504285.html >

Connolly, K. 2009, 'Germany approves €50bn stimulus package', *The Guardian*, 27 January, viewed 25 May 2009, <http://www.guardian.co.uk/world/2009/jan/27/germany-europe>

Der Spiegel 2008, 'Financial crisis puts Merkel in hot seat', *Der Spiegel*, 12 August, viewed 25 May 2009,
<http://www.spiegel.de/international/germany/0,1518,595044,00.html>

Dougherty, C. 2008, '3 European central banks cut rates', *The New York Times*, 4 December, viewed 1 May 2009,
<http://www.nytimes.com/2008/12/05/business/worldbusiness/05euro.html?_r=2&scp=11&sq=EU%20and%20%22financial%20crisis%22%20and%20%22trichet%22&st=cse>

Fincher, C. 2009, 'Brown, Merkel urge tighter global banking supervision', *Reuters*, 28 February, viewed 25 May 2009,
<http://www.reuters.com/article/idUSLS40256720090228>

Gow, D. 2009, 'EU leaders back clampdown on hedge funds and private equity firms', *The Guardian*, 24 February, viewed 10 July 2009,
<http://www.guardian.co.uk/business/2009/feb/23/eu-clampdown-on-private-equity>

Lindberg, L. N. and Scheingold, S. A. 1970, *Europe's Would-Be Polity: Patterns of change in the European Community*, Prentice-Hall, Englewood Cliffs.

McCormick, J. 2005, *Understanding the European Union: A concise introduction*, Palgrave Macmillan, New York.

Tallberg, J. 2006, *Leadership and Negotiation in the European Union*, Cambridge University Press, Cambridge.

Traynor, I. 2008, 'Europe announces €200bn rescue plan', *The Guardian*, 26 November, viewed 29 June 2009,
<http://www.guardian.co.uk/business/2008/nov/26/europe-economic-recovery-plan>

Trichet, J.-C. 2008, Introductory statement with Q&A, Announcement on interest rates, Brussels, 4 December, viewed 1 May 2009,
<http://www.ecb.int/press/pressconf/2008/html/is081204.en.html>

Trichet, J.-C. 2009a, A paradigm change for the global financial system, Speech to the International Colloquium, Paris, 9 January, viewed 1 May 2009,
<http://www.ecb.int/press/key/date/2009/html/sp090109.en.html>

Trichet, J.-C. 2009b, The financial crisis and our response so far, Speech to the Chatham House Global Financial Forum, New York, 27 April, viewed 1 May 2009,
<http://www.ecb.int/press/key/date/2009/html/sp090427.en.html>

Verbeek, B. (forthcoming), 'Leadership of international organizations', in J. Kane, H. Patapan and P. 't Hart (eds), *Dispersed Democratic Leadership: Origins, dynamics and implications*, Oxford University Press, Oxford.

Werdigier, J. and Dempsey, J. 2008, 'European leaders call for closer cooperation on economic crisis', *The New York Times,* 8 December, viewed 10 July 2009, <http://www.nytimes.com/2008/12/08/business/worldbusiness/08iht-summit.4.18499082.html>

Endnotes

[1] The effort to construct a media analysis in this case was hampered partly by practical difficulties. The author is monolingual and, while a combination of leading national papers and magazines in the main member states (such as *Le Monde, Le Soir, Frankfurter Allgemeine* and *Der Spiegel*) would constitute a credible proxy of 'European public opinion', their English-language web sites were either limited in their coverage or had inadequate search engines.

Part IV. No hiding place: the meltdown and the Asia-Pacific region

9. Australia: 'the lucky country' on a knife edge

Matthew Laing and Karen Tindall

1. Batten down the hatches

In October 2008, the All Ordinaries, Australia's oldest share index, having reached an all-time high in late 2007, went into free fall. By March 2009, it had halved in value—a record low. As the other polities studied in this volume fell into recession, the Australian public watched on, increasingly feeling the effects of the downturn. The lack of government debt and the apparent resilience of Australia's economy—tied as it was to the still-booming China—provided reasons for hope. As the crisis hit an increasing number of Australia's trading partners, however, the pinch was increasingly felt. Together, this highlighted the challenges leaders faced when trying to convince the public not to lose confidence in the economy. When in June 2009 the Rudd Government was able to declare that 'Australia is the only advanced economy as of today not in recession', the policy of pre-emptively tackling the economic downturn appeared to be vindicated.

Throughout these tense months, maintaining business and public confidence was a key concern of Australian Prime Minister Kevin Rudd, Treasurer Wayne Swan, and Governor of the Reserve Bank of Australia (RBA) Glenn Stevens. They sought to articulate the crisis to key stakeholders and the broader Australian public, to contain the crisis, to create support for the unprecedented measures they were taking and potentially to use it to their advantage. This chapter examines their public leadership during this period.

The Rudd Government had been in power since December 2007. In this period, several high-profile events abroad served to raise alarm bells in Australia. Three months before Rudd assumed office, the United Kingdom had experienced the most severe run on a bank in more than a century, and three months into Rudd's first term US investment bank Bear Stearns collapsed. The Australian economy was experiencing a continuing resource boom and, consequently, the RBA continued to raise rates to keep a lid on inflation (maintaining a 7.25 per cent interest rate until September 2008). Meanwhile, the US Federal funds rate was approaching zero and central banks around the world had begun to reduce their own rates. With increasingly dire economic news from abroad, Australians were watching the storm clouds gather. By September 2008, the crisis was well and truly on Australia's doorstep.

Box 9.1 Australia's financial crisis trajectory, March 2008 – March 2009

4 March 2008: Interest rates peak at 7.25 per cent, the RBA stating that there is a need to control inflation and slow growth.

20 March: Australian investment group Opes Prime collapses—the first victim in Australia of the global financial crisis.

10 April: The International Monetary Fund (IMF) predicts that Australia will not suffer from the same slump in growth rates that other nations will as a result of the global slowdown.

14 May: The 'responsible' and 'inflation fighting' 2008 federal budget is handed down in surplus. Beechwood, the largest home builder in New South Wales, collapses.

16 May: The All Ordinaries rises above 6000 points, driven by growth in mining stocks. Three days later, the Australian dollar hits a 24-year high of 95.71 US cents.

June: Australia is defying global trends, with gross domestic product (GDP) growing 0.4 per cent in the June quarter.

3 July: Borrowing for housing drops to its lowest rate since 1991.

10 July: The All Ordinaries drops below 5000 points on the back of investor concern about global recession.

25 July: The National Australia Bank (NAB) announces a write-down of almost $900 million worth of residential mortgage-backed securities. Within days, the ANZ Bank announces similar losses.

6 August: Consumer confidence levels and home-loan approvals are found to be in historic decline.

20 August: Opposition Leader, Malcolm Turnbull, claims that 'talking the economy down' by the government has had a deleterious effect on economic confidence.

2 September: The RBA cuts the cash rate back to 7 per cent.

15 September: The RBA injects $1.3 billion into the financial sector. Treasurer Swan warns that Australia will not be immune from the effects of the financial crisis.

16 September: Prime Minister Rudd states that the global financial crisis still has 'a long way to run yet' as the Australian dollar falls to 12-month lows and the share market falls to four-year lows.

18–21 September: Chaos on Wall Street starts another wave of dramatic tumbles at the Australian Stock Exchange (ASX). The Federal Government places a ban on the short-selling of stock.

26 September: In an address to the United Nations General Assembly, Rudd calls for a global response to the financial crisis

7 October: The RBA slashes interest rates to 6 per cent.

10 October (Black Friday): The All Ordinaries takes a 21-year record dive of 8.2 per cent to 3939, and $87 billion is wiped off the value of the ASX.

14 October: Rudd announces a $10.4 billion stimulus package to help Australia avoid going into recession.

24 October: Investment giant Babcock & Brown goes into trading insolvency.

November: Major companies Allco Finance, Freightlink and ABC Learning go bankrupt.

4 November: The RBA cuts rates to 5.25 per cent.

16 November: G20 Washington Summit announces the six-point economic plan. Rudd reiterates the need for international responses at the Asia-Pacific Economic Cooperation (APEC) meeting the next week.

21 November: The All Ordinaries sinks to a new low of 3235.

December: Australia's GDP growth rate contracts in the December quarter, falling to −0.5 per cent.

2 December: The RBA cuts its interest rate to 4.25 per cent.

8 December: The ANZ job advertisement survey and NAB business confidence index fall to their lowest levels since the 1991 recession.

January 2009: Unemployment rises to 4.8 per cent; building approvals fall almost 13 per cent nationally.

21 January: BHP Billiton lays off 3300 workers.

1 February: Swan announces that a budget deficit is now 'inevitable'.

3 February: The cash rate reaches a historic low of 3.25 per cent. The government announces the $42 billion National Building and Jobs Plan.

March: Unemployment hits a four-year high at 5.7 per cent; GDP recovers to 0.4 per cent.

13 March: The All Ordinaries hits its lowest point in nearly six years at 3052.

> **26 March:** The RBA announces its belief that the economic stimulus package is working.

2. Methodological considerations

This chapter follows the methodology laid out in Chapter 2. Twelve key speeches were chosen—four from each leader—from the period late March 2008 to March 2009. The speeches were selected primarily on their direct relevance to the crisis and the amount of coverage they received. Where possible, however, effort was made to include a spread of dates, thereby allowing insight into the evolution of the leaders' frames.

To gain a sense of the counter-frames and framing contests in Australia, this chapter considers a key sample of print media. The three prominent newspapers selected for analysis—*The Australian, The Age* and the *Australian Financial Review* (*AFR*)—were chosen for a number of analytical reasons. Fairfax owns two of the papers (the *AFR* and *The Age*), while News Corporation owns the other (*The Australian*). The *AFR*, a national paper, is the most prominent business daily, with an average daily circulation of 90,000 (92,000 on the weekend) (Australian Press Council 2008). Although its circulation was not as high as some of the other major broadsheets, its focus on economics and finance was desirable for this project. *The Australian*, with a circulation of 136,000 (301,000 on the weekend) (Australian Press Council 2008), has a centre-right editorial outlook and is the only other major national paper, often featuring more commentary on economic matters than the metropolitan dailies. *The Age*, with a circulation of 208,000 (and an average of 228,000 on the weekend) (Australian Press Council 2008), considered to be left-wing or centre-left, is a Melbourne-based paper circulated in other major centres.

Within seven days after each address, all references to the speech or its substantive content were extracted from these three publications and analysed. The extent of agreement with Rudd's, Swan's or Stevens' framing of the severity, causality, proposed policy and overall support for the speaker is discussed after each speech section. Using this qualitative analysis as a general indicator, it is possible to gain a sense of the responses to each speech and to identify the main framing battlegrounds. Public opinion data from Essential Research, Newspoll, Nielson and GlobeScan were also used to provide a contextual backdrop and, where applicable, were taken into account as indicators of the public's response to the leaders' framing.

3. Crisis exploitation and elite rhetoric in Australia

31 March 2008: the Prime Minister and the crisis abroad

Kevin Rudd had been Prime Minister for nearly four months when he embarked on the first major trip of his administration, arriving in the United States just weeks after the failure of Bear Sterns. Though Australia had to that point remained relatively unaffected by the sub-prime crisis, the shock collapse of Australian investment group Opes Prime on 28 March had begun to raise questions about the underlying stability of the Australian financial system (Urban 2008).

Speaking before the US Chamber of Commerce in Washington, DC, the Prime Minister summarised the Australian position by describing the 'current global financial crisis' as one of 'powerful cross-currents'. He described Australians as 'acutely aware' of the financial crisis and spoke strongly of its 'gravity'. His reporting of the Australian economy in the speech was, however, rosy, and he spoke at length about its sustained growth and strong fundamentals. 'Cross-currents', it seems, was a convenient turn of phrase here to reconcile the US and European economic turmoil with the boom conditions still being experienced in Australia. He highlighted the role that China and the developing economies had played in this regard.

The Prime Minister pinpointed cheap credit and the subsequent re-pricing of risk as chief causes of the crisis. A long period of economic expansion in the financial sector had led to 'lending extended without sufficient attention to risk'. The sophistry of lending instruments had outpaced the market's ability to understand and appraise them and the innate uncertainty of the situation had amplified the crisis by discouraging investors and recovery. Rudd chose not to assign blame to any particular government or body, instead treating the developments as somewhat of a fait accompli stemming from cycles of economic behaviour and the increasing complexity of international finance. He was also quick to point out the strong and well-regulated nature of the Australian financial system, implying at least that no blame for the crisis could be traced to Australia.

That explanation neatly dovetailed with his conclusion that the solution was 'a global response by our national regulators to a global crisis'. Though he recognised only minor implications for the Australian economy, his enthusiasm for participating in a global economic response was unequivocal. Australia was and would be participating at every level in formulating an international regulatory response: 'we *must* be an active participant in a coherent global economic response' (emphasis added).

Though the speech itself did not grab the headlines in Australia, its theme did not escape media commentary amid broader attention given to the Prime Minister's search for a 'global role' (Flitton 2008; Shanahan and Marris 2008;

Walker 2008). *The Australian*'s editorial commenting on the speech broadly agreed with Rudd's sentiments on the limited severity and unforeseeable cause of the crisis in Australia. It was, however, at best lukewarm about his policy response, admonishing governments not to be 'over-eager to find ways to get involved' in fiscal regulation (*The Australian* 2008a) and seeing the speech more cynically as part of a continuing strategy by the Prime Minister to eke out an increased global role for Australia (*The Australian* 2008b). The *AFR* went a step further; while supporting the free-trade aspects of the speech, it too was mildly critical of expanded prudential regulation (*AFR* 2008a; S. Turnbull 2008).

2 June 2008: the Treasurer's post-budget assessment of the global crisis

In June, three weeks after handing down his first budget, Wayne Swan presented a statement on Australia's financial stability to the House of Representatives. Although the US sub-prime crisis was yet to truly affect Australia, this speech represented one of the first tangible policy moves to address it. Swan's office simultaneously posted four media releases on policies summarised in this speech, regarding global 'outreach meetings', guarantees for depositors, continuing the four-pillars policy and the implementation of recommendations by an international body.

Swan highlighted the deterioration of the situation in the United Kingdom and the United States in the previous year. While acknowledging that 'to a much lesser extent, Australia also saw some of the impact', Swan played down the severity and externalised the causality. According to Swan, Australia had been impacted by the 'US sub-prime financial crisis despite our financial institutions not sharing its causes'. Swan's framing emphasised the role of 'declining confidence' and 'global uncertainty' in explaining 'so much of the downturn in the US economy overall'. Indeed, Swan stressed that although Australian banks were not threatened by any immediate risk, Australia was one of the last two Organisation for Economic Cooperation and Development (OECD) nations to have not yet guaranteed bank deposits and doing so now was a wise precaution. It was a simultaneous acknowledgment and mitigation of critical threat.

Claiming 'Australian Government agencies...performed their duties well in minimising the impact of this global crisis on the Australian economy', Swan's responsibility narrative focused on the reasons for Australia's relative success, rather than distributing blame for what had gone wrong. He credited Australia's 'sound financial institutions...supported by a strong prudential regulatory framework, and an adroit central bank'. At this point in the crisis, Swan believed governments' responsibility was not to intervene but to ensure these institutions 'have the tools they need to act swiftly and effectively'. The policies announced in June 2008 were not major departures from existing practices nor were they radical interventions. Swan framed the crisis as an incident, a 'long and difficult financial episode' with knock-on effects in Australia, but an episode nonetheless.

Swan's speech was a type-2 frame of sorts. It acknowledged problems and sought to strengthen the existing structures. The frame also demonstrated elements of a type-1 'business as usual' response, as he claimed the worst of the crisis was bypassing Australia and there were indications of improvement. In the speech, the few adjustments (such as guaranteeing bank deposits) in light of the crisis abroad were portrayed as precautionary steps taken to reduce anxiety.

The speech elicited a lot of response to the major policy implications in Swan's speech: the deposit guarantee and the continuation of existing banking policy (namely, the four-pillars scheme). Nearly all of these responses were critical (Colebatch 2008a; Cornell 2008; Harper 2008; Jury 2008; Williams 2008b). All three papers, but in particular the *AFR*, were unconvinced that Australia's success in weathering the crisis to that point had much to do with prudential policy, and strongly questioned Swan's explanation of Australia's crisis endurance (Cornell 2008; Durie 2008; Williams 2008b). A few other reports of the speech were nonchalant, offering only very weak support for the Treasurer, his explanation of the circumstances and his subsequent policy pronouncements (Patten 2008; Tingle 2008a). It seems, then, that the media attached *even less* severity to the crisis than the Treasurer, presenting a firmly type-1 counter-frame and taking the speech instead as test of the 'free-market credentials of a new government' (Tingle 2008a). Only a couple of articles were willing to support the Treasurer and a more serious framing of the emerging crisis (Patten 2008; Wood 2008a).

13 June 2008: the bank governor stating his priorities

In June 2008, inflation was still the focus of Glenn Stevens' speech to the American Chamber of Commerce in Australia. He did, however, address the issue of the US crisis, claiming that 'the worst fears of a serious financial collapse have abated somewhat', but acknowledging that 'considerable uncertainty' remained for the coming year or so. Stevens reassured his audience that Australia had different concerns to those about the US economy. This explanation also acted as justification for why the RBA was keeping cash rates high while the US Federal Reserve had halved rates in the past six months. Stevens partially divorced the US crisis from issues present in the Australian economy. He acknowledged the severity of the crisis in the United States and the United Kingdom and its impact on Australia (including causing households to 'adopt a more cautious attitude to borrowing and spending'). He also, however, described the reasons why Australia was not likely to have the same experience as the United States, the United Kingdom or Europe—in part because this suggested 'a moderation in growth in domestic demand is occurring' and there was the 'need for a moderation'.

Overall, the speech allocated neither blame nor credit for Australia's financial state. He stated that 'the seriousness of the sub-prime credit crisis, and the associated weak outcomes being experienced in the US, and thought to be in prospect in the UK and some parts of Europe, are well understood by Australian households and businesses', but this was not the case for the resource boom, the reasons behind inflation and how these factors interacted. As such, while this speech addressed the global financial crisis, it was largely to alert people about why it was not Australia's greatest economic concern.

Stevens framed the crisis as a passing phase: the US economy is struggling with a 'period of weakness' and a 'period of adjustment'. This did not mean, however, that the global economic status quo was going to remain the same. He pointed to 'the change in the trade experience of Australia…[as] an indicator of the way the weight in the world economy is gradually shifting to the Asian region'. In his view, the pace of demand growth needed to slow and 'domestic consumption…is being asked to make some room, for some period of time, for the rise in other forms of investment'. He explained that he was 'seeking to head off further problems'. Stevens indicated the need for a change—one that he had already been acting towards incrementally by trying to affect the economy through careful manipulation of the cash rate. With inflation remaining the focus and cash rates rising, it was still largely business as usual for Stevens.

The explanation, expectation, policy and strategy outlined by Stevens were generally supported in the media. Reporting in all three papers (*The Age* 2008a; Rollins 2008a; Wood 2008b) on the speech was largely positive and went along with the general theme of inflation dominating government economic pronouncements (Khadem 2008; Murdoch 2008). With reference to the spectre of 'stagflation' (high inflation and low growth) hitting the Australian economy, a broad spectrum of commentators sided with the governor in the belief that it was the low-growth fears that were unfounded, with one commentator proclaiming there was 'little to fear' (Bassanese 2008a). As with Swan weeks before, the media preferred the type-1 frame, and the occasional commentator saw storm clouds on the horizon (Gittins 2008).

17 September 2008: the bank governor insists on the big picture

By mid-September, cracks were starting to appear in the Australian economy's armour. In his first address after the Lehman Brothers collapse, Stevens chose to speak about the long-term perspective and positive outlook for Australia. In an immediate agenda contestation during a question and answer session after the speech, Stevens' attempt to set the agenda was derailed by questions about recent economic developments, the crisis abroad and whether Australians were receiving an overly optimistic narrative of the situation.

In this speech, Stevens minimised the impact of the crisis on Australia, which had 'been affected by these forces, but much less than the countries at the epicentre. Our financial system is weathering the storm well.' The crisis was articulated as a catalyst for shifts. For example, Stevens portrayed the complex factors surrounding the emergence of China as 'an opportunity and a challenge for Australian business and policymakers, and not just in the resource sector'. One of these factors was that 'we have had to absorb a massive income boost…of course, there are worse problems to have!'. These underlying forces were all argued in a positive (or neutral) light.

Because there was not much of a 'crisis' (according to Stevens), there was little reason to apportion blame or suggest policies to deal with it. Stevens attempted to calm Australians, urging them to 'step back…to focus on the bigger picture'. He sought to convince the audience that it was not an Australian crisis, 'even in the volatile conditions in which we all find ourselves at present'. He acknowledged the short-term fear, but even in the days after the Lehman Brothers collapse, he urged people not to make too much of the crisis as it was the collapse of US confidence, not Lehmans as such, that was the problem.

The somewhat out-of-step and cautiously optimistic frame from the Reserve Bank Governor triggered a divided media response. Far from the unanimous chorus of optimism in earlier months, by September, media confidence in Australia's ability to avoid the worst of the financial crisis had plummeted (Oatley 2008; Stammer 2008; Williams and Martin 2008). Stevens' presentation of the crisis as requiring some degree of reform and increased transparency was uncontroversial (Mitchell 2008a; Stutchbury 2008a). Interpreting the severity and implications of the latest turn in the financial crisis for Australia was, however, up for grabs, notwithstanding Stevens' posture. Stevens' comment in the question and answer session that the Australian banking system was 'light years away' from the crumbling US system set off a wave of commentary that was characterised by uncertainty about the future of the crisis (Bassanese 2008b; Hewett 2008; Stammer 2008). As an act of meaning making and in stark contrast with the speech made a few months earlier, Stevens' attempt to continue with a type-1 crisis framing now rang hollow with many commentators, the majority of whom now seemed to moving to a type-2 conception (Winestock 2008a).

10 October 2008: the Treasurer goes to Washington

On the day that Swan spoke at the Brookings Institution, the OECD released a report praising Australia as one of the economies to have 'so far' avoided major turmoil. On the same day, however, the All Ordinaries fell 8.2 per cent—the worst drop in 21 years. Still, this speech was used to explain the success of Australia, rather than explaining the crisis. Swan brushed over the potential severity of the crisis in Australia, simply saying 'our share markets have fallen'—despite the speech occurring after several days of bad news on the

Australian share market. He repeated his oft-voiced mantra that Australia was 'better placed than almost any other developed economy to withstand the fallout'.

His chief concern was with the health of the global system. Swan offered advice and lessons from an apparent success story, quoting the OECD report, which stated that 'thanks to prudent management' (as well as 'high profitability and strong capitalisation'), the Australian economy 'has stood up well to the ongoing global financial market turbulence. So far, the financial sector has withstood the crisis.'

This speech also demonstrated the shift that had occurred from his previous resistance to government intervention to a more activist stance. Swan claimed that the OECD 'endorses the new Rudd Government's ambitious reform agenda aimed at lifting our country's productive capacity and addressing climate change'. Swan's speech highlighted his aspirations for a shift towards a more global financial architecture and away from dominant ideologies and protectionism. He strongly advocated the utilisation of existing global forums and institutions to assist during this crisis and to prevent future ones. Swan made use of historical analogies to bolster his argument. He invoked the 'hard work' and 'plenty of sacrifice' in the post-World War II decades, which led to a 'level of prosperity [our] parents could scarcely imagine during the depths of the Great Depression'. He praised the Bretton Woods agreement as a 'great moral as well as economic achievement'.

Likewise, the current global problems required a 'long term solution not just a quick fix'. Type-3 rhetoric appeared when Swan attacked 'blind faith in markets' and put Australia forward as a lesson in 'successful regulation' and leadership, wondering how 'any responsible leader [could] observe all around us the wreckage of this latest bout of financial adventurism without being stirred to act'.

With this speech coming at a time when the crisis had reached fever pitch in Australia, media commentary was generally supportive of Swan's framing of the crisis as something created by the structure of the international financial system and the pressing need for reform (*The Age* 2008b; *AFR* 2008b; Guy 2008). With the media now rapidly escalating its estimation of crisis severity (O'Sullivan and Saulwick 2008; Uren and Stutchbury 2008), there was, however, continuing scepticism about the government's line and the solutions offered (Grattan 2008a; Grenville 2008), with one commentator noting that the government was doing little but 'jawboning to keep up confidence' (Grattan 2008a). As with its response to Stevens in the month beforehand, the media struggled to reconcile the apparent gap between economic events and the line coming from the government. Mirroring this concern, in the same week as this speech, the first polls were conducted on questions concerning the economic crisis. In the period 7 October to 12 October, 52 per cent of respondents were confident in Australia's ability to withstand the global financial crisis, with 42 per cent not confident. Approval of the government's response to the global financial crisis sat at 52 per cent, with 28 per cent disapproving (Essential Research 2008a).

14 October 2008: the Prime Minister addressing the nation

The four days between Swan's address in Washington, DC, and Rudd's address to the nation were a critical sense-making and decision-making period for the government. On 12 October, the government announced a guarantee for all deposits in Australian banks in an attempt to prevent capital flight. With talk of the economic crisis reaching fever pitch in the media and in the public sphere, however, Rudd took the initiative to realign the framing of the crisis around the government's response.

There are few acts of meaning making designed to be as dramatic as or more poignant than an address to the nation. The first theme of the address was one of severity. Stating that Australians had become 'concerned, anxious or even fearful as to the future', the Prime Minister spared nothing by describing the situation as 'the worst financial crisis in our lifetime' and compared it with 'a national security crisis'—a far cry from the contained and limited crisis talked of previously. As media reports pointed out, as little as a week beforehand the government had been conspicuous in its proclivity to avoid talking in emergency terms (Dodson 2008). With this speech there could now be no doubt about the high-stakes nature of the crisis.

If, however, Rudd was strong in emphasising that the 'tough times have now arrived', he was perhaps even stronger in treating the crisis as something that was affecting Australia through no fault of its own. The crisis was allegedly caused by news of the crisis impacting on other places. It was the fear of crisis more than any internal problem that was to blame. Indeed, the one statement that obliquely accounted for the onset of the crisis was: 'Nonetheless, as Prime Minister, I was not prepared to stand idly by while people's fears here were being fed by the stream of bad economic news from abroad.' Rudd's second major theme, then, in accordance with Swan and Stevens, was one of defensive reassurance—emphatically denying that any cause or blame for the crisis was on Australian shoulders and outlining the 'absolute confidence' Australians should have in their system.

The nature of the first and second theme strongly suggests the third—that the management of the impact of the crisis should be ameliorative rather than reformative. The address was used to announce the $10.4 billion 'Economic Security Strategy'—a package designed to inject funds into the economy to keep growth positive and jobs available. It fed into reassurance too, with a strong emphasis on decision making—including comments such as 'decisive action', to 'take whatever action is necessary' and 'responsible governments step in'.

213

The combination of these two themes served to highlight and strongly emphasise the severity of the crisis and to unambiguously absolve the government of responsibility and base its policy response on that mantra.

The address was met with nearly unanimous media support on all aspects—a unanimity that was itself commented on (Martin 2008a; Ricketson 2008). *The Age* came out strongly in support of the government's framing of the crisis (*The Age* 2008c; Grattan 2008b; Martin 2008a). The *AFR* was more subdued in its support for the Prime Minister, noting 'Rudd's repackaging of himself as a proactive Prime Minister always on the alert for a pre-emptive strike' (Tingle 2008b). Support for the government's stance on the severity, nature and management of the crisis was, however, strong—although not without some questions about potential deficit (*AFR* 2008c; Dodson 2008). Similarly, *The Australian* recognised the critical turning point in the treatment of the crisis rhetorically in Australia and was quick to welcome it and the government's response (Kelly 2008; Megalogenis 2008; Stutchbury 2008b). Just one commentary remained wary of Rudd's rhetorical framing, believing it to be a convenient way to exploit the crisis in order to implement programs in unrelated social areas (Shanahan 2008a).

Several major polls saw significant rises in the Prime Minister's approval rating in the aftermath of the speech (Newspoll 2009; Nielsen 2008). Most saliently though, approval of the government's handling of the global financial crisis rose 20 points from the previous week to 72 per cent, with disapproval dropping to just 12 per cent (Essential Research 2008b). Similarly, confidence in Australia's ability to withstand the financial crisis rose by 11 per cent from the previous week to 63 per cent (Essential Research 2008b). Evidently, the new type-2 severity frame presented by the government was one the public and media found far more amenable, despite the negative economic implications.

19 November 2008: the bank governor's plea for perspective

Even during Australia's worst period of the crisis to date, Stevens held firm to his frame: largely type-1, business-as-usual rhetoric. While noting the 'breathtaking turn of events' in mid-September, he used more measured language than Rudd and Swan. He placed it into the category of a 'cyclical event' that happened at a time when growth was slowing anyway and the most unpleasant frame he provided was that Australia was 'battling economic weakness'. The crisis was not caused by 'a sequence of financial events' but because these events 'led people to think it will turn out to be a bigger event than hitherto expected'. Continuing with this theme, he cautioned that 'the biggest mistake we could make would be to talk ourselves into unnecessary economic weakness'.

In the vein of a type-1, business-as-usual frame, Stevens did not feel that the situation in mid-November warranted significant policy moves because 'in facing the financial problems themselves, the most important steps have already been taken by countries at the epicentre of the crisis'. In a type-2-style frame, however, he asserted that 'these measures cannot avert a significant slowing in the global economy' (that is, there is still a threat, albeit not critical). In defence of existing structures, these policies averted 'potential systemic collapses that would have had massive repercussions throughout the world'. Towards the end of the speech, Stevens injected some type-3 rhetoric, noting that 'every episode of crisis provides some new lessons' that can be 'incorporated into regulatory and supervisory practice'. Although using the turn of phrase 'prudent borrowing', Stevens came out in support of the government running a deficit to 'continue worthwhile public investment'.

The speech concluded with the overarching type-2 frame that: acknowledged the severity of the crisis (the 'situation is serious'; 'we face difficult circumstances'); cited exogenous causes; and argued that the status quo was worth preserving ('we need not, and should not, abandon the well-established and tested policy frameworks that are in place').

The speech received ample commentary, with most headlines capturing the imputed prospect of either a recession (Colebatch 2008b; Martin 2008b) or a deficit (Rollins 2008b; Winestock 2008b). The media reacted strongly to Stevens' continuation of a largely type-1 crisis framing. Many commentators were critical, believing Stevens' framing to be unrealistic (Uren 2008b), and a strongly downcast view of the economic situation persisted (*AFR* 2008d; Korporaal 2008).

In presenting a domestic deficit as a management response to the situation, however, Stevens received wide support, with many commentators placing blame on the government for dodging the concept for so long (Colebatch 2008b; Grattan 2008c; Mitchell 2008b). The *AFR* was particularly supportive, seeing Stevens' comments on the matter as 'a healthy dose of realism' (*AFR* 2008d), with the media often contrasting it with the obfuscated government position on Australia's budgetary future (Colebatch 2008b). In Australia, it was the technocrat, not the politicians who gave the first mention of a deficit and started the debate before the government itself would volte-face on the subject a week later.

26 November 2008: the Prime Minister's 'temporary deficit'

Until mid-November, the Rudd Government had done everything it could to avoid the prospect of a budgetary deficit becoming a reality (*The Australian* 2008c; Uren 2008a). So, when Rudd was 'absolutely upfront' in Parliament on 26 November and made a single mention that the government would 'if necessary...use a temporary deficit', it awoke a political dragon that continued to dominate crisis discourse well into the next year.

It came as no surprise, then, that the Prime Minister's address to the House of Representatives outlining the potential for a deficit did so only after dedicating two-thirds of the speech to a sobering rundown of the economic context. The crisis 'has grown from a trickle to a flood'. It had affected 'every nation. Every government. Every economy.' A far cry from the rhetoric of Australian resilience to the crisis, Rudd here dismissed that period as 'the first part of the storm'. At this point, a 'quantum shift' had occurred and the decisions that would need to be made had much higher stakes because, although it was alluded to only implicitly, Australia was staring down the barrel of a recession.

The explanation for this change was one made in constant reference to other nations: everything Australia had experienced was what the rest of the world had experienced. In particular, Rudd cited the slowdown in China and the plunge in commodity prices as major factors impacting on Australia's downturn. These shifts had in turn 'had a profound effect on [the] budget position', with a $40 billion downgrading of anticipated tax income for the government.

Rudd stated that 'under [these] circumstances, it would be responsible to draw further from the surplus and, if necessary, to use a temporary deficit to begin investing in our future infrastructure needs'. Rudd justified this move at length. Undoubtedly cognisant of the fallout such an announcement would have, however, the Prime Minister also listed numerous measures the government had taken. He framed the administration in an active light, stressing in particular that 'the budget built a strong surplus' and its fiscal policy epitomised responsible governance.

A potential budget deficit was thus slotted rhetorically within the crisis frame. Rudd's account was that of a major crisis managed by a responsible government that was willing to take whatever ameliorative steps were necessary—and that this was a policy path that was not just the 'nation's mission', but 'the mission of the international community'. In a shift of rhetorical emphasis from previous speech acts analysed here, Rudd made it clear that there was no alternative to the path the government was setting out on. The alternative to deficit spending and Labor's fiscal policy was to 'sacrifice growth and jobs'. To *not* go into deficit would be 'irresponsible'. Specific stigmatisation of the alternative to government policy as job losses and economic depression was a powerful platform from which the government could define and subdue opposition. Doing so was important because, while most had accepted events so far as externally imposed on the Australian economy, a decision by the government to go into deficit was a risk and entirely within the government's choosing, thus creating a need to shift the frame of crisis meaning to better suit this new and riskier period of government policy.

The media responded rapidly and vociferously to the mention of a potential deficit. Many commentators felt that the speech merely shifted rhetoric to comport with what had already become understood economic reality and that the severity of the situation and inevitably of a deficit were unquestionable (Grattan 2008d; Ruehl 2008; Tingle 2008c). If anything, according to some, the speech was slightly disingenuous by playing up the crisis so much yet simultaneously burying and qualifying the use of the word 'deficit' (Grattan 2008d; Wood 2008c).

The media was quick to note the speech's political effectiveness as an act of framing and rhetoric and the difficulty it created for the opposition (Carney 2008). The media was, however, routinely divided on the degree to which it substantively agreed with the approach espoused. Several articles in the *AFR* and *The Australian* were sharply critical of the belatedness, lack of detail and sense of panic in the speech, which had the potential to undermine circumstances and provided a poor response to the crisis (*AFR* 2008e; Davidson 2008; Shanahan 2008b; Stutchbury 2008d). Others in the same papers arrived at different conclusions, supporting the Prime Minister's position and his willingness to use the deficit to relieve the effects of the crisis (*The Australian* 2008d; Steketee 2008; Wood 2008c). The media was, however, virtually unanimous on one point: that the speech heralded the entry of the government into new and far more politically tricky territory than it had previously been in (Stutchbury 2008e; Tingle 2008c).

23 January 2009: the Treasurer's visit to 'ground zero'

Speaking to investors in New York at a time when Australians had started to feel the economic pinch yet continued to strongly support the government, Swan needed to present an image that would appear positive to potential investors and would boost confidence back home in Australia, but would also not jar significantly with the reality of Australians feeling the effects of the downturn. He derided the 'false prophets' who had told the world 'that the only economic role for the state in a free market economy is to remove itself'. Furthermore, Swan insisted that the crisis was not caused by globalisation but by 'spectacular regulatory failure'. He claimed that Australia's 'realistic understanding of the role of government in the contemporary market economy' was key to its success in responding to the crisis, and he emphasised and detailed the policy implemented and action taken 'swiftly and decisively' by the Rudd Government in the onset of the global crisis.

By now, Swan was adamant that the crisis was not just an incident. Instead, 'the global financial crisis occurred at a time when our economies were already under pressure to change in profound ways'. Drawing an analogy with Hurricane Katrina, he claimed that the crisis 'shockwave' exposed underlying weaknesses in the system. Swan called for the global economy to be rebuilt into an 'economy that nations, their citizens, and their environment really need'—something that his government was already working towards. Speaking in type-3 mode, Swan therefore represented the crisis as 'an opportunity for reform that must be grasped…we must make the best of a bad situation'. Swan shared with the New York audience his 'picture of what we believe the post-crisis Australian economy will look like', with the focus shifting from strengthening existing financial systems or even addressing global economic structures to society-wide alterations and improvements in the wake of the crisis.

Response by the media to this speech was comparatively limited. This might be considered surprising given that, in hindsight, the speech flagged many of the elements that would eventually come together as the new ideological/interventionist philosophy that Rudd would expand on at length in *The Monthly* within a week. *The Australian* picked up on this in a couple of commentaries, linking the speech with the coming of a debate about the future role of government in the domestic economy (Franklin 2009a, 2009b; Milne 2009); however, in general, the speech went unnoticed. A global poll conducted a week before Swan's speech found that at this point Australians largely held similar views to those articulated by the Treasurer. According to the poll, 'more than three in four Australians (76 per cent) agree that the current economic crisis points to the need for major changes in the international economic system, while slightly less than half (48 per cent) agree that major changes are also needed for their own economy' (BBC World Service 2009). In any event, the speech would prove in retrospect to be a primer for the third major framing change undertaken by the government in February 2009.

February 2009: Rudd's essay

By early February, it was clear that Australia was not going to escape significant impact from the global financial crisis. The stock market had lost more than one-third of its value, unemployment was rising and the economy had temporarily dipped into recession. In the February edition of *The Monthly*, the Prime Minister published a lengthy essay redefining the terms of the crisis on an explicitly ideological basis. No longer simply blaming the work of greedy capitalists and irresponsible risk-takers, Rudd wrote that the global financial crisis was at that point the most salient symptom of a fundamentally flawed system—one underpinned by a discredited ideology and doomed to failure by virtue of its own design.

Rudd pointed out that the crisis was now so severe it would 'mark a turning point between one epoch and the next'. In his sentiments, the crisis was 'the greatest dislocation of our lifetime'. The underlying problem for Rudd now was no longer one of inadequate global regulation or poor practice; it was one of inadequate ideas. The crisis 'called into question the prevailing neo-liberal economic orthodoxy of the past 30 years'. The long leash given to the financial sector and lack of oversight led to systemic problems and irresponsible patterns.

This was not incidental though; Rudd posited that the crisis was 'generated by the system itself', implying the inevitability of the failure of the ideological regime.

Rudd now focused blame squarely on the proponents of neo-liberal ideology: the US Federal Reserve, investment banks, extreme capitalism and subscribing political parties. Rudd placed his opposition, the Liberal Party—'home of neo-liberalism in Australia'—within that broad grouping of blameworthy neo-liberal adherents. The ideology that the Liberal Party upheld had 'not served Australia well in preparing for the current crisis'.

The ideological antidote to the crisis was social democracy: 'the international challenge for social democrats is to save capitalism from itself.' While Rudd moderated his comments by seeing the need to 'recognise the great strengths of open, competitive markets', by and large, it was the social-democratic ideology that had to be employed in order to make things right again. Australia's specific role was somewhat consistent with earlier remarks: to 'provide international support for [US President, Barack Obama's] leadership' as part of a US-led reconstitution.

The allocation of blame to the neo-liberals was framed conveniently to avoid any blame falling on the so-called social democrats or the Labor Party in Australia. One government Rudd specified as upholding the values that had to be implemented in order to rebuild the economy was the 1983–96 series of Labor governments led by his predecessors, Bob Hawke and Paul Keating. 'They were able dramatically to improve the productivity of the Australian private economy, while simultaneously expanding the role of the state in the provision of equity-enhancing public services.' Many, however, would traditionally associate the Hawke–Keating governments with the global neo-liberal economic trend of the period and they arguably laid down most of the neo-liberal economic system that Australia had going into the crisis (Edwards 2009). In Rudd's meaning making, however, the political now took centre stage.

Given the nature of the essay, the significant response in the media tended to roll down more politically dispositional grooves. The moderately conservative *The Australian* was particularly critical, variously describing Rudd's essay as an 'ill-informed ideological crusade' (Costa 2009), a 'cheap attack' and 'arrogant promise' (Albrechtsen 2009a) and an ideological 'blame game' (Sheridan 2009). At the same time, *The Age* was more positive in its response (Colebatch 2009a; Gans 2009), with the *AFR* assuming a mixed but often critical stance (Crowe 2009a; Simes 2009).

Regardless of disagreement about the substantive line of the essay, most commentators were sceptical about the kind of rhetoric on display. Several articles (Albrechtsen 2009a; Hewett 2009; Tingle 2009a; Wright 2009) saw it as a nakedly political act designed to open up a previously muted argument about the ideological repercussions of the crisis. It was allegedly designed to first, bolster and justify a comprehensive and high-spending stimulus package and budget (which included numerous components that had little relevance to the recession); and second, to wed the political opposition to a supposedly failed ideology and discredited policies. Other articles expressed distaste for the 'blatantly political' timing and character of the essay (Edwards 2009; Sheridan 2009) and its numerous internal contradictions and misrepresentations (Burchell 2009; Hirst 2009). The essay was seen by some as symptomatic of a shift in rhetoric and strategy by both parties to 'score points' and assign blame for the crisis (Grattan 2009; Tingle 2009b).

There was, however, every indication that the shift was well received by the public. In polling conducted throughout February, support ranged as high as 84 per cent for certain 'social-democracy' measures such as education and infrastructure investment (Essential Research 2009a). Fifty-one per cent agreed specifically with the stimulus package as framed by Rudd, with only 33 per cent disagreeing (Essential Research 2009a). Irrespective of traditional resistance, the public did not reject the shift to a type-3 framing.

20 February 2009: the bank governor addresses the House

In late February, the bank governor had to face the House of Representatives Standing Economic Committee to account for the actions of the RBA in response to the crisis and the effects of these policies on the economy. Since his most recent statement to the committee in September 2008 (not analysed here), the crisis in Australia had escalated and the RBA had cut the cash rate by 3.75 per cent.

Stevens held firm to the various elements of the three frames seen in previous speeches. He acknowledged that the end of 2008 had witnessed 'the most intense financial turmoil seen in decades', but he minimised the severity by saying that the 'worst of the turmoil was actually fairly short lived'. He expanded on his optimistic prediction that Australia would likely 'have done well in comparison with most other countries'. He claimed that the policy action had been effective and insisted that the causes had been the public reaction to the shocks of 2008, not the shocks themselves. He remained adamant that the crisis was not as severe as many believed and even though the magnitude of the slowdown had come as a surprise, the slowdown itself was not unexpected.

He went on to exogenise the cause of the crisis by claiming that the 'deterioration in international conditions was so rapid that no policy response could prevent a period of near-term weakness in the Australian economy or, for that matter, other economies'. Furthermore, he asserted that the crisis was not as severe as it could have been and he vindicated the Rudd Government's response, stating that 'the extraordinary actions of governments and central banks in that period...helped to stabilise what could have been a catastrophic loss of confidence in the global financial system'. His message was one of near-term realism and long-term optimism.

Reporting on the Stevens speech, the media picked up on two themes: the RBA's apparent optimism in the face of continued negative news (Martin 2009a; Thornton 2009) and the governor's support for the government's policies in the crisis (Rumble 2009). The *AFR* captured in its editorial the continuing conflict between optimism and pessimism in the assessment of severity in that period (*AFR* 2009), though it was generally deferential to the governor's assessment and in broad agreement with the general direction outlined for RBA policy (Mitchell 2009; Rumble 2009).

Some commentaries, however, openly questioned Stevens' optimism, with one article commenting that it was 'his job to put a positive spin on things' and thus 'naturally the [governor] had no criticism of the Government's stimulus package or market interventions' (Colebatch 2009b). They pointed out that previous assessments of economic conditions had proved wrong through unforeseen events, and thus there was no reason to suspect that it could not happen again (Thornton 2009). In a similar vein to previous responses to Stevens' comments, therefore, the media was inclined to question his framing of the severity of the crisis, while being generally supportive of him personally and the management strategy espoused.

23 March 2009: the Treasurer's promise for the future

This speech reflected a treasurer resigned to the troubles of the economy but with a determination that the future would be bright, and a goal of rallying the nation. Speaking to the Sydney business community, Swan, in an address titled 'A future of promise', characterised the crisis as 'the worst the world can throw at us', insisting that 'no country in the world can hope to escape unscathed, including us'. This acted to reinforce his assurance that Australia was 'still faring better than almost all other developed nations'. He attempted to evoke patriotism and inspire a fighting spirit, telling the audience that to succeed 'we mustn't freeze in the face of immediate challenges, or use them as an excuse to retrench and retreat'. This theme was also present as he described the policy approach of the government—'to act early; minimise the depth of the problem; be in a position to recover faster. In short, stay on the offence.'

Swan tried to claim that the 'national mood' was one in which 'the short-term is full of challenges, the long-term is full of promise'. Swan's focus on the future was apt given the split in public attitudes about the hope for the short term. A poll conducted in the week before Swan's speech found that 43 per cent of respondents felt that the government's actions did not matter because 'the Australian economy cannot be protected from the effects of the global financial crisis'. However, 44 per cent still had faith in the government's influence, believing 'if the Government takes the right actions it can protect Australia's economy from the effects of the global financial crisis' (Essential Research 2009c).

While not attributing blame for the crisis, Swan deflected criticism that the Rudd Government was not meeting its election promises. Swan said that he would 'have preferred to have spent my time ticking off items on our "to do" list' and, after sitting 'in opposition during the boom years', he had to now 'chart a way through such an extraordinary international economic collapse', which he claimed the government was succeeding at. He asserted that the government's first stimulus package had kept Australia out of a recession and, having announced the $42 billion stimulus package a month earlier, this was a sort of vindication—or at least encouraging.

Swan did not stop there, however, criticising 'lazy and predictable arguments about deficits and government debt'. He claimed that the weakness of these arguments 'lies in their assumption that global economic conditions have not changed, when clearly they have, in the most damaging fashion'. Swan excoriated those who 'fall back on ideology', 'think we should let events run their course' and 'opportunistically deny our economy is being buffeted by global forces'. He even suggested they might be 'willing Australia to fail'. Swan claimed that he was not replacing one ideology with another but replacing an ideological approach with a 'pragmatic' approach. This speech, strongly projecting a type-3 frame, was an attempt to rally the public in unity against the exogenous crisis, discredit the opposition for working against the government's policies (and apparently Australia as a whole) and present an optimistic (and opportunistic) perspective on the crisis.

Coming on the heels of the announcement by Rudd that recession was now virtually unavoidable (Kerin and Walker 2009) and amid a series of other high-profile economic developments such as the 'Ruddbank' and state debt crises, the media did not find much in the speech to comment on—though it was reprinted in full in *The Australian* (*The Australian* 2009a). Much of the media was more concerned with announcements of budgetary implications after the Treasurer in his speech flagged that change would need occur (Kerr 2009; Steketee 2009). *The Australian* ran an article calling for 'rhetorical discipline', which was critical of the government's recent attempts to frame the crisis through newly politicised terms (*The Australian* 2009b). The majority of articles were interested far less in descriptions of the severity or explanation of the crisis, hanging out instead for specific policy prescriptions (for example, Crowe 2009b). It is interesting to note that this speech, which invokes the same type-3 framing that Rudd broached in the month before, seemingly raises far less controversy. Whether this was due to a tacit acceptance of this new frame or just a general lack of media interest is an interesting point to speculate on.

4. Framing the financial crisis in Australia: analysis and discussion

These speeches suggest that crisis framing during the period studied moved from a type-1 (severity minimised, incidental) to a type-2 (severity acknowledged, incidental) and finally to a type-3 (severity maximised, systemic problem) diagnosis. There were also a number of consistent themes that persisted in the framing of the crisis in Australia, which will be discussed further below.

In the speech acts from March to June 2008, the crisis was seen as something remote and with limited consequences for Australia. With confidence bolstered by high commodity prices and a strong Asian economy, the spectre of inflation and economic overheating was seen as the real economic management priority for the government. Explanation and blame for the crisis were diffused and sectoral, allocated to a runaway banking sector and poor decisions made by greedy financiers. In sum, the global financial crisis was still viewed very much as a sub-prime crisis, warranting only minor responses. This frame was consistent with what many other cases studied here maintained in the lead-up to the crisis manifesting as a global recession, where governments tended to play down the crisis to maintain confidence and contain political and policy consequences.

The undeniable seriousness of the crisis hit home fast in September 2008. As evidenced by the confused responses to Stevens' speech in that month, it was no longer tenable to deny the severity of the crisis. It stands to reason that this period was one in which the government itself was trying to make sense of the crisis. Within just four days of a relatively upbeat speech by Swan on 10 October, the Prime Minister appeared before the nation to dramatically revise the government's severity stance, lifting the political stakes along with it. By mid-November, both political actors had redefined the crisis squarely into a type-2 frame (severity acknowledged/incidental causes). This framing became politically necessary to justify the thorny issues of deficit and recession, both of which seemed inevitable by the end of 2008. Action was, however, framed as ameliorative; the government chose not to define the crisis as one of systemic problems, instead maintaining a line that Australia could not be 'immune' from international economic conditions in spite of having nothing to do with the genesis of the crisis.

This frame shifted slowly, however, to what began to look like a type-3 (severity maximised, symptomatic causes) categorisation by January 2009. The government began to point to something systemically wrong that led to the crisis: neo-liberalism. Rudd's essay in *The Monthly* marked a new and concerted effort to outline 'neo-liberal' ideology as the framework that allowed the crisis to occur and, as such, presented a justification for a new ideological policy platform from which the government must operate: social democracy. Though still finding little at fault with the financial framework in Australia per se, Rudd nevertheless found a common (if poorly defined) ideological enemy behind the crisis, suggesting its domestic adherents had to absorb some of the blame.

Finding a culprit: the political game

Having taken office in late 2007 after 11 years of their opponents' rule, the Rudd Administration could easily sidestep blame. If anything, the circumstances allowed the government to occupy the position of the 'critics' rather than 'incumbents' in the Boin et al. (2009) typology. Yet during the first two framing phases at least, arguably there were no clear 'incumbents' or 'critics'. Blame was made relevant only towards the end of the period studied. The overwhelming consensus in politics and in the media had long been that Australia was the innocent victim of world chaos, and indeed the strength of the banking system and financial regulations in Australia were the bulwarks that had warded off toxic assets. Even as the severity of the crisis increased, blame was absolved and responsibility was denied with little contention. It was only in January–February 2009 that the government rhetorically began to focus the blame—in this case, on its ideological opponents and its predecessors, by tying them in with the now 'guilty' intellectual edifice of neo-liberalism.

This was not just a Rudd effort. Swan's speech in January in particular indicated that oppositional forces were 'willing Australia to fail' (Swan 2009b) rather than abandoning their ideological platform. As a result, the political game moved to box III (Table 2.1 in Chapter 2): a blame showdown where, paradoxically, it was the government playing the critic and focusing blame and the opposition refusing to accept it. Indeed, Rudd's essay in February was enough to incite former Prime Minister John Howard to make his first post-government written commentary, denying responsibility, and he was joined in strenuous opposition by other prominent Liberal Party figures and conservative media. As a strategy of political exploitation, however, the government's action can be seen as effective, as the Liberal opposition struggled to distance itself from the label and to present a viable or acceptable counter-frame for the events.

Policy exploitation: Labor's new deal

Fitting the three framing periods, policy exploitation in the first two was designed mostly to be ameliorative. Incremental reforms—such as bank deposit insurance, a moderate stimulus package paid from the surplus and some minor fiscal policy adjustments—were the modus operandi under which the government proceeded (with little opposition) until major reframing in January.

The assignation of blame and identification of a systemic problem in early 2009, however, allowed (at least rhetorically) a much broader scope of policies to be justified as necessary to deal with the crisis. The government proceeded from here to generate a shopping list of tangentially related reforms such as a carbon-efficient economy, an education revolution, taxation reform and greater global cooperation (Swan 2009a). The new 'economic reform agenda', replete with a $42 billion stimulus entitled the 'Nation Building and Jobs Plan', was launched from this platform of rhetoric as essential to avoiding recession and warding off future crises. How politically opportunistic this was is a matter of conjecture; much of what has been implemented in the wake of the crisis is merely pre-existing election promises repackaged as recession busters. Other policies, however, have arguably gone through more smoothly than otherwise due to a convenient rhetorical frame. One example might have been the rolling back of the private health insurance rebate (in spite of an election promise to keep it), which was publicly framed as a crisis-borne necessity in the May 2009 budget. Swan and Rudd themselves obliquely referred to the policy opportunities offered by the crisis in their speeches (Swan 2009a) and there is plenty of evidence to suggest they have utilised them with considerable success.

With the media and public focused squarely on the financial crisis by October–November 2008, there was, however, perhaps no choice for a government whose election credibility relied at least in part on delivering on significant social promises. Crisis or no crisis, Labor faced a political bottom line and an election in less than two years.

Even before the height of the severity of the crisis in September–October, there was some degree of crisis exploitation for the purposes of policy. In the first of Rudd's speeches studied, and supported by Swan's speech in June 2008, the government used the foreign crisis to springboard itself into the international policy arena. By this stage, the sub-prime crisis had been extant for months. As such, at a time when Australia was seen to be soundly based and escaping the fate of many other Western nations, Swan and Rudd were eager to frame the crisis as an opportunity for Australia to participate actively in a global regulatory response. This was congruent with an existing internationalist agenda: bidding for a seat on the UN Security Council, setting nuclear disarmament talks and discussion of an Asian Union. The global financial crisis provided another opportunity for the Rudd Government to engage this policy platform. Evidently though, this international agenda was dropped as domestic conditions deteriorated.

The policy-exploitation game highlights the dangers for those tagged as the 'status quo' players. In Australia, while the government effectively framed itself as the proactive agent of change and reform, the rhetoric of the government meant that the opposition found it difficult to play the role of either incumbent or policy defender. By and large, it *competed* with the administration as an alternative agent of change. In this context, it was comparatively easier for the then new government to simply define its long-serving predecessors in the opposition as agents of the status quo. Throughout the first quarter of 2009, Rudd and Swan labelled resistance to government policy responses as merely adherence to defunct ideology—ideology accused of causing the crisis in the first place. This left the Liberal Party with hard choices. On the one hand, they risked the 'me-too' tag and a lack of definition if they sought to associate themselves with change and support government policy. On the other, if they sought to defend the status quo they risked irrelevance and association with the elements that were being blamed for the crisis. It was perhaps no wonder that by the end of March 2009, the Prime Minister had reached record approval ratings and there had been little change in the support for the opposition or its leadership. Key, then, to the unfolding of the framing contest was how the government seized the initiative; with the government defining the position of its opponents as status quo players, the opposition was cornered into playing the game from a side it would not necessarily have intended.

Exploitation objectives: politics and technocracy

As has been the case in other countries studied in this volume, the Reserve Bank Governor began with descriptions of the crisis quite similar to those of Rudd and Swan, but parted ways with his political counterparts as the crisis progressed. The technocrat has little to gain from engaging in political framing contests. The role of the RBA Governor was one where he was strategically interested in maintaining confidence and economic stability, and thus his interests congealed around presenting as supportive a picture as possible.

By the same measure, Stevens was afforded more room to manoeuvre in his framing. While he scaled up his assessment of the severity of the crisis alongside the government (though not to the same degree), it was his speech in November that first breached the topic of deficit spending to support growth. This came amid a fortnight in which the government almost farcically avoided mentioning the dreaded 'd' word—a fact commented on extensively in the press (Colebatch 2008b). Within a week of Stevens' speech, however, the Prime Minister had turned on a dime to signpost the government's intention to (if necessary) go into budgetary deficit to support fiscal policy.

By January, the political rhetoric was advocating a raft of policy changes, while Stevens remained stuck firmly to his definition of the crisis in Australia as a severe incident but part of the business cycle. Nonetheless, Stevens often spoke in tacit support of the government's approach to the crisis. To maintain credibility, the governor had to walk a fine line between expressing support for the government and becoming an unofficial cheerleader—a line, according to some reports from the period, that the governor was unable to keep to (Colebatch 2009b). While there was a clear differentiation between the framing undertaken by the government and the bank, innately there was a connection too. Their roles were separate, yet they relied on each other for certain rhetorical cues and leaned on each other for certain justifications. The relationship was a complex one, but it played an important role in the framing game.

Counter-frames: the media and the public

In an overall sense, the media and the public were solidly consistent in their support for the government during the crisis and there were plenty of indications that the government's framing of the crisis was largely successful. Though the media maintained certain editorial and political positions, the degree to which newspapers supported or critiqued the government appeared to be more case-by-case. In the first two framing phases identified (type-1 and type-2), this was understandable as government activity attracted little controversy. In the final stage, the blame allocation and ideological agenda pushing elicited a stronger response from the traditional right-leaning news media. Nonetheless, as public support for Kevin Rudd coasted at high levels for most of the period, it was probably unsurprising that the newspapers encapsulated that sentiment of general support. All through the time studied, the Rudd Government maintained consistently high polling figures. From May 2008 until March 2009, approval for Rudd's performance never fell below 61 per cent (Nielsen 2008, 2009). From the critical period of mid-October 2008 until mid-March 2009, between 53 per cent and 63 per cent of Australians were confident that the Australian economy could withstand the global financial crisis (Essential Research 2009b).

One exception to this pattern might be the government's earlier attempts to maintain a low-severity frame during the escalation of events in September and October. In was in these months of the period studied, after the Lehman Brothers collapse but before the Prime Minister's address to the nation, that the lowest levels of public support were observed. When a type-2 frame was belatedly adopted, the public rallied, despite the somewhat negative implications of such a change. Similarly, media commentaries on the speeches in the transition period were most consistently sceptical of the government's line on severity. In the area of severity, it seems the government had less room to move than elsewhere, and attempts to play down the crisis in the earlier stages appear to have made the government seem out of step rather than calming the situation.

When the government proactively seized the framing initiative in mid-October, however, and pursued a type-3 frame in early 2009, the public's mood largely rallied behind the government, indicating, if anything, that the later framing was a successful endeavour for the Labor Party. The Prime Minister's popularity and economic confidence remained in the high sixties (Newspoll 2009) and support for the new stimulus package in February was as high as 84 per cent for some measures (Essential Research 2009a). In contrast with attempts to frame the severity of the crisis, assigning causes and framing a response to the crisis were fairly successful endeavours for the government, even as it moved into otherwise controversial territory.

Also interesting is what agenda the media might have set for crisis definition. The most prominent example of this was deficit spending—a matter that required an extensive rhetorical frame to be set up to even introduce it as a possibility. That necessity was driven largely by a salience of the issue created by the media, as even the vaguest of references to this matter were latched onto with a ferocity that compelled the government to be well prepared.

Conclusion

In summary, the Australian story in this volume has been one of fluidity in framing and proactive adaptation. Coming on the back of 11 years of conservative government, the Rudd Administration was very successful in framing its new government as a dynamic agent of change. Astutely coming to embrace the severity and scale of the crisis, it was able to tailor its election promises, its policy platform and its broader ideological agenda to the circumstances and frame them as cures to the ills of the financial crisis. In the process, it tethered its erstwhile opposition to perceived historical failures and untenable ideologies. The Rudd Government adapted its rhetorical strategy to utilise the crisis, focus blame and embrace policy implications. The strategy has, however, been an evolving one. The significant shift in tone from mid-2008 to early 2009 demonstrates the complexity and situational nature of framing contests, and the government faced a difficult balancing act when creating a rhetorical frame that could be received as realistic by its constituency without shanghaiing the government agenda.

Though many observations have been discussed previously, one that seems critical to the success of the Rudd Government in this case is positioning. Flexibility to seize the initiative and define the players in the framing contests proved to be critical for the government. Despite starting as a defender of the system and playing down the crisis, the government was able to quickly recast itself as a champion of change and action by October 2008, and gave programmatic weight to that action by February 2009. Once accomplished, the framing battle itself was confined to light skirmishes as the opposition struggled to present an alternative frame and escape definition as a defender of a failed financial system.

In this chapter, we have been limited to examining just a slice of what occurred rhetorically during the escalation of the crisis (and how it was received). Nonetheless, while the global financial crisis undeniably increased the complexity of governing and created more difficult political and fiscal terrain, the Australian case demonstrates the significant political power of crisis framing and how, when harnessed well, crisis could be wind in the sails of the government, generating political momentum. In the middle of 2009, as the crisis continues to demolish the political capital of Western governments, their leaders can only look upon Kevin Rudd with envy.

References

Age 2008a, 'Sometimes a little bad news is actually good news', *The Age*, 16 June, viewed 17 June 2009, <http://www.theage.com.au/opinion/editorial/sometimes-a-little-bad-news-is-actually-good-news-20080615-2qwh.html>

Age 2008b, 'Step back, and look beyond the panic', *The Age*, 11 October, viewed 17 June 2009, <http://www.theage.com.au/opinion/editorial/step-back-and-look-beyond-the-panic-20081010-4yf7.html>

Age 2008c, 'Spending the surplus to suit the times', *The Age*, 15 October, viewed 30 June 2009, <http://www.theage.com.au/opinion/editorial/spending-the-surplus-to-suit-the-times-20081014-50l5.html>

Albrechtsen, J. 2009a, 'PM dumps facade for his ideological dream', *The Australian*, 4 February, viewed 15 June 2009, <http://www.theaustralian.news.com.au/story/0,,25004487-7583,00.html?from=public_rss>

Albrechtsen, J. 2009b, 'Hayek hatred a handy dog whistle', *The Australian*, 1 April, viewed 18 June 2009, <http://www.theaustralian.news.com.au/story/0,,25271550-32522,00.html>

Australian 2008a, 'Regulate lightly', *The Australian*, 2 April.

Australian 2008b, 'Rudd should take a long-term view', *The Australian*, 3 April, viewed 30 June 2009, <http://www.theaustralian.news.com.au/story/0,25197,23473729-16741,00.html>

Australian 2008c, 'The seven-letter word that dare not speak its dreaded name', *The Australian*, 27 November, viewed 16 June 2009, <http://www.theaustralian.news.com.au/story/0,,24712368-20261,00.html>

Australian 2008d, 'D-word beats r-word', *The Australian*, 28 November, viewed 16 June 2009, <http://www.theaustralian.news.com.au/story/0,,24717807-16382,00.html>

Australian 2009a, Editorial, *The Australian*, 23 March.

Australian 2009b, 'Rhetorical discipline would help', *The Australian*, 27 March, viewed 18 June 2009, <http://www.theaustralian.news.com.au/story/0,25197,25247874-16741,00.html>

Australian Financial Review (AFR) 2008a, 'Avoid response a la Sarbanes', *Australian Financial Review*, 1 April, viewed 29 June 2009, <http://www.afr.com/home/viewerSearch.aspx?ATL://20080401000020489278>

Australian Financial Review (AFR) 2008b, 'Now, to rise to the challenge', *Australian Financial Review*, 10 October, viewed 17 June 2009, <http://www.afr.com/home/viewerSearch.aspx?ATL:// 20081010000030404335>

Australian Financial Review (AFR) 2008c, 'The intervention we had to have', *Australian Financial Review*, 15 October.

Australian Financial Review (AFR) 2008d, 'Government's role is to support the economy', *Australian Financial Review*, 22 November, viewed 17 June 2009, <http://www.afr.com/home/viewerSearch.aspx?ATL:// 20081122000030562453>

Australian Financial Review (AFR) 2008e, 'Deficit requires serious thought', *Australian Financial Review*, 27 November, viewed 16 June 2009, <http://www.afr.com/home/viewerSearch.aspx?ATL:// 20081127000030580716>

Australian Financial Review (AFR) 2009, 'Australia must adapt to change', *Australian Financial Review*, 23 February, viewed 18 June 2009, <http://www.afr.com/home/viewerSearch.aspx?ATL:// 20090223000030865426>

Australian Press Council 2008, *State of the News Print Media in Australia*, Australian Press Council, Sydney.

Bassanese, D. 2008a, 'A recession-like feeling we have to have', *Australian Financial Review*, 14 June, viewed 17 June 2009, <http://www.afr.com/home/viewerSearch.aspx?ATL:// 20080614000020782248>

Bassanese, D. 2008b, 'Australian banks in sound condition', *Australian Financial Review*, 18 September, viewed 17 June 2009, <http://www.afr.com/home/viewerSearch.aspx?ATL:// 1221707147268>

BBC World Service 2009, 'Economic system needs major changes: global poll', *BBC World Service*, viewed 1 July 2009, <http://www.globescan.com/news_archives/bbc_economy09/ bbc_economy09.pdf>

Boin, A., McConnell, A. and 't Hart, P. 2009, 'Crisis exploitation: political and policy impacts of framing contests', *Journal of European Public Policy*, vol. 16, no. 1, pp. 81–106.

Burchell, D. 2009, 'Too many authors get Rudd into a write mess', *The Australian*, 2 February, viewed 15 June 2009, <http://www.theaustralian.news.com.au/story/ 0,25197,24992899-5013479,00.html>

Carney, S. 2008, 'Lib case in deficit—opinion', *The Age*, 29 November, viewed 16 June 2009,
<http://www.theage.com.au/news/opinion/lib-case-in-deficit/2008/11/28/1227491827373.html>

Colebatch, T. 2008a, 'Swan's promise is ready cash but not full protection', *The Age*, 3 June, viewed 16 June 2009,
<http://business.theage.com.au/business/swans-promise-is-ready-cash-but-not-full-protection-20080602-2kuy.html>

Colebatch, T. 2008b, 'Just say it: in a recession a deficit is not necessarily bad', *The Age*, 21 November, viewed 17 June 2009,
<http://www.theage.com.au/national/just-say-it-in-a-recession-a-deficit-is-not-necessarily-bad-20081120-6cu5.html?page=-1>

Colebatch, T. 2009a, 'Good, bad and the amoral', *The Age*, 4 February, viewed 15 June 2009,
<http://www.theage.com.au/national/good-bad-and-the-amoral-20090203-7wur.html>

Colebatch, T. 2009b, 'Contained but not doused, financial bushfires will be burning for months', *The Age*, 21 February, viewed 18 June 2009,
<http://www.afr.com/home/viewerSearch.aspx?ATL://20090221000030860241>

Cornell, A. 2008, 'Four pillars overlooks the real challenge', *Australian Financial Review*, 3 June, viewed 16 June 2009,
<http://www.afr.com/home/viewerSearch.aspx?ATL://20080603000020739779>

Costa, M. 2009, 'Rudd on a dangerous, ill-informed crusade', *The Australian*, 6 February, viewed 15 June 2009,
<http://www.theaustralian.news.com.au/story/0,25197,25013850-5013480,00.html>

Crowe, D. 2009a, 'Rudd's new deal', *Australian Financial Review*, 7 February, viewed 15 June 2009,
<http://www.afr.com/home/viewerSearch.aspx?ATL://20090207000030809563>

Crowe, D. 2009b, 'Swan wants bank reform', *Australian Financial Review*, 24 March, viewed 18 June 2009,
<http://www.afr.com/home/viewerSearch.aspx?ATL://20090324000030967862>

Davidson, S. 2008, 'Planning to go into deficit is misguided', *Australian Financial Review*, 1 December, viewed 16 June 2009,
<http://www.afr.com/home/viewerSearch.aspx?ATL://20081201000030594865>

Dodson, L. 2008, 'This time around it's no flight of fancy', *Australian Financial Review*, 15 October, viewed 10 June 2009, <http://www.afr.com/home/viewerSearch.aspx?ATL://20081015000030423227>

Durie, M. C. J. 2008, 'Knock over the four pillars policy and let ACCC decide', *The Australian*, 3 June, viewed 16 June 2009, <http://www.theaustralian.news.com.au/story/0,25197,23799742-5013408,00.html>

Edwards, J. 2009, 'Neo-liberal evils are exaggerated', *Australian Financial Review*, 2 February, viewed 15 June 2009, <http://www.afr.com/home/viewerSearch.aspx?ATL://20090202000030790955>

Essential Research 2008a, *Essential Report 13 October 2008*, 13 October, Essential Media, Sydney, viewed 1 July 2009, <http://www.essentialmedia.com.au/Media/EssentialReport_131008.pdf>

Essential Research 2008b, *Essential Report 20 October 2008*, 20 October, Essential Media, Sydney, viewed 1 July 2009, <http://www.essentialmedia.com.au/Media/EssentialReport_201008.pdf>

Essential Research 2009a, *Essential Report 16 February 2009*, 16 February, Essential Media, Sydney, viewed 1 July 2009, <http://www.essentialmedia.com.au/Media/Essential_Report_160209.pdf>

Essential Research 2009b, *Essential Report 10 March 2009*, 10 March, Essential Media, Sydney, viewed 1 July 2009, <http://www.essentialmedia.com.au/Media/Essential_Report_100309.pdf>

Essential Research 2009c, *Essential Report 23 March 2009*, 23 March, Essential Media, Sydney, viewed 1 July 2009, <http://www.essentialmedia.com.au/Media/Essential_Report_230309.pdf>

Flitton, D. 2008, 'The Rudd show goes on tour', *The Age*, 2 April, viewed 29 June 2009, <http://www.theage.com.au/news/national/the-rudd-show-goes-on-tour//04/01/1206850911106.html>

Franklin, M. 2009a, 'Wayne Swan calls for new controls on free market', *The Australian*, 24 January, viewed 18 June 2009, <http://www.theaustralian.news.com.au/story/0,24897,24955346-643,00.html>

Franklin, M. 2009b, 'Turnbull says let market decide', *The Australian*, 26 January, viewed 18 June 2009, <http://www.theaustralian.news.com.au/story/0,25197,24962641-601,00.html>

Gans, J. 2009, 'Forget ideology—common sense should prevail', *The Age*, 5 February, viewed 15 June 2009, <http://business.theage.com.au/business/forget-ideology--common-sense-should-prevail-20090204-7xyz.html>

Gittins, R. 2008, 'Prediction: next recession will be a severe one', *The Age*, 16 June.

Grattan, M. 2008a, 'Hoping to ride out the storm', *The Age*, 10 October, viewed 17 June 2009, <http://www.theage.com.au/opinion/hoping-to-ride-out-the-storm-20081009-4xir.html?page=-1>

Grattan, M. 2008b, 'Driving in thick fog, trying not to crash', *The Age*, 15 October, viewed 10 June 2009, <http://www.theage.com.au/national/driving-in-thick-fog-trying-not-to-crash-20081014-50no.html>

Grattan, M. 2008c, 'Deficit need not be a dirty word', *The Age*, 21 November, viewed 17 June 2009, <http://www.theage.com.au/opinion/deficit-need-not-be-a-dirty-word-20081120-6cs5.html?page=-1>

Grattan, M. 2008d, 'PM gets real on the d-word', *The Age*, 27 November, viewed 16 June 2009, <http://www.theage.com.au/national/pm-gets-real-on-the-dword-20081126-6is3.html>

Grattan, M. 2009, 'The great ideological divide', *The Age*, 6 February, viewed 15 June 2009, <http://www.theage.com.au/opinion/the-great-ideological-divide-20090205-7yx0.html>

Grenville, S. 2008, 'Soothing platitudes don't save the world', *Australian Financial Review*, 13 October, viewed 17 June 2009, <http://www.afr.com/home/viewerSearch.aspx?ATL://20081013000030414781>

Guy, R. 2008, 'Pressure rises for global crisis plan', *Australian Financial Review*, 10 October, viewed 17 June 2009, <http://www.afr.com/home/viewerSearch.aspx?ATL://20081010000030405398>

Harper, I. 2008, 'Four pillars, not much wisdom', *Australian Financial Review*, 3 June, viewed 16 June 2009, <http://www.afr.com/home/viewerSearch.aspx?ATL://20080603000020739587>

Hewett, J. 2008, 'Greater unravelling of a system already in crisis', *The Australian*, 18 September, viewed 17 June 2009,

<http://www.theaustralian.news.com.au/story/
0,25197,24364909-5013565,00.html>

Hewett, J. 2009, 'Manna from Kevin Rudd leaves the opposition unimpressed',
The Australian, 7 February, viewed 15 June 2009,
<http://www.theaustralian.news.com.au/story/
0,,25018554-28737,00.html?from=communities>

Hirst, D. 2009, 'Rudd gets his sources wrong', *The Age*, 7 February, viewed
15 June 2009, <http://www.theage.com.au/national/
rudd-gets-his-sources-wrong-20090206-7zzu.html>

Jury, A. 2008, 'Four pillars hold up the status quo', *Australian Financial Review*,
3 June, viewed 16 June 2009,
<http://www.afr.com/home/viewerSearch.aspx?ATL://
20080603000020739787>

Kelly, P. 2008, 'Two cheers for Rudd', *The Australian*, 27 September, viewed
17 June 2009, <http://www.theaustralian.news.com.au/story/
0,25197,24408103-12250,00.html>

Kerin, J. and Walker, T. 2009, 'Recession unavoidable: PM', *Australian Financial
Review*, 23 March, viewed 18 June 2009,
<http://www.afr.com/home/viewerSearch.aspx?ATL://
20090323000030964226>

Kerr, C. 2009, 'Wayne Swan flags budget bonus for pensioners, self-funded
retirees', *The Australian*, 23 March, viewed 18 June 2009,
<http://www.theaustralian.news.com.au/story/
0,25197,25229988-5017014,00.html>

Khadem, N. 2008, 'Boom a threat, says Reserve', *The Age*, 14 June, viewed
17 June 2009, <http://www.theage.com.au/national/
boom-a-threat-says-reserve-20080613-2qb9.html>

Korporaal, G. 2008, 'Positivity is profitable', *The Australian*, 22 November,
viewed 17 June 2009,
<http://www.theaustralian.news.com.au/business/story/
0,,24685780-30538,00.html>

Martin, P. 2008a, 'Songs of praise from all parties', *The Age*, 15 October, viewed
10 June 2009,
<http://www.theage.com.au/national/songs-of-praise-from-all-parties-
20081014-50nm.html>

Martin, P. 2008b, 'Recession possible, says Reserve Bank head', *The Age*,
20 November, viewed 17 June 2009,
<http://www.theage.com.au/national/
recession-possible-says-reserve-bank-head-20081119-6ble.html>

Martin, P. 2009a, 'Banks must not overreact: Reserve', *The Age*, 21 February, viewed 18 June 2009, <http://www.afr.com/home/viewerSearch.aspx?ATL:// 20090221000030860252>

Martin, P. 2009b, 'Reserve Bank flags wider brief to burst bubbles', *The Age*, 21 February, viewed 18 June 2009, <http://www.afr.com/home/viewerSearch.aspx?ATL:// 20090221000030860249>

Megalogenis, G. 2008, 'Borrowed ideas but higher stakes', *The Australian*, 15 October, viewed 11 June 2009, <http://blogs.theaustralian.news.com.au/meganomics/ index.php/theaustralian/comments/borrowed_ideas_but_higher_stakes/>

Milne, G. 2009, 'Swan concedes the worst is still ahead of us', *The Australian*, 26 January, viewed 18 June 2009, <http://www.theaustralian.news.com.au/story/ 0,25197,24961777-33435,00.html>

Mitchell, A. 2008a, 'Bank reform calls won't go away', *Australian Financial Review*, 20 September, viewed 17 June 2009, <http://www.afr.com/home/viewerSearch.aspx?ATL:// 20080920000030330039>

Mitchell, A. 2008b, 'Nothing dirty about "d" word', *Australian Financial Review*, 20 November, viewed 17 June 2009, <http://www.afr.com/home/viewerSearch.aspx?ATL:// 20081120000030556217>

Mitchell, A. 2009, 'It might all be left to central banks', *Australian Financial Review*, 23 February, viewed 18 June 2009, <http://www.afr.com/home/viewerSearch.aspx?ATL:// 20090223000030865299>

Murdoch, S. 2008, 'RBA chief highlights inflation threat', *The Age*, 13 June, viewed 17 June 2009, <http://business.theage.com.au/business/ rba-chief-highlights-inflation-threat-20080613-2pzx.html>

Newspoll 2009, *Opinion Polls: Political and issues trends*, Newspoll, viewed 1 July 2009, <http://www.newspoll.com.au/cgi-bin/polling/display_poll_data.pl>

Nielsen 2008, *Estimates of Voting Intention and Leadership Approval 2008*, Nielsen, Sydney, viewed 1 July 2009, <http://au.nielsen.com/news/documents/NielsenPoll2008_000.pdf>

Nielsen 2009, *Estimates of Voting Intention and Leadership Approval 2009*, Nielsen, Sydney, viewed 1 July 2009, <http://au.nielsen.com/news/documents/NielsenPoll2009.pdf>

Oatley, A. 2008, 'We forgot to keep a close eye on bubble trouble', *Australian Financial Review*, 19 September, viewed 17 June 2009, <http://www.afr.com/home/viewerSearch.aspx?ATL:// 20080919000030326048>

O'Sullivan, M. and Saulwick, J. 2008, 'Black Friday', *The Age*, 11 October, viewed 17 June 2009, <http://business.theage.com.au/business/black-friday-20081010-4yf9.html>

Patten, S. 2008, 'Swan treads well-worn path to financial safety', *Australian Financial Review*, 7 June, viewed 17 June 2009, <http://www.afr.com/home/viewerSearch.aspx?ATL:// 20080607000020755811>

Ricketson, M. 2008, 'Clarifying crisis without a stampede', *The Age*, 15 October.

Rollins, A. 2008a, 'RBA focus on curbing demand', *Australian Financial Review*, 16 June, viewed 17 June 2009, <http://www.afr.com/home/viewerSearch.aspx?ATL:// 20080616000020790629>

Rollins, A. 2008b, 'RBA gives green light to deficit', *Australian Financial Review*, 20 November, viewed 17 June 2009, <http://www.afr.com/home/viewerSearch.aspx?ATL:// 20081120000030556127>

Rudd, K. 2008a, Partners in the global economy—Australia and the United States, Address to the US Chamber of Commerce, Washington, DC, 31 March, viewed 10 June 2009, <http://www.pm.gov.au/media/Speech/2008/speech_0158.cfm>

Rudd, K. 2008b, Prime Minister's address to the nation, Parliament House, Canberra, 14 October, viewed 10 June 2009, <http://www.pm.gov.au/media/Speech/2008/speech_0553.cfm>

Rudd, K. 2008c, Ministerial statement in the House of Representatives, Parliament House, Canberra, 26 November, viewed 10 June 2009, <http://www.pm.gov.au/media/Speech/2008/speech_0635.cfm>

Rudd, K. 2009, 'The global financial crisis', *The Monthly*, issue 42 (February), viewed 10 June 2009, <http://www.themonthly.com.au/node/1421>

Ruehl, P. 2008, 'Live from skid row, Rudd utters a brave new word', *Australian Financial Review*, 29 November, viewed 16 June 2009, <http://www.afr.com/home/viewerSearch.aspx?ATL:// 20081129000030588428>

Rumble, T. 2009, 'Listen to Stevens, ignore the fundies', *Australian Financial Review*, 26 February, viewed 18 June 2009, <http://www.afr.com/home/viewerSearch.aspx?ATL:// 1235522403123>

Shanahan, D. 2008a, 'Black Friday marks Rudd's revolution', *The Australian*, 15 October, viewed 11 June 2009, <http://www.theaustralian.news.com.au/story/ 0,25197,24499038-17301,00.html>

Shanahan, D. 2008b, 'Rudd sails on perilous waters', *The Australian*, 27 November, viewed 16 June 2009, <http://www.theaustralian.news.com.au/story/ 0,,24713218-17301,00.html>

Shanahan, D. 2008c, 'D-word proof of Labor panic: Liberals', *The Australian*, 28 November, viewed 16 June 2009, <http://www.theaustralian.news.com.au/business/story/ 0,,24718597-36418,00.html>

Shanahan, D. and Marris, S. 2008, 'Rudd pursues global role', *The Australian*, 31 March, viewed 10 June 2009, <http://www.theaustralian.news.com.au/story/ 0,24897,23457510-601,00.html>

Sheridan, G. 2009, 'The global financial crisis is the ideologues' blame game', *The Australian*, 7 February, viewed 15 June 2009, <http://www.theaustralian.news.com.au/story/ 0,25197,25018200-7583,00.html>

Simes, R. 2009, 'We need better regulation, not more of it', *Australian Financial Review*, 3 February, viewed 15 June 2009, <http://www.afr.com/home/viewerSearch.aspx?ATL:// 1233621179619>

Stammer, D. 2008, 'Various shades of grey in the economic outlook', *The Australian*, 17 September, viewed 17 June 2009, <http://www.theaustralian.news.com.au/story/ 0,25197,24335195-5001942,00.html>

Steketee, M. 2008, 'Spend wisely to spur jobs and growth', *The Australian*, 27 November, viewed 16 June 2009, <http://www.theaustralian.news.com.au/story/ 0,,24712291-25072,00.html>

Steketee, M. 2009, 'Tax cuts: slash here', *The Australian*, 11 April, viewed 18 June 2009, <http://www.theaustralian.news.com.au/story/ 0,25197,25318147-7583,00.html>

Stevens, G. 2008a, Economic conditions, Address to the American Chamber of Commerce in Australia, Melbourne, 13 June, viewed 20 June 2009, <http://www.rba.gov.au/Speeches/2008/sp_gov_130608.html>

Stevens, G. 2008b, The director's cut: four important long-run themes, Address to the Australian Institute of Company Directors, Sydney, 17 September, viewed 20 June 2009, <http://www.rba.gov.au/Speeches/2008/sp_gov_170908.html>

Stevens, G. 2008c, The economic situation, Address to the CEDA annual dinner, Melbourne, 19 November, viewed 20 June 2009, <http://www.rba.gov.au/Speeches/2008/sp_gov_191108.html>

Stevens, G. 2009, Opening statement, Address to the House of Representatives Standing Economic Committee, Canberra, 20 February, viewed 20 June 2009, <www.aph.gov.au/house/committee/economics/rba2008/Hearings/Transcript1.pdf>

Stutchbury, M. 2008a, 'The disaster must be prevented from happening again', *The Australian*, 19 September, viewed 17 June 2009, <http://www.theaustralian.news.com.au/story/0,25197,24367743-5017885,00.html>

Stutchbury, M. 2008b, 'Quick fix a long-term punt for PM', *The Australian*, 15 October.

Stutchbury, M. 2008c, 'Get over your deficit hang-ups, but don't go crazy: RBA boss', *The Australian*, 21 November.

Stutchbury, M. 2008d, 'It's worse than they thought', *The Australian*, 27 November, viewed 17 June 2009, <http://www.theaustralian.news.com.au/business/story/0,,24713370-30538,00.html>

Stutchbury, M. 2008e, 'Rudd's temporary deficit claim needs framework', *The Australian*, 28 November, viewed 17 June 2009, <http://www.theaustralian.news.com.au/business/story/0,28124,24717720-5017885,00.html>

Swan, W. 2008a, Ministerial statement on financial stability, Address to the House of Representatives, Parliament House, Canberra, 2 June, viewed 20 June 2009, <http://www.treasurer.gov.au/DisplayDocs.aspx?doc=speeches/2008/016.htm&pageID=005&min=wms&Year=2008&DocType=1>

Swan, W. 2008b, Media releases 2008, *Treasury Portal*, 2 June, viewed 2 July 2009, <http://www.treasurer.gov.au/listdocs.aspx?pageid=003&doctype=0&year=2008&min=wms>

Swan, W. 2008c, Adapting our architecture to challenging times, Address to the Brookings Institution, Washington, DC, 10 October, viewed 20 June 2009, <http://www.treasurer.gov.au/DisplayDocs.aspx?doc=speeches/2008/039.htm&pageID=005&min=wms&Year=2008&DocType=1>

Swan, W. 2009a, The global recession and Australia's future economy, Address to the New York Investment Community, New York, 23 January, viewed 20 June 2009, <http://www.treasurer.gov.au/DisplayDocs.aspx?doc=speeches/2009/002.htm&pageID=005&min=wms&Year=&DocType=1>

Swan, W. 2009b, A future of promise, Address to the Sydney Institute, Sydney, 23 March, viewed 20 June 2009, <http://www.treasurer.gov.au/DisplayDocs.aspx?doc=speeches/2009/006.htm&pageID=005&min=wms&Year=&DocType=1>

Thornton, H. 2009, 'Whistling cheerfully', *The Australian*, 25 February, viewed 18 June 2009, <http://www.theaustralian.news.com.au/business/story/0,28124,25104440-5013868,00.html>

Tingle, L. 2008a, 'Balancing act has a light touch, for now', *Australian Financial Review*, 3 June, viewed 16 June 2009, <http://www.afr.com/home/viewerSearch.aspx?ATL://20080603000020739776>

Tingle, L. 2008b, 'PM recast as a man of action', *Australian Financial Review*, 15 October, viewed 11 June 2009, <http://www.afr.com/home/viewerSearch.aspx?ATL://20081015000030423316>

Tingle, L. 2008c, 'PM bites the bullet on the "d" word', *Australian Financial Review*, 27 November, viewed 16 June 2009, <http://www.afr.com/home/viewerSearch.aspx?ATL://20081127000030581409>

Tingle, L. 2009a, 'When clouds gather, spin hard', *Australian Financial Review*, 3 February, viewed 15 June 2009, <http://www.afr.com/home/viewerSearch.aspx?ATL://20090203000030794639>

Tingle, L. 2009b, 'Point scoring undermines battle of idea', *Australian Financial Review*, 6 February, viewed 15 June 2009, <http://www.afr.com/home/viewerSearch.aspx?ATL://20090206000030806003>

Turnbull, S. 2008, 'The blind leading the blind', *Australian Financial Review*, 3 April, viewed 10 June 2009,

<http://www.afr.com/home/viewerSearch.aspx?ATL://
20080403000020496951>

Urban, R. 2008, 'Little-known Opes, spectacular failure', *The Australian*, 5 April,
viewed 10 June 2009, <http://www.theaustralian.news.com.au/story/
0,,23485903-23850,00.html>

Uren, D. 2008a, 'We can avoid deficit: Treasurer Wayne Swan', *The Australian*,
21 November, viewed 17 June 2009,
<http://www.theaustralian.news.com.au/business/story/
0,,24683573-36418,00.html>

Uren, D. 2008b, 'Crisis no beat-up as bad news keeps flowing', *The Australian*,
24 November, viewed 17 June 2009,
<http://www.theaustralian.news.com.au/business/story/
0,,24694847-16965,00.html>

Uren, D. and Stutchbury, M. 2008, 'World finance D-Day', *The Australian*,
11 October, viewed 17 June 2009,
<http://www.theaustralian.news.com.au/story/
0,25197,24479265-2702,00.html>

Walker, T. 2008, 'PM to raise his voice in global councils', *Australian Financial
Review*, 2 April.

Williams, P. 2008a, 'Rudd targets Turnbull over RBA remarks', *The Age*,
18 September, viewed 17 June 2009,
<http://news.theage.com.au/national/rudd-targets-turnbull-over-rba-remarks-
20080918-4ir3.html>

Williams, P. 2008b, 'No dive for Swan when it comes to "four pillars"', *The Age*,
3 June, viewed 16 June 2009, <http://business.theage.com.au/business/
no-dive-for-swan-when-it-comes-to-four-pillars-20080602-2kxc.html>

Williams, P. and Martin, P. 2008, 'Hitting the wall—the market's global mayhem',
The Age, 20 September, viewed 17 June 2009,
<http://www.theage.com.au/national/hitting-the-wall--the-markets-global-mayhem-
20080919-4k8i.html?page=8>

Winestock, G. 2008a, 'How will Australia survive the storm?', *Australian
Financial Review*, 20 September, viewed 17 June 2009,
<http://www.afr.com/home/viewerSearch.aspx?ATL://
20080920000030331044>

Winestock, G. 2008b, 'Economists see red as the right response', *Australian
Financial Review*, 20 November, viewed 17 June 2009,
<http://www.afr.com/home/viewerSearch.aspx?ATL://
20081120000030556086>

Wood, A. 2008a, 'Four pillars lend stability: credit debacle shows big and global doesn't make banks better', *The Australian*, 7 June, viewed 16 June 2009, <http://www.theaustralian.news.com.au/story/0,,23823255-20501,00.html>

Wood, A. 2008b, 'Reserve would do well to target inflation', *The Australian*, 14 June, viewed 17 June 2009, <http://www.theaustralian.news.com.au/business/story/0,,23860387-30538,00.html>

Wood, A. 2008c, 'Embrace the deficit now', *The Australian*, 28 November, viewed 16 June 2009, <http://www.theaustralian.news.com.au/business/story/0,,24717614-30538,00.html>

Wright, T. 2009, 'Rudd's inquisition into neo-liberalism', *The Age*, 3 February, viewed 15 June 2009, <http://www.theage.com.au/national/rudds-inquisition-into-neoliberalism-20090202-7vrs.html>

10. New Zealand: electoral politics in times of crisis

Michael Jones

1. From crisis to crisis to elections

For the scholar of crisis leadership, the New Zealand Government's response to the 2008–09 global financial crisis represents a distinct and interesting case study. The combination of three characteristics in particular renders it unique. First, New Zealand's small, open economy is heavily dependent on trade, particularly in agricultural products; consequently, even in the best circumstances, it is hopelessly vulnerable to the vagaries of commodity prices in the international economy. Second, when the crisis hit New Zealand it was already in the grip of a home-grown economic downturn, attributable to a severe drought and a slowing of the housing market. Finally, the occurrence of the crisis immediately before a general election, on 8 November 2008, ensured that attempts by leaders to interpret economic events were intensely politicised and contested.

This chapter will analyse the leadership of key players in New Zealand's experience of the global financial crisis through an application of the theoretical framework advanced by Boin et al. (2009; see also Chapter 2, this volume). As a caveat to their theoretical model, Boin et al. (2009:95, 98–9) observe that situational and temporal factors can significantly influence the course and outcomes of a crisis. As suggested in the opening lines of this chapter, the course and outcomes of the global financial crisis in New Zealand are certainly no exception. Indeed, the three aforementioned characteristics, which render the case unique, have important implications for any attempted analysis.

The first situational factor—New Zealand's small, open economy—influenced crisis leadership in conflicting ways. In one sense, it allowed New Zealand's leaders to externalise blame for the crisis more easily, but at the same time, it gave them very limited ability to reduce its impact. Consequently, the master narrative of the crisis in New Zealand was not one of climactic, unforeseen events; indeed, domestic banking and financial institutions remained relatively strong (Bollard 2008c). Rather, it was a narrative of steady decline in growth and steady rises in oil and food prices—following developments in international markets—until a recession was declared on 5 August 2008. Tellingly, Morgan Research's (2008d) consumer confidence polling suggested that the New Zealand public, having felt the sting of an international downturn during the 1997–98

East Asian financial crisis, were aware of their vulnerability to international developments, and their confidence fell away accordingly.

The second situational factor—the home-grown downturn—was also significant. This was because it was in the interest of all political actors, at various times, for the framing of the two crises to become linked. Early in the period, the Clark Government sought to link the developing international crisis to the domestic downturn in order to escape blame for the latter. Later on, the new Key Government sought to establish a similar link in order to blame the Clark Government for the effect of the former.

Finally, the significance of the November general election as a temporal factor cannot be overstated. In particular, this was because all early pre-election polls strongly suggested that the vote would produce a change of government (Morgan Research 2008a; *One News-Colmar Brunton* 2008a; *TV3-TNS* 2008). The coincidental occurrence of elections heavily skewed all media coverage and popular perception of the crisis towards its impact as an electoral battleground. This resulted in two very different narratives running through the leadership of the crisis: one of a long-standing government desperately struggling against its decline; the other of a long-standing opposition seizing its first opportunity to govern in more than a decade.

2. Methodological considerations

The advent of a change in government during the period under study prevented this chapter from focusing on three central leaders, as in most of the case studies within this volume. Instead, in this chapter, the focus of analysis is on two key economic leaders within *each* of the two governments in office during the period: the Prime Ministers Helen Clark and John Key, and the Ministers of Finance Michael Cullen and Bill English. The New Zealand electoral context also renders problematic the figure of Dr Alan Bollard, the Governor of the Reserve Bank of New Zealand (RBNZ), whose equivalent is considered in the other case studies. By convention in New Zealand, the RBNZ Governor attempts to keep a low profile during the lead-up to an election so as to keep the office de-politicised. Bollard upheld this convention, limiting himself largely to the legally required monthly 'monetary policy statements' and biannual 'financial stability statements' during a period that was unfortunately simultaneous with the emergence of the crisis (Bennet 2008).

Additionally in New Zealand, the Department of the Treasury (*Kaitohutohu Kaupapa Rawa*) is charged with a unique, bipartisan public information function under Section 26T of the *Public Finance Act 1989*. This became especially significant in an electoral context when it was required to publicly release a *Pre-Election Economic and Fiscal Update* (*PREFU*) and a *Briefing to the incoming minister*, as it did at the height of the crisis. To account for these characteristics of the case, this chapter includes the two Treasury releases during the period of the election, as well as two speeches made by Governor Bollard when he resumed his public framing role after the election.

The analysis of each speech act contains two components situating it in terms of the framing contests and rhetorical strategies described in Chapter 2, and then gauges the public reception of the speech, through analysis of three of New Zealand's newspapers: the *Dominion Post*, *The Press* and the *New Zealand Herald*. Quantitatively, the media response is represented in tabular form with each responding article coded as agreeing, remaining neutral or disagreeing with four aspects of the speech's framing: 1) its framing of crisis severity; 2) its framing of crisis causation; 3) its framing of the proposed policy response; and 4) support for the speech-maker (for the references supporting each table, see the online appendix at <http://globalfinancialcrisis.wetpaint.com/>). This quantitative analysis is followed by qualitative analysis examining the degree to which the media responses accept, adopt or reject the frame's narrative of the crisis. In the case of the frames put forward by the Treasury and the RBNZ, which are apolitical and not widely covered in the media, the chapter will proceed directly to qualitative analysis.

The three papers selected for analysis were chosen to provide a representative sample of New Zealand's print media. First, according to polling by Nielson Media Research New Zealand (2008), they were the three highest-circulating papers in New Zealand in 2008. Second, they are published in each of New Zealand's three largest regional centres: the *Dominion Post* is published in the capital, Wellington (southern North Island); *The Press* is published in Christchurch (South Island); and the *New Zealand Herald* is published in Auckland (northern North Island). Moreover, Nielson's polling also suggests they have the dominant readership within the region surrounding their centre of publication. This was considered important to account for any regionally specific perspectives on the crisis. Finally, the three papers—while all centrist and more provincially than ideologically defined—represent a fair ideological spectrum.

Box 10.1 New Zealand's financial crisis trajectory, November 2007 – December 2008

November 2007: Reserve Bank of New Zealand (RBNZ) Governor Dr Alan Bollard, releases the biannual 'Financial stability report' reassuring New Zealanders that New Zealand banks have virtually no direct exposure to the US sub-prime market and have engaged in very little securitisation. He warns, however, that as funding costs rise, credit conditions will tighten (Bollard 2007).

6 March 2008: Bollard (2008a) warns that there is a risk that the slowdown in the US economy and international financial market turbulence could result in a sharper downturn in New Zealand.

7 May: Bollard (2008c) says New Zealand's financial system has so far withstood 'a severe test from global financial markets' and has 'very little exposure to offshore credit risk or structured debt products'.

22 May: The New Zealand Treasury (2008a) releases the *Budget Economic and Fiscal Update* (*BEFU*). Finance Minister, Michael Cullen, delivers the 2008 New Zealand budget.

5 June: Bollard releases his 'June monetary policy statement' in which he announces that the official cash rate (OCR) will remain unchanged and now projects little to no gross domestic product (GDP) growth in 2008 and only a modest recovery thereafter (Bollard 2008d).

27 June: Statistics New Zealand releases its quarterly GDP update, 'Gross domestic product: March 2008 quarter'; these are the first strong indicators that New Zealand is headed for recession (Statistics New Zealand 2008).

8 July: The New Zealand Institute of Economic Research's (NZIER 2008) *Quarterly Survey* suggests New Zealand is technically in recession.

5 August: The New Zealand Treasury's *Overview of July Economic Indicators* (2008b) predicts that the economy will slide into technical recession.

11 September: Bollard releases his 'September monetary policy statement' (Bollard 2008e) in which he announces that the OCR will be reduced by 50 points to 7.5 per cent and projects continuing inflation and possibly further OCR reductions.

6 October: The New Zealand Treasury (2008c) delivers its *Pre-Election Economic and Fiscal Update* (*PREFU*).

8 November: New Zealand General Election.

12 November: Bollard releases his biannual 'Financial stability report' (Bollard 2008f). He states that New Zealand's banks are well positioned to withstand the economic downturn. Deputy Governor, Grant Spencer, assures New Zealanders that their deposits are safe.

19 November: John Key's Government is sworn into office.

4 December: Bollard releases his 'December monetary policy statement' in which he announces reductions in the OCR to 5 per cent, bringing the cumulative reductions since July to 3.25 per cent (Bollard 2008g).

> **4 December:** The New Zealand Treasury releases *Briefing to the incoming Minister of Finance 2008: medium-term economic challenges* (Treasury 2008d).
>
> **18 December:** The New Zealand Treasury releases *Economic and Fiscal Forecasts: December 2008* (Treasury 2008e).

3. Crisis development and elite rhetoric in New Zealand

23 May 2008: Prime Minister Clark's budget speech

On 22 May 2008, Michael Cullen unexpectedly seized on gloomy forecasts in the Treasury's *Budget Economic and Fiscal Update* (Treasury 2008a) to cast his budget as a response to uncertain times (Cullen 2008a). The next day, in her traditional, post-budget address to the Auckland Chamber of Commerce, Clark went further than any New Zealand economic leader had to date. The Prime Minister book-ended her explanation of the budget with cautionary rhetoric. She opened by stating that 'this year's budget has been written against the background of a slower global economy which has obvious ramifications for New Zealand' and concluded with a reminder that the budget had been 'written against external factors which are not what any of us would want but which we have to work around'. She was not specific about the severity of the global financial crisis, which she described as 'the fall out of the sub-prime crisis in the United States', which 'has been felt around the world'. She did, however, place it at the centre of a confluence of externally caused factors that had resulted in a sufficiently severe 'backdrop' to which the budget had been tailored to respond. She supported the budget's combination of stimulus investments in infrastructure and tax relief for struggling families as the best policy response to this crisis.

Within the analytical framework, Clark's speech suggests that her decision to begin framing came well before she could have made accurate sense of, or decided on any response to, the global crisis (at least based on Treasury's numbers). Her frame emphasised the severity of the crisis, justifying an about-turn on tax cuts in the budget. It stressed the threat the crisis posed to the prosperity that New Zealanders had enjoyed under her (status quo) government. Clark's intention seems to have been to link the frame of the home-grown downturn to that of the international crisis, and thus exogenise any blame attributable to her government for the former.

Clark's framing highlights the dangers of viewing crises as discreet political episodes, particularly when calculating the intent of actors. Boin et al. (2009:85) posit that a political risk of overemphasising the severity of a crisis is to be accused of being 'alarmist' or 'opportunist'. Clark clearly accepted this risk, but she did so in order to superimpose a crisis her government could not control on a pre-existing one it should have controlled better.

	Severity	Causality	Proposed policy	Support for speaker
Agrees	*DP* (1); *NZH* (2)	*DP* (1); *NZH* (2)	*NZP* (1); *DP* (1)	
Disagrees			*DP* (1)	
No comment/ neutral	*DP* (1); *NZH* (1)	*DP* (1); *NZH* (1)	*NZH* (1)	*DP* (2); *NZH* (2)

Table 10.1 Media response to Clark's 23 May 2008 speech

Note: *DP = Dominion Post; NZH = New Zealand Herald.*

As the small numbers in Table 10.1 suggest, Clark's framing was to a degree buried by (perhaps more newsworthy) budget coverage focused on the content of Cullen's proposals. Where it was reported in detail, however, the papers largely accepted her emphasis on the severity of the global crisis (for instance, Janes 2008a). While Clark was successful in framing the importance of the global crisis, opinion polling suggests she was not able to escape blame for the home-grown downturn. Indeed, Labour suffered a shock drop in the polls (Morgan Research 2008b; *One News-Colmar Brunton* 2008b). Qualitative analysis can perhaps suggest the reason for this, with all of the articles analysed treating the budget as *the* key opportunity for Labour to reverse its poor approval ratings before the election. Clark's framing was widely perceived as a transparent attempt to pre-empt any generous tax cuts being offered by the National Party (*New Zealand Herald* 2008a). As such, while Clark's frame was accepted, she might have fallen victim to what the crisis literature describes as a 'credibility trap' through her overly partisan reading of the crisis (Boin et al. 2005:81).

27 June 2008: Treasurer Cullen's reassurance attempt

In the afternoon after the release of Statistics New Zealand's worrying quarterly GDP update, Finance Minister, Michael Cullen, delivered a brief speech reassuring New Zealanders that these data were attributable to a short-term shock. The framing within this brief speech was important, however, as it became a position Cullen would reiterate as a succession of concerning economic figures emerged in the next two months (Treasury 2008b). Cullen's speech was straightforward. He continued to attribute the crisis to external factors and to assert that the budgetary proposals were an appropriate policy response, as Clark and he had done earlier. Seeking to maintain confidence in the economy, however, he back-pedalled over its severity, which he now limited to the short term. Indeed, he described New Zealand's 'medium-term economic and social prospects' as 'very healthy and strong'. Cullen's downplaying of severity suggested that his sense making had advanced to the point that he was comprehending an international downturn creating a crisis of confidence in New Zealand, and that he decided to alter his frame in order to bolster confidence—a key part of the Finance Minister's economic leadership in any circumstance of uncertainty.

The most interesting aspect of Cullen's framing was its relationship to his sense making. He appeared to have backed away from the crisis rhetoric employed by himself and Clark in the budgetary debates, because he realised that the crisis was *more* serious than he had first appreciated. This could be attributable to Labour's punishment in the polls after the budget; however, it was just as likely to demonstrate an interesting unwillingness to curtail opportunistic crisis rhetoric if it could be detrimental to the economy.

	Severity	Causality	Proposed policy	Support for speaker
Agrees	*NZH* (1); *P* (1)	*NZH* (1); *P* (1)	*NZH* (1)	*NZH* (1)
Disagrees	*DP* (1); *P* (1)	*DP* (1); *P* (1)	*DP* (1)	
No comment/ neutral	*NZH* (1); *P* (1)	*NZH* (1); *P* (1)	*P* (3)	*DP* (1); *NZH* (1); *P* (3)

Table 10.2 Media response to Cullen's 27 June 2008 speech

Note: *DP = Dominion Post*; *NZH = New Zealand Herald*; *P = The Press*.

The spread of numbers in Table 10.2 demonstrates how open the 'event-significance' framing contest over the global financial crisis was at the time of Cullen's speech. It is noteworthy that all of those disagreeing with his framing of the severity of the crisis argued that it was more severe. Those disagreeing with his causation were unwilling to excuse the government for the earlier domestic downturn. Moreover, the small number of articles simply represents the fact that at that point in New Zealand politics, the global financial crisis had not yet made it from the business pages into the mainstream news.

Qualitative analysis of the articles supported the claim that Cullen's speech occurred at a time of genuine uncertainty among commentators in New Zealand. Given this context, an attempt to maintain confidence was probably a responsible act by the Finance Minister. When opinion crystallised a week or so later, however, Cullen's optimistic medium-term forecast began to attract criticism, and would have attracted more had not the opposition's forecast been equally disproved (Eaton 2008; O'Sullivan 2008). This indicates that all framing contests are relative.

6 October 2008: the Treasury's pre-election update

On 6 October 2008, after two and a half months of worsening crisis and with the New Zealand economy now technically in recession, the Department of the

Treasury released its *Pre-Election Economic and Fiscal Update* (*PREFU*), as required by the *Public Finance Act 1989*. Unparalleled among the cases studied in this volume, New Zealand's *PREFU* is a legally required, independent assessment of the nation's economic position before the beginning of the electoral period. As such, its sense making and framing of the crisis—while depoliticised and not an act of crisis exploitation—had a defining impact on subsequent acts of crisis exploitation by political leaders.

Within its projections, the *PREFU* defined the impact of the global financial crisis as 'severe', effectively closing off the event-significance framing contest to all subsequent frames. It projected that growth in the year to March 2009 was down to 0.1 per cent from 1.5 per cent in the May budget and would be rebounding in the next two years. Even more concerning for ordinary New Zealanders was its projection that unemployment was expected to rise to 5.1 per cent by March 2010 and could rise as high as 6.1 per cent in 2010. By necessary implication, the *PREFU* attributed the crisis to external factors, although it presented a range of policy options that left open the prospect of continued framing contests regarding management of the crisis.

The projections of the *PREFU* generally stood up to media criticism, although some reports cited independent research suggesting that the Treasury's projections could even have been slightly on the rosy side (Weir 2008a). The major effect of the *PREFU*'s frame was to set the crisis as the defining issue of the electoral period and to immediately begin another framing contest between New Zealand's two dominant parties.

6 October 2008: Cullen's response

At the *PREFU*'s release, and in direct response to its frame, Cullen gave a speech in which he abandoned his downplaying of the severity of the crisis and described the 'developments of recent weeks' as 'perhaps unprecedented in living memory'. This was, however, only partial abandonment, as he also stated that 'New Zealanders can feel a very high degree of confidence that New Zealand and Australia will emerge through these challenging times in better shape than many other developed nations'. He reinforced the Treasury's implicit attribution of causation to international developments, seemingly suggesting with the above statement that New Zealand's economic management before the crisis was superior to that of many other developed nations. Moreover, he strongly asserted that budgetary measures, such as 'the Government's strong infrastructure program' would be timely in their impact on this crisis. Simultaneously, he was expressly critical of any suggestion of further tax cuts in this context—a pointed attack on the advocacy of such cuts by opposition leader, John Key.

Situating Cullen's speech within the crisis-exploitation framework draws attention to the obvious connection between Cullen's speech and Labour's sense making after the *PREFU*. It is interesting to note, however, that this speech occurred before the decision to strongly exploit the crisis politically, which became evident five days later in Clark's 11 October speech act. The content of Cullen's frame was now type-2, following the emphatic demonstration of severity in the *PREFU*. In acknowledging severity, however, Cullen did not totally abandon the 'severity' framing contest, arguing that New Zealand's long-term prospects remained good, which would have significant implications in Clark's subsequent reframing. Cullen's clear intent was to mount a twofold pre-emptory defence: he aimed to demonstrate his budgetary measures were justified in the crisis while simultaneously using the crisis to pre-empt any National Party attempts to exceed his tax cuts.

Cullen's framing in this speech is perhaps most interesting for its restraint. This is especially true given the full-frontal assault against Key's economic philosophy launched in Clark's framing five days later. This suggests either that Labour had not decided yet to thoroughly exploit the crisis or, more likely, that they were waiting for Key to show his hand.

	Severity	Causality	Proposed policy	Support for speaker
Agrees	*DP* (3); *P* (1)	*DP* (1); *P* (1); *NZH* (1)	*DP* (1)	*DP* (1)
Disagrees	*DP* (1); *NZH* (4)		*DP* (2); *NZH* (3)	*NZH* (2)
No comment/ neutral	*NZH* (2)	*DP* (3); *NZH* (5)	*DP* (1); *P* (1); *NZH* (2)	*DP* (3); *P* (1); *NZH* (3)

Table 10.3 Media response to Cullen's 6 October 2008 speech

Note: *DP = Dominion Post; NZH = New Zealand Herald; P = The Press.*

Table 10.3 bears testimony to the polarising effect that such a momentous *PREFU* in an electoral context had within the commentariat. It is important to note, however, that all those who disagreed with Cullen's half-hearted framing of severity considered the crisis to be more severe, especially in terms of New Zealand's long-term economic prospects. Table 10.3 does evince a general dissatisfaction with Cullen's continued reliance on four-month-old budgetary solutions to a problem that now dwarfed the problems they were originally designed to address. This reliance on outdated framing was also significant in the qualitative analysis, which showed a general distaste among commentators for Cullen's attack on Key's further tax cuts—promised well before the crisis worsened (Cosgrove 2008; Oliver 2008). That said, much of the commentary on Cullen's frame, and certainly the opinion polling, was expectantly waiting for Key's post-*PREFU* response.

8 October 2008: the prime minister-in-waiting's big plan

After the *PREFU*, Key finally ventured a counter-frame to the Clark Government with his release of the 'National's economic management plan' on 8 October. While Key was not in government at this point, this speech has been included as one of his two speeches in this chapter's analysis because it was this initial framing of the crisis that carried him through the election and followed him into government. After the *PREFU*, Key acknowledged the severity of the crisis, although he chose to make only minor adjustments to his promised tax cuts—still outspending Labour. Unsurprisingly, Key sought to blame the incumbent government, suggesting that the 'suddenness and severity of the international downturn has exposed our economy's weaknesses more quickly than anyone would have expected', but asserting that those weakness had been 'present for some time'. He emphasised the need for the New Zealand economy to 'grow' out of the red ink and thus advanced policies directed towards long-term growth.

Key's speech is best characterised as a classic type-3, which attempted to utilise the economic crisis to expose deficiencies in Labour's economic management and economic policies. As such, Key's frame represents the first genuine challenge to Labour within the 'causality' framing contest. It is clear that Key's intent here was to frame the crisis in a manner favourable not just to a change in government, but to a major shift in macroeconomic management.

Within the crisis-exploitation framework, Key's framing demonstrated some of the advantages of opposition (see McCaffrie, this volume). As an opposition leader with a healthy (perhaps insurmountable) lead in the polls, Key was able to wait out the uncertainty of July and August 2008 until he had the data of the *PREFU* available to confirm his sense making (Morgan Research 2008c). His low-risk strategy also demonstrated the overarching narrative of the Clark Government's decline and the reality that the election was Key's to win or lose.

	Severity	Causality	Proposed policy	Support for speaker
Agrees	*DP* (1)	*DP* (1)	*DP* (1); *NZH* (3); *P* (2)	*DP* (1); *NZH* (2); *P* (1)
Disagrees	*DP* (1); *NZH* (3)		*DP* (1); *NZH* (5); *P* (2)	*DP* (1); *NZH* (3); *P* (1)
No comment/ neutral	*DP* (2); *P* (7); *NZH* (8)	*DP* (3); *NZH* (9); *P* (7)	*DP* (2); *NZH* (3); *P* (3)	*DP* (2); *NZH* (6); *P* (5)

Table 10.4 Media response to Key's 8 October 2008 speech

Note: *DP* = *Dominion Post*; *NZH* = *New Zealand Herald*; *P* = *The Press*.

Table 10.4 demonstrates the difficulties of attempting to adopt a low-risk strategy in framing a crisis. Key's unwillingness to water down too much his electorally popular tax cuts accounts for much of the criticism apparent in Table 10.4, which was surprisingly high given Key's continued 10-point lead in the polls (Morgan Research 2008c; *One News-Colmar Brunton* 2008c). Indeed, qualitatively, almost all of the disagreements with Key could be attributed to his inability to adequately recognise the severity of the crisis and change his outdated tax policy (*New Zealand Herald* 2008b). Running through the criticism of Key was a sense of disappointment that, with his poll lead so substantial, his policy was not bolder. Indeed, one headline described him as a 'Prime minister in waiting…with an albatross for his rival' (*New Zealand Herald* 2008c), which captured well the extent to which the onus was on Labour to take political risks with the crisis.

11 October 2008: Clark upping the ante

At the Labour Party campaign launch, on 11 October, Clark decided to aggressively reframe the crisis in a final effort to stave off electoral defeat. From the stage of Auckland's Town Hall, Clark resurrected analogies to the Great Depression of the 1930s before declaring 'a curtain is being drawn on the era of the free wheeling unregulated money traders and financiers whose greed has shaken the international financial system to its very core'. In rhetoric reminiscent of US President Franklin D. Roosevelt's first inauguration speech, in which he made reference to the malicious 'moneylenders' as key culprits of the Great Depression, Clark attributed blame to 'greed merchants' who had destroyed 'the lives of ordinary people in real jobs trying to put food on the table for their families'. She then announced two new policies—a retail bank deposit guarantee and an additional stimulus package—before concluding by asking voters to consider who they 'really trust with the future of our economy'.

Situated within the crisis-exploitation framework, Clark's speech can be characterised as distinctly anti-status quo framing by an incumbent government. Clark's aggressive reframing should be characterised as the result of her acknowledgment that without dramatic action Labour would suffer electoral defeat. Her frame itself is an interesting mix of type-2 and type-3, with the neo-liberal international status quo (and by implication its advocates within New Zealand) being identified as the critical threat to a still-prosperous domestic status quo produced under her government's stewardship. Clark's frame represented a decisive response to Key's contribution to the causality-framing contest three days earlier, with thinly veiled references to Key's background as a merchant banker in the description of 'greed merchants'. Finally, Clark's intention went further than just to exogenise blame from her government; she intended to apportion it to ideological stances similar to those advocated by the opposition.

	Severity	Causality	Proposed policy	Support for speaker
Agrees	*DP* (2); *NZH* (4); *P* (1)	*DP* (2); *NZH* (4); *P* (1)	*DP* (2); *NZH* (4); *P* (1)	*NZH* (1)
Disagrees				*NZH* (2); *P* (1)
No comment/ neutral	*NZH* (2); *P* (1)	*NZH* (2); *P* (2)	*NZH* (2); *P* (1)	*DP* (1); *NZH* (3); *P* (1)

Table 10.5 Media response to Clark's 11 October 2008 speech

Note: *DP = Dominion Post; NZH = New Zealand Herald; P = The Press.*

Table 10.5 attests to a generally positive reception for Clark's framing. In particular, the solid support for the severity and causality of Clark's frame suggest she tapped into a longing within the electorate for more meaningful engagement with economic issues of great concern. The disparity in 'Support for speaker' reflects criticism from some commentators of Clark's transparent exploitation of the crisis for electoral gain—in particular, her announcement of a deposit guarantee without consulting the opposition. Interestingly, however, any loss of credibility was confined to the media, as after Clark's speech, Labour enjoyed a brief surge in the opinion polls, gaining on the National Party for the first time in the period (*One News-Colmar Brunton* 2008d). Clark's aggressive and initially successful crisis framing—which was reinforced consistently by her party during the election—was, however, not sufficient to sustain the trend. By the end of October, Key's lead—which never shrank substantially—was again widening, leading to his emphatic victory on 8 November (Ministry of Justice 2008).

4 December 2008: the Treasury briefing to the incoming government

After the election of the Key Government on 8 November 2008, another of the New Zealand Treasury's public information functions became relevant: the *Briefing to an incoming minister*. Again unparalleled among the other cases studied in this volume, in the briefing, the Treasury issues its independent, 'frank and fearless' public advice to the newly elected Minister of Finance. In December 2008, this provided the public servants within the Treasury a second opportunity to provide an expert-driven, non-political view of the crisis.

In the briefing, Treasury defined the severity of the crisis as 'extremely challenging' and demanding of immediate action if the deterioration of the economy was to be stopped. Moreover, it argued against further short-term stimulus, claiming that the National Party's promised tax cuts went beyond what most other Organisation for Economic Cooperation and Development (OECD) nations were doing. It warned that living within the NZ$1.75 billion spending cap the National Party had pledged to maintain would be difficult. Instead,

Treasury suggested a shift in spending away from 'low-return' investments, such as lower staff–pupil ratios, to improving accountability for pupil achievement and the development of teaching practice; suggesting New Zealand superannuation might have to be less generous; and proposing alternative forms of tax restructuring.

Coming in the aftermath of the political game's climactic conclusion, Treasury's briefing represented a significant contribution to the framing of the crisis in the 'policy game' (see Chapter 2, this volume). As such, even though the new Finance Minister, Bill English, soundly rejected it (see below), the briefing provided an important alternative to the National Party's proposed structural reform of the economy.

5 December 2008: the new Treasurer's reform bid

On 5 December, English responded to the Treasury's briefing by advancing his own framing of the global financial crisis's impact on New Zealand. To give himself maximum room to manoeuvre, English opened his framing by acknowledging the severity of the crisis, stating that the government's books were likely to get worse before they got better. He then moved quickly to attribution of responsibility, which he placed squarely on 'Labour's complacency and refusal to address structural issues dragging down our growth potential', which increased the vulnerability of the New Zealand economy to global developments. English then advocated a policy response based on the removal of 'barriers that have prevented New Zealand becoming more competitive and achieving higher productivity growth'.

It was clear that English's framing followed recognition of the crisis as a critical opportunity for his party to advance its structural economic reforms early in its term. He sought to endogenise as much blame as possible, targeting the policies of the previous government. His intention appeared to be to build public sentiment behind neo-liberal economic reforms by discrediting the status quo. This framing of the global financial crisis to build support for centre-right, neo-liberal reforms was remarkable given that the same crisis had, in almost all other instances, been framed to the opposite effect. For example, in New Zealand's close neighbour and financial trading partner Australia, Prime Minister, Kevin Rudd, used the crisis to proclaim the death of 'neo-liberalism' (Rudd 2009; see further Laing and Tindall, this volume).

	Severity	Causality	Proposed policy	Support for speaker
Agrees			*NZH* (1)	*NZH* (1)
Disagrees			*P* (1)	
No comment/ neutral	*DP* (1); *NZH* (2); *P* (1)	*DP* (1); *NZH* (2); *P* (1)	*DP* (1); *NZH* (1)	*DP* (1); *NZH* (1); *P* (1)

Table 10.6 Media response to English's 5 December 2008 speech

Note: *DP = Dominion Post; NZH = New Zealand Herald; P = The Press.*

Table 10.6 shows the somewhat muted media response to English's framing. Much of this reaction can be attributed to the honeymoon period English was enjoying, with the neutral responses effectively meaning acquiescence to the National-led Government's mandated agenda. Qualitatively, it is remarkable the commentary did not address the extent to which English was going against the grain of international developments. This was especially significant given that the Treasury's briefing pointed out expressly that the National Party's program of tax cuts was out of step with the rest of the OECD (Treasury 2008b).

10 December 2008: the bank governor's warning

Having been compelled by convention to keep a low profile during the election, RBNZ Governor, Dr Alan Bollard, on 10 December 2008, felt at liberty to advance his framing of the crisis. He re-emphasised the severity of the crisis, warning that the road to recovery for New Zealand would be long. In particular, he expressed concerns about high inflation, which had to be reduced before the RBNZ could ease monetary policy to stimulate the economy. Moreover, he warned that falling international commodity prices could not be relied on to automatically reduce short inflation, as the operation of other factors such as the exchange rate, taxes and firms' margins could result in a lag of six months or more. Bollard, not just attributing the continuance of the crisis to external factors, warned that all sectors of the economy would need to refrain from adding inflationary pressures if New Zealand was to recover in the short term.

While it was not really picked up by the media, Bollard's post-election framing of the crisis was particularly significant for two reasons. First, after the electoral populism of the politicians, Bollard's speech represented the first attempt to advance a framing of the context specific to business leaders who—beyond the short-term calculus of an electoral contest—were a key audience for the government's economic management and for the outcome of the 'policy game'. The second reason for the importance of Bollard's framing was its focus on immediate challenges, which highlighted weaknesses in the more long-term, policy-oriented framing attempts by English and the Treasury. The immediacy of these short-term challenges was to become even more apparent eight days later with the Treasury's release of its *Economic and Fiscal Forecasts* (Treasury 2008e).

18 December 2008: further bad news from English

After the sharp deterioration of New Zealand's economic forecast in the Treasury's *Economic and Fiscal Forecasts*, Finance Minister English was compelled to reframe the severity of the crisis—in particular, for the next 12 months. English described the new Treasury forecast of 'sharply increasing public sector debt and higher fiscal deficits over the next five years' to be 'outside the range the government considered prudent'. This led English to hint at a policy response that appeared to be in tension with his government's promised tax cuts—notably: 'putting the economy on a strong medium to long-term footing, limiting spending growth, getting better value out of existing spending, ensuring that tax bases are maintained, and ensuring that government assets were managed as effectively as possible'.

It was clear that Treasury's December forecasts overtook English's initial sense making, particularly with regard to the short to medium-term urgency of the crisis. With this frame, English shifted his position and was now attributing far more blame to international developments (the Clark Government was not even mentioned). His intention was most likely to frame the crisis in a way that acknowledged the enormity of the challenge facing his government but also bolstered public confidence in their ability to achieve it.

	Severity	Causality	Proposed policy	Support for speaker
Agrees	*NZH* (2)		*NZH* (2)	
Disagrees	*DP* (2)		*DP* (1)	
No comment/ neutral	*DP* (1); *NZH* (1); *P* (1)	*DP* (3); *NZH* (3); *P* (1)	*DP* (2); *NZH* (1); *P* (1)	*DP* (3); *NZH* (3); *P* (1)

Table 10.7 Media response to English's 18 December 2008 speech

Note: *DP = Dominion Post*; *NZH = New Zealand Herald*; *P = The Press*.

The quantitative analysis in Table 10.7 reveals that when it came to the economic crisis, English's honeymoon in the press was cut short. Qualitative analysis emphasises this point. For the first time during the period, a genuinely alarmist didactic ran through much of the commentary as it began to come to terms with the prospect of sizeable budget deficits into the foreseeable future (for example, Weir 2008b). Some commentators looking further ahead warned of long-term difficulties such as accelerated infrastructure drift to Australia and even an unfavourable structural realignment of the international economy (for example, Janes 2008b).

27 February 2009: the bank governor at the 'Jobs Summit'

The final two speech acts to be analysed both occurred at the Key Government's 'Jobs Summit' on 27 February 2009. This summit was intended to generate ideas for the Key Government in preparing its first critically important crisis budget. Even though it occurred slightly after Key's opening address, Bollard's speech will be analysed first, as it provided the authoritative frame of the crisis for the summit.

In framing the impact of the global financial crisis at the Jobs Summit, Bollard re-engaged in the first framing context to curtail the sweeping use of historical analogy in describing the severity of the crisis. Bollard emphasised: 'to be clear, the state of the global economy and the outlook are very serious, but we are nowhere near Depression-level economic condition.' Using a more apt historical analogy, Bollard described the present crisis in world growth terms as 'somewhat below the early 1980s recession'. Bollard then framed the effect of the crisis as one of producing a 'new global balance', which in broad terms meant that economies such as New Zealand's would 'have to save more, reduce household deficits, build exports and improve their external balances'. Bollard concluded that within the Western world, 'New Zealand's economy and financial system are relatively well-placed to weather the adjustment. Our challenge will be to remain well-positioned to take advantage of the economic recovery when it comes'.

This framing by Bollard is significant in its context at the opening of the Jobs Summit. As the summit itself was an attempt to restore confidence in the economy through coopting New Zealand's business elite, it was critical to open with a relatively positive framing of the crisis. As the country's key financial technocrat, Governor Bollard was in a uniquely credible position to provide this. His authority was evident from universal acceptance of his frame.

27 February 2009: the new Prime Minister's call to action

The final speech act to be analysed in this chapter was delivered by Prime Minister Key in opening the Job Summit. The summit, a brainchild of his government, was intended as a forum to produce ideas before the delivery of his government's first budget in May, which inevitably was to be cast as a crisis-response budget. If nothing else, it represented a tremendous opportunity for the Key Government to close a credibility grab in bringing New Zealand's most respected economic minds into line behind its frame.

Key opened his address by framing the problem as one about which something could be done. He scolded that 'we will not gain anything today or in the months ahead if we become lost in hand-wringing and crystal ball gazing about how bad things are'. As such, he framed himself and the participants at the summit into the crisis as 'doers'.

The Job Summit followed from the sense making of the Key Government that the economic crisis was going to be a defining feature of its term, and from a decision to gain external credibility in order to assist its framing of the crisis. Key's framing represented a step back from the type-2 frame adopted late in December by English, in so much that blame for the crisis was not totally exogenised to international factors. It was important for Key to show that the government and the country's chief economic players would be able to 'do' something about it. Key appeared to be focused on gaining external credibility for his government's frame, while ignoring internal sources of credibility, such as the consistency of the frame itself.

	Severity	Causality	Proposed policy	Support for speaker
Agrees			*NZH* (1)	*NZH* (1)
Disagrees	*DP* (1); *NZH* (2); *P* (1)		*DP* (1); *NZH* (2)	*NZH* (2)
No comment/ neutral	*DP* (1); *NZH* (3)	*DP* (2); *NZH* (5); *P* (1)	*DP* (1); *NZH* (2); *P* (1)	*DP* (1); *NZH* (2); *P* (1)

Table 10.8 Media response to Key's 27 February 2009 speech

Note: *DP = Dominion Post; NZH = New Zealand Herald; P = The Press.*

Table 10.8 suggests that the media response to the Job Summit address, and indeed to the summit itself, was mixed. It is true that some of the 'No comment/ neutral' articles that merely reported the advent of such an august gathering would have served Key's purpose of increasing his government's credibility. The solid portion of articles that disagreed with the severity of Key's frame as well as his policy response can, however, be attributed to the sentiment that a summit was not an appropriate response to a crisis of this scale (for example, Van Beynen 2009). The pervasiveness of this critique of 'trivialisation' throughout the media coverage served to partially undermine the momentum Key might have hoped to obtain for his proposed reforms.

4. Framing the financial crisis in New Zealand: analysis and conclusions

Having analysed the attempts to frame the global financial crisis by key New Zealand leaders, it is possible to draw some conclusions about the impact of crisis exploitation within the case. In particular, it is useful to focus on the two 'games' that lie at the core of crisis exploitation: the political game and the policy game (see Chapter 2, this volume).

In terms of the political game in New Zealand, the impact of crisis exploitation was noted, but probably not decisive. The National Party, led by John Key, maintained its convincing lead in the polls throughout and was eventually electorally successful. In one sense, this could be seen as a justification for those who argue that already-popular leaders are more likely to emerge successfully from a crisis situation (Wilkins 1987; Seeger et al. 2003). Such an inference would, however, ignore two important conclusions from the case. First, the Clark Government's crisis exploitation—while unsuccessful—did have a noticeable impact on the polls. Its ultimate failure is explained just as well by the Key opposition's competent crisis leadership as it is by Key's general popularity. Moreover, throughout the period, the actions of all key players could be accommodated within a crisis-exploitation framework. This suggests, if nothing else, that the actors themselves considered crisis management to be of significant importance and they acted accordingly. In the terms outlined in the 'political game', an unpopular incumbent attempts first to minimise blame (box I) but then chooses to risk a blame showdown (box IV) in a last-ditch effort to reverse an imminent electoral defeat. This behaviour might be different to that posited as likely, *ceteris paribus*, in Chapter 2, but it can nonetheless be accommodated within the framework. Indeed, this chapter found such an accommodation to be illuminating.

It is in the context of the 'policy game' (see Chapter 2, this volume), however, that the utility of the framework is borne out. An interesting anomaly of the case, noted above in the analysis of English's first speech act analysed in this chapter, is the extent to which the Key Government was successful at exploiting the economic crisis to implement 'neo-liberal' economic reforms. Such reforms were anomalous because in almost all other countries, including New Zealand's close neighbour and financial partner Australia, the global financial crisis had led to the discrediting of neo-liberal economics.

Such a disparity in policy response between two close neighbours suggests the policy outcomes of crises are shaped by much more than the content of the crisis itself; it suggests the crisis framing is of the utmost importance to the policy outcomes. Boin et al.'s (2009) conception of a 'policy game' would seem an efficacious way to theoretically model this policy side of the framing contest. In the case of New Zealand, box III of Table 2.2 (Chapter 2) would seem to explain the neo-liberal outcome; there had been a major and swift rhetorical/symbolic change in New Zealand economic policy after the crisis, which was successfully framed as a consequence of New Zealand's lack of competitiveness in global markets.

The key question remains: what determined success in these framing contests? Considering the political and policy games in New Zealand together, it seems there was one factor that could incorporate the impact of popularity and that of a persuasive crisis in explaining causation: credibility. Elsewhere, credibility has been considered to constitute the key factor in determining the success of 'meaning making' after a crisis (Boin et al. 2005:79–83). In the New Zealand case study, its significance seems to be demonstrated. The insurmountable challenge for the Clark Government was not unpopularity so much as the 'credibility trap': any attempt to exploit the crisis to reverse this unpopularity without that intention becoming transparent. Moreover, the Key Government's early success in implementing significant neo-liberal policy reform would seem best explained by its ability to frame a crisis that struck during a home-grown downturn as being linked to the economic management that caused that downturn. If there is one salient lesson that the unique case of New Zealand should suggest to the scholar of crisis leadership, it is therefore the importance of credibility as a determinant in the political and policy outcomes of crises.

References

Bennet, A. 2008, 'Depositor's fears sparked savings pledge—Bollard', *New Zealand Herald*, 14 October.

Boin, A., 't Hart, P., Stern, E. and Sundelius, B. 2005, *The Politics of Crisis Management: Public leadership under pressure*, Cambridge University Press, Cambridge.

Boin, A., 't Hart, P. and McConnell, A. 2009, 'Crisis exploitation: political and policy impacts of framing contests', *Journal of European Public Policy*, vol. 16, no. 1, pp. 81–106.

Bollard, A. 2007, Financial stability report, Press release, 7 November, Reserve Bank of New Zealand, viewed 21 May 2009, <http://www.rbnz.govt.nz/finstab/fsreport/3162330.pdf>

Bollard, A. 2008a, March monetary policy statement, Press release, 6 March, Reserve Bank of New Zealand, viewed 21 May 2009, <http://www.rbnz.govt.nz/news/2009/3581433.html>

Bollard, A. 2008b, The New Zealand economic outlook, Press release, 28 March, Reserve Bank of New Zealand, viewed 21 May 2009, <http://www.rbnz.govt.nz/news/2008/3275909.html>

Bollard, A. 2008c, Financial stability report, Press release, 7 May, Reserve Bank of New Zealand, viewed 21 May 2009, <http://www.rbnz.govt.nz/news/2008/3310327.html>

Bollard, A. 2008d, June monetary policy statement, Press release, 5 June, Reserve Bank of New Zealand, viewed 21 May 2009, <http://www.rbnz.govt.nz/news/2007/3032038.html>

Bollard, A. 2008e, September monetary policy statement, Press release, 11 September, Reserve Bank of New Zealand, viewed 21 May 2009, <http://www.rbnz.govt.nz/news/2008/3416797.html>

Bollard, A. 2008f, Financial stability report, Press release, 12 November, Reserve Bank of New Zealand, viewed 21 May 2009, <http://www.rbnz.govt.nz/news/2008/3484984.html>

Bollard, A. 2008g, December monetary policy statement, Press release, 4 December, Reserve Bank of New Zealand, viewed 21 May 2009, <http://www.rbnz.govt.nz/news/2008/3504509.html>

Bollard, A. 2008h, Speech to the Wellington Chamber of Commerce, 18 December, Reserve Bank of New Zealand, viewed 9 May 2009, <http://www.rbnz.govt.nz/speeches/3509648.html>

Bollard, A. 2009, 'Speech to Jobs Summit', New Zealand Herald, 27 February, viewed 22 May 2009, <http://www.nzherald.co.nz/nz/news/article.cfm?c_id=1&objectid=10559061>

Clark, H. 2008a, Budget speech to Auckland Chamber of Commerce, 23 May, viewed 10 May 2009, <http://www.beehive.govt.nz/speech/budget+speech+auckland+chamber+commerce>

Clark, H. 2008b, Labour Party campaign launch speech, 13 October, viewed 10 May 2009, <http://www.scoop.co.nz/sotires/PA0810/S00261.htm>

Cosgrove, R. 2008, 'Labour horrific', The Press, 9 October.

Cullen, M. 2008a, Budget 2008: a fair economy, a strong future, Speech, 22 May, viewed 10 May 2009, <http://www.beehive.govt.nz/budget2008>

Cullen, M. 2008b, March GDP weak as expected, NZ future is strong, Press release, 27 June, viewed 7 May 2009, <http://www.beehive.govt.nz/release/march+gdp+weak+expected+nz+future+strong>

Cullen, M. 2008c, Pre-election economic and fiscal update 2008, Speech, 6 October, viewed 10 May 2008, <http://www.beehive.govt.nz/speech/pre-election+economic+and+fiscal+update+2008>

Eaton, D. 2008, 'Country now in recession', The Press, 6 August.

English, W. 2008a, Crown accounts show need for urgent economic action, Press release, 5 December, viewed 30 May 2009, <http://www.beehive.govt.nz/release/crown+accounts+show+need+economic+action>

English, W. 2008b, Government committed to plan for steering NZ through global turmoil, Press release, 18 December, viewed 30 May 2009, <http://www.beehive.govt.nz/release/government+committed+plan+steering+nz+through+global+turmoil>

Janes, A. 2008a, 'She's chalk and he's all cheese', Dominion Post, 24 May, p. 2.

Janes, A. 2008b, 'Capital punishment', Dominion Post, 20 December.

Key, J. 2008, National's economic management plan, 8 October, viewed 10 May 2009, <http://www.national.org.nz/ Article.aspx?ArticleID=28682>

Key, J. 2009, Opening address to the Jobs Summit, 27 February, viewed 30 May 2009, <http://www.nzherald.co.nz/ politics/news/article.cfm?c_id=280&objectid=10559036>

Ministry of Justice 2008, *Election Results 2008*, 9 November, Ministry of Justice, viewed 30 May 2009, <http://2008.electionresults.govt.nz/partystatus.html>

Morgan Research 2008a, New Zealand preferred party poll: 7–20 April, 24 April, Morgan Research, viewed 30 May 2009, <http://www.roymorgan.com/news/polls/2008/4288/>

Morgan Research 2008b, New Zealand preferred party poll: May, 5 June, Morgan Research, viewed 30 May 2009, <http://www.roymorgan.com/news/polls/2008/4298/>

Morgan Research 2008c, New Zealand preferred party poll: July 14–27, 1 August, Morgan Research, viewed 30 May 2009, <http://www.roymorgan.com/news/polls/2008/4311/>

Morgan Research 2008d, New Zealand consumer confidence drops 5.5pts to 100.1, 19 December, Morgan Research, viewed 30 May 2009, <http://www.roymorgan.com/news/polls/2008/828/>

New Zealand Herald 2008a, 'Cullen's ninth seeks to snooker the National Party over bigger tax cuts', *New Zealand Herald,* 23 May.

New Zealand Herald 2008b, 'Time now for Fiscal boldness', *New Zealand Herald,* 8 October.

New Zealand Herald 2008c, 'Prime Minister in waiting…with an albatross for his rival', *New Zealand Herald,* 8 October.

New Zealand Herald 2009, 'Challenges heavier than job solutions', *New Zealand Herald*, 28 February.

New Zealand Institute of Economic Research (NZIER) 2008, *Quarterly Survey of Business Opinion*, 8 July, New Zealand Institute of Economic Research, viewed 22 June 2009, <http://nzier.org.nz/includes/download.aspx?ID=95667>

Nielson Media Research New Zealand 2008, National readership survey results: newspaper readership, January–December, Nielson Media Research New Zealand, viewed 10 May 2009, <http://www.nielsenmedia.co.nz/MRI_pages.asp?MRID=35>

O'Sullivan, F. 2008, 'Muck but where's the pony?', *New Zealand Herald*, 6 August.

Oliver, P. 2008, 'Cullen rains on Key's parade', *New Zealand Herald*, 7 October.

One News-Colmar Brunton 2008a, 'Preferred Party Poll', April, *One News-Colmar Brunton,* viewed 30 May 2009, <http://tvnz.co.nz/view/page/425825/1728614>

One News-Colmar Brunton 2008b, 'Preferred Party Poll', May, *One News-Colmar Brunton,* viewed 30 May 2009, <http://images.tvnz.co.nz/tvnz_images/news2008/colmar_brunton/may08/May08_partysupport.pdf>

One News-Colmar Brunton 2008c, 'Preferred Party Poll', 5 October, *One News-Colmar Brunton,* viewed 30 May 2009, <http://tvnz.co.nz/view/page/1318360/2176207>

One News-Colmar Brunton 2008d, 'Preferred Party Poll', 19 October, *One News-Colmar Brunton,* viewed 30 May 2009, <http://tvnz.co.nz/view/page/576182/2216673>

Rudd, K. 2009, 'Essay: the global financial crisis', *The Monthly*, February, pp. 26–38.

Seeger, M. W., Sellnow T. L. and Ulmer, R. R. 2003, *Communication and Organisational Crisis*, Praeger, Westport, Conn.

Statistics New Zealand 2008, Gross domestic product: March quarter, Media release, 27 June, Statistics New Zealand, viewed 30 May 2009, <http://www.stats.gov.nz/store/2008/06/gross-domestic-product-mar08qtr-mr.htm>

Treasury 2008a, *Budget Economic and Fiscal Update*, 22 May, Department of the Treasury, viewed 14 May 2009, <http://www.treasury.govt.nz/budget/forecasts/befu2008>

Treasury 2008b, *Overview of July Economic Indicators*, 5 August, Department of the Treasury, viewed 14 May 2009, <http://www.treasury.govt.nz/economy/mei/archive/pdfs/mei-jul08.pdf>

Treasury 2008c, *Pre-Election Economic and Fiscal Update*, 6 October, Department of the Treasury, viewed 14 May 2009, <http://www.treasury.govt.nz/budget/forecasts/prefu2008>

Treasury 2008d, *Briefing to the Incoming Minister of Finance 2008: Medium-term economic challenges*, Briefing Paper, 4 December, Department of the Treasury, viewed 14 May 2009, <http://www.treasury.govt.nz/publications/briefings/2008/big08.pdf>

Treasury 2008e, *Economic and Fiscal Forecasts*, 18 December, Department of the Treasury, viewed 14 May 2009, <http://www.treasury.govt.nz/budget/forecasts/eff2008/eff08.pdf>

TV3-TNS 2008, 'Preferred Party Poll', 10-16 April, *TV3-TNS*, viewed 30 May 2009, <http://img.scoop.co.nz/media/pdfs/0804/3poll200408.pdf>

Van Beynen, M. 2009, 'Gabfest needs to be do-fest', *The Press*, 28 February.

Weir, J. 2008a, 'That "rainy day" has arrived', *Dominion Post*, 7 October.

Weir, J. 2008b, 'Watch your speedos when rain turns to a hurricane', *Dominion Post*, 7 October.

Wilkins, L. 1987, *Shared Vulnerability: The media and American perceptions of the Bhopal disaster*, Greenwood Press, New York.

11. Singapore: staying the course

Faith Benjaathonsirikul

1. Crisis management in a 'moderated democracy'

Singapore has presented itself as a unique and interesting case among nations deeply affected by the global financial crisis. The Lee thesis (after Lee Kuan Yew, who formulated it succinctly) argued in sum that freedoms and rights hampered economic growth and development (Sen 1999). The combination of a moderated democracy with limited governmental transparency and little freedom of the press, free speech or welfare rights has seen Singapore controversially typecast as a soft authoritarian and anti-democratic state. Singapore, however, has found its niche in its ability to foster liberal enterprise based on manufacturing, service and speculative investment. Singapore presents itself as a nation built on the business acumen of its people, harnessed through meticulous planning and shepherded by benevolent-paternalistic government.

The People's Action Party (PAP) has been the sole ruling political party in Singapore since 1959. Since the general election in 1963, with Lee Kuan Yew as its leader, the PAP has dominated Singapore's parliamentary democracy and has been central to the country's rapid political, social and economic development. Although the PAP professed a rejection of Western-style liberal democracy, it has, since its inception, accepted the need for some welfare spending and pragmatic economic intervention. Mauzy and Milne (2002) discern four major underlying principles of the PAP: pragmatism, meritocracy, multiracialism and communitarianism.

Singapore grew into South East Asia's wealthiest economy and, in 2008, had kept its rank for the third successive year as the easiest place to do business in the world (Brook 2008). Nevertheless, notwithstanding an average growth rate of 8 per cent between 2004 and 2007, Singapore was the first East Asian country to fall into a recession as a consequence of the global financial crisis. Due to conservative economic policies—a remnant of the 1997 East Asian financial crisis, combined with an existing well-regulated market—the exposure of Singapore's banks to sub-prime mortgages was limited. The country's reliance on foreign investment, however, and its heavy dependency on trade made it particularly sensitive to volatilities and shocks in the global financial markets, and in particular, to key exports of manufactured goods to the United States and Europe, which in the past few years accounted for nearly 33 per cent of total non-oil exports (Thangavelu 2009).

The huge losses in Singapore's wealth from the collapse of international stock markets further exacerbated already declining economic conditions. Although it was difficult to establish a true figure due to lack the of disclosure of their assets and trading activities, it was estimated that in 2008 alone the Government of Singapore Investment Corporation (GIC)—one of two government-funded institutions known as sovereign wealth funds—made an estimated loss of US$33 billion (Paris 2009). Temasek Holding Pty Ltd, GIC's sister agency, accrued an estimated loss of US$39 billion in the eight months between 31 March 2008 and 30 November 2008. The vulnerability of Singapore's two sovereign wealth funds was due mainly to heavy investments in distressed Western financial institutions such as Citigroup, UBS AG, Barclay's Bank and Merrill Lynch.

With the constraints on democratic accountability operating in the Singaporean political system, the potential scope for any particular crisis to threaten the political fortunes or policy commitments of incumbent leaders is limited. There is no credible opposition party and past voting behaviour in Singapore indicates that PAP office-holders are firmly in the saddle. Still, a crisis that has the potential to destabilise the key pillars of prosperity on which much of PAP's authority and public legitimacy rest, is worth closer examination. A crisis-induced rise in political disaffection among Singaporeans could have dented the long-term credibility of the PAP and, in particular, the Lee family.

Box 11.1 Singapore's financial crisis trajectory, December 2007 – March 2009

25 December 2007: Temasek Holding Pty Ltd (Temasek), a Singaporean investment fund and arm of the Singapore Government, buys a large stake in US financial services company Merrill Lynch at 13 per cent less than market value—spending $14 billion. Temasek also holds an option to purchase a further $600 million worth of shares by the end of March 2008.

25 June 2008: Temasek buys £200 million worth of shares in British bank Barclay's after the bank announced it would issue new shares worth £4.5 billion to bolster its finances, which had been hit by losses on US mortgage-backed securities.

29 July: Temasek increases its stake in Merrill Lynch. Temasek had previously paid $5 billion for new shares in the company; it is now entitled to a discount totalling $2.5 billion on this purchase. Temasek spends the discount returned to it by Merrill Lynch on an additional purchase of $900 million worth of shares in the company at a price of $24 a share—half of the purchase price paid in December 2007.

Mid-September: The Monetary Authority of Singapore (MAS) pledges to hold inquiries into potentially wrongly sold Lehman Minibond notes, though it does not indicate any commitment to order financial institutions to buy back the notes and denies having authority to compel financial institutions to compensate consumers. The total size of the Lehman Minibond program was S$508 million, of which S$375 million was sold to approximately 8000 retail investors through nine distributors. These notes are considered growth stock, as opposed to income-producing assets, of a high-risk nature.

October: Easing of monetary policy; lowering of trading band to allow depreciation of currency.

10 October: The MAS issues a statement that Singapore's policy of modest and gradual appreciation of the Singaporean dollar's nominal effective exchange rate policy, standing since April 2004, has been tightened to help mitigate inflationary pressures in lieu of sustained growth and rising commodity prices. Advanced estimates released by the Ministry of Trade and Industry show, however, that Singapore's gross domestic product (GDP) has declined by 6.3 per cent—due mainly to external shocks transmitting into a domestic slowdown in financial and trade channels.

20 October: The government moves to guarantee all Singaporean dollar and foreign currency deposits of individual and non-bank customers until 31 December 2010. The PAP sets aside S$150 billion as sufficient to back S$700 billion of individual deposits and non-bank customers. This is a precautionary measure to avoid any potential erosion of Singaporean banks' deposit base and to ensure an international playing field for Singapore.

Late October: The MAS establishes a US$30 billion swap facility with the US Federal Reserve as a pre-emptive measure to ensure dollar liquidity for the Singaporean banking system.

Early November: Singapore's DBS Bank retrenches 450 workers to cut costs.

November: The government pledges $1.5 billion to help firms secure credit, followed by a further announcement that it is ready to run a bigger budget deficit to boost the economy.

11 January 2009: Temasek acquires shares in Bank of America by converting shares it had purchased in Merrill Lynch (see 25 December 2007 and 29 July 2008) into shares in Bank of America, which had recently purchased Merrill Lynch. Temasek now owns 3.8 per cent of Bank of America.

22 January: The government announces its 2009 'Resilience Package' totalling $20.3 billion (8.2 per cent of GDP) made up of five components: jobs for Singaporeans; stimulating bank lending; enhancing business cash flow and competitiveness; supporting families; and building homes for the future.

6 February: Board of Directors of Temasek announces CEO, Ho Ching (wife of Lee Hsien Loong), is stepping down after Temasek's ailing performance in 2008.

2 March: United Overseas Bank shares fall about 6 per cent to S$9.38—the lowest level in almost six years.

6 March: *Recent Economic Development in Singapore* report states that GDP has further contracted by 16.4 per cent in the fourth quarter of 2008 after the 2.1 per cent decline in the preceding quarter. It is reported as the steepest sequential contraction on record and is marked by rapid deterioration in trade-related industries and a sharp drop in financial services. Reported retrenchment of 13 400 workers in 2008 (a rise from 7700 in 2007).

2009: Government expects budget deficit of $8.7 billion (3.5 per cent of GDP) for FY2008—a significant rise from the budget deficit of $2.2 billion for FY2007.

2. Methodological considerations

In a bid to downplay Singapore's dire economic situation, there was marked concurrence in commentary about the unravelling of Singapore's economy by the three most significant actors in economic policy: Prime Minister Lee Hsien Loong, Finance Minister Tharman Shanmugaratnam, and the Managing Director of the Monetary Authority of Singapore (MAS) Heng Swee Keat. Below we describe and analyse the development of their rhetoric as the crisis unfolded. Analysing its reception in Singaporean public opinion, however, presented a challenge unique to the case studies in this volume.

Official censorship of the Internet, media reporting and newspapers was the primary obstacle to gauging public opinion. Although the *Singaporean Constitution* provides for freedom of speech and expression, it permits official restrictions on these rights. In practice, the government has significantly restricted freedom of speech and freedom of the press (US Department of State 2009:2a). High-level censorship and lack of credible opposition parties in Singapore ultimately had the effect of limiting, and possibly skewing, publicly expressed opinion. Although the *Straits Times* (Singapore's highest-selling newspaper), *Channel News Asia* and *Business Times* were consulted as sources of information, it must be noted that the government has a significant influence on the printed, electronic and televised media in Singapore; thus, these three news media sources could be only loosely consulted as general indicators of public opinion.

The nine speech acts were chosen based on the grounds that they addressed the main stakeholders or, in the case of the Singaporean budget speech for 2009, provided a template for other meaning-making processes. The speech acts were analysed in accordance with the volume's analytical framework (see Chapter 2)—that is, considering their representation of the severity and causes of the crisis, the allocation of responsibility for the crisis (and its handling) and the articulation of its policy implications. In using the heuristic of the political crisis exploitation game, the degree to which the three key actors' credibility was affected by the public reception of their crisis rhetoric is also assessed. Finally, the policy crisis exploitation game was used to assess the possibility of a shift in policy away from the status quo as a result of (un)successful framing of the crisis by the three key actors.

3. Crisis development and elite rhetoric in Singapore

27 June 2008: Finance Minister Shanmugaratnam blaming (foreign) hubris

In his address to the Association of Banks (ABS), Tharman Shanmugaratnam attributed the cause of the global financial crisis to hubris after the boom of the past two decades. The long period of macroeconomic stability had led to heightened risk-taking behaviour and leveraging reaching unprecedented levels in global finance, while credit spreads on risky assets fell to exceptionally low levels. Financial engineering and the search for higher yields led to an explosion of complex financial derivatives, as such high-yield securities backed by sub-prime mortgages originating in the United States found their way into the books of financial institutions in other parts of the world, especially Europe.

Shanmugaratnam emphasised the exogenous origins of the global financial crisis, stating that Singapore's experience had been somewhat exceptional in that:

> Singapore's challenges mirror those faced elsewhere in Asia, but are in some ways more pronounced. We are a price taker in the true sense, given our small size and the openness of our economy and financial markets. We cannot insulate ourselves from global prices of food or fuel, or anything else.

He alluded to the possibility that the global financial crisis would trigger a new phase in the globalised world. Monetary policy in the past had been too loose and with this as the fundamental flaw, symptoms such as boosted aggregate demand and increased leveraging in financial markets had surfaced. He alluded to a systemic problem with Western practices of neo-liberalism—in particular, in the United States.

Although at this stage the depth and implications of the global financial crisis in Asia had not yet materialised, and the speech featured no new policy commitments, it was interesting to note Shanmugaratnam's defence of the non-prescription of fiscal policy at this early stage of the crisis. Later, Singapore's stimulus policy intervention would come to pass in the form of the so-called 'Resilience Package', totalling S$20.5 billion, creating the largest budget balance deficit ever incurred in the city-state.

24 July 2008: monetary authority managing director Heng's 'business as usual'

At the time of Shanmugaratnam's address to the ABS General Meeting in June 2008, the depth and implications of the global financial crisis in Singapore had not been fully realised. Crisis rhetoric and framing processes in mid 2008 were largely subdued in comparison with later speeches. At a press conference marking the release of the MAS's *Annual Report*, Heng Swee Keat referred to the crisis as 'unusual market volatility' and maintained that despite external market volatilities, Singapore had still recorded strong growth, though economic activity had moderated. No radical policy had been introduced to combat the early stages of the global financial crisis.

In this press conference, Heng attributed Singapore's economic slowdown to factors beyond the control of the Singaporean Government. The rise in inflation was imputed to external developments, such as high oil prices, continued high prices of food and inflationary pressures on trading partners. Although the cause of the rise in basic living expenses and inflation was attributed to external influences, at this point, blame was not a large factor in the framing of the crisis. As Heng commented on the United States and Europe: 'The international financial system and the global economy are still facing significant challenges and downside risks. So far, prompt action by financial authorities in the US and Europe has helped avert a wider crisis. But financial markets remain uncertain and volatile.'

Overall, Heng's remarks at the press conference typified a type-2 'crisis as critical threat' posture. Although no blame had been allocated, causation had been attributed to external factors. Heng's address represented a defence of the status quo. He reassured his audience of the soundness of past MAS policies in combating rising inflation. Reminiscent of Lee's stance, Heng expressed that in the face of increasing volatility globally, there was no room for complacency and that the MAS had tightened its monitoring of financial markets and supervision of financial institutions:

> We need to remain vigilant in the face of a number of risks in the global economic and financial environment. We will continue to work closely with the industry to identify vulnerabilities and threats to financial stability through macro surveillance and stress testing. MAS' work in the coming year will continue to be driven by our mission of supporting non-inflationary economic growth, and fostering a sound and reputable financial centre.

17 October 2008: Heng managing blame

In October, Heng gave a press conference in response to stakeholders' concerns about the suspect sale of high-risk financial instruments to poorly informed retail investors, the effects of which became evident only in lieu of the global financial crisis, forcing many to forgo their entire savings, including many who could not afford to do so. This speech represented a crisis within a crisis. The PAP professed to have well-regulated financial institutions, but in light of the global financial crisis, flaws became evident.

Heng began by recognising the significance of the inappropriate selling of bonds, especially to vulnerable customers unable to absorb adverse market fluctuations without risking financial ruin. He also largely externalised the blame for the fiasco to the private sector financial institutions and their representatives, portraying the regulator (MAS) as well meaning and proactive in finding a solution to protect the most vulnerable of Singapore's investors.

The speech also highlighted, however, the pragmatic ideology of Singapore's elite. Although stressing that the MAS required financial institutions 'to have a rigorous process to look into every complaint and resolve them fairly', Heng delegated the responsibility for investigating the scandal to the very financial institutions that had sold the products to begin with. This left him open to questions about the MAS's commitment to aiding those affected. Although Heng assured his audience that there would be an independent third party overhearing complaints, he did not give operational details about how this third party could audit the decisions of financial institutions' review panels. He emphasised a self-regulating approach in putting his trust in the review panel and their chairs to conduct thorough reviews of each case and communicate their decision to their customers within a short time.

Given the PAP's traditional emphasis on detailed regulation to achieve economic prosperity and social stability, the MAS, as Singapore's de facto central bank, might have been identified as having failed to monitor closely enough the activities of financial institutions. Heng's posture in this speech was clearly a defensive one. Damage control was the name of the game.

22 January 2009: Shanmugaratnam's budget statement

Shanmugaratnam's 2009 budget statement foreshadowed the government's intended policy responses to the global financial crisis, which had begun to hit Asia hard in the preceding months. He opened by mentioning the uncertain times Singapore had fallen into and that the prospect for 2009 remained uncertain as all major economic regions of the world were experiencing a simultaneous recession. He re-emphasised that the global financial crisis had descended on Singapore from outside, as its economic fortunes were so closely tied to those of the global market: 'We had known and had highlighted the downside risks of a US recession and a worsening global credit crunch. But like other governments and the vast majority of private forecasters, we did not anticipate the speed and scale of the deterioration in the global economy in the last six months'.

Acknowledging the far-reaching implications of the global financial crisis, Shanmugaratnam mentioned systemic changes happening right across the financial sector, including in Singapore:

> Several of the foreign banks, especially those with weak balance sheets globally, have been focusing on re-capitalisation in their head offices...even the stronger players, including our local banks, have taken a step back to reassess their lending strategies because of the uncertainty over the depth and duration of this recession.

He maintained that the credit situation in Singapore had held steady until October 2008, when there was a decline in credit due to a decrease in demand as well as banks becoming more cautious about the prospects of loan recovery.

Although in 2008 growth in Singapore had been much faster than in any other Asian newly industrialised country, and the government's strategy had kept unemployment low, Shanmugaratnam predicted that the worst manifestation of the global financial crisis in Singapore would be in terms of job losses. Attempting to soften the bad news, he emphasised Singapore's advantage in the global crisis in that the government was able to provide resources to respond to the immediate needs of businesses and households while not compromising long-term investment. On this issue, Shanmugaratnam claimed credit for the government having 'rigorously adhered to a prudent fiscal policy, spending within [its] means, maintaining a stable base of revenues, and building up a nest egg of reserves for contingencies'.

Shanmugaratnam also mentioned that the government, while it could help sound companies weather the storm of the global financial crisis and sharpen their competitiveness, would 'not be able to save companies that are inefficient or whose products have lost relevance or appeal in the marketplace'. In other words: the government would allow the crisis to cull inefficient or lagging businesses, while its own interventions would be aimed at supporting thriving industries.

He emphasised that the major measures taken by the government were not necessarily aimed at preserving the status quo. How well companies were able to benefit from the government's support would depend largely on how well they were able to review their business models, restructure and put efforts into improving their products and exploring new markets. This was in line with PAP's longstanding meritocratic ideology of finding Singapore's niche strength through a form of market-based natural selection. In a bid to reduce unemployment, workers were also encouraged to make significant adjustments to allow businesses to cut costs, such as accepting pay cuts, and businesses also were responsible to 'cut costs to save jobs, not cut jobs to save costs'.

To aid productivity, Shanmugaratnam detailed the Resilience Package totalling $20.5 billion, aimed at saving jobs and helping viable companies stay afloat. He outlined that this package would not bring Singapore out of recession, but would help avoid a sharper downturn and lasting damage to the economy. Unlike the fiscal policies of foreign countries, Singapore's Resilience Package entailed a supply-side approach aimed at helping businesses retain workers by strengthening cash flow in order to provide more support and confidence for the domestic sector. This strategy reflected the government's desire to bolster Singapore's service sector in order to, like Hong Kong, develop a more competitive service and retail industry. As such, the global financial crisis provided the opportunity for the PAP to restructure and retrain the labour market so that the country could 'emerge stronger and ready to seize new opportunities, just as [we] did when [we] responded to the Asian Financial Crisis a decade ago'.

19 February 2009: Prime Minister Lee's pride in fiscal prudence

Throughout Prime Minister Lee's speech to the Standard Chartered gala dinner on 19 February—his first major utterance in recognition of the crisis—he moulded his crisis rhetoric to stress the superiority of the Singaporean model. The crisis, he said, was due to a systemic problem with Western practices of neo-liberalism. Careful not to criticise neo-liberalism itself, he found fault with the ways in which Western governments had managed their financial institutions, the effects of which were now spilling over into the local economy:

> In Singapore, it is unlikely for a bank to fail due to domestic problems, but problems elsewhere may affect its operations here. If it is a major financial institution, there could be large ripple effects on the health of other banks and confidence in the entire financial sector. We will therefore need to watch for contagion and deal with systemic risk.

Lee's criticism of the West's lack of prudential care and responsibility implied a belief that its culture bred an acceptance of unnecessary risk taking and careless disregard for the flow-on effects of individualistic behaviour that epitomised Western neo-liberal culture. This was clever politics, serving to exogenise the causes of the economic problems and at the same time reaffirm that the PAP's apprehensiveness about Western-style liberal democracy was justified and the alternative model of a controlled, phased liberalisation of the financial industry had served Singaporeans well.

In the wake of the 1997 East Asian financial crisis, the PAP had taken a pragmatic approach to liberalising the banking sector. Unlike the policies of foreign governments that installed more protectionist measures in times of recession, Singapore had eased its competition policy, exposing its banking sector to overseas rivals. Combined with consolidation of the banks, these measures served to create a stronger and more dynamic local banking sector. At the same time, however, prudent and conservative regulatory policies were implemented, which Lee now claimed had buffered Singaporean banks from exposure to toxic assets and non-performing loans (NPLs). Lee claimed credit for preparing Singapore with a well-developed 'disaster subculture' and 'safety culture' that ensured protection of banks and resources through conservative lending policies and high levels of government surveillance and interference—otherwise referred to as 'vigilance'. As a result, Singapore had been able to put away reserves in the form of high past surpluses that ultimately helped the State weather the global financial crisis.

Although Lee acknowledged that the collapse of Lehman Brothers had an unexpected impact in Singapore (and around the world) through credit-linked structure products, he ascribed this not to the failure of government supervision, but to the poor conduct of financial institutions grounded in a lack of understanding of the failing instrument they had sold. Lee took the opportunity to warn investors against future investments in complex securitisation products or investing in risks they could not bear, as such high-risk investments 'can destabilise the whole financial system in unforeseeable ways'—a reminder to Singaporeans that their foremost duty was to their country.

22 February 2009: Lee's defence of the Singaporean way

Just three days later, Lee continued his meaning-making efforts. In his speech on 22 February, he focused on the strength of Singapore as a nation and, by association, the strength and conviction of its government in looking after the best interests of Singaporeans. He acknowledged that the global financial crisis was the worst economic crisis experienced in Singapore in the past 60 years. He exogenised the causes of the problem and the responsibility for its solution by saying that in order for Singapore to recover, other economies must first recover—in particular, the United States and the European Union—which he did not expect to happen any time soon. Communication of these sentiments achieved a dual objective: it acted to absolve the government from any blame while also playing down public expectation about the government's ability to resolve the crisis.

Lee reiterated the success of his policies that had enabled the government to store reserves from past surpluses, which fully financed the current Resilience Package, as well as the so-called Skills Programme for Upgrading and Resilience (SPUR), aimed at retraining Singapore's workforce to make it more competitive.

Lee highlighted the government's intervention through the introduction of the Credit Scheme, which had helped businesses avoid wage cuts, defer retrenchments or reduce the number of workers that had to be retrenched, while other businesses had used it to expand. With expected growth of 2–3 per cent in GDP in the next four to five years, Lee emphasised his government's proactive stance in buffering Singaporeans against the massive job losses seen in other countries—again, juxtaposing Singapore's situation with that overseas. He often drew comparisons with 'other countries' to attempt to reassure the audience that Singapore had not suffered badly comparatively, and moreover, that the PAP had been prepared and well funded to aid Singaporeans through programs to help the unemployed find jobs through training and professionals through their Professional Skills Programme (PSP). This stance was reminiscent of Singapore's rejection of a welfare state. Instead of proposing monetary aid for the unemployed, the PAP encouraged the workforce to retrain.

Lee maintained that only in Singapore could a company cut costs without massive retrenchment and he gave three reasons for this: the Job Credit spurt, Singapore's flexible wage system and flexible work arrangements. As such, Singaporean workers must aspire to be 'better than the cheaper ones, and cheaper than the better ones'. Although the global financial crisis was an exogenous problem, Singapore must endogenise its long-term interests. Instead of hiring foreign workers, jobs could be found for Singaporeans by reducing the cost of hiring Singaporeans and upgrading the skills of each Singaporean employee through training.

4 March 2009: Heng's gloomy outlook

With the local economy nosediving, Heng's address to the International Institute of Finance offered dire prognoses, designed to communicate a sense of urgency that had been lacking in Lee's and Shanmugaratnam's speech acts. Consistent with Lee and Shanmugaratnam's crisis rhetoric, Heng emphasised the unprecedented and exceptional nature of the crisis, and recognised the unconventional measures taken by financial authorities in efforts to arrest the unfolding events.

> The epicenter of this crisis is the US—it is the world's largest economy, holder of the international reserve currency, and home to the largest and most sophisticated financial system. So we are talking about the core of

the global financial and economic system where severe problems arose and have since spread across borders.

The combination of European banks' and other financial institutions' significant exposure to US assets, over-leveraging and dependence on benign conditions for liquidity aided the rapid financial stresses that had travelled from the United States and into the European Union. Japan, having relied on external demand, had also been derailed by the contraction in the US and EU markets. With its own domestic activity afflicted, Japan's capacity to support other emerging economies had diminished, thus damaging those emerging economies. In 2007 alone, the United States, the European Union and Japan had accounted for 50 per cent of global GDP.

Heng predicted the possibility of a new global order, as US households might no longer be able to function as the engine for the world economy—and with no clear alternative yet in sight. On this point, his view interestingly, though subtly, deviated from that of Lee and Shanmugaratnam. For the Prime Minister and Minister for Finance, it had not been a matter of whether the United States would regain its position in the status quo, but when.

In his address, Heng called for a proactive, decisive and coordinated response from Asian financial leaders in order to counter the effects of the global financial crisis in Asia. Although he believed that since the 1997 East Asian financial crisis, fundamentals in the Asian financial system and economy had become generally sound—banks had been well capitalised and, unlike their Western counterparts, had limited exposure to toxic assets—Asian economies that were more reliant on external demand were expected to contract more sharply. Heng emphasised that although it had been important to focus on the 'here and now', structural weaknesses could emerge from short-term measures, damaging the long-term viability and health of Asian economies. As such, leaders were encouraged not to base their actions on sequential responses that had underestimated the severity of the global financial crisis. Remedial action that was too tentative or lacking in conviction could trigger renewed bouts of panic and thus delay recovery.

24 March 2009: Shanmugaratnam finetuning the message

In a speech to the Singapore Business Awards on 24 March, Shanmugaratnam acknowledged the significance of the global financial crisis as likely the deepest recession in history. The Minister for Finance did not, however, offer the same optimistic view of Singapore's situation as had the Prime Minister. Recognising that Singapore's growth had been notably affected by the global financial crisis, he did not expect the worst of the recession to surface within the next two quarters. He forecast that growth for Singapore would remain weak until at least the end of 2010. This admittance of the dire situation of Singapore's economy was not unexpected, as the economic indicators were there for all to see.

Echoing his own and the other two leaders' assertions that the blame for the crisis lay elsewhere, Shanmugaratnam was explicit in his criticism of foreign governments and foreign politicians for not taking a hard policy line to discipline their constituencies, as well as not having provided much boost to their economies by way of discretionary spending. Their tightening of credit, according to Shanmugaratnam, had acted as a drag on the global economy and Singapore would suffer the consequences.

In contrast, he congratulated the incumbent PAP for taking forward measures during the 1997 East Asian financial crisis, which had cushioned the impact of the global financial crisis in Singapore. Furthermore, Shanmugaratnam praised Singapore's entrepreneurs. As this was an address to the Business Awards, Shanmugaratnam's audience would likely have consisted of stakeholders who would find most benefit from the PAP's measures to counter the effects of the global financial crisis. Some of the measures included supporting cash flow through reduction in corporate tax, property tax rebates, the enhanced-loss carry-back scheme to help companies making losses and foreign-sourced income exemption. He also foreshadowed a suite of other business-friendly measures—for example, a reduction in administrative speed bumps and reducing regulatory roadblocks. Shanmugaratnam also highlighted small and medium enterprises (SMEs) as a point of focus for future growth whereby they would be encouraged to expand globally, at the same time appealing to foreign SMEs to invest in Singapore. He also proposed to introduce an integrated system of financial reporting to lighten the regulatory compliance burden of companies, especially SMEs. Most significantly, he highlighted the government's decision to enter into a risk-sharing scheme with banks to encourage banks to continue lending to SMEs by moderating the risks. Although these measures were proposed to encourage competition and coordination among businesses, it is interesting to note that some of the measures proposed would draw corporate governance away from the democratic issue of corporate transparency.

28 March 2009: Lee's call for unity

In Prime Minister Lee's speech to the Manual and Mercantile Workers' Union (the biggest and one of the oldest unions in Singapore) on 28 March, he took a defensive stance. This presented a significant variation from his previous speeches, revealing deeper concerns about the local impact of the crisis. In what by now had become a familiar mantra, Lee first exogenised responsibility and blame for the global financial crisis and attributed Singapore's current plight to the United States and Europe, omitting more endogenous contributing factors such as Singapore's heavy dependence on speculative trade. Lee acknowledged that while recent US Government crisis measures were helpful, the global storm had, inevitably, produced a surge in unemployment, particularly in Singapore's manufacturing sector, tourism and transportation businesses. Although job losses had so far not affected the service sector, Lee advised Singaporeans to brace themselves, as eventually the service sector would also be affected.

Lee's thinly veiled concern in this speech was about social stability. Pointing to France, where three million people had taken to the streets in protest against the policies of President, Nicolas Sarkozy (see further Windle, this volume), Lee feared the discontent of the unemployed and impoverished would trigger fear and frustration. Eventually the unemployed would look for someone to blame and would lash out at governments. Highlighting the social impact of recession in this way, Lee betrayed an awareness of the growing unrest among the Singaporean workforce. He then attempted to address this issue before it could potentially become a crisis situation in itself, urging Singaporeans to unite in times of duress. He stressed that tripartite cooperation between the government, workers (and unions) and businesses had never been more important. Its strength had to be preserved in these times of economic decline.

Lee reiterated once again that Singapore had no control over its external environment and must do the best with what was available to it. Singapore, being a 'price taker', had to accept and operate within global economic constraints. As such, the PAP had been capable of only buffering Singaporeans from the worst effects of the global storm—limiting their overall responsibility.

Policies covered by Lee in this speech were largely in line with the PAP's longstanding rejection of protectionist measures and welfare payments to the aged or unemployed. Rather, Lee encouraged workers to accept demotions, pay cuts and, alternatively, retrain to work in a different industry as job opportunities presented themselves. The government had, as part of its Resilience Package, set up agencies to help reallocate the unemployed to available jobs—at times in different fields—as well as encouraging the aged to continue working.

As such, based on a loose assessment of the employment situation, the likely outcome of the crisis-exploitation game would be elite escape with little change in public opinion regarding Lee's credibility. In part, this could be attributed to Lee's and the PAP's consistent and established political and economic ideology, which had been endogenised by the majority of Singaporeans. Based on the issue of unemployment alone, a paradigm shift would be an unlikely event, thus a policy stalemate between the opposition and the PAP would likely endure.

4. Framing the financial crisis in Singapore: analysis and conclusions

Perhaps not surprisingly in a highly centralised system of government, there was a great deal of consistency between the messages of the three leaders. The core refrain was as follows: this is a nasty crisis; it has been caused overseas; we are well placed to weather the storm; we are doing everything we can to enhance business competitiveness, but we have to accept that our dependence on our major trading partners' economies is overwhelming; as long as they are in recession, we will face significant uncertainty and unemployment; but we cannot allow this to diverge us from our tried and tested approach to creating long-term prosperity.

In the majority of speeches analysed in this chapter, the speakers directed the cause and responsibility towards the United States as the origin of the global financial crisis. Further to this, with varying degrees of explicitness, they lamented the failure of US legislators and regulators to diagnose and manage the health and viability of its financial markets and banking system. Heng even expressed some doubt about the United States' ability to fully recover—alluding to possible long-term changes in the world order, the substance of which might become clear only after the global financial crisis and its effects had fully dissipated.

Singapore has been known as the financial and business hub of East Asia. With the pride of the nation hinging on its commercial success and high standard of living, economic crises pose an existential threat to this small city-state. In what could be construed as an attempt to regain consumer confidence and confidence in its leaders, the most prominent hallmark of the three key actors' crisis framing was the propensity to deflect blame—mostly towards foreign governments and organisations, but also, to a lesser extent, to naive domestic investors and misconduct within some domestic financial institutions.

Though comparatively small, some differences in tone and emphasis are notable. Lee's unflinching optimism about Singapore's capacity to weather the storm was not fully met by Shanmugaratnam and Heng, who were more inclined to stress the fragility of the situation (while sharing Lee's staunch defence of the government's past and present economic policies). Overall, however, the impression one gets is that whether spontaneously or by purposeful coordination, the speeches all served the same underlying purpose: to consolidate and strengthen the PAP's political capital and at the same time advance and defend longstanding PAP policies. On this line, the PAP has, arguably, successfully turned a crisis situation into an opportunity to implement pragmatic, and perhaps otherwise unacceptable, policies that will redirect and reshape Singapore's business community in ways that fit the PAP's vision for the future of Singapore.

At the same time, the proactive attitude shown by the PAP in its attempts to buffer Singapore from the worst of the effects of the global financial crisis might not have been for purely pragmatic purposes. With Prime Minister Lee often being accused of attaining his position through nepotism, the global financial crisis might have come at a good time for him to prove himself as being as indispensable to Singapore as Lee Kuan Yew had been, and that the PAP's role in Singapore society was still viable and not yet redundant. Even in a 'managed democracy' political leaders must, to a considerable extent, accept the discipline of public criticism and social opposition (Dreze and Sen 1989).

In their meaning-making efforts with regard to the global financial crisis, the ruling party injected their values into their depiction of the situation and their narratives of severity, causality and responsibility. Whether Lee's or the PAP's private sense making coincided with their public pronouncements remains unclear. With the memory of the 1997 East Asian financial crisis and Singapore's vigorous and largely successful response to it still looming large in their own (and, presumably, the Singaporean public's) minds, they might have believed their own, self-confident rhetoric. Politically, barring a total economic collapse, it is unlikely that there will be any significant paradigm shift or substantial damage to the long-term image of the Lee family or the PAP as a result of this crisis.

References

Boin, A., 't Hart, P. and McConnell, A. 2009, 'Crisis exploitation: political and policy impacts of framing contests', *Journal of European Public Policy*, vol. 16, no. 1, pp. 81–106.

Brook, P. J. 2008, *Doing Business 2009: In Singapore*, 28 October, The World Bank, Washington, DC, viewed 8 May 2009, <http://siteresources.worldbank.org/INTSINGAPORE/Resources/DB09_Singapore_Rev-3.pdf>

Dreze, J. and Sen, A. 1989, *Hunger and Public Action*, Oxford University Press, Oxford.

Heng S. 2008a, *A More Challenging Global and Domestic Economic Environment*, 24 July, Bank for International Settlements, Basel, viewed 21 May 2009, <http://www.bis.org/review/r080725e.pdf>

Heng, S. 2008b, Sale of structured products to retail investors: opening remarks, Press conference, 17 October, Monetary Authority of Singapore, viewed 11 April 2009, <http://www.mas.gov.sg/news_room/statements/2008/Opening_Remarks_by_Heng_Swee_Keat_Managing_Director_MAS_at_the_MAS_Press_Conference_on_the_Sale_of_Structured_Products_to_Retail_Investors.html>

Heng, S. 2009, Keynote Address, International Institute of Finance Asia Regional Economic Forum: The impact of the global financial crisis on Asia, 4 March, viewed 20 April 2009, <http://www.mas.gov.sg/news_room/statements/2009/Keynote_Address_by_Mr_Heng_Swee_Keat_MD_MAS_at_the_International_Institute_of_Finance.html>

Lee, H. 2009a, Speech by Mr Lee Hsien Loong, Prime Minister, Standard Chartered 150th Anniversary in Singapore Gala Dinner, 19 February, viewed 11 April 2009, <http://www.mas.gov.sg/news_room/statements/2009/ Speech_By_PM_Lee_at_Standard_Chartered_150th_Anniversary_ in_Singapore_Gala_Dinner.html>

Lee, H. 2009b, Speech, Singapore Tripartism Forum: Coping with the crisis. Part 1, 22 February, viewed 5 May 2009, <http://www.youtube.com/watch?v=wC8kAReAc3U&feature=channel_page>

Lee, H. 2009c, Speech, SMMWU 50th Anniversary Gala Dinner, 28 March, viewed 20 April 2009, <http://www.pmo.gov.sg/News/Speeches/Prime+Minister/ Singapore+United+the+way+to+go.htm>

Mauzy, D. and Milne, R. S. 2002, *Singapore Politics Under the People's Action Party*, Routledge, London.

Paris, C. 2009, 'Singapore government fund's loss pegged at $33 billion', *The Wall Street Journal*, 18 February, viewed 6 May 2009, <http://online.wsj.com/article/SB123486651894698861.html>

Sen, A. 1999, *Development as Freedom*, Oxford University Press, Oxford.

Shanmugaratnam, T. 2008, Speech, Association of the Banks in Singapore Annual General Meeting, 27 June, viewed 21 May 2009, <http://app.mof.gov.sg/news_speeches/speechdetails.asp?speechid=240>

Shanmugaratnam, T. 2009a, Keeping jobs, building for the future, Budget speech 2009, 22 January, viewed 11 April 2009, <http://www.singaporebudget.gov.sg/>

Shanmugaratnam, T. 2009b, Speech, Singapore Business Awards 2009, 24 March, viewed 20 April 2009, <http://www.news.gov.sg/public/sgpc/en/media_releases/ agencies/mof/speech/S-20090324-1.html>

Thangavelu, S. 2009, 'Riding the global economic crisis in Singapore', *East Asia Forum*, 5 January, viewed 20 April 2009, <http://www.eastasiaforum.org/2009/01/05/ riding-the-global-economic-crisis-in-singapore/>

US Department of State 2009, '2008 human rights report: Singapore', *2008 Country Reports on Human Rights Practices*, 25 February, US Department of State, Washington, DC, viewed 8 May 2009, <http://www.state.gov/g/drl/rls/hrrpt/2008/eap/119056.htm>

Part V. Comparisons and reflections

12. Contesting the frame: opposition leadership and the global financial crisis

Brendan McCaffrie

1. Whose crisis?

The global financial crisis has dominated inter-party political contests in almost all major democracies, presenting challenges and opportunities to executive government leaders and opposition party leaders alike. In their public responses to crises, opposition leaders complete many comparable framing tasks to those of executive leaders. Opposition leaders, however, typically have lesser resources, fewer political weapons and limited responsibility for the real crisis response. These differences create a distinct and difficult challenge for opposition leaders in crises. Despite these restricted opportunities, opposition leaders can exploit crises for political gain. This chapter demonstrates how opposition leaders in three different political systems utilised the public sphere to do this, and explains their consequent political successes and failures.

Political opposition is understudied in political science, while opposition leadership is almost entirely neglected. This is unfortunate, as oppositions and opposition leaders are crucial to maintaining the accountability and legitimacy of governments, and as such should be better understood than they are. Opposition leadership can be defined in many ways. Traditionally, the term 'Leader of the Opposition' has been used in Westminster systems to refer to the leader of the largest non-government party in parliament. Moving beyond Westminster systems, this conception becomes problematic.

In presidential systems such as the United States, it is very often unclear who is leading the non-government party. In situations of divided government, when the president's party does not hold a majority in both houses of Congress, it can also be unclear which is the non-governing party. As Dahl (1966:34) notes of the United States, '[t]o say where the government "leaves off" and "the opposition" begins is an exercise in metaphysics'. Additionally, the definitional restriction to the largest non-government party cannot accurately represent different oppositional configurations displayed in multiparty coalition systems. For instance, after the 2005 German federal elections, the centre-right Christian Democrats (CDU/CSU) became the senior governing partner in a 'grand coalition' government with the centre-left Social Democratic Party (SPD). The CDU/CSU's preferred coalition partner, the Free Democratic Party (FDP), was the largest non-government party although it held only 61 of 614 Bundestag seats and was ideologically similar to the CDU/CSU. Moreover, it was clear from the post-election posturing of the SPD that the most significant opposition to the leadership of Chancellor, Angela Merkel, would come from within her own grand coalition government (Richter 2006).

This chapter does not investigate the roles of minor-party oppositional leadership or extra-parliamentary oppositional leadership in the financial crisis. The simplest term to describe the types of opposition leadership investigated here is 'alternative executive leadership'. Each of the opposition leaders discussed has been engaged in a legitimate attempt to replace the incumbent head of government. With this as the common goal, and bearing in mind the nature of the global financial crisis, it is unsurprising that opposition leaders focused on the third and fourth framing contests described in Chapter 2. Apportioning blame (third contest) and providing alternative policies (fourth contest) are opposition leaders' two strongest weapons.

They might find the first framing contest, which centres on defining the significance and severity of events, a more fruitful avenue of attack in other types of crisis than it was at the onset of this financial crisis. This is because oppositions typically rely on the same economic data as governments and have fewer economic experts at their disposal to interpret those data, making it difficult to contest government statements about the severity of negative economic events. Furthermore, offering a bleaker picture of the state of the economy than government leaders do leaves opposition leaders susceptible to claims that they are acting irresponsibly by diminishing consumer confidence and thereby damaging the economy. This difficulty was exemplified by Britain's Shadow Chancellor of the Exchequer, George Osborne, who warned of the potential for a run on the pound, only to be pilloried by the government, media and even his own party (Helm et al. 2008). This was a rare example of an opposition attempting to make a mark in the first framing contest. Given the outcome, this rarity is hardly surprising. In the cases studied, the first framing contest is a relatively minor one and therefore it is excluded from the analysis.

The second framing contest—in which political actors attempt to define the cause of a crisis—is crucial to opposition leaders' abilities to blame the government for the disaster. If a government leader effectively defines the crisis as caused by external events, it becomes virtually untenable for an opposition leader to claim that the government or its leader is culpable for the negative effects of the crisis. In the specific case of the financial crisis, it made little sense to define an opposition leader's causal frame as distinct from their blaming frame. Alternative government leaders gain nothing by offering a causal frame that does not, either directly or indirectly, apportion blame to the government. As such, these two framing avenues—causality and blame—will be examined together in section three of this chapter.

2. Cases and context: opportunities and expectations

The three nations selected for analysis—the United Kingdom, the United States and Germany—are each considered archetypes for different systems of government. The United Kingdom has the original Westminster system and its opposition behaves almost exclusively as an alternative government. Since World War II, there has not been a coalition government and its only major deviation from a classic binary government–opposition dichotomy is a fairly strong third party, though typically it is not strong enough to prevent a majority government. The United States has a presidential system with a pure separation of powers. As such, it presents significant challenges in locating an opposition, let alone its leader. This chapter examines the period of the 2008 US presidential election campaign, as elections are perhaps the only time when both major parties have an obvious leader. They are certainly the only times when alternative government leaders can be readily identified. Germany is seen to epitomise consensus systems, with a proportional representation voting system and a growing history of coalition governments. The rise of the minor parties at the expense of the two major parties in recent times led to only the second German 'grand coalition' government, in 2005, although at the time of writing Germany was approaching an election with another grand coalition one likely possibility. This chapter defines the German alternative executive leader as the leader of the junior coalition party, which during the onset of the financial crisis was the SPD. Ordinarily, this would present a difficulty in that much of its opposition to the Merkel-led 'union' of CDU and CSU parties is not conducted in the public realm. Fortunately, the proximity of the September 2009 election and the SPD's decision to choose its chancellor candidate an entire year before the poll escalated the public nature of the SPD's opposition to the union parties.

United Kingdom: a besieged government and a vulnerable economy

The United Kingdom entered the financial crisis with a more immediately vulnerable economy than either Germany or the United States. Under the Labour Government, Britain had enjoyed a decade of immense prosperity, with the International Monetary Fund (IMF) declaring that between 1996 and 2005 the United Kingdom's 'growth of real GDP per capita was higher and less volatile than any other G7 country' (IMF quoted in Lee 2008:17). The consistently high exchange rate of the pound against other currencies in that period, however, discouraged exports and resulted in a poor balance of trade. Even with booming financial and business services sectors, which delivered almost 30 per cent of gross domestic product (GDP) (*The Guardian* 2007), the United Kingdom ran consistent trade and current account deficits (Lee 2008). This reliance on financial and business services coupled with a dependence on overseas borrowing meant that the financial crisis, with its sharp decline in lending, damaged Britain's economy severely and rapidly.

The Labour Government entered the financial crisis after more than a decade in office, but with the experienced Prime Minister, Tony Blair, having stepped aside for his long-time Chancellor of the Exchequer, Gordon Brown, in June 2007. Brown performed well in the polls during his first few months as leader, with Labour consistently leading its rival Conservative Party by single-figure margins (UK Polling Report 2009). Despite this leadership transition, Brown's long tenure as Chancellor meant that he was inextricably linked with the economic performance of the nation, especially as he had long boasted that his stewardship of the economy had resulted in 'the longest period of sustained economic growth since records began' (Brown quoted in Milne 2007).

Traditionally, the governing Labour Party was a centre-left social democratic party. The 'New Labour's' third-way politics broadly accepted a move towards a neo-liberal economic strategy (Heffernan 1999), although some commentators contested the extent to which this was the case (cf. Beech 2008). This meant that little distinguished the Conservative Party from the Labour Government on economic matters except for Labour's slightly greater predilection for public spending.

For Conservative Opposition Leader, David Cameron, who took on the role in December 2005, the economic situation and the length of the Labour Government's tenure combined to create strong opportunities to attack Brown and his government using blaming tactics. Brown essentially had responsibility for the economic system and had claimed responsibility for its successes. The severe hardship that Britain was to face in comparison with many other Western European nations would mean that as long as the public accepted Brown and his government as responsible for the crisis, or even just for its severity, Labour's popularity would slip. In the policy contest, however, the Conservatives would likely be hampered by their ideological proximity to the failing economic policies of the Labour Government. Cameron would be unable to press for a paradigm shift in economic policy and would be forced to focus on technical issues and specific policy failings of the Brown Government. Thus, the global financial crisis would provide significant but by no means unlimited opportunities for Cameron as opposition leader.

United States: competing opposition leaders

When the sub-prime mortgage crisis visibly struck the financial sector in March 2008 with the collapse of Bear Sterns investment bank, President, George W. Bush, was suffering unremittingly low approval ratings. A Gallup Poll published on 20 February 2008 (Saad 2008) found that 31 per cent of respondents approved of Bush's performance—a result that was strikingly similar to those of the preceding months. The Bear Sterns failure also coincided with the 2008 presidential election campaign. Polling suggested that presumptive Republican nominee, Senator John McCain, was roughly level with eventual Democratic nominee, Senator Barack Obama, with some polls favouring the Democrat and others the Republican (Real Clear Politics 2008). These polls should be treated with caution, as McCain had won the Republican nomination, while Obama was still battling Senator Hillary Clinton for the Democratic nomination, but they do show that each leader was in a reasonable position to utilise the crisis to their political advantage.

The financial crisis struck the United States at the end of the two-term Bush Republican presidency. In terms of apportioning blame, the unpopularity and apparent culpability of Bush made him an obvious target. With two presidential contenders who had not been part of the Bush Administration and had explicitly opposed it on many issues in the past, each could use blame tactics against Bush. This would be easier for Obama than McCain, as Obama could repudiate the entire Republican Party. It is also important to note that blaming the incumbent, though likely damaging to Bush, would be far less relevant than blaming the opposing candidate. This meant that the relevant argument could either shift to blaming the partisan ideology behind the crisis or to focus on the policy contest. Either argument would again likely favour Obama. The vehemently free-market Republicans were intractably associated with the ideology that public debate increasingly blamed for the crisis. They were also unlikely or even unable to argue for a policy shift, whereas the more centre-left Democrats could plausibly argue for stricter regulations of the finance sector. Therefore Obama had greater opportunities to use the weapons of blame and policy to exploit the crisis to his political advantage than did McCain.

Germany: spot the opposition

Compared with the other nations examined in this chapter, Germany felt the early effects of the financial crisis fairly moderately. Admittedly, the government was forced to bail out IKB Deutsche Industriebank AG on several occasions from mid 2007, and to rescue Hypo Real Estate in September 2008, after the Lehman Brothers collapse in the United States because of each of these lenders' exposure to the sub-prime crisis. Financial problems in Germany, however, remained largely distinct from the rest of the economy, which led Europe in managing 1.5 per cent growth in the first quarter of 2008 (Dougherty 2008). This was due largely to its strong and varied export sector. When the crisis made other nations less able to buy its goods, the German economy did falter (*The Economist* 2009). An idiosyncratic factor of the political and economic context in Germany is a deep fiscal conservatism that leads politicians to shun state intervention through stimulus packages and other similar measures (Bovensiepen et al. 2008).

The German political context at the time of the crisis was intriguing. The 'grand coalition' government of SPD and union parties was an uneasy alliance between parties that had been staunch competitors since the State's founding in 1949—bar one period of an equally uneasy coalition imposed by political circumstances from 1966 to 1969. Condemned to collaboration by the election outcomes, the parties forged the coalition in a difficult negotiation process subsequent to the 2005 election. The masterful posturing skills of outgoing Chancellor, Gerhard Schröder, secured for the SPD a majority of cabinet positions, among them the highly important Finance Ministry, which was taken by Peer Steinbrück (Richter 2006). The negotiation phase also saw the Christian Social Union (CSU), the Bavarian sister party to the Merkel-led Christian Democratic Union (CDU), awarded the Economics Ministry, and from the time of the election until February 2009, the Economics Minister was the reluctant and economically uninterested Michael Glos. As a result of Glos's lack of economic acumen and Merkel's lack of trust in him, Steinbrück had far more involvement in economic decisions throughout the crisis (Nelles and Neukirch 2008). Glos's frustration at his own lack of influence led him to call publicly for the government to change policy and introduce tax cuts (Bovensiepen et al. 2008), and ultimately to resign in an unorthodox manner designed to embarrass Chancellor Merkel (cf. Crossland 2009). The significant input of Steinbrück had allowed the SPD a far greater opportunity to affect government policy in response to the crisis, but consequently limited its ability to blame the government for failing to prevent the crisis, or respond appropriately.

The SPD's legacy as the previous governing party further limited its potential to advocate a policy shift. Under Schröder, the SPD Government implemented a largely neo-liberal set of economic proposals known as 'Agenda 2010', which cut taxes, reduced welfare programs and reformed the labour market. Schröder's SPD was very strongly associated with the neo-liberal ideology and had been the senior governing party in a coalition government with the Green Party until 2005. Seemingly, it was in a poor position to cast blame on a centre-right party that had been in government for a comparatively short period. When Frank-Walter Steinmeier became the SPD chancellor candidate, this connection to the Agenda 2010 reforms intensified. Steinmeier had participated in the design of the program in the bureaucratic post of head of the Office of the Chancellor, where he was one of Schröder's political confidantes.

A further limitation on the SPD was its waning popularity. After performing better than expected in the 2005 election—garnering 34.3 per cent of the vote and forcing the grand coalition situation—the SPD's polling numbers declined. In the last few months of 2007, major polling agencies consistently recorded its support at between 25 and 30 per cent compared with the CDU/CSU's polling in the very high 30s (*Der Spiegel* 2009). Worse was to come after then party leader, Kurt Beck, reneged on a promise not to deal with the far-left Left Party and backed the bid by State of Hessen's SPD leader, Andrea Ypsilanti, to form a government there with the support of the Left Party. The Left Party's strong connections with the former East German regime made this a politically fraught situation. It caused ructions within the SPD on a national level and ultimately failed when rebel SPD member Dagmar Metzger in Hessen refused to accept her own party as a government (*Deutsche Welle* 2008a). Beck's popularity plummeted. A poll in March suggested that he was the preferred chancellor for only 13 per cent of voters, while also showing just 23 per cent support for the SPD Party (*Der Spiegel* 2008a). Beck was replaced as party leader in September 2008 by Franz Müntefering, while Foreign Minister and Deputy Chancellor, Frank-Walter Steinmeier, was announced as the SPD's chancellor candidate for the 2009 election, thus becoming the alternative government leader. The weak position of the SPD would appear to limit its ability to attack the CDU/CSU even further, particularly in the last months of Beck's party leadership, when speculation about his future was frequent.

Of the cases discussed here, the German opposition leadership was in the worst position to use the weapons of blame and policy change. It was handicapped by its high level of responsibility for the economic situation in having a two-term neo-liberal economic policy legacy to defend and in providing the most important minister in German economic matters to the current coalition government. Although traditionally the SPD had been the party of centre-left social democracy in Germany, it was in no position to advocate a major ideological shift in economic policy because of its close ties to the neo-liberal system in place. Furthermore, the political landscape was dominated by fiscal conservatism—with Merkel and Steinbrück each motivated by the long-term goal of a balanced budget rather than short-term attempts to ward off recession (*Deutsche Welle* 2008c).

3. The second and third framing contests: causality and blame

United Kingdom: winning a blame showdown

Opposition leaders rarely if ever treat causality as distinct from blame. This was exemplified by David Cameron's contention immediately after the run on Northern Rock bank in September 2007: that this was caused by too much public and private debt—a problem fostered by the Brown Government (Elliot and Seager 2007; Harding 2007). Cameron repeated this claim like a mantra throughout the financial crisis, clearly seeing an opportunity not only to blame the government for its part in creating the crisis but to undo the public perception that the Labour Government had managed the economy successfully in the past decade. He therefore claimed that the previous boom had been 'built on a mountain of debt' (Cameron quoted in Webster and Elliot 2007).

In the immediate aftermath of the Northern Rock failure, Cameron struggled to make a political impact. In the first week or two after the news broke, Labour advanced from its slim advantage to a double-figure lead in several polls. This government bounce was short-lived, however, and by the second week in October most polling agencies showed the Conservatives in front (UK Polling Report 2009). The Northern Rock issue lingered for months. It was mid-February 2008 by the time the government decided to nationalise the institution, leading Cameron to argue that Chancellor of the Exchequer, Alistair Darling, should resign and that the Brown Government had failed by dithering over the nationalisation (Watt 2008a).

In continuing to promote the message that the Labour Government had done little to restrain debt, Shadow Chancellor of the Exchequer, George Osborne, noted in March 2008 that Brown had failed to prepare the country for possible tough times. Here, Osborne was careful not to suggest that a downturn had begun, merely claiming that there should always be emergency funds in case of one (Riddell 2008a). This allowed the Tories to avoid the appearance of a reckless party that endangered the economy by reducing public confidence. It also allowed them to avoid the risk of appearing economically ignorant by suggesting a major economic slump was on its way when it might not happen. In April, Osborne continued the pressure over the public debt, claiming that the United Kingdom had the largest budget deficit in the developed world. This statement, though perhaps not entirely accurate given the size of the US deficit (Milne 2008b), was an effective one, because it distinguished the UK situation from that of the rest of the developed world. It damaged counterclaims by Brown that the real cause of the financial crisis was the United States. Osborne and Cameron repeated this claim several times over many months, although eventually Osborne altered the phrasing from 'largest deficit' in the developed world to 'worst public finances' in the developed world (Webster et al. 2009).

The excessive-debt narrative served Cameron and Osborne well for the best part of six months, as the Conservatives continued a steady climb in the polls. From 4 May 2008 to 14 September 2008, in 40 voting-intention polls taken by major polling agencies, the Conservatives led by an average of 19 percentage points. The next week, the crisis reached its climax. The failure of Lehman Brothers in the United States and the ensuing market turmoil sparked a Labour poll revival (UK Polling Report 2009). At this point, the crisis changed in nature, and to help explain the collapse of financial institutions, a secondary causal and blaming tool became prominent. The Conservative leadership used the idea of a failure of financial regulation to blame the government for the financial crisis. Cameron and Osborne continued to make debt the principal issue, most likely because the Tories had little intention of making substantial alterations to the system of financial regulations themselves. Nevertheless, Osborne did take the opportunity to attack Brown for a failure of regulation (Webster and Elliot 2008; Wintour 2008).

On 30 September 2008, Cameron announced an unlikely policy of bipartisanship (Elliot and Wintour 2008). This was apparently in response to the failure of the United States to pass a bank bailout bill through Congress because of ideological party divisions. British bipartisanship was short-lived, lasting a little more than two weeks before the opposition leader began criticising Brown's crisis response, reverting to the debt narrative and labelling Brown's solution to the crisis 'borrowing and borrowing and borrowing' (Cameron quoted in Stratton 2008). Neither the bipartisan strategy nor the subsequent reversion to the political contest appears to have had any impact on poll results.

Immediately after the September–October turmoil, the Labour Party rallied in the polls and throughout December 2008 they had closed the gap to within single figures (UK Polling Report 2009), prompting talk about Brown calling an early election to profit from the favourable view of his international crisis-management leadership. This also proved short-lived and in the New Year the Tories re-established their double-figure lead. At this time, Cameron unveiled a new blaming strategy. He spent a considerable amount of time calling for Brown to admit to mistakes in his response to the crisis and to apologise for them (Rawnsley 2009). As well as bluntly implying that Brown was culpable for the United Kingdom's parlous economic situation, this tactic played at a popular characterisation of Brown—that he was chronically unable to admit mistakes. Furthermore, it was a useful way to harness anger felt by those in the electorate who had suffered through the crisis and direct it towards the Prime Minister.

The opposition's blame frame led to a revival in its fortunes soon after the September 2007 Northern Rock episode. The advanced age of the Labour Government and its willingness to take responsibility for the perceived successes of the British economy in the preceding decade made it an easy target when that economy began to falter. This was especially salient given that the United Kingdom's situation appeared worse than in many other European nations. The debt message that Cameron and Osborne proffered was simple to understand and consistently applied. Circumstances assisted the Conservative opposition leader, but he still had to apply a plausible and consistent message against a political opponent who was not prepared to accept blame for the crisis.

United States: blame as a fait accompli

At first glance, the US situation was a contest between two challengers with an outgoing incumbent, making it impossible for one candidate to blame the other for the financial crisis and fruitless to blame the President. Senator Obama, however, managed to blame not just the President, but the broader ideology of his party and thereby include McCain in the blame frame. In a March 2008 address, after the Bear Sterns collapse, Obama blamed the Bush Administration, including its tax cuts for top earners and the war in Iraq—two major policies on which McCain agreed with the President—as causative factors in the crisis. Obama also blamed nameless 'lobbyists and politicians' who had dismantled the regulatory framework governing the financial sector (Obama 2008).

In contrast, McCain blamed the behaviour of lenders in financial institutions for the deteriorating economic situation, but also somewhat surprisingly, those who took out loans. His heaviest focus was on financial institutions' 'rampant speculation', but he also suggested that homeowners had engaged in dangerous borrowing (Rohter and Andrews 2008). Unsurprisingly, McCain spent the entire campaign attempting to distance himself from Bush. It was easier for Obama to deliver a clear message of blame towards Bush and the man who followed him with a similar economic philosophy.

In September 2008, after the Lehman Brothers failure, the competition for blame intensified. Obama persisted in denouncing the Bush Administration's 'failed philosophy' (Landler and Stolberg 2008) and equating McCain with Bush on economic policy (Healy 2008; Page 2008). He repeated this message ad nauseam, though conspicuously seeking to moderate the personal attack element inherent in the statement, arguing, 'I certainly don't fault Senator McCain for these problems, but I do fault the economic philosophy he subscribes to' (Obama quoted in Calmes 2008a).

McCain continued to deflect blame towards the bankers and Wall Street greed (Calmes 2008a). Obama's strategy of equating his opponent with Bush was clearly hurting McCain. In the last weeks before the election, Bush removed himself almost entirely from the public eye, attending only a handful of relatively minor events. He avoided making policy pronouncements or discussing the state of the economy (Stolberg 2008). The President's invisibility was clearly a deliberate Republican strategy. A humiliation for Bush, it was a clear sign that the McCain campaign knew it was losing the blame contest. McCain was always going to struggle to win this contest as Obama had the advantage of being able to create an ideological separation between himself and the events that led to the crisis, as well as between himself and the incredibly unpopular President. McCain was not only inextricably linked to the apparently failing ideology and the President, he was unable to find a similar angle with which to blame Obama for the events of the crisis. Neither Obama's party nor the relatively inexperienced candidate had been in control of the political system for the previous eight years. In these circumstances, only an extraordinary failure of public performance could have seen Obama lose the blame contest.

Germany: blame dilemmas

Superficially, it seems highly unusual that in Germany a weakened social democratic party was virtually unable to blame a governing centre-right party nearing the end of its term. As noted above, the nature of the grand coalition government, the fact that the SPD controlled the finance ministry throughout that government and the party's recent alignment with the neo-liberal consensus meant that if there was blame to be apportioned to a political party in Germany, the SPD was more likely to be receiving it than dispensing it. For the SPD under Beck and later Steinmeier to blame the government that it was a part of would risk having its charges reflect poorly on itself. Merkel and the CDU could rebuff any specific public complaints about the government's response to the crisis with the contention that the junior governing partner should have raised its concerns in cabinet. Furthermore, the leaders could not blame Finance Minister Steinbrück, who was instrumental in announcing and defending government economic and financial policy, but was also a senior member of the SPD.

The SPD still had the capacity to make political headway during the crisis but these achievements were unlikely to be won in the public sphere unless Merkel failed in her response to the crisis. This last possibility would have been more likely had the SPD contested the severity-framing contest. For then party leader Beck to dispute the significance of the crisis, however, would have invited criticism that he was diminishing public confidence in the economy.

The German causal and blame frame that emerged early in the crisis was a consensus position, with Merkel and Steinbrück each blaming the United States for the crisis. Merkel claimed that it was a result of the United States' resistance to stricter regulations on its financial sector (*Deutsche Welle* 2008b). Steinbrück concurred with this exogenised frame: 'The United States is the source of the crisis, and it is the focus of the crisis' (*Der Spiegel* 2008b); 'More than anything, the finance market is an American problem' (*Der Spiegel* 2008c).

Eventually, with Steinmeier as chancellor candidate, the SPD began to blame the ideological commitments of the CDU/CSU parties, claiming, 'The rule of radical market ideology that began with Margaret Thatcher and Ronald Reagan has ended with a loud bang…This new time that is dawning now must become our time—the time of social democracy' (Steinmeier quoted in Moore 2008). While the SPD's shift to the left appears to have been a cynical and opportunistic exercise in crisis exploitation, the advantages of the move away from the free market are to be found in greater party unity rather than in a newfound capacity to win the blame contest. Unlike Obama, who was successfully able to blame his opponent by blaming his ideology, Steinmeier and his party had recently been committed to a neo-liberal economic program.

4. Opposition by looking forward: the politics of policy change

United Kingdom: the rewards of doing nothing

Despite the Tories' huge advantage in being able to successfully blame the Labour Government for the crisis, Cameron faced repeated criticism for his failure to articulate alternative policy (*The Guardian* 2008a, 2008b; Riddell 2008b). Cameron, however, well understood that winning was 'not really about your policies and your plans' (Cameron quoted in *The Guardian* 2008b). Still, the consistency of this criticism raises two important questions. First, why were the Tories unable to articulate an alternative policy platform? Second, did they really need to articulate an alternative policy platform?

The Tories had an ideological commitment to the neo-liberal economic program that was already in place. It is difficult to make a personal pledge to betray one's own principles and it is even harder to drag an entire party along against its will (Oborne 2009). One of the greatest problems Cameron had to face was that there were powerful arguments for stronger financial regulations to prevent destabilising lending practices, but his party's free-market advocates had long argued for less regulation (Elliot 2008). This philosophy was apparent when George Osborne stated that 'no one takes pleasure from people making money out of the misery of others, but that is a function of capitalist markets' as he opposed the government's proposal to ban the practice of short selling, in which shareholders sell shares they expect to drop in price, then repurchase them when they do (Osborne quoted in Milne 2008a; *The Observer* 2008). The Labour position was likely to be popular and it was hard to see what the Tories' tacit encouragement of short selling would achieve in policy terms, but the Conservative ideological belief that governments should not interfere with the market overwhelmed each of these concerns. Similarly, Osborne and Cameron consistently opposed the temporary government ownership of the failing lending institution Northern Rock (Watt 2008a).

Considering the second question, does it matter that the Tory Party failed to create a consistent regulatory or stimulus policy with which to oppose Labour? The answer is that in this case it did not. Voting-intention polls showed that the Conservatives had a double-figure lead over Labour in all but one poll throughout the second quarter of 2009. The last time the Labour Party had been in front in a single poll was 23 January 2008 (UK Polling Report 2009). With such consistent poll leads, who needed good policy to convince floating voters?

That is not to suggest that Cameron acquiesced on all government proposals and neglected to announce policy at every juncture; there were several interesting policy contests. Opposition policy was, however, piecemeal. Rather than offering a coherent alternative and advocating radical reforms to the government policies that it said were failing, the opposition suggested only minor alterations. This included broader intervention and takeover powers for the Bank of England to use in the case of failing financial institutions. This policy seemed reasonable, but Cameron announced it at the same time as he opposed the government's takeover of failing bank Bradford & Bingley. This was a confusing stance. It did not completely oppose nationalisation of failing institutions, but merely changed who was to decide to nationalise them (Elliot et al. 2008). Presumably, the free-market Tories preferred banks not to be nationalised but, forced to accept its necessity in some circumstances, would allow it as long as they did not have to take responsibility for it if in government.

Brown's policy failures as prime minister contributed to the opposition leader's success despite lacking an organised policy strategy. The government's removal of the '10p tax rate' for the lowest income earners was particularly harmful. This meant that instead of paying 10 per cent income tax, the lowest earners would be paying 20 per cent—a change that the Commons Treasury Committee considered to be an 'unreasonable' way to raise tax revenue (Duncan 2008). Months later, Brown made an uncharacteristic admission that the policy was a mistake (Watt 2008b). This policy led to bitter infighting within the Labour Party, allowing the Conservatives to calmly watch on as Labour attacked itself (Webster 2008).

Cameron's Conservatives did not advocate a paradigm shift because of their ideological support for the spluttering free market. Instead, they sought to contain policy change and retain a broadly neo-liberal economic system. Cameron selectively contested certain policies and certain aspects of policies, but never outlined a broader vision of what the new British economy would look like should he win office. Labour's occasional policy gaffes and sporadic infighting helped Cameron, whose Conservative Party, as of mid 2009, remained heavily favoured to win the next election. It seemed that this eventuality would likely be a result of the ability of the Tory leader to win the third framing contest, while at best drawing the fourth.

United States: the other guy blinked

In one respect, Republican Presidential Candidate McCain was in the same situation as David Cameron. Like the Tories, the Republicans subscribe to a free-market ideology, perhaps even more fervently so. As noted in section three, Obama had success in tying McCain and the neo-liberal agenda to Bush and presenting it as a failure of ideology. Like Cameron, McCain had very little room to manoeuvre on his economic position. He could afford neither to abandon his free-market ideals and lose his core constituency nor to maintain too rigid a neo-liberal position for fear that he would be compared with the outgoing President and coupled to an apparently failing ideology. Also like Cameron, he was criticised for lacking an overarching plan or vision for the future of the economy (Brooks 2008).

All of these factors combined to make it difficult for McCain to respond to the rapidly changing events of the financial crisis. Initially, he opposed the bailout of insurance brokers AIG. Two days later, when the Bush Administration pushed the bailout through, McCain accepted it as 'unavoidable' (Calmes and Zeleny 2008). Similarly, in response to the Bush Administration's $250 billion injection into the banking sector, McCain initially expressed opposition and then grudgingly supported the move (Calmes 2008b).

McCain made other errors in his public leadership that added to his policy mistakes and allowed Obama to depict him as erratic and risky (Bumiller and Healy 2008). He was ridiculed for declaring at the time of the Lehman Brothers disaster in mid-September 2008 that the fundamentals of the US economy were strong (Balz and Barnes 2008; Jackson 2008). Even worse was his unusual tactic to suspend his campaign and arrive in Washington, DC, to help broker a solution on the late-September $700 billion bank bailout bill. This bid largely backfired, as McCain appeared to be an unhelpful member at the negotiating table, hardly speaking at all (Nagourney and Bumiller 2008). He then sought to have the first presidential debate postponed, attracting an attack from Obama, who contended, 'It is going to be part of the president's job to deal with more than one thing at once' (Barnes 2008).

One policy position that McCain consistently maintained throughout the campaign, though not necessarily beforehand, was his commitment to continuing the high-income earner tax cuts introduced by President Bush. This was a policy that he needed in order to retain the right-wing segment of his party's supporters. Perhaps, given the circumstances, it was unfortunate that the economic policy that he was best known for was regularly referred to as the 'Bush tax cuts', unwittingly exacerbating McCain's unwanted association with the unpopular President.

In stark contrast with McCain's general vacillation, Obama spoke after the Lehman Brothers' calamity, stating clearly, 'What we've seen in the last few days is nothing less than the final verdict on an economic philosophy that has completely failed' (Zeleny 2008). Obama spoke consistently of the failure of inadequate regulation and advocated a new regulatory approach (Harwood and Cooper 2008). Although he left the policy details until after the campaign, it was clear that Obama was advocating a stricter system of regulation and he did not waver from that.

The delicate balance McCain had to strike between keeping supporters on side and maintaining distance from an unpopular president and a faltering ideology was awkward, and ultimately proved too difficult. McCain could not maintain a consistent position in the face of rapidly changing events. Obama was able to repudiate the failing ideology, to repudiate the failing President and to offer a consistent message of change. It was unimportant whether his policies were better in theory or better in detail than McCain's, as the mistakes and inconsistencies in McCain's policies ensured that he lost the policy contest even if Obama was not particularly impressive. Like Brown, McCain blundered into disaster; Obama like Cameron could win merely by looking on, and he had the additional advantage of greater consistency in repudiating the unrestrained free market.

Germany: missed opportunities

In the German polity there was great potential for an alternative government leader to pressure the Chancellor to create a stimulus package after the government implemented a surprisingly small package of €5 billion per annum in November 2008. As noted above, the consensus in Germany was for the government not to spend on such matters. Finance Minister, Peer Steinbrück, was a firm believer that stimulus packages did not work, as evidenced by Germany's efforts in the 1960s and 1970s, and he was known to be a difficult man to bypass (Bovensiepen et al. 2008). The strong exogenised causal frame that he and Merkel created early in the crisis, when each blamed the United States, implied that there was nothing the German Government could do to fix the crisis (*Deutsche Welle* 2008d). In December, the government finally introduced a €50 billion stimulus package of public investment and tax cuts. This was partly a result of international pressure from European nations that felt the German Chancellor had not done enough to curb recession in the largest economy within the European Union (*Der Spiegel* 2008e). Other leaders of major European nations even excluded Germany from a summit on the response to the crisis (*Deutsche Welle* 2008e). CEOs of leading German companies also pressured the government to stimulate the economy (*Der Spiegel* 2008f).

Further opportunities to oppose the Chancellor on economic policy materialised, with Merkel's failure to make a convincing speech explaining measures taken to address the crisis (Nelles and Neukirch 2008). Merkel also erred in mid-October 2008 when creating an independent board of economic experts to draft new financial regulations by choosing Hans Tietmeyer to head the group. Tietmeyer had been a member of the supervisory board of Hypo Real Estate, a lending company that the government had bailed out with a rescue package only a few weeks earlier. The SPD expressed outrage and Tietmeyer chose to withdraw from consideration for the position (*Der Spiegel* 2008d).

The failure of the SPD to do more publicly to oppose their rival governing partners began to cause internal tensions, with the left wing of the party claiming that Steinbrück was not adhering to SPD values and was preventing the SPD from taking its natural approach (*Der Spiegel* 2008e). That the SPD did not behave as a genuine alternative government party in offering a policy paradigm shift was entirely understandable because of the grand coalition. Steinbrück's approach to his position as Finance Minister was refreshingly non-partisan. The international and national media pilloried his refusal to consider a stimulus package in the early stages of the crisis, but he acted from conviction instead of taking a populist stance and attempting to damage the Chancellor and her party. The ideological position of the party was another major factor in preventing the SPD from pressing for a policy shift. The SPD's strong ties to the neo-liberal economic system through its work as senior coalition partner in the Schröder-led government reinforced this stance.

Steinmeier, on the occasion of his official confirmation as SPD chancellor candidate, announced his determination to lead a social-democratic campaign, spurning neo-liberalism and the free market. This, as of mid 2009, has had no discernable impact on the party's polling status. Many German commentators viewed it as a manipulative attempt to exploit the crisis (Moore 2008). Steinmeier's campaign launch in April 2009 continued the SPD's shift to the left, including proposals to increase taxes on the rich and cut taxes for lower income earners. This was met with indignation even from the Green Party, the SPD's preferred coalition partner, which issued a statement asserting, 'What the SPD is proposing today is the opposite of what they did during four years in the grand coalition. So we have to ask them: "Are you really serious?"' (*Deutsche Welle* 2009). The SPD might have been better off at this point had it been in a non-government opposition arrangement, rather than part of the grand coalition. It would certainly have been more able to utilise the crisis politically without being admonished for its cynicism. Moreover, it might have been able to emerge from the crisis as a victor of the policy-framing contest, which so far it clearly had not.

5. Conclusions: opposition and crisis exploitation

Alternative government leaders seeking to exploit financial crises have two weapons to use in the public sphere. The first is the negative weapon of blame, while the second is the more constructive weapon of policy creation. It is clear from the cases in this chapter that the ability to use these weapons is constrained by the different political systems and political contexts within which opposition leaders operate. Furthermore, it is clear that an opposition leader can exploit a crisis successfully while using only one of these weapons effectively. This was certainly the case for David Cameron, who won his blame-framing contest convincingly but was rather less dominant in the policy-framing contest, either breaking even or winning by default. The implication is that a different British prime minister might have been a tougher challenge for Cameron in this contest.

This research suggests that to win the blame contest does not necessarily require a direct link between an opponent and the crisis itself. The indirect links from John McCain to George W. Bush and from McCain to the neo-liberal ideology were more than enough to give Barack Obama a resounding victory in this contest. Moreover, leaders' success in the blame contests presented in this study hinged on the ability to hold an opponent responsible for the economic system presently in place. This appeared to be a function of how long an opposing party had been in power in recent years.

The findings of this study suggest many potential avenues of research and this chapter has only begun to open up the field of opposition leadership in crisis situations. A larger study is needed to determine whether its core finding—that in a crisis the blaming contest is politically more productive for oppositions than the policy contest—holds. It would also be valuable to investigate whether it is possible to win the policy contest without already having won the blame contest.

Perhaps the most interesting finding of this research is that party leaders who could take a committed ideological stance against the neo-liberal economic program attempted to do so, and this created a pathway to victory in the policy-framing contest. Parties that were ideologically aligned with the neo-liberal program tended to have great difficulty offering an effective alternative. This led such parties to focus on the third contest, as the Tories did, or suffer the consequences of appearing manipulative, as the SPD will probably do in the September 2009 elections. Although opposition leaders have limited avenues through which to exploit financial crises, they can make political gains, particularly if they can blame their opponents for the downturn and if they can repudiate the orthodox ideology.

References

Balz, D. and Barnes, R. 2008, 'Economy becomes new proving ground for McCain, Obama', *The Washington Post*, 16 September.

Barnes, R. 2008, 'First debate's fate unclear as Obama resists McCain's call to postpone', *The Washington Post*, 25 September.

Beech, M. 2008, 'Introductory preface', in M. Beech and S. Lee (eds), *Ten Years of New Labour*, Palgrave Macmillan, Basingstoke, pp. xix–xxiv.

Bovensiepen, N., Hawranek, D. and Reiermann, C. 2008, 'German government "has to step into the breach"', *Der Spiegel*, 24 November.

Brooks, D. 2008, 'Thinking about McCain', *The New York Times*, 26 September.

Bumiller, E. and Healy, P. 2008, 'McCain joins attacks on Obama over radical', *The New York Times*, 10 October.

Calmes, J. 2008a, 'In candidates, 2 approaches to Wall Street', *The New York Times*, 16 September.

Calmes, J. 2008b, 'From 2 rivals, 2 prescriptions', *The New York Times*, 15 October.

Calmes, J. and Zeleny, J. 2008, 'For rivals, finance crisis is posing on-the-fly tests', *The New York Times*, 19 September.

Crossland, D. 2009, 'Merkel "has egg on face" over cabinet chaos', *Der Spiegel*, 9 February.

Dahl, Robert A. 1966, *Political Oppositions in Western Democracies*, Yale University Press, New Haven.

Der Spiegel 2008a, 'Social Democrats' support sinks to record low', *Der Spiegel*, 12 March.

Der Spiegel 2008b, 'Merkel says Washington helped drag Europe into the credit crisis', *Der Spiegel*, 22 September.

Der Spiegel 2008c, 'Our economy will also suffer', *Der Spiegel*, 25 September.

Der Spiegel 2008d, 'The danger had not yet been averted', *Der Spiegel*, 15 October.

Der Spiegel 2008e, 'Merkel urged to act before it's too late', *Der Spiegel*, 9 December.

Der Spiegel 2008f, 'Top CEOs urge Merkel to take action on economy', *Der Spiegel*, 9 December.

Der Spiegel 2009, 'Spiegel online poll barometer', *Der Spiegel*, viewed 24 June 2009, < http://www.spiegel.de/flash/0,5532,13290,00.html >

Deutsche Welle 2008a, 'Social democrat abandons bid to become Premier of Hesse', *Deutsche Welle*, 7 March.

Deutsche Welle 2008b, 'Germany calls for cooperation to tackle financial crisis', *Deutsche Welle*, 18 March.

Deutsche Welle 2008c, 'Germany's election year budget draft light on spending cuts', *Deutsche Welle*, 2 July.

Deutsche Welle 2008d, 'Germany says it sees no need for own US-style bailout', *Deutsche Welle*, 23 September.

Deutsche Welle 2008e, 'Germany absent from London mini-summit on financial crisis', *Deutsche Welle*, 8 December.

Deutsche Welle 2009, 'Steinmeier determined to topple Merkel in German elections', *Deutsche Welle*, 19 April.

Dougherty, C. 2008, 'Led by Germany, Europe closes a strong quarter', *The New York Times*, 16 May.

Duncan, G. 2008, 'Darling is accused of complacency over full scale of threat to economy', *The Times*, 7 April.

Economist 2009, 'The export model splutters', *The Economist*, 7 May.

Elliot, L. 2008, 'If a week is a long time in politics, it's an entire career in economics: the prime minister's luck may have turned as the financial crisis worsens', *The Guardian*, 22 September.

Elliot, L. and Seager, A. 2007, 'Spread of banking panic forces ministers to guarantee savings', *The Guardian*, 18 September.

Elliot, L. and Wintour, P. 2008, 'Government moves to calm consumers by protecting savings up to £50,000: government to protect savings up to £50,000', *The Guardian*, 1 October.

Elliot, L., Treanor, J. and Wintour, P. 2008, 'Another day, another bail-out', *The Guardian*, 29 September.

Guardian 2007, 'Speculative horse that bolted the stable: Credit spree encouraged by the Tories has reached its apogee under Labour', *The Guardian*, 17 September.

Guardian 2008a, 'Conservatives: Unnerving numbers', *The Guardian*, 27 September.

Guardian 2008b, 'Conservative conference: The glassy void', 2 October.

Harding, J. 2007, 'An American crisis that could harm a lot of reputations here—including Gordon's', *The Times*, 17 September.

Harwood, J. and Cooper, M. 2008, 'McCain and Obama urge greater oversight in a financial bailout plan', *The New York Times*, 22 September.

Healy, P. 2008, 'Obama wraps his hopes inside economic anxiety', *The New York Times*, 9 October.

Heffernan, R. 1999, *New Labour and Thatcherism: Political change in Britain*, St Martin's Press, New York.

Helm, T., Elliot, L. and Hinsliff, G. 2008, 'Osborne faces storm over warning of run on pound', *The Observer*, 16 November.

Jackson, D. 2008, 'Candidates pin blame in financial "crisis"; but rivals don't agree on causes of Wall St woes', *USA Today*, 16 September.

Landler, M. and Stolberg, S. 2008, 'As fingers point in the financial crisis, many of them are aimed at Bush', *The New York Times*, 20 September.

Lee, S. 2008, 'The British model of political economy', in M. Beech and S. Lee (eds), *Ten Years of New Labour*, Palgrave Macmillan, Basingstoke, pp. 17–34.

Milne, S. 2007, 'This crisis spells the end of the free market consensus', *The Guardian*, 13 December.

Milne, S. 2008a, 'Whether Brown survives, Labour has already changed: the financial meltdown has allowed the prime minister to shift his rhetoric. The question now is if he will act on it', *The Guardian*, 25 September.

Milne, S. 2008b, 'The Tories have shown they are irrelevant to this crisis: Cameron's calls for a smaller state ring hollow when only intervention and nationalisation can halt financial collapse', *The Guardian*, 2 October.

Moore, M. 2008, 'Social Democrats tap Steinmeier as chancellor candidate', *Der Spiegel*, 20 October.

Nagourney, A. and Bumiller, E. 2008, 'McCain leaps into a thicket', *The New York Times*, 26 September.

Nelles, R. and Neukirch, R. 2008, 'Financial crisis exposes German leader's weaknesses', *Der Spiegel*, 27 October.

Obama, B. 2008, 'Renewing the American economy', *The New York Times*, 27 March.

Oborne, P. 2009, 'Cameron plans to transform Britain and has what it takes: but just as Mrs Thatcher courted unpopularity to achieve her ideals, he must do the same if he wants to gain office', *The Observer*, 4 January.

Observer 2008, 'The Tories must condemn the City's moral failure', *The Observer*, 28 September.

Page, S. 2008, 'Today round 2: candidates take off gloves; casual setting doesn't dull pointed jabs at forum', *USA Today*, 8 October.

Rawnsley, A. 2009, 'The cabinet's quarrels are a warning of the storms ahead: behind closed doors, ministers are locked in fierce arguments over the best way to get the voters behind them once again', *The Observer*, 15 February.

Real Clear Politics 2008, 'General Election; McCain vs. Obama', *Real Clear Politics*, viewed 24 June 2009, <http://www.realclearpolitics.com/epolls/2008/president/us/general_election_mccain_vs_obama-225.html#polls>

Richter, M. W. 2006, 'Elements of surprise: the 2005 election and the formation of the grand coalition', *German Politics*, vol. 15, no. 4, pp. 500–19.

Riddell, P. 2008a, 'A tricky case of economic schadenfraude', *The Times*, 12 March.

Riddell, P. 2008b, 'Bouncing along the bottom, and looking out for big bumps ahead', *The Times*, 8 November.

Rohter, L. and Andrews, E. 2008, 'Unlike rivals, McCain rejects broad US aid on mortgages', *The New York Times*, 26 March.

Saad, L. 2008, 'Disapproval of Bush spans the issues', *Gallup*, 20 February, viewed 24 June 2009,
<http://www.gallup.com/poll/104458/Disapproval-Bush-Spans-Issues.aspx>

Stolberg, S. 2008, 'A presidential vanishing act, by design', *The New York Times*, 31 October.

Stratton, A. 2008, 'Cameron shatters cross-party truce over banking meltdown: Tory leader attacks PM's competence on economy; criticism akin to student politics, say Labour', *The Guardian*, 18 October.

UK Polling Report 2009, 'Voting intention', *UK Polling Report*, viewed 24 June 2009, < http://ukpollingreport.co.uk/blog/voting-intention >

Watt, N. 2008a, 'Nationalisation is best deal for the taxpayer—Brown: Cameron accuses government of creating "economic calamity"', *The Guardian*, 19 February.

Watt, N. 2008b, 'Serious and contrite, Brown pledges fairer Britain for a new age', *The Guardian*, 24 September.

Webster, P. 2008, 'Chancellor to rush out cash payments for 10p tax losers', *The Times*, 13 May.

Webster, P. and Elliot, F. 2007, 'Chancellor admits reputation is at stake as Tories go on offensive', *The Times*, 18 September.

Webster, P. and Elliot, F. 2008, 'Brown's had his boom, now he's bust, says Cameron', *The Times*, 29 September.

Webster, P., Elliot, F. and Duncan, G. 2009, 'Darling "out of control" as borrowing leaps to £75 billion', *The Times*, 20 March.

Wintour, P. 2008, 'Tories blame PM for the "age of irresponsibility"', *The Guardian*, 29 September.

Zeleny, J. 2008, 'Obama looks to shift focus of campaign to economy', *The New York Times*, 17 September.

13. Crisis leadership in terra incognita: why meaning making is not enough

Arjen Boin

1. Managing a financial tsunami

The global financial crisis that started some time in 2007 and continues to unfold is a pure example of a trans-boundary crisis: it washes over geographical boundaries and leaves no sector of economic and social life untouched. It is hideously complex and thus hard to map and comprehend; it escalates through 'tipping points' and rides reversed feedback loops. The damage is staggeringly high and mounting. The 'new normal' that will emerge after this crisis will likely look very different from the one we had before.

Comparisons with the depression years of the 1930s often suggest the current crisis is not nearly as bad and is mostly under control, but the debate raging among economists tells a different story: nobody knows how bad it really is and what is still in store for us (for instance, Bradley et al. 2009). Economists disagree about how many toxic assets are still out there, what the consequences of worldwide stimulus packages will be, whether lost manufacturing jobs will ever return to Western economies and when it will be over. For political leaders, the global financial crisis is terra incognita.

How can political leaders navigate this unknown terrain? Traditional crisis-management skills—making 'hard calls' under pressure and with little information—are no longer sufficient according to crisis researchers. It is not just what they do or decide; what truly matters is what leaders say, the way they say it and the way it is understood by others. Great crisis leaders—Abraham Lincoln, Franklin D. Roosevelt, Winston Churchill and John F. Kennedy—are remembered for their eloquence and their words of consolation and inspiration when it mattered most.

In the early months of his presidency, Barack Obama was frequently referred to as the 'cheerleader in chief' and the 'psychologist in chief' (tellingly, perhaps, it remained unclear who the 'economist in chief' was). The US President was chastised alternately as being 'too pessimistic' and 'naively optimistic'. The attitude and words of leaders still matter a great deal in times of crisis.

Crisis leadership, in this perspective, is essentially about the use of discourse aimed at shaping a shared understanding of adverse events and providing guidance for dealing with them ('t Hart 1993). The underlying assumption is that incumbent elites try to frame the events and persuade the public (through the media) to accept their definition of the situation. The hypothesis is that a well-executed *meaning-making* strategy will help win the framing contest and thus shore up political capital and the policy commitments of leaders (Boin et al. 2009).

2. Management by discourse: does it work?

How did leaders fare during the global financial crisis? Surprisingly, perhaps, most survived the period under study; there were a few changes in the ruling party following elections held during the crisis, but it is not clear how the electoral outcomes relate to the actual management of the crisis. The lasting impression that emerges from this book, however, is of a group of leaders that stumbled and fumbled in their pursuit of an ever-escalating crisis.

The starting position of all leaders was similar: they downplayed or denied that there was a crisis. They thus placed the burden on those who sought to convince the public that there was a crisis. This initial defensive position would greatly limit their room for rhetorical manoeuvring.

In their subsequent descriptions of the evolving crisis, the leaders under study used very similar wordings: they pointed to 'outside forces' and spoke of 'very challenging', 'unprecedented' times—the 'worst since the Great Depression'. They admonished people not to panic: 'we are well placed' to manage these times, much better than other countries, as 'the fundamentals of our economy are strong'. And, of course, they promised that 'we will come out better than we were'.

They also displayed a strong tendency to moralise: many could not resist the temptation to blame the US system (US leaders, in turn, could not hide a hint of satisfaction when the European economies took a nosedive). When more and more financial institutions disclosed their 'toxic assets', the blame quickly shifted to greedy banks and their bankers.

The leaders seemed constantly behind the curve: by the time they recognised that there was a crisis, it had already spun out of control. After they failed to 'talk up the economy', they failed to 'talk down the crisis'. When they were finally ready to admit that the situation was bad, they were forced to emphasise how strong 'the fundamentals' were in fear of adding fuel to the fire.

An intriguing observation of this book is that the selected media apparently showed little interest in the speech acts of these leaders. The newspapers, in other words, did not recognise any news value in the meaning-making efforts of political leaders.

This could mean that leaders 'make meaning' through different media—local media, television and the Internet—or in different venues (parliamentary debates, informal conversations, op-ed pieces). It could also mean that leaders were not trying very hard to offer a distinct interpretation of events—one that would deviate from the tired rhetoric described above and would therefore generate 'news'.

A reading of the chapters suggests that leaders were caught in a prisoner's dilemma. If all leaders are trying to make meaning of the same event, it becomes dangerous to offer radically different interpretations (especially if everyone is aware that their statements can directly affect the process of crisis escalation). Timely and realistic assessments of existing vulnerabilities, evolving problems and escalating downturns can, after all, chase away investors, drive down the currency and sink the stock markets.

3. Crisis exploitation: how, then, does one exploit a global crisis?

US presidential candidate Obama used the evolving crisis to his advantage, attacking his opponent, John McCain, for declaring repeatedly that the 'fundamentals of our economy are strong'. Obama did not, however, win the election on a bad economy alone. Moreover, President Obama found it hard to exploit the crisis to further his political agenda (his stimulus bill was watered down considerably to please Republicans). If anything, the continuing crisis is seriously hampering his reform objectives (think of a new health system or a greener climate).

The global financial crisis did come in handy for those leaders who were already facing an economic downturn due to longstanding vulnerabilities. Those leaders were relatively quick to recognise the global financial crisis, making sure to stress its 'unprecedented' and exogenous nature. In a similar vein, we can conclude that the global financial crisis relieved some leaders of the responsibility for dealing with complex policy problems that could now be branded 'unaffordable under the current circumstances'. While all this can be categorised as a form of crisis exploitation, it has little to do with the timely use of 'opportunity windows' (Kingdon 1997) to push through otherwise unpalatable or infeasible reforms.

The dearth of targeted and timely reforms in the wake of a global crisis—supposedly a great time for deep reform (Hall 1993)—suggests crisis exploitation might be harder or less prevalent than theory sometimes suggests it is (Kingdon 1997). In spite of cheerful comments that a 'good crisis should not be wasted' (*'il faut utiliser une crise'*), few fundamental proposals were successfully initiated to redesign the financial system.

The idea that leaders can and do exploit crises to further their political interests thus merits renewed scrutiny (cf. Boin and 't Hart 2000). A successful effort would require a serious understanding of crisis dynamics; leaders would have to grasp how and why these crises escalate and what they can do to arrest the process. Moreover, they must have a firm grasp of the way journalists, opposition leaders and interested citizens perceive and assess their frames and actions. They would have to persuade people that they could shift a crashing economy this or that way.

This book shows that crisis exploitation is not without risks. Leaders who try can become caught in so-called credibility gaps. For instance, emphasising external causes might divert attention from home-grown failures, but it also undermines the legitimacy of subsequent reform proposals. Overplaying the crisis to push through a reform package can create expectations that the proposed reforms cannot meet. Botched efforts to exploit a crisis might fuel public cynicism with regard to the functioning and performance of the political system.

4. Reconsidering crisis leadership

Lest we become too gloomy about the prospects for crisis leadership, we should perhaps apply a wider and more balanced leadership perspective. In the introductory chapter, the editors helpfully define crisis leadership in terms of nine challenges (meaning making is only one of them). The global financial crisis—still in full swing at the time of writing—has tested world leaders on the first five: the challenges of sense making, meaning making, decision making, coordination and delimitation. Apart from meaning making (discussed above), how did leaders perform on those other four challenges?

Perhaps one of the most glaring failures of global leaders—and especially US leaders—is found in the *sense-making* domain. 'The field of economics is anything but an exact science,' 't Hart and Tindall correctly note in the introductory chapter. At the same time, no PhD in economics was required to recognise that the US economy was bound to run into serious trouble. Indeed, many journalists mapped the deep vulnerabilities as far back as 2005. When the economy was spiralling into recession, former President Bush and Senator McCain continued their talk of 'strong fundamentals'.

It took leaders of all countries a remarkably long time to diagnose the situation correctly. Hindsight does not make this assessment harder than it perhaps should be. The knowledge—as any analysis of op-ed pages, economic headlines and serious news reports will confirm—was widely available. One would have to conclude that leaders did not want to acknowledge or confirm an uncomfortable and inconvenient truth.

Leaders performed much better when it came to *critical decision making*. Once the extent of the potential damage had become undeniable, leaders acted with remarkable speed and courage. US leaders infused the system with unprecedented sums of money after the failure of the Lehman Brothers Bank threatened to take the system down in September 2008. 'If we don't do this, we may not have an economy on Monday,' Federal Reserve Chairman, Ben Bernanke, reportedly told US law-makers (Nocera 2008). This was only one of the many drastic decisions taken across the world. It serves as a reminder that decision making is still a critical part of the crisis leadership package.[1]

A global crisis that cascades across policy boundaries requires *crisis coordination*. This has traditionally been viewed as somewhat of a holy grail: it is hard in good times and nearly impossible in bad times—or so the thinking goes (Boin et al. 2005). It was thus impressive to see the level of coordination that was achieved across sectors, administrations (the remarkable cooperation between the outgoing Bush Administration and the incoming Obama Administration) and between countries. The role of international organisations such as the International Monetary Fund (IMF), the World Bank and the European Union grew quickly and with little controversy.

It is hard to prove, but leaders seemed much less adept at managing expectations (the challenge of *delimitation*). With few exceptions (such as Singapore's leader), leaders consistently avoided telling the public flat-out that an economic crisis of this size and scope would drag down a society's level of wellbeing. (Compare this with the frank talk delivered by US President Roosevelt in his 'fire-side chats'; 'Yes, we shall have to give up many things entirely,' Roosevelt told his fellow countrymen after declaring war on Japan in December 1941.) The hardest-hit countries will have to learn to live within their means. That usually means more taxes and less government spending. The rhetoric of world leaders—as analysed in this book—suggests nothing of the kind.

Taken together, it would seem that leaders are better at doing than talking during a crisis. They find it hard to admit a crisis has arrived. Their crisis rhetoric is often bland and cliché ridden, as this book documents so well. And, when they finally address the crisis, leaders shun the cold, hard truth.

What can we learn in terms of trans-boundary crisis management? As the classic tasks of crisis management at first glance appear to have been fulfilled reasonably well, most mileage can be gained from an improvement of early warning and sense-making capacities. This crisis had all the markings of an announced crisis. The key question, once again, is therefore: why did they not see it coming (Turner 1978)?

A preoccupation with the functional dimensions of crisis management—getting a clear picture of the situation, making critical decisions, coordinating multiple parties—has long prevented crisis scholars from recognising the importance of the symbolic dimension of crisis management. This book demonstrates how far crisis researchers have come. This empirical study also signals the limits of meaning making: the inescapable conclusion is that the management of crisis symbolism is not enough; trans-boundary crises demand the full execution of all crisis tasks.

References

Boin, A. and 't Hart, P. 2000, 'Institutional crises in policy sectors: an exploration of characteristics, conditions and consequences', in H. Wagenaar (ed.), *Government Institutions: Effects, changes and normative foundations*, Kluwer Press, Boston, pp. 9–31.

Boin, A., 't Hart, P., Stern, E. and Sundelius, B. 2005, *The Politics of Crisis Management: Public leadership under pressure*, Cambridge University Press, Cambridge.

Boin, A., McConnell, A. and 't Hart, P. 2009, 'Crisis exploitation: political and policy impacts of framing contests', *Journal of European Public Policy*, vol. 16, no. 1, pp. 81–106.

Bradley, B., Ferguson, N., Krugman, P., Roubini, N., Soros, G. and Wells, R. 2009, 'The crisis and how to deal with it', *The New York Review of Books*, vol. 56, no. 10 (11 June).

Hall, P. 1993, 'Policy paradigms, social learning, and the state: the case of economic policymaking in Britain', *Comparative Politics*, vol. 25, no. 3, pp. 275–96.

't Hart, P. 1993, 'Symbols, rituals and power: the lost dimension in crisis management', *Journal of Contingencies and Crisis Management*, vol. 1 no. 1, pp. 36–50.

Kingdon, J. W. 1997, *Agendas, Alternatives and Public Policies*, 2nd edn, Pearson, Upper Saddle River, NJ.

Nocera, J. 2008, 'The reckoning: a credit crisis spiraled, alarm led to action', *The New York Times*, 1 October.

Stern, E. and Sundelius, B. 1997, 'Sweden's twin monetary crises of 1992: rigidity and learning in crisis decision making', *Journal of Contingencies and Crisis Management*, vol. 5, no. 1, pp. 32–48.

Turner, B. A. 1978, *Man-Made Disasters*, Wykeham, London.

Endnotes

[1] For a similar description of drastic crisis decision making in the Swedish financial crisis of 1992, see Stern and Sundelius (1997).

14. Framing dilemmas in the quest for successful crisis management

Allan McConnell

1. Why the cacophony?

Many science fiction films feature a scene where an alien lands on Earth and is puzzled by the bizarre antics of human beings performing even the simplest of tasks. Perhaps aliens would struggle to make sense of how leaders of the world have responded to the global financial crisis. In the face of arguably the biggest single threat to world stability in recent times, some leaders virtually ignored it (former US President George W. Bush), some said the system was near to collapse (Australian Prime Minister, Kevin Rudd), some said they did not help cause the crisis in any way (Singaporean Prime Minister, Lee Hsien Loong), others said they held a degree of culpability (UK Chancellor, Alistair Darling) and almost everyone started with one position only to take a contrary stance some months later. What is going on? Why have the leaders of the world responded in a multitude of different and constantly changing ways to essentially the same problem?

This puzzle goes to the heart of political science and public policy. As Shapiro and Bedi (2007) suggest, we can see the world as little more than the product of a series of disparate contingencies or we can see it primarily as the operation of certain laws or at least tendencies in political behaviour. Most political science seeks to impose some sense of order on the world to explain patterns of continuity and regularity, as well as change. Hence, we have perspectives such as new institutionalism, rational choice, group and network theory, socioeconomic power and ideational-based models. All attempt to explain the world and its patterns of political behaviour. Many such analyses of the global financial crisis will no doubt emerge in the years to come.

This chapter is not the opportunity to dive into these models and apply them to the global financial crisis. It is, however, an opportunity to put forward a framework that I would argue does help identify a constant amid the diversity and dynamics of framing responses. It is based on the assumption that leaders will always attempt to successfully manage a crisis. It does not claim to be the only constant, or that leadership 'agency' is all powerful, but I consider it to be an important finding that has the potential to be factored into many different policy models. Part of the thinking here is derived from work I have been undertaking on policy success in relation to non-crisis issues (Marsh and McConnell forthcoming; McConnell forthcoming). Let me explain further.

2. Striving for success in crisis management

Crises present extraordinary challenges for political leaders. Amid threats, uncertainty and urgency, they must undertake a number of tasks, such as making sense of what is going on and articulating its depth and scope to a wider public. I would argue, however, that such tasks are means towards ends, rather than ends in themselves. The goal of leaders is to successfully manage a crisis. After all, who would want to fail, except as an interim measure towards a longer-term success? The focus of this book is 'framing' and therefore we need to ask: if leaders strive to produce frames in order to successfully manage a crisis then what does a 'successful' frame look like from their perspective? The clues are already in Chapters 1 and 2, but I want to draw them out:

• *Crisis-management frame for political success*: a frame that is intended to ensure political survival and protect or even enhance reputation.
• *Crisis-management frame for policy success*: a frame that is intended to steer policy down a desired track, whether it be continuity, change or a combination of both.

Of course, it is not possible to get inside the minds of leaders to prove these assumptions. Even interviews have limitations. A large element of crisis leadership is based on instinct rather than a rational appraisal of objectives and all the possible means of achieving them (Flin 1996). Nevertheless, it is a relatively straightforward task to look at the global financial crisis case studies and attribute, with a high degree of plausibility, 'success' motives. For example, in terms of the political game, the initial 'business-as-usual' frame (type-1) of Canadian Prime Minister, Stephen Harper, could be read as an attempt to play down the crisis, while playing up his credentials as an experienced economist who was strongly placed to lead the country at the forthcoming election. This frame suited his quest to hold onto office and enhance his reputation. With regard to the policy game, New Zealand Prime Minister Helen Clark's framing of the crisis as both threat and opportunity (type-2 and type-3) can be read as an attempt to pave the way for policy reform. The fact that an election was looming illustrates that a striving for political success can be contingent on policy success—in this case, the need to demonstrate that the existing Labour-led government was best placed to manage the global financial crisis.

Importantly, no frame is guaranteed to succeed. Some strategies are riskier than others. Risks relate to the likelihood that goals will not be met (Drennan and McConnell 2007). Context is crucial to assessments of risk (Douglas 1992; Althaus 2008). The same activity—walking slowly across the road—is low or even no risk when the road is empty, but high risk if done on a busy motorway.

Leadership framing of crisis is little different. A frame can be at low risk of failing to achieve 'success' in one context, but that same frame can be high risk in another. We need to think, therefore, about 'context'.

Context can be all manner of phenomena such as culture, time, political mood and economic activity. For the purposes of focusing on framing, I consider context to be the existence or otherwise of strong and credible counter-frames to those articulated by leaders.

If leaders strive for political success by projecting a frame that is intended to ensure their political survival and protect and even enhance their reputation then—all things being equal—a lower risk context is when there is no strong and credible counter-frame in existence. Clearly, this is typically the case in the early sense-making and meaning-making stages of a crisis when leaders need to be out in the public sphere with statements on issues of crisis severity, causes, responsibilities and remedies. Many of the chapters in this volume reveal early attempts to exogenise the global financial crisis and play down its severity (for example, in Canada, the United Kingdom and Ireland), although such frames can survive intact for long periods when there is no credible opposition to produce authoritative counter-frames (for example, in Singapore and to a large extent Canada). When the context is different, however, these same framing strategies can become barriers to political success. It seems clear, for example, that former US President George W. Bush's initial business-as-usual response (playing down the crisis as little more than a market correction) was understandable in terms of his low popularity and a desire to protect his political capital. With corporate failures and increasingly worse economic indicators leading to credible counter-frames, however, his framing became a barrier to achieving his political goals—for example, ending his term in office on a relative 'high' in terms of job approval. His conversion to a type-2 'crisis as threat' frame was a logical move if he was to have any hope of protecting his political reputation and avoiding the label of being chronically 'out of touch' with every major crisis in the United States after 9/11.

A similar logic applies to contexts, risk and the policy game. If leaders strive for policy success by seeking to steer policy down their desired route (stability, reform or a combination) then—all things being equal—a lower risk context is when there is no strong and credible counter-frame. In the United Kingdom, Prime Minister, Gordon Brown, and Chancellor, Alistair Darling, adopted a type-2 'crisis as critical, global threat' frame, a move that was suited to conserving the British policy status quo and, in the political game, circumnavigating questions of the 11-year-old Labour Government's co-responsibility for the occurrence of the crisis. A type-2 frame on its own does not, however, provide the legitimating framework when strong counter-frames are emerging from opponents and the media that policy reforms are needed to tackle a crisis. With the Conservative Party ascendant in the polls—though not necessarily pushing a radically different and more popular line on the financial crisis—and the media sceptical towards the government, the move of Brown and Darling to a type-3 frame becomes understandable. They started presenting the crisis more explicitly as a trigger for regulatory reform. A quest for policy success seems evident in both phases, but frames need to be aligned with goals, otherwise risks of failure are generated.

One might be led to believe, therefore, that crisis framing is a simple task. All that leaders need to do is think about what they want, assess the strength of and support for counter-frames and then opt for the lowest-risk framing strategy with the highest likelihood of political and policy 'success'. As I will explain below, however, leadership is never simple and crisis leadership is doubly complicated.

3. Hot spots: crisis-framing dilemmas

After reading the case studies in this volume, it seems evident to me that there are three main 'hot spots' in terms of the leadership challenge of crisis framing. I use the term hot spots to refer to dilemmas of crisis framing that are particularly tough because they put leaders under pressure to perform with decisiveness and conviction at a time when they are being pulled in different directions.

Fast versus successful framing

Crises shatter our understanding of the world ('t Hart 1993) and create political space that political actors seek to fill rapidly with efforts at meaning making. They present frames designed to tell stakeholders and the general public of what happened and what needs to be done. Crises, however, generate uncertainties (knowledge deficits, ambiguous and contradictory information) that do not lend themselves easily to quick framing that will protect political credibility and guide policy action (or inaction). During crises, leaders seldom have the luxury of picking 'the right time' to offer their accounts, as they normally would. If leaders do not produce credible frames to fill the information and interpretation vacuum triggered by the occurrence of unscheduled events with great speed then others will step in and dominate the discourse.

Crisis-management research has identified various potential leadership pathologies in crises (Boin et al. 2005; Drennan and McConnell 2007). In sense making, for example, leaders can (be led to) misunderstand crucial dimensions of the crisis. Basing their initial public meaning-making efforts on a faulty or incomplete diagnosis of what is going on presents a major risk to leader credibility in a crisis. Despite logic leading us to assume that leaders will initially engage in low-risk framing strategies, they might veer towards high risk through, for example, publicly under-reacting or overreacting. The need to fill a crisis-induced meaning-making vacuum places extraordinary and sometimes unrealistic pressures on leaders, who, like anyone else, are confronted with surprising, bewildering, ambiguous, sometimes contradictory signals and expert opinions. Amid all the pressures of crisis management, they might misjudge the accuracy of their own sense making or the persuasiveness of their meaning making.

The latter can occur when they fail to pay enough attention to the evolution of the context in which their frames are being received, interpreted and challenged. Former Spanish Prime Minister José Maria Aznar fell prey to this in the framing contest that developed in relation to the 2004 Madrid bombings. Coming just before general elections, the attack did not just traumatise the nation, it divided it. Aznar's quick and emphatic claim that the attacks were perpetrated by the Spanish State's long-time adversary, the Basque nationalist extremists of ETA, was quickly construed by opposition groups as an opportunistic move to 'cover up' the true causes of the attack—namely, 'payback' by al-Qaeda for Spanish participation in the US-led war in Iraq. The opposition was very effective in dramatising the force of its counter-frame; and it was helped along by a trickle of information from the police investigations into the attacks, which began to point in the direction of Muslim extremists. Aznar persevered regardless and his party paid the price at an election a few days later (Olmeda 2008). Likewise, George W. Bush's initial business-as-usual frame with regard to the financial crisis began to crumble politically as the material realities of the crisis unfolded and lent credence to voices much more pessimistic than Bush's.

Frame consistency versus frame adaptability

Once leaders espouse a particular crisis frame, subsequent events and their interpretation lead almost inevitably to the emergence of counter-frames. Initial crisis frames rarely stand the test of time. In other words, the context changes and a low-risk frame becomes high risk unless action is taken. This presents leaders with two key challenges: a) to know when the context is changing, and b) to know when the context has altered sufficiently that a new frame really is needed. There is a danger of holding on tightly to an outmoded frame when events and counter-frames lead to a serious questioning of the credibility of the author of the original frame. Canadian Prime Minister Harper's tenacious assertions (type-1 frame) that the crisis was 'elsewhere' and would have little effect on Canada were discredited when the country slid into recession and his political authority was severely challenged in Parliament.

Framing for political versus policy success

I have suggested that political leaders always strive for success in two domains: 'politics' and 'policy'. These are often not necessarily complementary, and in crises the tensions between them can become stark. Framing a crisis in order to ensure political survival or enhance political reputation might jar with a framing strategy designed to shape the future direction of policy. Producing a frame that satisfies both can be difficult. The Irish Government was fairly quick in settling into a crisis-as-threat frame (type-2) with an element of opportunity emerging later (type-3). These frames were better at providing the foundations for the successful achievement of policy reforms (cuts to pensioner medical benefits, public service reforms and a modernisation of the Irish economy) than they were for shoring up political credibility. Political frames and policy frames do not always go hand in hand. Judging how to blend them while striving for political and policy success can put political leaders under immense pressure.

4. Conclusion

Perhaps if the mythical alien came down to Earth, armed with an understanding of how leaders will always strive to ensure political and policy success in response to crisis, it would not be particularly puzzled by the multiple and conflicting leadership responses throughout the world to the global financial crisis. Crises push human beings in all sorts of directions as they struggle to 'succeed' and find their way out. Framing is a way of attempting to succeed in political and policy terms, even though the journey can become rather heated and mistakes can be made along the way.

References

Althaus, C. 2008, *Calculating Political Risk*, University of New South Wales Press, Sydney.

Boin, A., 't Hart, P., Stern, E. and Sundelius, B. 2005, *The Politics of Crisis Management: Public leadership under pressure*, Cambridge University Press, Cambridge.

Douglas, M. 1992, *Risk and Blame: Essays in cultural theory*, Routledge, London.

Drennan, L. T. and McConnell, A. 2007, *Risk and Crisis Management in the Public Sector*, Routledge, London.

Flin, R. 1996, *Sitting in the Hot Seat: Leaders and teams for critical incident management*, John Wiley & Sons, New York.

't Hart, P. 1993, 'Symbols, rituals and power: the lost dimension in crisis management', *Journal of Contingencies and Crisis Management*, vol. 1, no. 1, pp. 36–50.

Marsh, D. and McConnell, A. (forthcoming), 'Towards a framework for establishing policy success', *Public Administration*.

McConnell, A. (forthcoming), *Understanding Policy Success: Rethinking public policy*, Palgrave Macmillan, Basingstoke.

Olmeda, J. 2008, 'A reversal of fortune: blame games and framing contests after the 3/11 terrorist attacks in Madrid', in A. Boin, A. McConnell and P. 't Hart (eds), *Governing After Crisis: The politics of investigation, accountability and learning*, Cambridge University Press, Cambridge, pp. 62–84.

Shapiro, I. and Bedi, S. 2007, 'Introduction: contingency's challenge to political science', in I. Shapiro and S. Bedi (eds), *Political Contingency: Studying the unexpected, the accidental and the unforeseen*, New York University Press, New York, pp. 1–18.

15. Managing trans-boundary crises: leadership challenges for the EU Presidency

Bengt Sundelius

1. Crises without borders

In the bulk of this book, research findings have been presented on how national leaders have handled the many aspects of the recent international financial collapse and its multiple effects on their societies. Theoretically informed empirical examinations of several political systems have shown the perils of leadership under severe financial conditions. We expect much from our public leaders in the national hot seats.

In this chapter, I heighten the stakes of top-level crisis management even further. Trans-boundary crises such as the financial meltdown in 2008–09 or the likely pandemics of the 2009 influenza season are even more complex than more common disasters that are by and large bounded by space and time. The global financial crisis of 2008–09 as examined in this volume is an early example of a type of fast-paced and vastly diffused development that leaders are likely to experience more frequently in future years.

Trans-boundary phenomena require that multiple actors in distinct jurisdictions, in coherent ways, jointly handle the shared crisis and its often-unexpected aftershocks. The leaders of the G8 and G20 member states were activated in the global financial crisis for this reason. In the European Union, the European Commission and the European Central Bank were very active (see Fletcher, this volume). The French Presidency during the second half of 2008 headed the common crisis-management efforts that involved a number of initiatives, top-level meetings and financial support packages (see Windle, this volume).

In Europe, a multilevel form of crisis management is emerging. Effective crisis coordination must here be fostered across levels, sectors, institutions and sovereign jurisdictions. It would be prudent to strengthen European networks of crisis coordination before events overtake the capacity for effective joint management. This type of preparatory work is well under way and it seems to have been given some priority by current and recent presidencies. The legitimacy of the European Union can be strengthened and the social distance to its citizens can be shortened when the common union capacity to manage crises is put to the test by unexpected trans-boundary phenomena.

The Presidency of the European Union is responsible for multinational, multilevel, multi-sector and multi-institutional leadership in situations of severe stress for the union, its 27 member states and almost 500 million people. During the second half of 2009, Sweden serves in this capacity. In his program statement of 1 July, the Swedish Prime Minister and EU President, Fredrik Reinfeldt, listed the top-priority issues facing his six-month tenure: finding a durable solution to climate change and overcoming the financial collapse. Reinfeldt concluded the manifesto boldly: 'We must also be prepared to manage the unexpected. Sweden is ready to meet this challenge.' Many observers claim that the test of the performance of an EU President rests on the ability to excel in public leadership in the high-stakes and very visible media setting of dealing with gravely consequential problems that are not yet known. Some presidencies do very well—such as the French term during 2008—while others fare less well.

This memo is directed to the holders of the EU Presidency. I am convinced that research into crisis management has practical value. Recognising all the limitations of trying to turn research findings into 'how-to' (or more often 'how-not-to') recommendations, this essay draws on the scholarly evidence for reflections and advice to the incumbent EU Presidency. Leaders have to face the challenges, make choices and live with the consequences of their action or inaction. After many years of observation of crisis leadership, I have considerable respect for the difficulties and burdens of exercising authority and upholding credibility in crisis—in particular, when facing trans-boundary phenomena. My normative stand is that I applaud crisis leadership practices that help minimise human and material losses and other societal costs, while also upholding fundamental values of democratic governance, the rule of law and citizen rights. When our academic understanding can in modest ways enhance crisis leadership, along the above criteria, so much the better.

2. Making sense of uncertainty and complexity

Before a political leader can engage in exploitation strategies to build public credibility, one must engage in individual and shared sense making. Uncertainty and complexity are key early parameters of a rapidly evolving trans-boundary challenge (and the chapters in this volume clearly illustrate how leaders around the world have grappled with these parameters in making sense of the escalating financial crisis). Crises are characterised by communications overload and by information shortage. In spite of vast investments in information-gathering agencies, intelligence analysts and a close reading of the daily news, public leaders appear genuinely taken by surprise over and over again.

As the leader of the union, you should be aware of how information is filtered and summarised before it reaches your desk. You should probe behind the seductive phrases in texts and the compelling charts in briefings. Examine how the information given to you is being framed. Time spent on a critical dialogue over how to diagnose the rapidly evolving situation is an investment in your remaining years as a leader in good public standing.

The institutional features around you matter for how you can deal with crises. As EU President, you are clearly not a free agent but an institutionally embedded policy shaper. Your leadership must be connected not only with proactive crisis responses, but with strategic questions of institutional design. The implementation of your national decisions is in the hands of the professionals. Coordination in crises across professional boundaries has proven to be at least as difficult as cooperation across geographical borders. The mandarins of the union's sprawling bureaucracies can hold the presidency hostage to their preferred line of action or inaction.

Crises can drive you out of control and literally out of office. Beware not to lose control of your own team. Stay proactive with your organisation and with the media. This is not the time to hide; rather, you must remain visibly on top of the dramatic situation. Do not allow yourself to be driven by events. Seize the formative moment to shape the course of events. Relate the crisis to the fundamentals of your public mission, to the storyline of your presidency.

Crises cast long shadows. Prepare yourself and your staff for dealing with cascading effects over the long haul. Monitor from the beginning the second-order consequences, which will come back to haunt you if you remain unprepared. Check how the crisis, and your handling of it, is reflected through the media. The press mirrors your actions and the appearances of action or inaction. Fluid images of success or fiasco are framed through media reports of what you seemingly did and did not do in the crisis. Is your preferred narrative the dominant one for the public meaning-making process?

Public officials often regard the media as an adversary in crises. Much of the attention of your staff is devoted to how to meet the demands of journalists. You get instant reports from your associates about how the coping effort plays out in the media. Bad reviews invite commentary within your inner circle about unfair treatment and poor journalistic styles. The crisis scenario can turn into a script of them against us. A comforting myth is created that 'we are the victims of circumstances, who are trying our best to handle a grave situation'.

Crises are not only threatening challenges to be coped with. Exploitation processes can be identified and explored, as covered in this book. Crises and their aftermaths also offer space for changes of policy, procedures and institutional designs. A period of serious inquiry, evaluation and recommendations that are based on this analysis is needed between crisis and public reform. Leadership in crisis should include a personal and organisational capacity for engaging in meaningful accountability proceedings and evaluation processes.

Leadership in crises will sometimes invite the taking of draconian measures. Forging effective and visible action might take precedence over other equally vital considerations. Quick, forceful and possibly effective intervention in a crisis, however, might come at the price of eroding the legitimacy of democratic governance and the rule of law. At what cost to democracy, civil liberties, freedom of the press and public stature at home and abroad will your strong crisis leadership image be earned? What kind of value base do you want to embody as president, and—when push comes to shove in a crisis—do you propose the union makes trade-offs between effective and appropriate governance?

In the heat of the dramatic moments of urgency and immediacy, strategic considerations must be part of decision making. When the ordinary grind of political life again takes hold after the urgent phase has passed, draconian crisis measures will, however, appear in another light. How then to account for the choices made in the heat of the moment?

3. Accepting the heat at the top

The craft of governing a multinational union requires a judgment call between rash moves in the heat of crisis and sliding into the avoidance of responsibility. By emphasising certain procedural priorities, arrangements or regulations, attention can be shifted away from the substantive controversy at hand. Delays can be created through exercises in consensus building or legal requirements of unanimity. You should distinguish between a calculated postponement and a drift into avoidance by fear of taking responsibility for the whole.

The danger of entrapment at the top, rather than of splendid isolation, seems to characterise crisis decision making by European public leaders. You might find yourself highly vulnerable to the restrictions of the normative and regulatory frameworks and procedures that the professionals claim have bearings on the crisis at hand. Political leadership, however, requires sensitivity to the more ambiguous symbolic and politically charged elements of a crisis. These dimensions are rarely on the horizons of the sectoral specialists or operational professionals that might do much of the advice giving in an acute crisis. The presidency should therefore enforce a holistic view of the requirements for crisis leadership, in contrast with national concerns or sector-based perspectives grounded in distinct professions. It is best to build such a shared paradigm for trans-boundary coordination in advance of the next major crisis.

When matters go wrong, it is comforting to be able to point the finger at somebody or something else. It is tempting in the aftershock of a crisis to engage in blame shifting. One can claim that the media created a hostile event or inflamed a difficult situation in the union into a crisis. One might rationalise that with a more responsible media role, the crisis would not have erupted at all or our ability to manage the situation would have been much better. Crisis research shows time again, however, that it is counterproductive to blame the media for your possible shortcomings or for inflaming a situation or affecting the outcome of a crisis. You can meet the media only through a proactive posture. You cannot hope to silence journalists or crush the impact of the rapid flow of news images on the public.

If you cannot blame the media, why not point the finger inside the less than perfect construct that you have been obligated to lead? Finding scapegoats lower down the hierarchy or across the institutional or partisan divide would seem a prudent post-crisis strategy for a political leader. History is filled with examples of how mid-level officials face charges linked to crises, while the top leadership escapes from any public accountability claims. Not only is such a blame-management strategy normatively problematic, it will turn the bureaucracy against you, making it fearful of being frank when the next crisis comes along. Avoiding responsibility is short sighted. Leaders and their organisations alike thus forgo the opportunity for self-evaluation, learning and institutional reform that crises create. Teflon leadership comes at a price.

4. Practice makes perfect

A leader's success in a crisis rests heavily on the ability under uncertainty and time pressure to make informed choices among competing priorities. In part, this skill can be developed through experience. Seasoned officials thrive in the hectic pace of deliberations and decisions. Many tend to develop astute self-confidence in their abilities to handle high-pressure situations. The French Presidency of 2008 excelled in this skill, while the subsequent Czech Presidency paled in comparison.

The distinctive feature of national and multinational crisis decision making, however, is the onslaught of qualitatively new challenges. There are limits to the ability of political leaders to prepare for crisis coping through on-the-job experiences. You also need systematic training through scenario-based simulations to instil a sense of the unique features of crisis decision making compared with other and more frequently experienced types of policymaking situations. It is better to discover your shortcomings coping with a crisis in discrete training settings than expose them live in the media limelight.

Giving strong verbal commitment to an improved crisis-management capacity in the immediate aftermath of tragic events, such as 9/11, 11/3 or 7/7, is commonplace among leaders. How many of them, however, really follow it up? The responsible public leader commits to the task of continuous capacity enhancement long after such dramatic events. Without a leadership commitment, the work towards improving the organisational capacity for low-probability but high-consequence events will soon slide into a low-prestige ritual without adequate staff motivation.

5. Beyond the thrill ride

Crisis management is a highwire-balancing act without a safety net; one wrong step and your political life could be over. Successful tiptoeing along the suspended wire might just buy you the thrill of strong public endorsement and the envy of your peers. From a democratic governance perspective, two competing dimensions must be balanced in order to enjoy the fruits of the thrill. One element of good governance is the capacity to deal effectively with crises affecting the security of societies and the safety of people. Another necessary element is the ability to strengthen the legitimacy of democratic governance through crisis-management actions within the realm of publicly accepted laws, norms and practices. Consequential actions based on urgency and immediacy must pass the scrutiny of post-crisis investigations and the ensuing accountability debates. In high-stakes situations, your leadership integrity is being put to the test—and in full public view

Crisis management also stands between stability and change. Many of the operational concerns of crisis performers are focused on dealing with traumatic events in terms of threats to political stability, public order or economic disaster. The slide is not long in crises from defending stability to becoming locked into a posture of rigidity. The imminent threat of fundamental change is then met by avoidance or by draconian measures. This fixation on ensuring stability is merely one side of the calculus of high-performance crisis management.

Leader rigidity in the face of political or financial challenges can be counterproductive to system-level transformations benefiting society and citizens. One question is often asked ex post facto by informed observers, such as scholars or journalists: a crisis for whom? As the responsible leader of the union, you should also raise this fundamental and thorny issue, while in the midst of crisis coping. What are the stakes and who are the stakeholders of this unfolding event? Where do I, as the temporary caretaker of the union of 27 democratic societies, fit into this unfolding script of turmoil between stability and change? Taking the time for some strategic reflection while in the eye of the storm is a good investment in a political future after the crisis has passed.

Crisis leadership presumes the skill to balance often overwhelming information and expert recommendations with other equally important perspectives. Sensitivity to the wider political and indeed international landscape within and beyond the union is an important quality. A robust normative compass is a source of inner strength. Political leadership often means the ability to grasp and connect with the fleeting public view of what constitutes a reasonable course of action in a given high-stakes situation. Crises offer windows of opportunity to move a nation or a union and to be able to take credit for having done so.

16. Public leadership and the social construction of economic catastrophe

Paul 't Hart and Karen Tindall

1. Meaning-making predicaments

In a study of Alan Greenspan's rhetorical leadership, Bligh and Hess (2007:98) state:

> It is entirely possible that in a post-crisis situation characterised by tremendous uncertainty, no prior cases or precedents to examine, or previous experiences to draw upon, leaders grapple with not only how to make sense of a situation but also how to frame the situation when they themselves may not have a firm grasp of what it means for the future.

Precisely this predicament—how to engage in persuasive public meaning making when your own backstage sense making is continuing and problematic—has been faced by the leaders studied in this volume. It formed the core of the interest with which this study began.

How do leaders resolve this predicament? It depends. Crisis communication scholars tell us that

> leadership can have a positive or negative impact on the development of a crisis. Leadership can be a positive force by helping to frame the meaning of a crisis event, expressing appropriate concern and support, overseeing mitigation, coordinating support, and facilitating timely, open communication. In many cases, however, crisis leadership is characterised by strategies minimising harm, denying responsibility, and shifting the blame (Seeger et al. 2003:241).

The crisis exploitation model presented in Chapter 2 and used by the case study authors to interpret the verbal behaviour of the chief economic policymakers of nine polities offers some ideas about why crisis leadership can evolve in one way or another. Put in Clausewitzian terms, it claims that crises constitute the continuation of politics as usual by other means. When extraordinary events occur, continuing struggles for political ascendancy do not cease; they can intensify. The same goes for continuing debates about public policy, which can be jolted in one way or another by the challenges crises pose to the resilience of existing governance ideas and practices.

When the unexpected happens, public leaders become the focus of intense attention. In a context of uncertainty and stress, they have to act on the public stage—to talk sensibly, to steer people's beliefs and emotions, to project authority. They have to do so, however, in the knowledge that the very occurrence of a crisis puts them under intense scrutiny. Their past and their present performances will be judged in a new light. The political price of a slip of the tongue, bad timing or clumsy dramaturgy can be considerable—for government leaders and their chief rivals alike. There are, however, also considerable gains to be achieved from capturing the public's ear and gaining its support for one's portrayal of the crisis and the ways in which it could best be managed.

It was in this high-stakes, mixed-motive context that the leaders studied here talked about the economic catastrophe that was unfolding before their and our eyes. Some might have felt overwhelmingly threatened by the crisis, whereas others might rather have sensed the opportunities it presented to them. Some were good at reading the writing on the wall and did not hold back in depicting the depth of the problems. Others were keen to keep the wolves at bay by projecting optimism. Some were keen to publicly justify their past policy stances; others focused on using the crisis to leverage policy change. In this chapter, we reflect on what these studies can teach us about the nature, use and limits of rhetoric in taming and exploiting crises.

2. Hard realities versus soft talk

And what a crisis it was. Once it went beyond its origins in the US mortgage market, the financial meltdown hit most of the Western world hard and fast. It presented governments and citizens with a set of stark, undeniable, immediate realities. Share markets tumbled, with hundreds of billions of dollars wiped off capital assets day after day. Real estate prices came tumbling down in places such as New York, London and Singapore. Once mighty corporate empires filed for bankruptcy. Others came hat-in-hand to the government to be bailed out or were taken over. The International Monetary Fund (IMF), the Organisation for Economic Cooperation and Development (OECD) and other global economy watchers weighed in with ever more pessimistic outlooks. The world saw bank runs, Iceland going broke, Wall Street suicides, mass sackings, repossessed homes, abandoned construction sites. In 2009, virtually all major economies were experiencing what economists awkwardly called 'negative growth'. And for those who cared to look for them were the shattering consequences of falling Western demand in the developing economies of the world.

During the months scrutinised most closely in this volume, these were the hard realities of the financial collapse and the economic downturn it triggered. With 'the facts' so incontrovertibly on display for all to see, and so many to acutely feel, there were definite limits to what leaders could aspire to when it came to shaping and bending public perceptions of the severity of the economic problems that had arisen. The upbeat, euphemistic 'business as usual' talk that some of the leaders studied here used to downplay the crisis during its initial stages was so patently disproved by the material realities of the downturn that—sooner rather than later—most of them staged a rhetorical retreat from crisis denial (type-1 rhetoric, in Table 2.1) to crisis acknowledgment (type-2 rhetoric).

Although ours has been a study of rhetoric as the main instrument of crisis leadership, the findings of the case studies teach us an important lesson: if material realities are hard, immediate and widespread enough, political and even expert talk becomes soft in comparison. In terms of framing the problem and putting it right at the top of the political agenda, the brute facts lead and public discourse has to follow, leaving less scope for 'spin' than politics in normal times does.

In this, the financial crisis stands in marked contrast with the other great crisis of the present era: climate change. The politics of climate change have long been dominated by framing contests about the very nature of the problem (Pettenger 2007). Does it exist? How bad is it now and how much worse will it become? What is causing it? The reasons for this difference are not hard to spot. Whereas the downturn hit the very financial centres of the Earth first in immediate and devastating fashion, the realities of climate change were much harder to spot and interpret. Much of the debate was based on models and projections, not directly observable facts. Some of the more conspicuous forms of ecosystem change (mostly degradation) that did occur in real time were found mostly in far-flung places such as the polar zones or tropical rainforests. Moreover, even when such effects were registered and caused wider public concern, it was not immediately obvious that 'climate change' was the prime cause. Softer facts, longer timelines, more selective and ephemeral impacts, tenuous causal links—climate change was bound to offer much more of a rhetorical battleground than the global financial crisis. It had to be 'sung into existence' (Patterson and Stripple 2007) rather than imposing itself abruptly and non-negotiably on the world, as the financial meltdown by and large did. The framing contest around the existence of climate change and its deleterious effects has long been the main game; the framing of the severity and causal nexus underpinning the financial meltdown quickly became a sideshow. It was a space that almost all of the policymakers studied here abandoned quickly, leaving it to small tribes of ideological warriors—masking as economists—to fight over what the rest of the world now felt was a trivial question. However flimsy their arguments are gradually becoming, after decades of research and debate, there are still numerous climate change deniers in the world today; but there never have been and never will be global financial crisis deniers.

The fact that the existence of a severe crisis that had its roots in the US sub-prime mortgage sector and spilled over into its financial institutions at large quickly became a non-issue did not mean that there was no space for social construction and thus political contestation in the management of the financial crisis. On the contrary: as the case studies demonstrate, policymakers within and across countries often proposed markedly different interpretations when it came to questions of responsibilities and remedies.

Consider the question of responsibilities first. There was much scope for externalising versus internalising that issue and (de-)politicising the accountabilities of public office-holders and institutions accordingly. Even if the root causes were exogenous (in the United States, in the market sector), were our own financial systems resilient enough to absorb the market distress? Were our regulatory practices instrumental or detrimental to this resilience? Were the incumbent policymakers alert enough to spot the problems early on and did they take sensible measures to curb their impacts? Or did their early interventions in effect aggravate the crisis rather than contain it (for example, Taylor 2009)? These questions were never far from the minds of the speech-makers we studied and were certainly on the minds of those reporting their speeches and holding them accountable politically.

The same goes for the question of policy implications. In all the countries studied, policymakers faced the same predicament: what do we do *now*? Nationalise banks? Subsidise or take over 'strategic' corporations more widely? Slash taxes; which ones and by how much? Offer cash payments? Redesign financial regulation? Go at it alone in protecting domestic industries? Or develop economic stimulus and pursue reforms in regional and global arenas? Bewildering as the sheer magnitude and hitherto unthinkable nature of some of these policy predicaments might have seemed, astute policymakers would have been quick to see possible silver linings behind the clouds of the current crisis. Perhaps it was a good time to use the crisis as cover for one's pet policy innovations that would otherwise be politically impossible to achieve?

In the remainder of this chapter, we dig a little deeper into these two clusters of questions, corresponding to what we in Chapter 2 call the political game (about responsibility and accountability) and the policy game (about preserving and innovating modes of governing) of crisis exploitation. In these games, elite rhetoric inevitably plays a key role, no matter how 'hard' are the facts of the crisis at hand. In the latter part of the chapter, we tease out some recurrent patterns in the crisis rhetoric of the public office-holders studied here. We conclude by reflecting on the limitations and implications of this study.

3. Who done it? Rhetoric of responsibility and blame

In his book *Credit and Blame*, Charles Tilly (2008:13) reminds us that

> responsibility does not necessarily equal cause. Your judgment, my judgment, and a medical specialist's judgment as to what actually caused a given hospital patient to die often turn out to be irrelevant for the assignment of blame. Cause–effect connections usually play only a secondary and contingent part in determination of responsibility. That determination typically emphasises judgments of intent and competence.

Likewise, Bovens and 't Hart (1996:137–8) observe:

> The crucial—but often implicit—question in…debates [about the causes of disasters] is where, when and how misfortune stops and mismanagement begins…Some failures have such grave consequences or pose such a threat to our worldview or sense of justice that 'bad luck', however appropriate in empirical terms, will not be accepted as an explanation. Especially those who have been injured will continue to look for someone to blame.

Anticipating and managing blame have become second nature to contemporary politicians and public servants. In an era of high visibility, floating voters, declining trust in traditional elites and institutions and collective obsession with risk and danger, those who govern and their servants are answerable for an awful lot. They have learned that when the news is bad, and the policies they have to sell are about retrenchment, contraction, redistribution benefits or allocating risks, the 'politics of pain' set in, with 'blame avoidance' being the name of the game (Pierson 1994; Hood 2002; Pal and Weaver 2003). So, when confronted with the biggest financial and economic breakdown in well more than half a century, the holders of executive office studied here knew there would be blame games to play. No matter that there was little dispute about the causal narrative of the crisis: this problem was 'made in America'. This put former US President George W. Bush et al. on the spot, but implied that all the others were essentially off the hook. Nevertheless, most of them must have known that the story would not end there. Although the root causes of the credit crunch might have been beyond their control, nasty questions might still present themselves. Why did you not see it coming? Was our financial system really as resilient as it could have been? Did you do enough to mitigate the impact of the crisis once it was under way? Why have you not been leaning much harder on corporate excess? In making meaning about the developing financial crisis, therefore, our policymakers were not just managing the issues themselves; they were managing the potential political fallout from the issues. They also knew that other public voices—oppositions, sceptical journalists, expert *besserwissers*—would weigh in on the framing of responsibility.

As Table 2.1 suggests, they had roughly two options: deny all responsibility or accept that they could have done more and better in at least mitigation. Likewise, journalists, non-governing parties and other actors in the debate had the options of absolving government actors from (co-)culpability or pinpointing blame on them. Depending on the configuration of their choices, different types of blame games could ensue. And although there were some notable differences, the similarities stood out most. Careful study of the speeches across the nine jurisdictions reveals the following general pattern.

- Issues of responsibility and blame do not enter the official discourse until the crisis is well under way, as the first impulse of most policymakers is to *downplay the severity* of the problems. They thus sidestep the very need for blame.

- Once past the denial stage, speech-makers make a concerted attempt to *exogenise the causes* of the crisis across territorial ('it's the Americans' or, in the case of Singapore, the West) and institutional ('it's the market') borders. The fallback position is thus to attempt to deflect blame.

- At the same time, virtually all of the politicians—unlike the national bank governors—attempt to *moralise the issue*, by accusing key corporate actors of 'greed', 'recklessness', 'unscrupulousness' and the like. They do some 'pinpointing' of their own. Like all blamers, they draw moral lines between 'them' and 'us' (Douglas 1992; Tilly 2008), so as to erase any doubt among their audiences about who is at fault (and who, by implication, should get off scot-free).

- Virtually all speakers engage in attempts to *'jump over' blame*, by moving straight from assessments of severity and causes to talk about the need for regulatory reform in the financial sector, domestically but most emphatically at the international level (see further below). This is a rhetorical feat: the system is broken and should be fixed, but let's not talk about who should bear responsibility for it being broken in the first place.

- And finally, a limited number of speakers engage in some form of *admission*—not of 'guilt', but of the presumably lesser evils of naivety (about the extent to which perverse incentives in the financial sector have bred deep cultures of corporate irresponsibility) and lack of vigour in tightening regulation. All stop well short of public contrition, though a few acknowledge and empathise with the extent of suffering borne by the ordinary citizens who have been the losers in the crisis.

In all, this pattern corresponds closely with the findings of other studies of blame management—namely, a pattern of 'staged retreat': the potential blamee tries to keep the discussion about blame as far away as possible from themselves, but as the pressure on them increases (because new facts become known, more people have become angry or credible other voices are starting to question their involvement, competence or intent), they retreat to less ideal but still potentially workable forms of blame avoidance (Bovens et al. 1999; Brändström and Kuipers 2003; Hood et al. 2007). It is important to note that none of the policymakers engaged in proactive acceptance of responsibility, forfeiting the option of ending up in the relatively benign 'blame minimisation' game type, in which early and forthright public acknowledgment of responsibility gets the blamee 'off the hook' in the media and parliamentary arenas (see Table 2.1; for empirical illustration, see Brändström et al. 2008).

This general pattern was punctuated by several differences of timing and emphasis. For example, Singaporean and European Commission leaders did not budge in their responsibility rhetoric; in contrast, UK policymakers, particularly Chancellor, Alistair Darling, eventually did engage in some acknowledgment of responsibility. What factors might have caused such differences? They are mainly contextual, underlining that there is truth in the cliché that where one stands depends on where one sits. On the basis of the case studies—and other than obvious factors such as personal beliefs and styles or being in versus outside government—we would nominate the following factors.

- *Salience of accountability pressures*: lacking real media or legislative scrutiny in these matters, Singaporean and European Commission policymakers could afford to gloss over questions of responsibility.
- *Type of office held*: much of the political heat of accounting for the crisis fell on the politicians and there were at times marked differences in the responsibility rhetoric of heads of government and finance ministers on the one hand, and bank governors on the other (only the retired US Federal Reserve chairman Alan Greenspan, in a Congressional hearing in October 2008, came out with a highly publicised acknowledgment of responsibility). The bank governors, as bureaucrats, were able to concentrate more on diagnosing and managing the operational crisis. They therefore generally steered clear of statements that could lead others to question their past prudence, lest these might spill over into doubts about their present competence in crisis response.
- *Length of incumbency*: obviously, policymakers such as UK Prime Minister, Gordon Brown, former New Zealand Prime Minister, Helen Clarke, and Irish Taoiseach, Brian Cowen, who had held an executive leadership position for several years before the occurrence of the crisis, were more at risk in discussions about responsibility than their counterparts such as Australian Prime Minister, Kevin Rudd, incoming New Zealand Prime Minister, John Key, and US President, Barack Obama (and their treasurers), who took office just before or in the middle of the crisis. The latter were far better able to credibly shift blame to others—notably, their predecessors. Some in effect presented themselves primarily as blamers, not blamees, with US Treasury

Secretary, Timothy Geithner, and Rudd the most conspicuous examples. Conversely, some opposition politicians during the crisis were muted in their criticism of government passivity in the face of a growing bubble that was waiting to burst only because they themselves had been in government in the years leading up to the meltdown. It shows that Table 2.1 ignores the crucial influence of temporal factors (and thus possible role changes and factors mediating media predispositions towards the responsibility rhetoric of various elite actors) in its prediction of the nature of crisis-induced blame games. Determining who blames and who accounts is not a matter of taking a snapshot view of a crisis; it instead requires understanding crises in terms of the unfolding of a much longer political scenario.

In the end, there was surprisingly little hardball politics of blaming going on during the period under study. Yes, the crisis became a prominent election issue in New Zealand, the United States and, to a lesser extent, Canada. In Canada, however, the incumbents survived, whereas in New Zealand and the United States, one had the distinct impression that the loss of the incumbents (or their parties) was over-determined to begin with by a host of other factors.

Perhaps the immediate challenges of absorbing and taming the crisis were too overwhelming (and controversial). This suggests that blame still needs to be apportioned later—for example, in the context of the inevitable inquiries that are being announced in various countries at the time of writing. Perhaps blame was effectively privatised in this case, with impoverished account holders and investors chasing financial executives in the courts. Perhaps, however, there simply was not enough semantic space and political appetite left for pinpointing blame domestically for a fiasco that has widely become labelled as the *global* financial crisis. Anthropologists might be on the mark in observing that those who have been injured will always look for someone to blame; but if the victims are in their millions scattered across the planet, the more likely it is that the search will be fruitless. It is the ultimate 'many hands' problem: the more 'global' the crisis, the larger the number of hands that have helped bring it about and the easier it is for incumbent elites to successfully engage in blame-avoidance rhetoric, with blame ultimately evaporating rather than crystallising.

4. What now? Rhetoric of policy and reform

The global financial crisis spawned a wide array of ad hoc measures and policy interventions. More broadly, the crisis produced a great deal of reform rhetoric from leaders and from opposing parties and interest groups. The presence of such contests forced leaders into the position of status quo player or change advocate, and choose between preserving or innovating modes of governing.

Previous research into economic crises suggests that governments react strongly to the prospect of mass unemployment. Moreover, the negative public sentiment that comes with the threat of mass unemployment provides governments with a greater mandate for action (Keeler 1993). Furthermore, economic crises produce 'opportunity windows for reform' that governments can harness (Baumgartner and Jones 1993; Kingdon 1995; Wilson 2000). Therefore, while economic crises might limit governments' budgets, they also allow policymakers greater scope to implement reforms that would otherwise be met with fervent opposition. The reason is simple: ever since former US President Franklin D. Roosevelt stepped in to stem the tide of the Depression through proto-Keynesian government activism, the public expected governments to 'do something' in times of recession and rising unemployment. Governments can capitalise on that momentum by packaging tailor-made reactions to the current economic circumstances along with additional policies it had wished to implement all along but which can now be reframed as forming an integral part of the recession-busting strategy (Rodrik 1996). This was evident in many of the polities studied in this volume. In Australia, the 'education revolution' and climate change technology became part of the reform rhetoric, as did European unity and integration in the EU leaders' reform rhetoric.

Kuipers' (2006) work on policymaking and 'competing crisis narratives' claims that crises open up space for actors to construct their own crisis narrative. A leader or opposition group can utilise crisis narratives to describe their own version of events and propose reform to adapt the system to meet the exogenous changes and the new challenges. Nevertheless, to be effective, the narrative must be in sync with, or speak to, the experience of the broader public (Hay 1999, 2002). Kuipers (2006:181–2) notes four indicators that a crisis narrative is being constructed: the use of the word 'crisis' to describe an undesirable situation; claims that the situation is urgent and requires drastic action; when the broader public is asked to comply with reforms or the leader appeals to solidarity during the crisis, as in wartime; and when the complex crisis situation is simplified or the leader makes use of metaphors and historical analogies to explain the situation. When these narratives catch on and are accepted by the public, they pave the way for reform in the system. Each of the polities studied in this volume displayed some if not all of these elements of crisis narratives in relation to policy and reform.

The leaders studied here needed to determine what they believed to be the right course of action. At the same time, however, they were held accountable for their decisions and had to articulate their strategic actions and their policy moves (or even others' policy moves) to the public. Their policy moves were at times reactive and improvised, as they needed to rhetorically prime their audiences in the rapidly evolving situation.

The policy game laid out in Chapter 2 of this volume suggests that leaders take one of four rhetorical positions. As a 'change advocate', they might press for a policy paradigm shift or for incremental reform, or as a status quo player, they might attempt to resist or contain policy change. Opposition parties, unions and interest groups, sections of the media and/or demographics of the public might take up the other side of the contest.

The case studies demonstrate that the model's assumption needs to be refined. We encountered a couple of interesting situations where both sides of the contest were pro-reform. Disagreement and contest instead centred on the specific policies that should be implemented—or more often, the scope and pace of the proposed reforms (incremental versus paradigm shift). For example, in the United Kingdom and Australia, the head of government and the opposition leader both claimed to favour some kind of reform. At the same time, Prime Ministers Brown and Rudd both attempted to portray their opposition leaders, David Cameron and Malcolm Turnbull, respectively, as advocates of the old 'failed' system. In Australia, this caused problems for Turnbull, particularly as the media remained largely supportive of the government. In contrast, for Cameron, Brown's strategy did not make much of a dent as the media and public were quick to note that Brown had had 11 years in which to offset the alleged flaws of the 'neo-liberal' economic philosophy of the previous Conservative governments and had apparently missed the opportunity to do so. Blaming predecessors is simply not credible in these circumstances.

At times, the media was more focused on the leader's behaviour and style than on the government's policy. For example, in Canada, Prime Minister Stephen Harper's alleged lack of sensitivity to the suffering of ordinary Canadians became a key storyline, much more so than the critical vetting of the substance of his statements—at least for a while.

Our case studies suggest some recurrent patterns in the policy component of leaders' crisis rhetoric. One was the prevalence of bricolage: combining tailor-made responses with essentially policy initiatives that were thrown in because they fit the leader's election promises or prior convictions or were skilfully brought to the leader's attention by advisers, bureaucrats and interest groups. As predicted by models of agenda setting and policymaking that stress the role of contingency and opportunism (for example, Cohen et al. 1972; Baumgartner and Jones 1993; Kingdon 1995), the economic crisis spurred actors to advance ideas and proposals that would otherwise not be accorded the same attention or levels of funding. For example, in Australia and the European Union, the crises speeded up initiatives to (re)invest in green technology. In Ireland, it provided momentum to Prime Minister Cowen and Finance Minister Brian Lenihan's 'Framework for Economic Renewal'.

Some leaders managed to successfully incorporate non-economic policy into crisis rhetoric. After the Australian Government's announcement of the major stimulus package that would send the economy into deficit, opinion polls indicated that the public was strongly in favour of spending on renewable energy, tax cuts and other projects for the betterment of society, which made up the package, but comparatively, they were somewhat less supportive of the package as a whole or of the notion of large-scale deficit spending. As such, it was rhetorically prudent for Australian leaders to highlight the benefits of the package to particular, high-priority policy sectors. This highlights the importance of matching the crisis narrative to the felt experiences of those on the ground (Kuipers 2006)—something at which some leaders, such as Obama, excelled and others, such as Brown and Harper, failed.

Second, the policy contests that ensued in the course of the crisis were to a considerable extent fuelled by underlying ideological disagreements. In some cases, leaders spent considerable rhetorical effort attacking 'neo-liberalism' and its free-market policies, with the Australian and Singaporean Prime Ministers leading the way. Conversely, the New Zealand case demonstrated how the same set of events was utilised by incoming Finance Minister, Bill English, to push for less rather than more government regulation of financial markets. This position was taken up by some Republicans and Hayekian economists in the United States, but was clearly repudiated by Obama and Geithner. Debates about the merits of stimulus packages in most of the countries studied appeared to hinge not on the size of projected deficits, but on the underlying beliefs about the relative merits of 'big' versus 'lean' government.

Third, the global nature of this economic downturn created an extra dimension for political leaders—one that they could use to their advantage. The majority of political leaders highlighted the international dimension of the crisis, not simply to blame exogenous forces, but when discussing reform or policy implementation. During a crisis, there is often a need for leaders to appear action orientated, but domestic opposition might tie their hands in taking bold initiatives. Calling for, organising and visibly working with peers, however, in ad hoc meetings of international forums such as meetings of the G7, G8 and G20, EU conferences and regional summits provides national leaders with excellent opportunities for 'self-dramatisation' (Edelman 1977). It also helps supranational leaders (such as European Commission President, José Manuel Barroso) make the case for the pivotal role their institutions can play in forging common approaches to what are clearly trans-boundary crises.

Advocating international reforms also allowed leaders to perform the balancing act of appearing as proactive change agents while in the same breath talking up the strength of their domestic economies and defending their record in regulating their national financial sectors. It also shifted part of the policy game to international arenas where domestic opposition forces had no seat at the table. Internationalisation of crisis rhetoric was evident to a different degree and for a different purpose in each of the cases. For French President, Nicolas Sarkozy, the EU Presidency was a chance for France (and Sarkozy) to be heard; for the United Kingdom, hosting the G20 was a chance to appear in charge and at the centre of the solution. For the open economies of Singapore, New Zealand and Ireland, however, the global dimension of the crisis was mainly a source of despair rather than a feasible source of relief.

Fourth, the leaders' past records greatly shaped and constrained their ability to credibly advocate particular policy stances. Some leaders had been in charge of their country's financial regulation and economic policy for a long time when the crisis materialised. For example, UK Prime Minister Brown and Irish Taoiseach Cowen had both been treasurers in long-serving governments before taking over as party leader and head of government. Canada's Prime Minister Harper had built much of his authority on his reputation as an astute economist. The public deference this generated appeared to buy him time when the crisis first materialised, but then appeared to backfire as his optimistic predictions were defied by growing unemployment cues. In Ireland, it was impossible for Cowen to escape criticism for his old policies when attempting to introduce new ones.

Fifth, the least prominent yet also the least criticised speech-makers in our set were the bank governors. Although in normal times bank governors are key figures in interpreting economic realities to investors and entrepreneurs, during the hottest months of the global downturn, their speeches were often eclipsed by the attention paid to the words and actions of the heads of government. When the going gets tough, it is clearly the politicians rather than the technocrats who are monitored most closely by the media and the public.

Though perhaps their relative visibility was low, their credibility might have been higher than that of the government leaders, particularly the long-serving ones for whom the crisis was first of all a source of potential electoral embarrassment. In contrast, the bank governors' statutory independence and reputation as non-aligned technocrats protected their credibility, with media coverage of their speeches on balance far less critical than that of politicians' speeches. In the US case, the picture was more complicated. Former US Federal Reserve Bank Governor Alan Greenspan's very public admission of having made critical errors of judgment that had allowed the monster of the mortgage bubble to grow unchecked could have dented public confidence in his successor, Ben Bernanke. Bernanke moreover struggled with having to manage the biggest crisis of the financial system he is supposed to help preserve while at the same time having to adjust to the political transition from the Bush to the Obama Administrations.

Some bank governors were vocal and visible. In Australia, Reserve Bank Governor, Glenn Stevens, was the first of the Australian leaders to broach the issue of deficit spending, and only after the media picked up on this did the Prime Minister and Treasurer actively discuss in public what would later become a reality. Most governors were not publicly known figures before the crisis but came to be seen as significant players. In the United Kingdom, Bank of England Governor, Mervyn King, became part of a media-perpetuated controversy speculating on a rift between him and the government. In Ireland, Governor of the Central Bank and Financial Services Authority, John Hurley, was respected for staying on past his retirement date. In many cases, including Ireland and Australia, the central bank governor was seen to 'inject reality' into the rhetoric. In contrast with the coverage of the politicians' speeches, the overwhelming tendency was for journalists not to focus on the personal characteristics and political beliefs and interests of the governors, and instead concentrate on the substantive merits of their policy arguments.

Finally, the speeches were notable for their strategic uses of the past. Popular in leader rhetoric during the global financial crisis was the use of historical analogies to simplify explanations and manage public sentiments. Australia's Treasurer, Wayne Swan, used the analogy of Hurricane Katrina to convince his audience that through crisis came a better understanding of underlying weaknesses in a system. Various leaders likened the crisis to an 'economic tsunami', tapping into recent global memory to underline the severity of the crisis. Predictably, virtually all leaders invoked the Great Depression of the 1930s when attempting to maximise the severity of the recent downturn, but they also used historical analogies to 'sell' policy. Brown and Darling tried on several occasions to sell their policy proposals using the analogy of the Bretton Woods agreement (as did leaders in France and Australia) and even the Marshall Plan. President Obama drew analogies from throughout US history of economic policy that spurred great change and modernisation, and this rhetoric seemed to resonate. The Singaporean Prime Minister tapped into the well of the Asian financial crisis of the 1990s to highlight his government's preparedness and the claimed superiority of the country's regulatory regime (which had already incorporated the lessons the Western countries would now be forced to learn all over again).

The point about using analogies in meaning making is not that they are correct; it is that they resonate—as opposed to their use in the leaders' own sense making, when incorrect analogies can fatally wound the diagnostic capacity of leaders (Brändström et al. 2004). When analogies are widely challenged, they backfire. When they appeal to universal symbols and are carefully crafted and timed, however, their metaphorical power in weaving a crisis narrative (Kuipers 2006) can do more to shape public perceptions of a crisis than any set of facts and charts is able to.

5. So what? Final reflections

We need to place this study in proper perspective. Our findings are to be regarded as setting the stage rather than speaking the final word on the power and limitations of elite rhetoric in the global financial crisis. For all its faults, however, this study does raise a few larger questions about leadership, rhetoric and crisis that we will flag in this last section of the book, as a potential bridge from this study to its as yet unwritten successors.

Nostra culpa: flaws and limitations

There is no denying that our effort has been a limited one in several key respects. In particular, we should note that we studied only three public office-holders per country—those who were most intimately involved in macroeconomic management—and thus possibly failed to register publicly voiced differences and disagreements within the government. We selected only a limited number of speeches per office-holder, not replicating Wood's (2007) towering effort of studying each and every word they uttered on the crisis, so there is a risk of sampling bias. The speeches we selected here might not have captured the full breadth or all the twists and turns over time in the rhetoric of the leaders involved. We focused exclusively on speech-makers on the government side of politics, thus excluding the voices of non-governing parties and interest groups. We adopted a fairly crude set of measures of assessing media responses, focusing on newspapers, and concentrating on broadsheets at that, for the most part ignoring the electronic media and the tabloids whose reach alone might have made them at least as salient a venue for registering the 'vox populi' when it came to the public reception of crisis rhetoric. We looked at public opinion data where available and to provide a contextual backdrop, but we know that caution should be exercised when attributing (changes in) leaders' approval ratings to a particular speech or action by that leader.

We hope—and expect—that in years to come, others will revisit the ground covered in this study more comprehensively and methodically than we have been able to in the short time frame we imposed on ourselves. It remains to be seen whether such exercises will refute, complement or merely reinforce the conclusions of the case studies and the general observations offered here. For the moment, the obvious limitations of this study will not stop us from leaving the reader with a few final questions and reflections that have emerged from it.

Does rhetoric matter?

This leads into a larger question: does leader rhetoric matter at all? Allan McConnell's chapter reminds us that leaders always strive for political and policy success, and rhetoric is one of the tools they employ to achieve it. The question is how powerful a tool it really is. Or, perhaps more sensibly, to wonder whether crises lend themselves well to management by speech. It is hard to deny that there are times when rhetoric—words plus the dramaturgy involved in their delivery—matters a great deal in politics. No one who closely followed the dramatic 2008 US election campaign—overshadowed by the cascading financial crisis shattering its corporate giants—which delivered the United States its first African-American President, Barack Obama, would have failed to register the galvanising effect of his persona and presentation on a crisis-ridden nation desperately looking for new leadership. How powerful, however, was the rhetoric of the leaders studied here in naming, framing and taming the financial crisis? Can leaders speak 'words that succeed' even though the economic indicators of the day suggest that their policies are failing (Edelman 1977)?

This question is of interest to those scholars in political science and international relations who argue on either side of the debate between 'realism' and 'constructivism'. This debate comes in many guises and the proponents of the two positions use different labels to describe themselves. The main bone of contention, however, is whether political contests and outcomes are driven first and foremost by the material realities that they purport to shape or by 'ideas' (cognitions, beliefs, norms, tacit knowledge, models) that people have in their heads and that exist quite independently of those material realities (Bevir and Rhodes 2005, 2006a, 2006b, 2006c, 2008; Marsh and Furlong 2002; Furlong and Marsh 2007; Marsh 2008).

Our study would be of interest to each side in this debate. As we intimated in the opening section of this final chapter, the brute facts of economic breakdown that were unfolding on a daily basis during most of 2008 and the early months of 2009 greatly constrained the ideational space when it came to answering the question 'Is something bad the matter?'—as something so obviously was. And consequently, the heads of government, finance ministers and bank governors who initially attempted to do what they normally did when faced with a sluggish economy—talking it up—were forced to stage fairly rapid and significant rhetorical retreats. The leaders who had confidently asserted that their country was better prepared than anywhere else to withstand the temporary turbulence caused by problems in US financial markets (and words to that effect) did not offer a pretty sight. All had to back down from their repeated and emphatic assertions about their own system's resilience and admit that this crisis was not going to pass them by. They received a hard lesson in the full extent of economic globalisation: along with sharing the benefits of open markets and interdependencies comes a share of negative spill-overs—and little can be done to avoid them. Only in Singapore and Canada did leaders hold out a bit longer—in Canada because the Prime Minister genuinely seemed to believe he knew better and was not convincingly corrected by experts or credible opposition counterparts, and in Singapore because of the lack of opposition. By late 2008, even their staunch optimism had to give way to preparing the public for pain.

There is also much in this study for constructivists to consider. The differences within and between countries on how to combat the crisis were sometimes stark. They were the product of pre-existing beliefs, more so than of material realities or interests. Regardless of how badly their particular country was affected by the downturn, fiscal conservatives and free marketeers blamed misguided regulation and ill-designed bailouts for the escalation of the problems. They consequently advocated a less-constrained market rather than government intervention as the ultimate solution for the crisis. They deplored the level of indebtedness their ideological opposites were getting taxpayers into as a result of the stimulus packages they were proposing. In contrast, 'neo-Keynesians' and other advocates of activist government saw this crisis as the perfect bankruptcy of their ideological opponents' long dominance in political-economic thought and policy. They therefore dubbed the crisis the greatest market failure in modern history and their rhetoric readily adopted the language of government as pivotal regulator and wealth defender.

Whatever happened to rallying around the flag?

One of the conventional wisdoms of political science is that in times of crisis, people 'rally around the flag'. That is, they lend their support to whoever happens to be in charge of the government. The first Gulf War was a classic case in point. American and global public opinion wholeheartedly embraced the White House's definition of the situation: evil dictator invades harmless, oil-rich neighbour, and it is the duty of the world community to not let him get away with it. The 9/11 attacks in the United States generated pretty much the same response—as the 1982 Argentinean invasion of the Falklands Islands had done within the United Kingdom (Lai and Reiter 2005). The phenomenon has been associated in particular with international security crises, although detailed studies have demonstrated that the strength of the effect is highly variable depending on, among other things, whether the conflict involves real war and the way in which it is reported in key media outlets (Oneal and Bryan 1995). The phenomenon has parallels in the world of natural disasters, where researchers observe the emergence of 'altruistic communities' and 'prosocial behaviour'—people setting aside their daily routines and their political differences to help those affected by the destruction (Dynes 1970:84; Tierney et al. 2001).

Leader rhetoric can help bring about the effect and in return leaders can be important beneficiaries of its occurrence (Schubert et al. 2002). That is why leaders like to 'securitise' problems: framing them as threats to core national values and interests (Buzan et al. 1998; Eriksson 2002). Doing so successfully lifts these issues above the fray of day-to-day politics and elevates the leaders in question to key managers of the national interest (rather than spineless, poll-following opportunists).

This being the case, a puzzle presents itself: why did we see so little of this in evidence in the case of the global financial crisis? A striking feature of media and public opinion responses to the leader speeches is how guarded or even overtly critical the majority of them are. This surprised us. Surely a crisis of this magnitude lent itself to securitisation, in that a credible case could have been made that the very foundations of national prosperity were at stake? It is perhaps not so surprising that a fading leader such as Bush, who arguably had already gone 'one war too far' in Iraq (McAllister 2006) and whose reputation for crisis management was fatally tarnished in the wake of the Hurricane Katrina fiasco (Preston 2008; Boin et al. forthcoming), could not pull this off—but neither could his much-vaunted successor nor many of the other heads of government studied here. In his October address to the nation, Rudd certainly tried to rally Australians in 'the economic equivalent of a national security crisis', but this did not remain a dominant theme. Perhaps it is because economic downturns come without enemies that can be stigmatised and inflated to mobilise support for the government ('corporate greed' was tried by almost all leaders, but never really settled in the public's mind as the prime culprit).

In fact, although they might feel counterintuitive, our impressions are in fact in line with the results of public opinion research that suggests that head-of-government popularity takes a dive when the economy does likewise. The leadership lesson that can be drawn from this appears to be as follows: you might be able to frame your way into popularity during war and disaster, but you cannot frame your way out of unpopularity in a recession (nor should you expect to get the credit for economic booms in the same way that you might for winning wars; cf. Kinder 1981). As Bengt Sundelius reminds us in his chapter, inconvenient or ill-managed crises can drive leaders out of a job and governments out of office.

A crisis in progress

The 'quick response' approach to the social science research of this volume deconstructs a process that is still evolving. In that sense our study is shooting at a moving target. At the time of writing, the majority of polities studied in this volume had not undergone a major post-crisis election. It will be a process worth observing as the rhetoric of blame and reform is likely to be brought to the fore. Political careers and institutional futures will inevitably rely on the result of the continuing political and policy framing contests triggered by the economic downturn. It is too early to tell whether the paradigm shifts or overhauls of current regulatory institutions and practices advocated by some will materialise. A considered answer to one of this volume's central questions—concerning the success of the meaning-making efforts of these leaders—can be provided only by a subsequent study, conducted when the waves produced by the current crisis have fully settled.

One thing is clear, however: the economic downturn has opened the floodgates of economic orthodoxy and regulatory practices underpinning the political management of the market economy within states and across the international system as a whole. Time will tell who will emerge as the winners and losers among the elites and institutions most closely involved in the framing contests that lie at the heart of the reform struggles that are picking up momentum as this book comes to a close.

References

Baumgartner, F. R. and Jones, B. D. 1993, *Agendas and Instability in American Politics*, University of Chicago Press, Chicago.

Bevir, M. and Rhodes, R. 2005, 'Interpretation and its others', *Australian Journal of Political Science*, vol. 40, no. 2, pp. 169–87.

Bevir, M. and Rhodes, R. 2006a, 'Defending interpretation', *European Political Science*, vol. 5, no. 1, pp. 69–83.

Bevir, M. and Rhodes, R. 2006b, 'Disaggregating structures as an agenda for critical realism: a reply to McAnulla', *British Politics*, vol. 1, no. 3, pp. 397–403.

Bevir, M. and Rhodes, R. 2006c, 'Interpretive approaches to British government and politics', *British Politics*, vol. 1, no. 1, pp. 1–29.

Bevir, M. and Rhodes, R. 2008, 'The differentiated polity as narrative', *British Journal of Politics and International Relations*, vol. 10, no. 4, pp. 729–34.

Bligh, M. C. and Hess, G. D. 2007, 'The power of leading subtly: Alan Greenspan, rhetorical leadership, and monetary policy', *The Leadership Quarterly*, vol. 18, no. 1, pp. 87–104.

Boin, A., McConnell, A., 't Hart, P. and Preston, T. (forthcoming), 'Leadership style, crisis response and blame management: the case of Hurricane Katrina', *Public Administration*.

Bovens, M. and 't Hart, P. 1996, *Understanding Policy Fiascoes*, Transaction, New Brunswick.

Bovens, M., 't Hart, P., Dekker, S. and Verheuvel, G. 1999, 'The politics of blame avoidance: defensive tactics in a Dutch crime-fighting fiasco', in H. K. Anheier (ed.), *When Things Go Wrong: Failures and breakdowns in organizational settings*, Sage, London, pp. 123–47.

Brändström, A. and Kuipers, S. 2003, 'From "normal incidents" to political crises: understanding the selective politicization of policy failures', *Government and Opposition*, vol. 38, no. 3, pp. 279–305.

Brändström, A., Bynander, F. and 't Hart, P. 2004, 'Governing by looking back: historical analogies and contemporary crisis management', *Public Administration*, vol. 82, no. 1, pp. 191–210.

Brändström, A., Kuipers, S. and Daléus, P. 2008, 'The politics of blame management in Scandinavia after the tsunami disaster', in A. Boin, P. 't Hart and A. McConnell (eds), *Governing After Crisis: The politics of investigation, accountability and learning*, Cambridge University Press, Cambridge, pp. 114–47.

Buzan, B., Waever, O. and de Wilde, J. 1998, *Security: A new framework for analysis*, Lynne Rienner, London.

Cohen, M. D., March, J. G. and Olsen, J. P. 1972, 'A garbage can model of organizational choice', *Administrative Science Quarterly*, vol. 17, no. 1, pp. 1–25.

Douglas, M. 1992, *Risk and Blame*, Routledge, London.

Dynes, R. R. 1970, *Organized Behavior in Disaster*, Heath, Lexington.

Edelman, M. 1977, *Political Language: Words that succeed and policies that fail*, Academic Press, New York.

Eriksson, J. (ed.) 2002, *Threat Politics*, Ashgate, Aldershot.

Furlong, P. and Marsh, D. 2007, 'On ontological and epistemological gatekeeping: a response to Bates and Jenkins', *Politics*, vol. 27, no. 3, pp. 204–7.

Hay, C. 1999, 'Crisis and the structural transformation of the state: interrogating the process of change', *British Journal of Politics and International Relations*, vol. 1, no. 3, pp. 317–44.

Hay, C. 2002, *Political Analysis: A critical introduction*, Palgrave Macmillan, Hampshire.

Hood, C. C. 2002, 'The risk game and the blame game', *Government and Opposition*, vol. 37, no. 1, pp. 15–37.

Hood, C. C., Jennings, W., Hogwood, B. with Beeston, C. 2007, *Fighting fires in testing times: exploring a staged response hypothesis for blame management in two exam fiasco cases*, CARR, London, viewed 20 June 2009, <www.lse.ac.uk/collections/CARR/pdf/DPs/Disspaper42.pdf>

Keeler, J. 1993, 'Opening the window for reform: mandates, crises, and extraordinary policy-making', *Comparative Political Studies*, vol. 25, no. 1, pp. 433–86.

Kinder, D. R. 1981, 'Presidents, prosperity and public opinion', *Public Opinion Quarterly*, vol. 45, no. 1, pp. 1–21.

Kingdon, J. 1995, *Agendas, Alternatives, and Public Policies*, 2nd edn, Longman, New York.

Kuipers, S. 2006, *The Crisis Imperative: Crisis rhetoric and welfare state reform in Belgium and the Netherlands in the early 1990s*, Amsterdam University Press, Amsterdam.

Lai, B. and Reiter, D. 2005, 'Rally around the flag, Jack: public opinion and the use of force in the United Kingdom, 1948–2001', *International Studies Quarterly*, vol. 49, no. 5, pp. 255–72.

McAllister, I. 2006, 'A war too far? Bush, Iraq and the 2004 US presidential election', *Presidential Studies Quarterly*, vol. 36, no. 2, pp. 260–80.

Marsh, D. 2008, 'What is at stake? A response to Bevir and Rhodes', *British Journal of Politics and International Relations*, vol. 10, no. 4, pp. 735–9.

Marsh, D. and Furlong, P. 2002, 'A skin, not a sweater: ontology and epistemology in political science', in D. Marsh and G. Stoker (eds), *Theories and Methods in Political Science*, Palgrave, Basingstoke, pp. 17–44.

Oneal, J. and Bryan, A. L. 1995, 'The rally round the flag effect in US foreign policy crises, 1950–1985', *Political Behavior*, vol. 17, no. 4, pp. 379–401.

Pal, L. A. and Weaver, K. R. (eds) 2003, *The Government Taketh Away: The politics of pain in the United States and Canada*, Georgetown University Press, Washington, DC.

Patterson, M. and Stripple, J. 2007, 'Singing climate change into existence: on the territorialization of climate policymaking', in M. E. Pettenger (ed.), *The Social Construction of Climate Change: Power, knowledge, norms, discourses*, Ashgate, Aldershot.

Pettenger, M. E. (ed.) 2007, *The Social Construction of Climate Change: Power, knowledge, norms, discourses*, Ashgate, Aldershot.

Pierson, P. 1994, *Dismantling the Welfare State? Reagan, Thatcher and the politics of retrenchment*, Cambridge University Press, Cambridge.

Preston, T. 2008, 'Weathering the politics of responsibility and blame: the Bush administration and its response to Hurricane Katrina', in A. Boin, A. McConnell and P. 't Hart (eds), *Governing After Crisis: The politics of investigation, accountability and learning*, Cambridge University Press, Cambridge, pp. 33–61.

Rodrik, D. 1996, 'Understanding economic policy reform', *Journal of Economic Literature, American Economic Association*, vol. 34, no. 1, pp. 9–41.

Rudd, K. 2008, Prime Minister's address to the nation, Parliament House, Canberra, 14 October, viewed 10 June 2009, <http://www.pm.gov.au/media/Speech/2008/speech_0553.cfm>

Schubert, J. N., Stewart, P. A. and Curran, M. A. 2002, 'A defining presidential moment: 9/11 and the rally effect', *Political Psychology*, vol. 23, no. 3, pp. 559–81.

Seeger, M., Sellnow, T. L. and Ulmer, R. R. 2003, *Communication and Organizational Crisis*, Praeger, Westport.

Taylor, J. B. 2009, *Getting off Track: How government actions and interventions caused, prolonged, and worsened the financial crisis*, Hoover Institution, Stanford.

Tierney, K. J., Lindell, M. K. and Perry, R. S. (eds) 2001, *Facing the Unexpected: Disaster preparedness and response in the United States*, Joseph Henry Press, Washington, DC.

Tilly, C. 2008, *Credit and Blame*, Princeton University Press, Princeton.

Wilson, C. 2000, 'Policy regimes and policy change', *Journal of Public Policy*, vol. 20, no. 3, pp. 247–74.

Wood, B. D. 2007, *The Politics of Economic Leadership: The causes and consequences of presidential rhetoric*, Princeton University Press, Princeton, NJ.

www.ingramcontent.com/pod-product-compliance
Lightning Source LLC
Chambersburg PA
CBHW061226270326
41928CB00025B/3359